RISE
AND
BE
SEATED

THE UPS AND DOWNS
OF JEWISH WORSHIP

JOSEPH A. LEVINE

JASON ARONSON INC.
Northvale, New Jersey
Jerusalem

This book was set in 11 pt. Centaur by Alpha Graphics of Pittsfield, NH and printed and bound by Book-Mart Press, Inc. of North Bergen, NJ.

Library of Congress Cataloging-in-Publication Data

Levine, Joseph A., 1933–
    Rise and be seated : the ups and downs of Jewish worship / by Joseph A. Levine.
      p. cm.
    Includes bibliographical references and index.
    ISBN 0–7657–6137–8 (alk. paper)
    1. Worship (Judaism)   2. Judaism—Liturgy.   I. Title.
  BM656 .L48 2000
  296.4'5—dc21   99–059863

Printed in the United States of America on acid-free paper. For information and catalog, write to Jason Aronson Inc., 230 Livingston Street, Northvale, NJ 07647-1726, or visit our website: www.aronson.com

Contents

Acknowledgments

My indebtedness to many individuals accompanies the initial mention of—or quote from—their work in the text proper. Indirect references are credited in the Bibliography. Technical or Hebrew terms are listed in a Glossary, whether or not they are defined at first appearance or left undefined due to their wide common usage. I locate citations from Scripture, post-biblical writings, Talmud, Commentaries, Codes, and prayerbooks by specific location as they appear. Talmudic sources are identified as either BT (Babylonian) or JT (Jerusalem). All translations not credited are my own. I employ a readable transliteration system that avoids diacritical markings above or below the words. It was formulated by the late Hebrew Union College Librarian Werner Weinberg and adopted by the American National Standards Institute in 1976.

My thanks go to a number of professional colleagues who generously shared their wealth of knowledge with me at various stages of this project: Aviva Astrinsky, librarian of the YIVO Institute in New York; Eric J. Bram, senior rabbi of Indianapolis Hebrew Congregation; Edward Feld, chair of the Rabbinical Assembly Machzor Committee; Robert Freedman, the University of Pennsylvania's Jewish music archivist; Margot Gruenstein, a former research associate at the Fels Institute; Mark Kushner, cantor of Congregation Beth Zion-Beth Israel; Solomon

Mendelson, past president of the Cantors Assembly; Rochelle Morse, former senior psychologist at Gouverneur Hospital; Hayim Shaynin, associate librarian at Gratz College; Eliyahu Schleifer, professor of sacred music at Hebrew Union College; Stephen Stein, executive vice president of the Cantors Assembly; David Tilman, cantor of Beth Sholom Congregation; Barbara Wachs, late consultant at the Auerbach Jewish Education Center; Saul Wachs, professor of liturgy at Gratz College; and Akiva Zimmermann, Israel's leading authority on the literature of prayer responsa.

In addition, I am grateful to the following experts in their own fields of endeavor who graciously consented to critique working versions of the manuscript partway through its many incarnations: Dr. William C. Freund; Judy Freund; Adele Aron Greenspun; Donna Harlev; Dr. Michael Heilbron; Rabbi Richard Marcovitz; Edward A. Phillips; Aaron Priest; Dr. Robert E. Shepard; and Cantor Bernard Walters. For all that I learned from their insightful comments, I have my editorially minded daughter Rona Levine to thank; it was her idea to survey a representative cross-section of the well-informed readership for whom this book is intended. Thanks are due my students at New York's Academy for Jewish Religion as well as the director of its cantorial program, Kenneth Cohen. Had they not so willingly accepted my basic premise of an ongoing creative cycle that continues to govern the way Jews approach God, it would never have evolved into the general-field theory that I advance here.

I owe more than I can ever repay to Rabbi John Moscowitz, who took the first rough draft in hand and wouldn't let go until assured I would attend to every one of the "small details"—many of them major gaffes—that he felt needed fixing. A brother could not have been more helpful, nor more firm in his conviction that the book's unique point of view deserved a hearing.

Proper reward for my dear and perceptive wife, Doris, who—as always—was first and last to offer words of encouragement along with well-chosen advice as I wrestled with making what I wanted to say intelligible, will have to await a more equitable world than this one.

The place of honor on this personal roll call belongs to Cantor Benjamin Maissner of Toronto's Holy Blossom Temple. Beny's consummate skills as a synagogue musician and religious leader have been a continuing inspiration, his loyalty and friendship a constant source of encouragement. More to the point, his frequent invitations for me to lecture before his community and colleagues are what initially prompted the writing of this work.

Joseph A. Levine
Philadelphia

Foreword
Rediscovering a Norm

Much of what transpires in today's synagogues
is unconscious activity, a series of actions
without relation to each other or to anything else.
—Dr. Abraham Bronson Feldman,
Psychoanalytic Observations on a Conservative Service,
Personal communication to the author, 1979

*H*ow is it that a worshiping congregation can appear to be seated while standing, and vice versa; a paradox, no? Yet whenever we appear before God, we come
not as blameless and upright but as poor in deed and lowly in spirit. Through our
collective prayer we resolve to do better, and our spirits are uplifted even while at
their lowest. Yiddish playwright Sh. Anski immortalized this truth in a dramatic
legend about the ever-present possibility of spiritual redemption. A single candle
alleviates the gloom of an ancient study hall from whose depths the voices of young
seminarians moan in ecstatic communing with God.

> Though the soul may fall
> from highest heights
> to the depths below,
> within its fall
> lies the power to rise again!

This opening line, drawn from generations upon generations of our ancestors' life
experiences, also echoes their religious practice. Just as we never considered the

rise or fall of our people's fortune as anything more than a reflection of passing circumstance, so, too, have we not viewed the ups and downs built into our worship as permanent states of being.

AN ALARM SOUNDS ON SHABBAT

I found myself questioning that truism some twenty years ago while attending Sabbath services as an interested observer, to see how the dynamic of worship played itself out in a self-styled "Progressive Conservative" congregation. An occurrence alerted me to the possibility that contemporary synagogue practice might have drifted off course by more than a few degrees. It wasn't anything startling—just a momentary bit of byplay between pulpit and pew—but noticeable enough to signal a definite turn from the main road.

Outwardly, things could not have appeared more serene on that sunlit May morning. The synagogue's stone-and-glass facade glittered above scattered saplings and freshly built split-levels that dotted one of the burgeoning suburban developments surrounding Greater Philadelphia. Inside was a reverse image of the exterior brilliance: twenty or thirty elderly worshipers dwarfed by the starkness of a rather dark, oak-paneled sanctuary. An usher who greeted me at the door apologized for the sparse attendance, adding by way of explanation that no Bar or Bat Mitzvah celebration had been scheduled for that day. I considered myself fortunate, since it afforded an opportunity to participate in the liturgy without any social distractions.

A single lasting impression remains from that service: only once during its three hours did I hear the sound of human voices spontaneously raised in prayer. When the rabbi announced *Yehi Ratson*, the blessing for Rosh Chodesh (New Moon), several old-timers began to murmur the text half-aloud—to *daven* it—as is customary before the *chazan* (cantor) took up his chant. Because the rabbi had merely specified the prayer and for once omitted any instructions as to its performance, the momentum of worship had inadvertently passed from him back to the congregation. But not for long; like a drill sergeant whose recruits had begun to parade without awaiting his marching orders, he barked into the microphone, "We read together in English!" One might normally characterize that sort of pulpit activity as a mechanical function: telling what will happen, even when any need for such information has been superseded by an alert congregational reaction. Having aborted the morning's lone manifestation of religious fervor, however, it merited the label *counterproductive* as well.

A SUKKOT THEATER OF THE ABSURD

I considered the incident an aberration, reasoning that surely such a warp in the universe of Jewish worship could not be endemic. That supposition was proved wrong a few months later. I happened to be vacationing in Montreal during the late-harvest Pilgrimage Festival of Sukkot, when our people are directed to take up a bouquet of four species—citron, palm, myrtle, and willow—and rejoice before God (Leviticus 23:40). In the Time to Come, prophesied Zechariah (14:16), not only Jews but all nations will celebrate the Fall Festival. This may apply to every other nation, but evidently not to Jews worshiping in that particular Reform temple on the first day of Sukkot—a Sunday morning, in fact—for its rabbi announced, "Good *Shabbos* ['Sabbath' in colloquial parlance] everyone; we begin with the singing of *Sholom Aleichem*, page 735." As worshipers dutifully filled the chapel with sounds of that Friday Night hymn (Chapter 4 . . . "Music to Get Things Started"), an aroma of gefilte fish and roasted chicken seemed to replace the autumnal fragrance normally encountered during Sukkot.

A SEARCH FOR PRECEDENTS

The two incidents—one on the heels of the other—set off a warning bell in my mind, along with Metaphysical poet John Donne's caution never to inquire for whom it tolls. Because I was retired from active cantorial duty, however, any implicit understanding about not reacting to what I had witnessed no longer applied. It was nothing less than *ritual murder*, the ceremonial snuffing out of accepted synagogue practice while congregants stood by with folded hands. The research prompted by that realization would reveal that over a quarter-million North American Jews worshiped in synagogues weekly and over a million and a third of them attended once or twice a year (Chapter 6 . . . "Bridging the Gap"). Was it possible that all those good people were so unaware of their historical role as active partners in worship that they acquiesced under a misapprehension that their own diffidence represented the norm? I determined to find out by visiting as many different types of service as I could throughout the United States and Canada. Luckily, not every visit proved noteworthy, or this study would be interminable. Yet each synagogue provided a unique learning experience that, when coupled with further research, convinced me that I was not the first student of Jewish religious practice to harbor reservations about the way worship was conducted.

In 1913 a young German-Jewish scholar, who after much deliberation had decided to convert out of the faith, attended what he thought would be his last services on Yom Kippur, the Day of Atonement. He detested the radically altered services to which his semi-assimilated parents had occasionally taken him as a child, presided over by black-robed clergy in funereal grimness. Instead, he preferred a religious setting where any Jew—even one bent on leaving the fold—"knew he had his chair behind him and could sit down without looking around." Seeking the most authentic place from which to enter Christianity the same way most of its New Testament founders had entered it 1900 years before—as a Jew—he chose a small, far-away Orthodox synagogue.

That long night and day of Atonement proved an epiphany, for when it was over the would-be convert had determined to remain within the fold. He never mentioned the experience, but from his later writings we learn indirectly that Franz Rosenzweig (1886–1929) regarded it as the revelatory first phase in a process of self-discovery. Subsequently, during the process' deliberative phase, he would re-trace each step of his fateful Yom Kippur experience—particularly its culmination—which he described as having "attained eternity within the moment, seeing the light which God separated at Creation and put away for safekeeping so that pious ones might enjoy it in the world to come."

As a result of his experience Rosenzweig became convinced that the key to Judaism's survival lay in its God-ordained yearly liturgy, "a public service" of God through worship, whose "supreme component is not the common word but the *common gesture*, something more than speech." He believed that the most accessible gesture of all is re-enacted every Sabbath, when Jewry commemorates the three elements of its eternal life: Creation on Friday night (the heavens and the earth were finished); Revelation on Sabbath morning (Moses stood before God on Mount Sinai); Redemption on Sabbath afternoon (God will crown His people with salvation). All three elements commingle at the Sabbath meals taken in common by family or community, through quasi-liturgical table hymns (*zemirot*) that help make these ritual dinners the most inclusive of events. The nostalgic songs reconcile any ideological differences that might otherwise separate more diligent religious practitioners from those whose standard of observance flies somewhat lower.

MAKING WORSHIP MORE INTERACTIVE

Echoes of Rosenzweig's philosophy reverberate throughout this book, which shows how his "common gesture through liturgy" has provided a never-ending source of raw material for Jews to build their covenantal relationship with God. Rather than settle in occasional valleys while telling the 3,300-year story of our people's public devotions, *Rise and Be Seated* alights upon a far greater number of historic peaks. From these it is able to observe and analyze in greater detail the shifting interplay between a religious community and its appointed emissary in prayer, an essentially antiphonal dynamic that has enabled Jews to approach God directly for almost seventy generations.

Chapter 1: "Cycling Creatively" takes the unique position of viewing Jewish worship as part of a creative process in all art. The process—as spelled out in the Bible—is cyclical, rotating constantly between spontaneity and predictability. At various times and in different places its oscillation has quickened along that continuum to merge imagination with intellect in dynamic reciprocity.

Chapter 2: "A Few Ground Rules" demonstrates how an increasing mechanization of services through pulpit directives has dissolved the age-old partnership in which worshipers—as well as their leaders—set the pace and tone of prayer. This produces chronic lassitude on the part of those few who attend synagogues regularly, and indifference among the majority who stay away. A hugely successful outreach program is described, which retrains dysfunctional worshipers of all ages through example rather than instruction.

Chapter 3: "The Latest Road Maps" suggests a modern revival of the democratization instituted in ancient Judea during the centuries immediately preceding the Common Era: the burden of worship, formerly borne by priests and Levites alone, was shared with qualified lay leaders. Nowadays that means apportioning a good deal more of the liturgy to the congregation. Current prayer books reserve over 80 percent of most services for recitation by a rabbi or cantor.

Chapter 4: "Changing Lanes" shows how congregations can be meaningfully engaged in prayer through a Judaization of liturgical melodies derived from secular sources. Branches of flourishing popular music are as easily grafted onto the sturdy trunk of synagogue tradition today as they were in the past, provided the foreign elements bear more than a superficial resemblance to that tradition. Resultant hybrids often adjust the texts' stress patterns to conform to contemporary speech rhythms with which worshipers are most familiar.

Chapter 5: "Castles in Time" advances another idea worthy of consideration: an interactive alternative to the tedious readings by individuals that worshipers must now sit through. Long and complicated stretches of statutory prayer were historically handled as musical dialogue between cantor and congregation. The contour of this lively exchange imitates the parallelistic structure of Hebrew prayer: expressing the same idea differently in a verse's antecedent and consequent phrases.

Chapter 6: "Melodies in Space" explores a long-standing Jewish mystical belief that has at last gained credence in synagogues of every persuasion—namely, that the soul speaks through melody whereas words only serve to interrupt its emotional outpouring. Since a service cannot proceeed without words, the mystical strains have been wrapped around brief liturgical phrases that repeat over and over. Easily learned, they have come to occupy a pre-eminent place in current synagogue practice.

Chapter 7: "A State of Mind" spotlights the two most potentially disruptive moments during a service: processionals that bear Torah Scrolls from—and return them to—the Ark (*Aron*). With some few exceptions these interludes are too often taken as signals to socialize and invariably degenerate into unrestrained free-for-alls. A more reverent procedure, practiced for centuries by the Spanish/ Portuguese rite, is advocated for these ceremonial passages through the synagogue.

Chapter 8: "Sacred Circles" discusses the lack of a golden mean between well-meant but often amateurish involvement of the few who regularly frequent small prayer fellowships and the comfortable disinterest of a majority who sporadically attend established synagogues. It remains to be seen whether large synagogues will accept the fellowship approach of validating multiple religious viewpoints under one roof. At the very least, these intimate groups' do-it-yourself activism has proved that worship need not be controlled to the point where spontaneity is off-limits.

The Epilogue, "Touching the Infinite," reviews more recent efforts to recapture the vibrant mix of feeling and thought in our liturgy, through its more imaginative performance by the entire assemblage. The challenge of freshening words that Jews have traditionally repeated every day of their lives is being met on an individual basis by rabbis and cantors within their own congregations. Without exception, the solutions that they are devising find expression in collective acts that merge religious yearning with aesthetic fulfillment.

HOW IT WILL HAPPEN

I remain cautiously optimistic that this type of synthesis will occur with greater frequency in the future, knowing that Jewish worship has always been able to reconcile traditional demands with contemporary preferences. The "new" approaches I cite derive from historically documented usage and are not in the least beyond reach. Nor do I marshal them as ammunition for preaching to the converted. While some suggested options may already have occurred to readers of this book, they have never before been examined in the context of their aesthetic—as well as doctrinal—integrity. My purpose is to strengthen the hands of both regular and occasional synagogue goers who until now have held back from being the first in their community to broach these workable solutions openly. I hope that after seeing some of their own thoughts validated in print, they will be spurred into seeking out more of the common liturgical gestures that Jewish worship demands, today more than ever.

In that sense *Rise and Be Seated* can serve as wake-up call for a generation of worshipers asleep at the switch. Its message is loud and clear. To help ensure Jewish continuity on this continent we had best retain enough of the traditional liturgy along with its normative modes of practice so that tomorrow's worshipers may inherit something sufficiently viable with which to experiment on their own.

To help us attain that end, the book adopts an expository approach made famous by the late director Akira Kurosawa in his 1950 film *Rashomon*. Every time the narrative seems to be covering familiar ground it is really offering a different perspective that might better explain the historic ups and downs of Jewish communal prayer, pinpointing where it has recently gone off track and providing a wealth of ideas for getting it back on again. By highlighting past compromises, it shows how contemporary Jewish worship can sustain pluralistic values within an overarching religious unity. In comparing Judaism's habitual response to the religious impulse with that of other cultures it cross-references certain universal procedures, all of which Jewish worship followed until recently. In advocating a reclaiming of those common liturgical practices the book taps something permanently embedded in human consciousness, the need for expressing our innermost feelings to God, and offers ways of doing so that are in touch with our time.

CHAPTER I

Cycling Creatively

Intuitive knowledge precedes logical knowledge . . .
art is ruled by imagination
long before it is defined by intellect.

Benedetto Croce,
Esthetic, 1909

The urge to create always rings twice. Shortly after the Israelites fled Egypt over 3,300 years ago, God called upon Bezalel ben Uri, an artisan of the tribe of Judah, to oversee construction of a wilderness sanctuary for His Holy Presence (Exodus 35). God's instructions to Bezalel—as recounted by Moses—summarize the bipolar experience that creative individuals have undergone ever since:

a. think artistic thoughts
   [*lachashov machashavot*, verse 32]; and
b. be willing to teach them
   [*ulehorot natan belibo*, verse 34].

THE SUCCESSIVE STAGES OF CREATIVITY

First comes *discovery*, an instinctive and solitary event. Systematic *modification* follows, a by-product of passing on the discovery to others. In the beginning conceive your own heaven and earth, the Bible is telling us, then refine them. Give birth to an idea—your brainchild—then raise it as you would an infant, through teaching, during which you and others learn. Folk wisdom would phrase it in earthier terms: First hatch your chickens, then count them. The hatching and counting stages—conception and refinement—are interconnected. There is perpetual vacillation between them, a cognitive swing that reflects the way we first acquire knowledge in our formative years.

Psychologist Anton Ehrenzweig found that very young children's perception of the world is syncretistic, that is, all-encompassing and hence unfocused. Only as they mature does their view of things narrow, becoming more analytical and conscious of detail. Adults, on the other hand, have learned to move back and forth between these two types of awareness, alternating the *dispersed scanning* of early childhood with the *focused attention* that comes from life experience. They engage in this sort of mental gymnastics automatically when confronting any elaborately executed masterpiece of art, whether graphic, tonal, structural, or multimedial. Temporarily relinquishing the analytical half of their perceptive powers, they attempt—in novelist Henry Roth's well-chosen phrase—to again "behold with the eyes of childhood, the wondering gaze" they exercised so unself-consciously as preschoolers. Doing so even for a moment allows them to grasp at once everything the artist has included in his or her first-stage effort: figure and background; melody and accompaniment. This is the teaching-to-others phase that Exodus 35 tells us inevitably follows the thinking of artistic thoughts.

But here, too, the creative process demands that when imparting his or her unconscious insight, the artist does not limit others to gathering information through conscious scrutiny and precise visualization alone. It is preferable that audience members create their own order out of the seemingly unstructured first-stage chaos an artist may have left them, by a series of split-second subliminal scannings. Creative work is never "finished"; intuitive delving into the subconscious occurs at the receptor end of the line as well as at its transmitter station. Listeners or viewers receive what appear to be varying signals from artists' individualized translations of reality, because they each reinterpret the same signals according to their personal sensibilities and experiences. In addition, the circumstances and conventions that influence artists as well as their audiences periodically tend to reverse direction, effectively canceling themselves out. Calm gives way to frenzy, form to disarray, and objectivity to abstraction at clearly discernable intervals. Popular taste changes constantly as part of an outer ring surrounding a series of concentric circles containing the unending interplay between artists creating cause and audiences registering effect. This reactive spiral—constantly shifting with prevailing fancy—winds its way through every art form, including Jewish public worship.

SONG AT THE SEA: TWO VERSIONS

In a broad sense the creative cycle of ancient Israel's worship was set in motion even before God formulated it for Bezalel: at the shores of the "Reed" Sea (*yam suf*; Exodus 15). When its waters receded and our forebears crossed over to freedom, they celebrated their deliverance by singing; Moses-and-the-Israelites' "Song at the Sea" (*Shirat Hayam*) represents Judaism's first communal religious expression. If so, was it articulated through an ungoverned primal scream (one possibility for an instinctive first phase of the cycle) or through controlled music-making (the cycle's systematic-modification phase)? The answer, I believe, is both. Overcome by the immensity of God's deliverance, Moses' soul erupted in an emotional lava flow of thanksgiving and glory. At that early stage of the creative process our people—by their tens of thousands—followed as best they could. This was the first reaction to their inconceivable victory, a synoptic glance which instantaneously registered everything that had transpired: the east wind; the standing waters; the Israelite's crossing; the Egyptians' debacle. Moses' impassioned recounting of it—incorporating disbelief, gratitude, and praise—stirred a mighty chorus of on-the-spot improvisation, with no hint of an organized refrain.

> *I sing to the Lord for He has triumphed,*
> *horse and rider   has He thrown in the sea . . .*
> *Your fury, O Lord, shattered the foe . . .*
> *In love and in strength   You led forth Your people . . .*
> *Your reign, O Lord, is for ever and ever!*

The final form of Moses' song did not emerge until after his sister Miriam, biding her time while she internalized its essence, made the hymn her own (Verse 21). Her rendition, different from the original, occurred sometime after its initial performance. From the Bible's choice of object pronoun—*vata'an lahem miryam* (Miriam answered *them*)—we learn that she, too, led the entire assemblage and not only its womenfolk. Third person plural in Hebrew, when it describes a mixed gathering, is as a rule masculine (*lahem*). Had the Bible been referring to women exclusively, it would have used the feminine *lahen*.

To go by our textual evidence, Moses-and-the-Israelites' outburst—in unison—represented the first impulsive step in a creative process. Miriam-and-the-Israelites' later refinement—responsive singing reinforced with timbrel and dance—embodied its subsequent (teaching) step. From her having *answered* the people (*vata'an lahem*), we infer that Miriam's was not another unison rendition. By then everyone was familiar with the song, and Miriam could alter its manner of performance. This is reflected in its new opening: *shiru* (*you* sing), that is, respond to my cue rather than listen to me improvise, which would have begun with *ashirah* (*I* sing), as did the original.

Without Miriam's reworking, Moses' effort would have retained an unfinished quality that is characteristic of creativity's intuitive first stage. While vitality and expression may be discernible in imperfection, art critic John Ruskin deemed its opposite—perfection—a necessary companion to it. He defined the latter as a female complement to male endeavor, equally valid while remaining unalike. To Ruskin, man is "eminently the doer, the creator, the discoverer," while "woman's power is for sweet ordering, arrangement, and decision." So much so, observes contemporary biblical scholar Phyllis Trible in an essay on Miriam's crucial role in the Israelites' liberation, that "only after her words do we get closure from the Exodus and then move into the wilderness." Miriam gave Moses' Sea Song the lasting, well-ordered arrangement by which it has been recognized ever since. Indeed, its graphic representation in Torah scrolls—as I have reproduced it here—is called "long brick over two short bricks" (*ari'ach al gabei leveinah*; BT, *Megillah* 16b). Its staggered transcription recalls the alternating-line dialogue of classical Greek drama, strongly implying an antiphonal performance style that can prove just as riveting, if rendered with the same degree of intensity. Exodus, Chapter 15, transmits only the opening of Miriam's finalization, but it seems logical to conclude that what has come down to us reflects her input: the people reiterating a constant chapter heading—*I sing to the Lord for He has triumphed*—after each succeeding half-verse (BT, *Sotah* 30b; R. Akiva).

Which version was more effective, the initial unison hymn or the later call and response? Neither, because each suited different circumstances: unexpected triumph followed by delicious retelling. Both versions proved so apt—for their specific circumstances—that they set two precedents for approaching God: through immediately passionate inspiration; or through delayed interaction that allowed for reflection. After the Sea Song, one or the other type of prayer held sway, successively.

WORSHIP IN BIBLICAL ISRAEL

The planned, interactive approach still endured when Israel was ruled by Judges (Chapter 5). In praising God for bringing them victory over Canaanite forces at Kishon Brook, the Prophetess Deborah and Barak ben Avinoam—who had led the fighting men of Naphtali—echoed Miriam's antiphonal scheme:

[Barak]—Awake, Deborah, utter your song . . .
[Deborah]—Arise, Barak, lead your captives!

Shortly thereafter, inner passion prevailed once again. A barren Ephraimite woman named Hannah, who was destined to bear the future prophet Samuel, readopted unrestrained fervor when year after year in the Sanctuary at Shiloh she petitioned God to grant her a child:

Hannah spoke only in her heart,
her lips moved but her voice was not heard.

So intense was her prayer and so oblivious was she to her environs that the priest Eili thought she had been drinking (I Samuel I).

When David lamented the deaths of King Saul and his son Jonathan, in battle with the Philistines on Mount Gilboa (2 Samuel I), he reverted to a measured, grief-filled antiphony, evoking from his listeners the periodic refrain

how are the mighty fallen
in their zeal to do God's will.

King David's son Solomon reintroduced manic exhilaration at the First Jerusalem Temple's inauguration, having hundreds of instrumentalists and singers perform at top volume while tens of thousands attending joined in unbridled rejoicing as an equal number of sacrifices was offered (2 Chronicles 5):

the trumpets and singers were as one
to make a single sound in praising the Lord.

It was a reprise of Moses-and-the-Israelites' unison singing at the Sea of Reeds.

WORSHIP IN CLASSICAL ISRAEL

By the Second Temple era, proceedings had quieted down completely (post-Apocryphal Letter of Aristeas: 95).

A general silence reigns so that one might think there was not a single man in the place, although the number of ministers in attendance is more than 700.

It was a meticulously directed ceremonial, with string-accompanied Psalm singing filling gaps between offerings to the Lord. From the way Psalm texts are worded, musicologist Alfred Sendrey infers a strong probability that they were sung responsively by a precentor (who led the chant) and chorus. Over a third of the 150 Psalms alternate their subject pronoun between "I" and "We" and in addition append an instructional heading: "To the Leader" (*Lamenatsei'ach*). Simultaneous with sacrificially oriented rites, prayer services that did not include burnt offerings were held throughout the Judean hinterland, according to the codified Oral Law known as the Mishnah (*Ta'anit* 4:2; Commentary of R. Obadiah di Bertinoro). In due time the texts recited at those services were formally organized into fixed Orders of Prayer or *sidrei tefillah* (BT, *Berakhot* 26b). That culminating transition from chaotic to controlled ritual took over fourteen centuries to accomplish in all, from about 1350 B.C.E. to 70 of the Common Era.

When Jerusalem and the Temple were laid waste, worship transferred to local synagogues scattered throughout the ancient world. The real intent of bringing sacrifices, (*korbanot*): *lehakriv*, "drawing nearer to God," was thereafter realized through prayer alone. The antiphonal Psalm singing of Levites lived on in the responsive *prayer chant* of myriad precentors and their congregations.

WORSHIP IN THE MIDDLE AGES

The cyclical pattern of that first millennium and a half would replay itself during succeeding centuries, as synagogue practice either adopted Second Temple restraint or opted for First Temple rambunctiousness. The tendency toward one or the other extreme did not limit itself to any single locale or custom but affected the ritual of Judaism's two principal streams: Sephardic (originating first in Spain—*sepharad*, in Hebrew—later the Levant); and Ashkenazic (stemming from Germany—*ashkenaz*, in Hebrew—and Northern Europe). It even permeated a fantastic report late in the ninth century, of worship among the Ten Tribes who had been carried away from Northern Israel by Sennacherib, King of Assyria, almost 1,600 years before.

Between the years 880 and 883 a Jew who claimed East African descent from the tribe of Dan produced a detailed account of the Lost Tribes having survived in various parts of Africa and the Middle East (*Travels of Eldad the Danite*). As Eldad told it, half the tribes worshiped elegantly and the other half—geographically separated from them—did so rather noisily. In the Wilderness of Paran (mentioned in Genesis 14:6) along the eastern portion of the Sinai Peninsula, the tribe of Reuben "read the Law according to the *te'amim* [Masoretic symbols indicating melody and accent]: the text in Hebrew; its interpretation responsively in Persian." A thousand miles farther south on the Red Sea coast, Eldad's own tribe of Dan assumed an opposite worship stance. Descendants of the biblical strongman Samson, "they had no employment but war, and just before fighting they would strengthen their heart unto God, all of them shouting aloud several times in unison: *Shema, Yisrael* . . . [Deuteronomy 6:4] 'Hear, O Israel, the Lord our God is One'!"

In tenth-century Babylonia (ca. 930), historian Nathan ben Isaac minutely recorded the service that accompanied installation of a *resh galuta* or Exilarch, the community's civil leader. "The precentor put his head under the Exilarch's canopy in front of the pulpit and . . . blessed him with a low voice . . . and the youths who were under it responded 'Amen.' All the people were silent . . . there was not a sound in the congregation." That account of serenity and wholeness—with ritual acts proceeding like clockwork—contrasts starkly with what the Spanish traveler Benjamin ben Jonah of Tudela presumably experienced during a visit to Rome in 1165. Its shattering effect must be imagined by the reader, for Benjamin chronicles nothing but desolate ruins: "catacombs . . . and a cave on the bank of the River Tiber containing the graves of martyrs . . . and another where Titus the son of Vespasian stored the Temple vessels which he brought from Jerusalem . . . and two bronze columns taken from the Temple, which exude moisture like water every year on Tishah B'Av [the Ninth of Av; date of both Temples' destruction]."

A probable worship response on the part of Roman Jewry to such dread evidence of past disasters would have echoed an earlier lament by Solomon bar Simson, who witnessed the Crusaders' slaughter of 1,100 innocent men, women, and children in the Rhineland town of Mainz (1096).

> Why then did the heavens not grow dark,
> and the light of the stars not go out,
> and the sun and moon not die in their stations?
> Can Thou let such things happen, O Lord?
> Were they not slain for Thy sake?
> Avenge, O Lord, the blood of Thy servants
> soon, in our day, for our eyes to behold! Amen.

To counterbalance such openly expressed outrage, we must turn to a different culture sphere and the travel journal kept by Petachiah of Regensburg (1170–1180; annotated by Rabbi Judah the Pious). Petachiah found that the Jews of Baghdad "all walk about wrapped in their fringed woolen prayer shawls . . . there is no one in all of Babylon, Assyria, Media, and Persia who is not conversant with the Twenty-Four Books [of the Hebrew Bible] and with punctuation, grammar and the superfluous and omitted letters [in Scripture]. Nor does the synagogue precentor read the Torah portion, for every one called up recites it himself." In this intellectually driven worship system nothing was left to chance, and from the testimony given by Petachiah, nothing unexpected ever transpired.

Rabbi Obadiah di Bertinoro discovered a similar situation in the course of his journey from Italy to the Land of Israel (1485–1490). The synagogue in Palermo, Sicily, was exquisite, surrounded by a collonaded courtyard "complete with a splendid fountain." Obadiah writes of "five permanent readers in the community, who on Sabbaths and Festivals chant the prayers more sweetly than I have ever heard it done in any other congregation." The rituals he observed there and on the Island of Rhodes and in Alexandria, Cairo, and the Holy Land were models of the most precise and elaborate execution imaginable.

WORSHIP IN POST-RENAISSANCE EUROPE

By the seventeenth century, worship elsewhere had evolved quite differently, growing increasingly louder and more uninhibited. Following general expulsion from Spain in 1492 and periodic migrations from Portugal between 1497 and 1578 (Chapter 6 ... "Sephardic Real Time; The Portuguese Experience"), Iberian *Sephardim* settled not only along the Mediterranean shores but secretly in countries of Western Europe that had earlier banished entire Jewish populations: England in 1290; France in 1394. When King Charles II openly readmitted Israelites to the British Isles in 1660, enterprising Spanish/Portuguese exiles were first to return. They were initially allowed to worship only in the cramped confines of private homes, where their prayers shocked the famous diarist Samuel Pepys (October 14, 1663).

"But, Lord, to see the disorder, laughing, sporting, and no attention, but confusion in all their service, more like brutes than people knowing the true God. I never ... could have imagined there had been any religion in the world so absurdly performed as this."

Italy, one of the initial destinations to which Spanish Jewry had fled, immediately permitted the refugees to establish synagogues and hold worship services. But these, too, did not escape denigration by knowing observers like the Renaissance composer Adriano Banchieri, who slipped a rather mean-spirited parody of Hebrew sacred chant into one of his comic madrigals *La Sinagoga* ("The Synagogue," 1623) opens with a satirical imitation of prayer heard in the Venetian ghetto—*nai-nai, nai-nai*—and segues abruptly into a raucous heterophonic babble of Oriental-sounding nonsense:

> *ot zorocot balacot, asak mustak,*
> *ogog umagog, cala malacot, baruk aba.*

The last phrase of that musical caricature, which surely won no friends for Sephardic prayer, is an approximation of *baruch haba*, "Blessed are you who come in the Lord's name" (Psalm 118:26); with which Priests and Levites greeted pilgrims to the Jerusalem Temple.

Nor was Ashkenazic practice immune to ridicule, mainly from within its own ranks. Two centuries after Banchieri's musical slight of Sephardic ritual, Ashkenazic leader Meyer Israel Bresselau skewered the Hamburg community's prevalent style of service in his blistering pamphlet, *Avenging Sword of the Covenant*.

> Three stand, one raises a lion's voice that can cause hinds to bear calf . . .
> the second roars, the third chirps . . . will God listen to your yelling?

The first one (*chazan*), who raises his "lion's voice," was evidently a professional cantor who led prayer. The second one (*meshorer* or chorister), who "roars," accompanied the *chazan* in a bass register. The third one (*singer* or boy soprano), who "chirps," harmonized against both in a high falsetto. This generic trio must have brought German synagogue worship to its nadir, for communities referred to the ensemble facetiously as *klei cho-m-os* (condensing *chazan-meshorer-singer* into an acronymic adaptation of the biblical epithet "instruments of violence," Genesis 49:5).

SEVENTEENTH- AND EIGHTEENTH-CENTURY SEPHARDIC ASCENDANCY

Yet at the very moments when both branches of synagogue practice had succumbed to relative anarchy, they would undergo rebirths that stand as systematic paradigms even today. Mantua—an Italian duchy ruled by the art-loving Gonzaga family during the seventeenth century—for the first time heard Jewish music specifically written for performance during prayer, chiefly by the Sephardic court composer Salamone Rossi. It was sung by a four-part choir (often subdivided into six or eight separate vocal lines) accompanied by an orchestra. Gala performances avoided the rabbinic injunction against musical instruments through adroit scheduling; they either concluded just before Sabbath began or commenced an hour after it ended. In the neighboring commercial hub of Venice, annual celebrations of Purim—the late-winter festival commemorating Persian Jewry's deliverance from annihilation in the fifth century B.C.E.—were so colorful that Gentiles regularly attended them, their private gondolas gliding up to Fisherman's Quay on the Canareggio just off the Grand Canal, only a few paces away from Europe's oldest ghetto. There masked characters straight out of the *Megillah* (Scroll of Esther; plural: *Megillot*) re-enacted the religious drama to specially composed music. For Christian spectators it served as a second inaugural of their Lenten season, which had already begun, a kind of Jewish *Carnevale* (Carnival).

The eighteenth century saw festive religious processions wind their way through Amsterdam's Jewish Quarter on the eves of Shavuot (early-summer Pilgrimage Festival commemorating God's Revelation—and Israel's acceptance of the Torah or "Law" at Sinai), Shabbat Nachamu (following Tishah B'Av), and Simchat Torah ('Rejoicing of the Law' on Sukkot's final day), accompanied by original hymns. After embracing Protestantism in 1578, the Dutch port city had become a haven where Portuguese/Sephardic expatriates, posing at first as practicing Christians, were later able to openly re-embrace Judaism and prosper in diamond cutting and overseas trade. Acclaimed as Jerusalem of the North, the Amsterdam community fostered a level of Jewish scholarship that also valued the humanities and arts. Its communal religious school taught poetry alongside Talmud, and its most highly regarded sages played regularly in instrumental ensembles. Receptions for visiting dignitaries and installation ceremonies for newly elected officiants of the Great Synagogue featured liturgies custom-written for each occasion, the words distributed to guests—Jew and non-Jew alike—who were invited to sing along. Specially composed cantatas with string, woodwind, and brass accompaniment were performed at circumcision banquets and dedications of Torah scrolls. If surviving manuscripts like those edited and published by musicologist Israel Adler are any indication, these events engendered an exquisite blend of ritual observance and artistic expression, catching the worship cycle at its creative zenith.

Northern Italy and the Netherlands from the mid-seventeenth to the mid-eighteenth century marked the only times and places in the West where Jews of Sephardic extraction (*Sephardim*) outnumbered those of Ashkenazic derivation (*Ashkenazim*) since the Expulsion. It resulted in a burgeoning of artistry and learning that ranked second only to the earlier Sephardic Golden Age, which had lasted from the tenth through the twelfth centuries. This time the oscillating pendulum paused for 100 years, long enough for those involved to finalize their achievement in a notated form that could be revived by future generations. Then it moved on. The light of benignly regulated artistic license dimmed—first over Mantua and Venice, then over Amsterdam—from noon blaze to burnished sunset.

NINETEENTH-CENTURY ASHKENAZIC ASCENDANCY

Things brightened again during the nineteenth century when another cycle of creativity hovered over Hapsburg Austria/Hungary and afforded *Ashkenazim* the opportunity to secure their own moment in the sun. Vienna had always been fascinated with the stage above every other art form, hence its preoccupation with festive occasions, balls, parties, fireworks, and exhibitions. Psychoanalyst Alfred Schick associates Vienna's love of pageantry and the glitter of bygone years with its "world-view of the Baroque . . . as manifested in the splendor of painting, music, theater, and the ecstacy of architecture." It was no accident that Viennese Jewry's attainment of a highly impressive synagogue ceremonial coincided with a theatrical revival spearheaded by the Romantic playwrites Grillparzer, Schickaneder, Hauptmann, and Maeterlinck. It also rode a crest of musical inventiveness that had washed over Vienna in the vocal and instrumental outpouring of Mozart, Haydn, Beethoven, and Schubert. A predominantly Catholic city, Vienna's many church choirs regularly presented musical programs on the highest level, and their performances were open to everyone.

Ashkenazic worship's amazing recovery had been made possible by Hapsburg Emperor Joseph II's Tolerance Decree of 1781, permitting Jews to resettle in Vienna after an exile of 111 years. This time the returnees set a place for themselves at the city's cultural table as well. Jewish community leaders mingled in high society and quickly developed a taste for the finest in art. That preference extended to a gem-like temple—still standing today—that they erected at number 4 Seitenstettengasse in 1826. The Vienna Temple's first religious leaders were Isaac Noah Mannheimer and Salomon Sulzer, two innovators who together fashioned a ritual that reconciled the habitual dichotomy between predictability and impulse. Rabbi Mannheimer's sermons, motivated by the urge to inspire and unite—rather than indoctrinate and divide—his listeners, appealed to all elements of Viennese Jewry. The homilies were grounded in aggadah, the Talmud's non-halachic narrative component. Cantor Sulzer's performance of the liturgy, in a high baritone voice of heroic dimension dramatically employed to evoke all the brilliance of its upper register, awed even non-Jews who visited the Vienna Temple. Writer Frances Trollope and musician Franz Liszt were so deeply moved by his "fiery persuasiveness" and "luminous faith" that even without knowing Hebrew they found themselves participating in the prayers.

The service developed by Mannheimer and Sulzer showed what a moderate reform that based itself on accepted synagogue procedure could accomplish. Known as the Vienna Rite, it owed its immense popularity to an astute combination of formal and informal practice, managing to take wing often enough to satisfy recent emigres from the economically poorer—though Jewishly rich—Upper Austrian province of Galicia, but not too often to offend those who had arrived from there a decade before and zealously guarded their newly acquired "native" status. Everyone was expected to join in prayer without prompting. Pulpit discourses were delivered in vernacular, but the congregation prayed almost exclusively in Hebrew. The liturgy regularly featured choral settings that, although written in the latest style, scrupulously preserved an age-old stock of prayer melodies. Those sacred chants dated back hundreds of years and had been officially approved and deposited in the archives of Viennese Jewry's organized religious community (*kehillah*, in Hebrew). All participants acknowledged the parameters of their assigned roles in worship (Chapter 4 . . . "Fuzzing Edges"). As a result the Vienna Rite never exceeded limits set by either religious or aesthetic propriety.

Essentially a compromise between the demands of tradition and modernity, the Vienna Rite proved so workable a solution that its best features were as widely imitated among *Ashkenazim* as the Mantua/Venice/Amsterdam *Minhag* (worship practice) had been among *Sephardim*. Both represented historic compromises that called a momentary halt in the perennial tug of war between overregulation and chaos. Each lasted as long as it took for time and circumstance to eventually loosen the bonds that held its components in dynamic reciprocity. Coupled with the steady erosion of ancient European Jewish communities, the requirements of an increasingly secular Jewry that arose in North America would lead to novel solutions never before contemplated.

EARLY AMERICAN/JEWISH WORSHIP: A SEPHARDIC MONOPOLY

Viewed from the perspective of an endlessly rotating creative cycle, our worship experience in the New World has faithfully mirrored the vacillating preferences of Judaism's distant past, ranging from the impromptu excitement of Moses' Sea Song through the Second Temple's serene Psalm singing. Continuing changes in North American synagogue procedure are traceable largely to the freedom that citizens in this part of the world enjoy to practice the religion of their choice in a manner with which they are comfortable. They are also due to the specificity of Jewish immigration here during different periods.

The first to arrive were Portuguese-descended Sephardic Jews living in Holland who had migrated to the colony of Recife on the Brazilian coast, then under Dutch control. In the mid-seventeenth century, Portugal recaptured its former New World outpost, and before reinstating Catholicism as the official and only religion to be practiced, it gave Jewish settlers who had been developing the virgin territory under contract with the Dutch government permission to sail home. The last of sixteen vessels carrying them northeastward was blown off-course by a storm, captured by Spanish pirates, and sunk, its human cargo taken to be sold as slaves. Rescued by a French merchant vessel, the impoverished former settlers were allowed to disembark—upon forfeiture of all their personal belongings to the captain—at the Dutch colony of New Amsterdam in what is now New York Harbor, on September 1, 1654. With help from their coreligionists in Holland, they quickly gained an economic foothold. They built homes and instituted an extremely sedate worship rite, known today as the Amsterdam/London *Minhag*, which features aristocratic processionals paced off as if by nobility in the presence of royalty (Chapter 7 . . . "The Pace of Sephardic *Tefillah*"). *Sephardim* consider themselves descendants of Grandees, and the melodies that accompany their ritual may conceivably emanate from storied centers of learning in Medieval Spain.

COMPETITION ARRIVES; TENSIONS INCREASE

Until 1825 the dignified Sephardic rite prevailed among 10,000 Jews scattered in a vast and untamed American republic. It was soon eclipsed by a wave of Ashkenazic immigration from the German-speaking lands of Central Europe—250,000 by the Civil War's end. In the absence of qualified leadership the newcomers' disorganized prayer ritual proved anathema to the Sephardic Old Guard and prompted widespread demand for religious reform from its own camp. It was lack of decorum that initially spurred the growth of American Reform Judaism, hardly the content of services, because even forward-looking congregations adhered to Orthodox practice and Hebrew prayer until the late 1800s. From the radical changes that were then introduced, we may surmise that the typical non-Sephardic worship experience up to that time had been a rather free-wheeling affair.

Indeed, the crudest sort of service prevailed in the United States at mid-nineteenth century, when many newly arrived German Jews had no choice but to rough it along a frontier moving rapidly westward. In the absence of a well-schooled cantorate, those who took it upon themselves to serve as prayer surrogates were generally unversed in Jewish Law or custom, relying instead on raw emotion and their own quick wits. Not surprisingly, they drew richly merited opprobrium from one of the first ordained rabbis to arrive, Isaac Mayer Wise, who dubbed the early American cantor "half priest, half beggar, half oracle, half fool, as the occasion demanded."

Rabbi Wise was being overly complimentary, according to an 1857 letter that appeared in Philadelphia's weekly periodical *The Occident and Jewish Advocate*. The anonymously authored letter excoriated American synagogue worship as lacking in content as well as decorum, and called for categorical abolition of the cantorate, whose "miserable operatic music has usurped the place where religious instruction and mental reflection should be found." Yet in all fairness to the pioneers of those days, living as they did outside the moderating influence of an established and functioning *kehillah*, we must ask ourselves how worshipers could be expected to reflect upon religious instruction that remained—more often than not—at odds with itself? It was, after all, the great age of congregational dissention concerning the very nature of Judaism.

In 1846 Rabbi Wise—newly settled in Albany—initially attempted to preserve a semblance of Jewish religious propriety by demanding that a Board member resign if he persisted in keeping his business open on the Sabbath. Outraged by Wise's presumption, the congregation's *parnas* (president) forbade him to continue officiating. Ever the rebel, Wise appeared on the *Bimah* the first morning of Rosh Hashanah and as he went to open the Ark, the *parnas* hit him so hard with his fist that the rabbinical cap fell from Wise's head. In 1859 when Rabbi Benjamin Szold—a moderate innovator—arrived in Baltimore, he devoted his inaugural sermon to an earnest plea for rapprochment between "the spirit of the times on one side and tradition on the other." Rabbi David Einhorn, a more radical colleague, thereupon took to his own pulpit—Har Sinai Temple—and maliciously derided Szold's timidity, predicting a swift demise for the newcomer's recently founded congregation, Oheb Shalom.

Ande Manners, a chronicler of this tumultuous period in American Jewish history, records that in 1883, Cincinnati's Hebrew Union College served a biblically prohibited menu at the dinner honoring its first class of rabbinical graduates. Orthodox leaders immediately decried the ever-widening rift within American Jewry and castigated as *meshumadim* (apostates) those who were causing it. In defending their ceremonial public consumption of Little Neck clams, softshell crabs, shrimp salad, and creamed frogs' legs, the Reformers disparaged "Kitchen Judaism" and, led by Rabbi Kaufmann Kohler, issued a manifesto that abrogated the bulk of Mosaic Law. In 1902, Reform philanthropists Jacob Schiff and Louis Marshall imported the Rumanian-born talmudist Solomon Schechter from Cambridge University to head middle-of-the-road Conservatism's rabbinical school (Chapter 2 . . . "Reactions to Radical Reform"). They hoped he would "refine" the Old World Orthodoxy to which millions of Russian immigrants still clung. Instead, Dr. Schechter accused Reform rabbis—by name—of doing "terrible mischief downtown" by missionizing for their own brand of Judaism among the huddled masses.

JEWISH CIVIL WARS

Doctrinal contention and internecine backbiting went on unchecked here for almost a century. In Europe the *kehillah* had been governmentally sanctioned, and it supported multiple institutions that accommodated the religious, educational, philanthropic, and social needs of the Jewish populace. But in North America, local synagogues were called upon to shoulder all of these separate functions unaided. In the absence of a central authority that might have deflected and mediated the rancorous charges and counter-charges, every service turned into an impromptu battleground where wars were fought over the claims of time-honored *Minhag* versus an even stronger urge to blend into a free and open society. Because synagogues had to bear the brunt of every attack, it is easy to see why their religious practice was in disarray. With the exception of Reform, self-expression among the membership grew ever more unruly—peppered with violent fisticuffs and confrontational name-calling over such comparatively minor matters as seating claims and congregational dues. This lasted until more threatening external pressures induced the contending parties to effect a *pax in bello* that relegated all intramural squabbles and interdenominational disputes to a back burner for the duration of World War II.

The cease-fire continued to hold afterward, as awareness of our people's irreplaceable loss sank in. Without a steady influx of European-trained leadership, Jewish worship in the United States and Canada was forced to find its own salvation. While Reform, Conservative, and Orthodox seminaries had grown to the point of being able to supply North American Jewry with a sufficient number of rabbinical functionaries, they now recognized an urgent need for establishing cantorial schools without delay. In record time—the six years between 1948 and 1954—Hebrew Union College's School of Sacred Music, the Jewish Theological Seminary's Cantors Institute (now the H. L. Miller Cantorial School), and Yeshiva University's Cantorial Training Institute (now the Philip and Sarah Belz School of Jewish Music) all opened their doors.

WHERE WE STAND IN THE CYCLE

Over time, a dilution of content in all three training seminaries has tended to dampen the fire of synagogue worship. One might think this is at least partly due to a mass entry into the rabbinate and cantorate by women, who according to historian Israel Abrahams have had no available role models of their own sex leading synagogue prayer for the past 700 years. Abrahams documents the fact that women in the Rhineland town of Worms conducted their own worship as late as the thirteenth century but were not permitted to do so thereafter. At that time, according to talmudist Rabbi Samson ben Tzadok, women were even allowed to hold their infant sons in their laps for the Brit Milah (circumcision) performed during synagogue services (*Tashbetz*, number 397 after Rabbi Meier of Rothenburg). By the late-fourteenth century, whatever minor privileges women formerly enjoyed in public worship had been rescinded. The sixteenth-century Galician authority Rabbi Moses Mat (*Sefer Matei Moshe, Inyanei Milah* 4:5) credits his predecessor Rabbi Jacob Moellin, head of the Jewish communities in Germany, Austria, and Bohemia, for this ruling.

Contemporary liturgist Rabbi Lawrence Hoffman attributes rabbinic banishment of women from the synagogue—including their infant sons' Brit ceremonies—to the halachic system of imposing order on Creation. Women were thought not to fit into this system. "For the rabbis," writes Hoffman, "women pose a constant threat of disorder, compulsive behavior, a failure of self-control." This is truly ironic, for we have noted that in every instance of public worship from biblical through classical and medieval times, religious impetuosity is as characteristic of males as it is of females, depending on the circumstances. Conversely, neither Miriam's prayer at the Reed Sea nor Deborah's at Kishon Brook, nor Hannah's at Shiloh lacked for intensity simply because they were formulated and offered by women. Whether tranquil or tempestuous, women's leadership of public worship was unwelcome even in Liberal Judaism until just a generation ago (Chapter 3 . . . "Rewriting Road Manuals to Accommodate Women Drivers").

Today, after a quarter-century of women functioning as rabbis and cantors, serenity reigns supreme on the devotional front. Yet the fact that exuberance during worship is now considered an unwelcome guest has little to do with feminine proclivity, for it is equally true of services led by men who were trained at the same institutions. Logic has won out over intuition in North American synagogues across the board because of a societally influenced shift in Judaism from imitative to *text-based* practice. A generally better-educated class of worshipers seems content to read dispassionately *about* the liturgy rather than display emotion while praying.

The creative cycle's latest turn signifies a revival of Second Temple sedateness in North American synagogue practice. Sterile silence pervades most sanctuaries, and worshipers—as if under mass hypnosis—react only to logistical directives: rise; be seated; turn to page such-and-such. Even to the extent that such mass puppetry signifies the recycling of an historical imperative in the creative life of our people, can it truly be defined as normative Jewish worship after so many centuries? Like the concerned relative of a patient awaiting test results on what could be a life-threatening condition, anyone reading these lines must hope the crisis will pass. Notwithstanding its severity, I would not diagnose our case as terminal. While present-day lassitude may indicate a retreat from the intense passion that erupted when World War II ended and a Jewish state was established soon afterward, our communal prayer has endured the malady for some twenty-five years and promises to survive it, if need be, for a bit longer. Call the status quo critical if we must, but let us qualify it as being stable, for it remains safely within the limits of past cyclical digressions. Nor should we view it in any more permanent a light than the countless deviations that preceded it during our people's 2,000–year dispersal.

WHEN RITE WAS CONSIDERED WRONG IN THE PAST

Historian Samuel Abba Horodetzky assures us that this is by no means the first time Jewish worship so over-organized itself that a clamor for deregulation arose in protest. Indignant voices have regularly questioned similar ritualistic inflexibility during the past two and a half millennia. From the eighth to the fifth centuries B.C.E., the rallying call of every Hebrew Prophet was that God prefers imperfect *righteousness* to unblemished sacrifice (Hosea 6:6). Between the first and seventh centuries of this era, talmudic authorities declared that the All-Merciful One looks to the *heart* rather than the mind (BT, *Sanhedrin* 106b). Jewish mystical thinking has always agreed with Rabbi Joseph (BT, *Niddah* 61b) that "in the Hereafter, rules and prohibitions will no longer hold sway."

That teaching resurfaced in eighteenth-century Russia/Poland. Grinding poverty combined with bitter memories of the previous century's massacres (1648–1654) at the hands of Ukranian Cossack leader Bogdan Chmielnicki, as well as disillusionment over the failed "messiah" Shabtai Zevi (1626–1676), to remove all hope from the bulk of Eastern European Jewry. Endemic ignorance only added to the general despair, for without the knowledge to properly observe God's commandments one could never aspire to true piety in this world or salvation in the world to come (*Daily Prayer Book*, ed. Philip Birnbaum, 1949, page 15).

Amid the pervasive misery there arose a group of charismatic religious leaders who lifted the yoke of ritual requirements so that their unlearned adherents might have easier access to God. One of the more innovative dispensations was to permit singing without words as an acceptable form of prayer when worshipers could not read the liturgy (Chapter 6 . . . "Wordless Song"). Among proponents of this extenuation, *Rav* (rabbi) Nachman the Bratslaver held primacy of musical place. He taught the importance of everyone having his own personal melody, independent of specific text, and his greatest pleasure was to savor the musical inventiveness of others as they stood before a prayer lectern. *Rav* Nachman's abiding passion for the right melody sung at the right moment informs an incident (described by novelist Curt Leviant) that may well have occurred on one of his prolonged journeys through the Ukraine.

Nachman arrived in a strange town one Friday evening just before sundown and hurriedly made his way to a nearby synagogue. A cantor was concluding the prayer that officially ushers in Shabbat ("Sabbath" in modern Hebrew): Psalms 92; A Song for the Sabbath Day. As the murmur of worshipers' collective *daven'n* died down, the cantor began intoning a wordless melody. Slowly at first, he sang it again and again, and with each repetition added more heartfelt trills and anguished turns, soul-searing roulades that erupted into otherworldly cascades of sound suspended between heaven and earth. When it reached the point where all Creation seemed to skip a beat, he suddenly stopped and continued with *Maariv*, the Evening service proper. Afterward, Nachman went over to the man and told him: "One more note, and you would have brought down the Messiah."

From our remove of 200 years and 4,000 miles we may well ask: Was such ecstatic display in the midst of public prayer usual or unusual among Jews? The answer, dear reader, you have probably guessed by now. It depended on when and where the synagogue stood, who led prayer, and who constituted the congregation. Jewish worship is always in pursuit of either individuality or conformity. The improvisational style expressed through explosive fervor—which Nachman experienced—still survives as a style known as *tefillat haregesh* (prayer of feeling), which we might characterize as Dionysian. Its antipode, well-ordered recitation that is elegant but entirely predictable, is designated *tefillat haseder* (orderly prayer) and would fall under the heading Apollonian.

AD LIBITUM—VERSUS DISCIPLINED—ART

The terms *Dionysian* and *Apollonian* point to a confrontation between the instinctual and the contemplative in all art, including religious ceremonials. In ancient Greece, Dionysian rites gave free rein to wild emotional outbursts and paroxysms of intoxification, whereas worship of the sooth-saying god Apollo displayed calm and measured restraint. Order and disorder co-exist to varying degrees in every great work, often tempting others to suggest changing the mix. Philosopher

Friedrich Nietzsche advocated smoothing the texture and lowering the temperature of Beethoven's choral outburst at the finale of his *Ninth Symphony* (1824) by converting it into a quieter art: painting. Perhaps Nietzsche took his cue from French Symbolist poet Theophile Gautier, who had capped someone else's transformation of mood and medium with one of his own. Gautier described in verse a fiery musical air—*Le carnaval de Venise*—composed by violin virtuoso Niccolo Paganini, who had been inspired by land and seascape painter Antonio Canaletto's placid visual tableau of the same subject.

Most artists limited themselves to single transposition. Georges Seurat, who painted with pointillist dots of pure color to capture the effect of solar light on canvas, expressed graphically certain abstract metaphysical polarities normally encountered in philosophical treatises. His 1884 masterpiece *Sunday Afternoon on the Island of La Grande Jatte* sets a formal scene treated in Apollonian fashion, yet redolent with an underlying Dionysian tension. Seurat's forty-odd strollers, boaters, and picnickers constitute a lonely crowd caught between two powerfully contending motifs of Far Eastern cosmology: nature's passive element, Yin; and its active counterpart, Yang. Seurat's Yin-like clouds, vapors, bonnets, and parasols effectively counter the upthrust of yang-like tree trunks, torsos, smokestacks, and sails.

Inner-directed and outer-directed elements are similarly facing off in contemporary Jewish worship, where we find a centripetal inclination toward the dispassionate keeping centrifugal visionary tendencies in check. This temporary stalemate runs counter to the previous pattern of *tefillat haregesh* and *tefillat haseder* exerting hegemony at different times and in different places. Sixty years after Nachman of Bratslav's death in 1811, a seminal pull toward emotionally demonstrative—as opposed to intellectually reserved—worship sprang up in the traditionalist synagogues of Berdichev, Ukraine. It was a natural reaction to the more formal *chorshul* or "Choral Synagogue" rite that had evolved in the Black Sea port of Odessa. Yiddish novelist Mendele Mocher Sforim, who lived in both centers, satirized their differences.

Berdichev (regesh)

The *chazan* would first growl in a low register, then shake the rafters with a couple of high notes that crackled like pistol shots. Suddenly, with a tender Rumanian shepherd song that might appeal to God's softer nature, he shifted into falsetto: *oi tatenyu*, "Dear Father"!

Odessa (seder)

The *Kantor* barely earned his keep. No sooner did he utter a note when the choir would swoop in and scoop it up, mix it with some groats and poppy seeds and dish it out again in little portions. They called that: "services."

FINDING COMMON LITURGICAL GROUND

While noticing surface ripples of incongruity between the two disparate worship styles, however, we ought not overlook a deeper level of underlying similarity. As far back as nineteenth-century Russia, well-regulated services flourished right along-side freewheeling prayer; one was not in decline nor the other in ascendancy. This meant that the lead time separating cycles had already foreshortened considerably when compared to prior swings. In addition, the locale for every contest between chaotic and organized worship had shrunk to a single tonal space where voices joined in prayer, a field of sound upon which the liturgy took shape.

Interaction with God through vocal means is the norm in most cultures. Islamic sacred song recognizes the common tonal ground of Divine communication as *Makamat*, a system of sung patterns revolving around a more-or-less fixed *tonic*, or principal note, toward which all chants gravitate and to which all voices adjust. The Roman Catholic Church uses a comparable device in its Psalm Tones, formulas for reciting liturgy during the daily Offices. Jewish worship attains the same end through prayer *modes*, chains of age-old musical motifs commonly used in synagogue chant (Chapter 2 . . . "Words and Music"; Chapter 4 . . . "Crossing a Boundary without Realizing It"). This is no accident; all three religious traditions are bound by natural laws that govern the way sound works. Acousticians have long known that specific musical pitches cause the interior space in narrow, high-ceilinged stone buildings to vibrate sympathetically. When a worshiping multitude follows the service in an undertone on any of those pitches, a kind of buzz seems to accompany the leader's recitation. The multiphonic effect provides just enough reinforcement to encourage both congregation and precentor, and their vocal output keeps growing because it fuels itself. This phenomenon involves two or three pitches—sympathetic notes—and occurs mainly in old-style mosques, cathedrals, and synagogues. As we might expect, the notes that trigger it coincide with the most frequently sung fixed-tonic notes of Islamic, Ecclesiastic, and Hebraic chant; the pitch levels upon which human voices generally intone prayer.

One need not be a trained musician to get the feel of those pitch levels. I invite you to recite aloud any of the following invocations, with conviction, as if leading a multidenominational *Minyan* (prayer quorum of ten adults).

Requiem aeternum dona eis Dominum
Grant them eternal rest, O God
(Catholic Mass for the Dead);

Allahu akbar, la ilaha illa Allah
God is great, there is no God besides Allah
(Moslem Call to Prayer);

Yeheh shemeh raba mevarach le'alam ul'almei almaya
May His great Name be blessed forever and ever
(Jewish response to *Kaddish*, praising God).

Notice how your recitations all gravitate toward the same two or three pitch levels, appropriately called *reciting tones*. Opera lovers might draw an analogy with the pious maidservant, Suzuki, in Giacomo Puccini's *Madama Butterfly*. As this humble minor character implores a host of deities on behalf of her doomed mistress, Cio-Cio-San, she consistently prays on reciting tones that are most sympathetically resonant: treble G, G#, and A.

Just so, the tonic note of music that has just been completed by a worshiping congregation can indicate to rabbis or ministers where they might best pitch a reading that follows. It will require a bit of risk taking for those who are accustomed to speak on their own level and let everyone else make the necessary adjustment. But the small initial inconvenience of casting their verbal bread upon congregational waters will at the end of the day return to them manifold. All it takes to have people sit up and notice what they might otherwise have merely rote-read is for the leader to speak an opening line on the tone everybody has just sustained in singing prayer.

THE GROUND SHIFTS

We see, then, that the aural space in which worship takes place is universal. But the spoken or sung matter that fills the space can vary as greatly as do the different religious traditions from which it derives, often readjusting from generation to generation even within a single tradition. The devout ear that once heard a *muezzin* (crier) pour out his heart calling the Muslim faithful to prayer five times a day in all kinds of weather must be shocked by the amplified recordings that have now supplanted that live functionary. The *muezzin* tapes are lately played at decibel levels more suited to repelling—rather than attracting—worshipers traditionally known for their reverence and introspection. Staunch Catholics of an older generation, raised on the sublime symmetry of a Mass whose rolling Latin cadences bespoke majesty, might understandably be put off by contemporary debasing of its language to the level of a child's catechism. Today's Jewish worshipers, many of whom were exposed to the dynamic interplay of antiphonal Hebrew prayer chant in their youth, now find themselves as adults listening passively to a service read mostly *at* them, in English.

These changes—unrelated to one another at first glance—all arise out of a societal shift, from people simply doing what had to be done, into a coasting gear where everyone expects to reap benefits without an undue expenditure of effort. Hence the prerecorded Muslim prayer calls, the rudimentary Catholic wordings, the robotic Synagogue readings. Instead of purposefully obtaining hands-on experience in a given discipline, individuals now sit back and absorb endless amounts of information concerning it. Especially in the sphere of Jewish religious practice, venerated custom has yielded to lengthy discussion of its underlying reasons. Familiarity with ritual performance has disappeared; acts that sacrilized our daily lives, which we formerly acquired by imitating our elders, must now be researched. Since our elders for the most part can no longer serve as pedagogical models, an entire generation of worshipers has grown up uninitiated in traditional ways of praying. Our synagogues have adjusted to their consumer-oriented society as just another service industry (pun intended), proffering religion to clients who have forgotten what Jewish piety is all about.

Given the present over-analytical climate, no art form—including prayer—can subsist for its own sake. A half-century ago the infant medium of television totally captivated a wide audience despite its lack of substantive programming. That didn't matter, as social critic Marshall McLuhan soon realized, since the new technology entered our lives on such an all-encompassing scale that the medium itself was the message. Today, television and every other medium must carry a message of political correctness or risk losing its audience. Imagination is out, conformity is in. All art forms, including prayer, are currently being manipulated to advance social causes ranging from the protection of unborn fetuses to the curing of AIDS sufferers. Simply stated, messages have taken over their media of transmission.

But this tendency is about to end in Jewish worship. As I see it, we have spent sufficient time recollecting in tranquility the deep feelings that drove our prayer immediately after the horrors of mid-century came to light. Now we are again ripe for the spontaneous overflow of our long pent-up emotions. In other, more secular areas of artistic endeavor the creative pendulum is already swinging back toward a median range between its customary extremes of intuition and reason. That comfort zone may already have been reached in what critics dub *postmodern*, characterized by a softening of intellectually induced rigidity and the introduction of whimsical elements previously considered embarassingly out of date. Literary critic John Lanchester captures the essence of this latest seesawing.

> Modernism was about finding out how much
> you could get away with leaving out;
> post-Modernism is about how much
> you can get away with putting in.

Writers are again stressing narrative, architects are now re-enlisting ornamental references to the past, painters have returned to representational figuration, and composers are once more crafting melodies that smack of tonality. In art—as in fashion—stylistic preferences come around, if one has the patience to wait. With that in mind, let us look a bit more closely at the densely nuanced cyclical pattern of Jewish worship that is presently teetering on its fulcrum and seems ready to resume its overarching bi-millennial trend toward extroversion.

THE AMERICAN CENTURY OF JEWISH WORSHIP REVISITED

In order to time our current cycle's imminent closure, we might refer to the circumstancial forces that propelled two previous oscillations. The developing economies of eighteenth-century Amsterdam and nineteenth-century Vienna lacked sufficient manpower to sustain rapid growth, a demographic need that happened to coincide with the fortuitous arrival of Jewish immigrants in substantial number. Yet in each case the seeds of synagogal creativity germinated for 100 years before they burst into bloom. Turn-of-the-century America occasioned a similar convergence, with one important variant. Immediately after the Civil War, as German-Jewish immigrants prospered along with general industrial expansion, a grave and dreary formalism seemed to fly in and perch just above their prayer rite. Reform, with which most of the Central Europeans affiliated, set the twentieth-century cycle in motion by adopting a nonparticipatory, church-inspired service. Professional clergy were appointed to lead prayer after almost 200 years of *laissez faire* in the New World. Liturgy congealed along the lines of a readily accessible Protestantism, with services stressing reading and preaching. Congregants sank comfortably into cushioned pews surrounded by a carpet of wall-to-wall organ music, content to maintain a silence of glacial proportions.

Just as the creative pendulum of American Jewish worship creaked into its non-participatory backstroke, there arrived more than two million Jews fleeing persecution in Eastern Europe. Once here, the Easterners initiated a groundswell of sentiment for the culture they had left behind in Russia, Poland, or Rumania. That ethnic atmosphere was replicated by the Yiddish Theater, which employed a rich jargon of Middle High German, Hebrew, and Slavic elements, and which enjoyed its greatest popularity between 1891 and 1920. The sacred sounds of that culture were reproduced by a host of accomplished European cantors who emigrated here in numbers sufficient to prompt claims for a new Golden Age of synagogue singing. The American cantorate's heyday began in 1912, two years before the outbreak of global war in Europe, and peaked in 1921 when a quota based on national origins limited entry in a given year of any group to 3 percent of the foreign-born of that group present in the United States in 1910. Mass Jewish immigration ended in 1924 when the Johnson-Lodge Act completely cut off its source of supply, but it lasted a bit longer in Canada, blessed with an abundance of natural resources spread over ten underpopulated provinces.

During the twentieth-century's early years, American stages and pulpits were unlikely rivals for patronage by the Eastern European "Greenhorns," especially on Sabbath Eve, family night at New York's Yiddish theaters. In contrast to the stuffiness of Reform temples at that time, Yiddish theaters provided an intimate atmosphere where newly arrived families could come as if to a picnic, laughing through their tears at the melodrama onstage. For those more habituated to strict religious observance, Orthodox worship offered the theater its most direct competition, particularly if it featured a superstar like the dramatic-tenor cantor Josef Rosenblatt, whom an adoring public dubbed "the Jewish Caruso" after he declined an offer from the Chicago Grand Opera Company because of his religious convictions. Jewish immigrants readily identified with this diminutive prototype of a bearded Jew, whose warmhearted prayer chant was laced not only with intricate vocal filigree work and folk melodies of a genre familiar to them from childhood, but with aria-like cadenzas and bravura passages that rivaled anything then available on the lyric stage.

In the years of rapid growth preceding and following World War I, rabbis and cantors from both the Orthodox and Reform movements (Conservatism had not as yet come into its own; Chapter 2 . . . "Reactions to Radical Reform") alternated between their congregations' newer and older branches, officiating one Sabbath uptown and the next one downtown. Due to the proximity of first-settlement area synagogues to Yiddish theaters in every large urban center, nostalgia for consoling rituals like the *Havdalah* ("separation") ceremony at Sabbath's end—with its braided candle and aromatic spicebox—began to figure dramatically in plays like *Green Fields*, which toured the American Midwest in 1929. The reverse was true as well; a noticeable element of theatricality began creeping into Jewish houses of worship. The vulgarity of nineteenth-century frontier days permeated the Roaring Twenties as the synagogue's sacred chant played to a national audience via Hollywood's first "talkie," *The Jazz Singer* (1927), concerning a cantor's son whose rebellion takes the form of a career in show business. The creative pendulum was swinging into its emotive upstroke.

BETWEEN THE WARS

A decade later, global conditions would conspire to change the course of synagogue worship once again; widespread economic hardship led to an epidemic of blatant anti-Semitism and a retrenchment within the Jewish segment of the population on all visible fronts. Though growing steadily in number, North American Jewry still felt itself weak and ineffectual when singled out for incessant attack. Memories of childhood persecution persisted, bolstered by horror stories of Pogroms along the Russo-Polish border which appeared daily in the press. Between 1917 and 1919, over 150,000 Jewish civilians were massacred in the Ukraine by peasant mobs who used opposition to the Bolshevik takeover as an outlet for their long-harbored Jew hatred. This wanton bloodshed came on top of the half-million Jews who had fallen throughout Europe during the Great War.

In the United States, rampant bigotry was furthered by the leading industrialist Henry Ford. He lent credence to an earlier scurrilous defamation, *Protocols of the Elders of Zion*, by publishing several hundred thousand copies of it in his newspaper, *The Dearborn Independent*. This only encouraged rabble-rousers like the Detroit-based pro-Nazi Roman Catholic priest Reverend Charles E. Coughlin. Through a weekly radio program that reached sixteen million listeners, Father Coughlin branded the few thousand destitute Jewish refugees who were admitted during the Depression years as dangerous subversives responsible for every problem faced by out-of-work Americans. Unrest north of the border drove Canada's Parliament to severely limit immigration in 1932 and paved the way for Fascist-leaning politicians like Minister of Labour Adrien Arcand to publicly urge the boycotting of all Jewish businesses.

It seemed a good time for Conservative Judaism to make its move. Heeding the adage of Russian/Jewish Enlightenment's poet laureate, Judah Leib Gordon,

"be observant at home, but unobtrusive at large"
heveh yehudi beveitecha, ve'adam betseitecha,

Conservatism maintained a low public profile. During the 1930s its modulated tone of worship laid the foundation for future growth by staking out a middle ground, less intimidating than Reform's ecclesiastical pomp and more inviting than Orthodoxy's storefront hurly-burly. Its congregations borrowed from Reform only the innovations that still allowed them to preserve the statutory liturgy within a dignified modern setting. Conservative rabbis, mainly American born and trained, sermonized in English. Since there were no cantorial schools, Conservative *chazanim* (plural of *chazan*) often came from European Orthodox backgrounds. Forced to officiate facing worshipers who wanted to join in, they lowered both volume and virtuosity to a level that suited communal participation.

Modern Orthodoxy, which was in the process of emerging as a more progressive faction among Traditionalists, followed the Conservative lead by insisting on synagogue decorum and greatly expanding the amount of congregational singing during services. Modern Orthodox men shaved their beards and although they wore Yarmulkes (skullcaps) in synagogue, when appearing in public they sported hats. Their sons attended the recently opened Yeshiva College (1929), whose dual curriculum strove for a synthesis of religious teaching and secular knowledge: *torah umada.*

A national chain of Young Israel synagogues reflected the same urge to straddle the Old and New Worlds in worship. The *mechitzah* (partition) that separated men from women remained, but at a height so minimal that it amounted to a legal fiction. Kabbalat Shabbat ("Receiving the Sabbath") services began at twenty minutes before sundown. After the dinner hour there followed a lecture-and-collation, called Oneg Shabbat ("Sabbath delight"; after Isaiah 58:13), which provided Modern Orthodox families with a viable alternative to Reform and Conservative Late Services held at 8:30. Key prayers were sung by the entire assemblage—men, women, and children—to melodies so enjoyable they formed an enduring species known as Young Israel tunes. Professional part-time cantors were engaged only for the High Holy Days of Rosh Hashanah and Yom Kippur, while musically gifted congregants—many of whom had sung in synagogue choirs during their youth—rotated as prayer leaders for the balance of the year. Rabbis served as arbiters of *halachah* (Jewish Law; literally, "going," a continuous process), but a weekly Devar Torah—learned talk based on the weekly *sidrah* (Torah portion)—was just as often delivered by a knowledgeable member or a national leader of the movement. To the youthful immigrants who founded it, Young Israel was an oxymoron realized: "liberal" Orthodox worship, sans oratorio or oratory.

THE CENTURY WANES

The tide of Jewish liturgical modification continued to ebb and flow on these shores during the twentieth century, one generation of newcomers introducing a *Minhag*, the next generation taking an opposite tack, if only for a brief while. The near-total absence of immigration in the 1930s disrupted this accelerated sequence at its halfway mark. As a beleaguered North American Jewry sought solace in more understated devotions, it appeared for a fleeting instant as if the middle ground between erratic fancy and predictable polish that flourished in the seventeenth and eighteenth centuries had been regained. The Holocaust changed all that. Soon afterward, a feeling of breast-beating introspection emerged over what had not been done to mitigate the slaughter. Orthodoxy pulled back from modernity and adopted the rigorous standards of its decimated European counterpart: rigorous *glat* ("smooth" or unblemished, referring to an animal's lungs) kosher standards in the slaughterhouse; overtly emotional prayer in the synagogue. Worship in New York City, mecca of most survivors, was frequently led by cantors who had somehow made it through the war in Europe and arrived here with little more than the clothes they wore. Having been spared, they seized upon any prayer that could serve as vehicle for the despair they felt over the fallen ones, often at great length and on the spur of the moment.

Now, a half-century later, extemporaneity has run its course and given way to a more tightly supervised rendition of the liturgy. Gone from the plea recited on High Holy Days by every denomination—*Avinu Malkeinu*, "Our Father, Our King"—is the anthropomorphic personal God Whom we worshiped with such warmth. In place of "remove . . . famine . . . from *the children* who obey Thy covenant" (Conservative *High Holiday Prayer Book*, tr. Morris Silverman, 1951:94), we have depersonalized first ourselves: "exterminate . . . famine . . . from the *members* of your covenant" (Orthodox *Art Scroll Machzor*, tr. Nosson Scherman, 1986:121), then God: "*make an end* to . . . famine" (Reform *Gates of Repentance*, tr. Chaim Stern, 1978:121), and finally the very concept of human hunger in our well-stocked microworld (Reconstructionist *Prayerbook for the Days of Awe*, tr. David A. Teutsch, 1999:452), where *the verse no longer appears*.

Most tellingly, gone from Orthodox services is the knowing smile that came to one's lips with every Young Israel tune; in fact the entire notion of a Modern

Orthodoxy has—with rare exceptions—seemed like an anachronism in recent decades. In today's Young Israel synagogues the number of congregational refrains has shrunk in reverse proportion to the height of the *mechitzah*. Both the treatment of women and pronunciation of the Hebrew language have reverted to the dark days in Russia/Poland prior to Enlightenment; it is as if the twentieth century never arrived. But it did—as Orthodoxy is only too well aware—bringing with it a multicultural permissiveness that has eroded the everyday ritual skills we once acquired at home. Now ritual requirements are taught in the religious academy (yeshivah), and exacted in full measure during worship that is deliberately made as unpleasant an ordeal as possible. This is Orthodoxy with a vengeance.

And yet, if one but recognizes the early-warning signals, even Orthodox Revisionism is beginning to relent somewhat as our worship pendulum arches away from intellectual formalism to greet another century. Brandeis University historian Stephen J. Whitfield relates an incident that inspired his latest book on American Jewish culture and the performing arts. While conferring with a Yarmulke-wearing student who wanted to write a paper on the *rat-a-tat* Southern school of early Rock and Roll, he became fascinated with "how one can feel . . . a connection with something which in strictest terms should speak in no way to an Orthodox Jew . . . the very sort of uninhibited musical style that is very much at variance with the traditional Jewish concern for restraint and decorum." Professor Whitfield had discerned the first bubblings of a creative geyser being superheated underground by the igneous desire for a re-infusion of impulsiveness into our ritual practice.

As to what the future might ultimately hold for us, if our past record is any indicator it is a bit early to foretell. Historian Salo W. Baron reminds us that Jewish life had gone on uninterrupted in the Nile Valley since the seventh century B.C.E., but it took fully 600 years to produce a Philo of Alexandria. In Babylonia a Jewish community flourished from the sixth century B.C.E., and 500 years later its population increased to over a million. But until the founding of Rav's academy in Sura during its ninth century of existence, Babylonian Jewry had left no permanent mark. The Golden Age of creativity among Sephardic Jewry first bloomed in the tenth century, after 700 years of settlement in Spain. The same is true of Western European Ashkenazic Jewry; nothing much was heard until Rabbi Gershom, "The Light of the Exile," began issuing halachic directives around the year 1000. Eastern European *Ashkenazim* settled in the Caucasus as early as the eighth century, but 800 years had to pass before they began writing works of enduring scholarship. By comparison, three and a half centuries in North America would seem a relatively short time.

WHAT LIES IMMEDIATELY AHEAD

Over thirty years ago Anton Ehrenzweig penned the following prescient warning: "We cannot depend on history's cycles to get the job done for us." If we are to awaken from our present ritual sleep we shall have to start thinking of ourselves as players and not as spectators, an attitudinal shift that is already in progress. On the upper West Side of Manhattan, B'nai Jeshurun, a Conservative congregation that was about to fold during the mid-1980s has since managed to refill its reservoire of human potential to overflowing. Down to forty families, it set out to attract the professional young singles of its neighborhood through an interactive Kabbalat Shabbat experience conceived by its late rabbi, Marshall Meyer, who taught it to his successor, Rolando Matalon. A decade later, when I attended a Friday Night service, the almost completely sung liturgy was led by two student rabbis and a cantor—Ari Priven—who accompanied them on the keyboard; all three engaged in steady musical interaction with the worshipers. At the first prolonged hymn, *Lecha Dodi* "come, my beloved [Israel], to greet the [Sabbath] bride," half of those present rose to form a dancing column that encircled the huge room. (The congregation had been renting a Methodist church since 1993, when the ceiling of its own 75-year-old building collapsed.)

This was the 5:30 or Family service, at which many more adults would have joined the human chain were they not cradling infants and minding slightly older toddlers. The children are living proof of the experimental service's drawing power, for in most cases their parents met while attending it during the preceding decade. At its height the original 6:30 service drew a crowd of over 1,200. That was more than either the restored synagogue or rented church could seat, and a second service—mostly for singles—now accommodates the overflow at 7:00. Even knowing they must vacate in time for the later service to begin, the early crowd is in such a convivial mood at the end—singing and socializing—that ushers have to gently but firmly prod people toward the front exits while a second, much larger throng that stretches around a city block enters from the rear. Because of the "Singles" service's popularity it continues at its present venue even after the congregation's return to its own rebuilt—but smaller—sanctuary.

The demand for a worship setting in which young families, students, and especially singles can reconnect to their religion and to each other is so great that every synagogue on the Upper West Side has been affected by it. Ohab Zedek, an Orthodox congregation situated ten blocks from B'nai Jeshurun, could barely muster a *Minyan* in the late 1980s. When its newly appointed rabbi, Allen Schwartz, began to meet young folk in the neighborhood on his way home from Kabbalat

Shabbat, he invited them to come along with him for a homecooked meal and some Jewish camaraderie. His members did likewise, reviving both an honored tradition of *hachnasat orchim* ("extending hospitality to strangers"; BT, *Shabbat* 127a) at Ohab Zedek along with attendance at services. Word quickly spread that nobody left "O. Z." on Friday night without being royally fed, and the under-thirty set started showing up en masse. A thousand eligible men and women partial to Orthodox worship now regularly make the Oheb Zedek Kabbalat Shabbat something to behold, their spirited participation raising the echoes of postwar years when prayer was wholeheartedly sung in North American synagogues.

The idea of again encouraging unrestricted congregational participation in the liturgy has already spread to other cities. In 1997–98, seven Conservative, Reconstructionist, and Reform synagogues in Greater Philadelphia hosted a rotating monthly service patterned after the ones in Manhattan's thirty blocks between West 65th and 95th Streets. Funded privately at first and then by a local Federation of Jewish Philanthropies grant, *Friday Night Alive!* was led by a team of young rabbis who happened to be trained as musicians. They stumbled occasionally. At *Lecha Dodi*, one rabbi earnestly exhorted: "You will now feel the spirit move you into leaving your seat and join in spontaneous dancing." The specially prepared prayer booklet mistakenly implied that God was "jealous" of all Creation instead of its "Master," by ending the key word *vekoneh* with *Aleph* instead of *Heh* (*Friday Night Alive!*, ed. Joe Lewis and Ellen Bernstein, 1997, page 28). But the underlying purpose was a noble one: to give heretofore disenfranchised—or even defected—Jews along the entire social spectrum a reason to come back and identify through accessible, jointly sung worship. The service improves constantly, guided by comments systematically elicited from attendees. Midway through its first year the two laymen whose idea it was—Mark Solomon and Paul Silberberg—were receiving detailed inquiries from congregations as far afield as California (Chapter 8 . . . "Havurot and Bilingual/Transliterated Prayer"). A year later, six of the original congregations were able to continue on their own while the series expanded to include twelve new venues.

A bit earlier, the Bathurst section of Toronto had experienced something similar. In 1989 Holy Blossom Temple offered a special 45–minute service on the second day of Rosh Hashanah to those in the community who were hearing-impaired. The 100-or-so who showed up told their friends about it and by the following year, attendance had so increased that a liturgy had to be constructed that would allow for more singing. Today the optional service draws an overflow crowd—as I learned while trying to reserve a seat—in a Classical Reform congregation that never worshiped on more than one day of Rosh Hashanah during its 140–year history. No longer is that Second Day event specifically geared for the handicapped; in fact, its regular attendees now look upon the *first* day's more conventional Reform worship as singing-impaired by comparison.

It is not that less English appears in the specially constructed liturgy. In actuality, it presents more readings than in either of the two Morning Service alternatives offered by *Gates of Repentance* (ed. Chaim Stern, 1978), Reform's official High Holy Day prayerbook. The difference lies in this special service's use of its English, as supplementary—rather than integral—to prayer. Worshipers, who have put themselves above-and-beyond the call of Liberal duty to express their religious feelings in as traditional a manner as their leadership will currently permit, vault the massive blocks of solo readings like camels galloping across desert gullies. Searching for whatever oases of Hebrew sparingly dot the folio-sized pages of their booklet (*In Praise of God*, gleaned from many sources, 1993), they slake their thirst only in spring water that gushes from the familiar words their parents and grandparents recited.

> *Zochreinu Lechayim,* "remember us unto life";
> *Le'eil Oreich Din,* "You search the heart on Judgment Day";
> *Vechol Ma'aminim,* "we believe that You are a Righteous Judge";
> *Hayom Te'amtseinu,* "hear our supplication this day."

The tools for liturgical reclamation were lying there all along; people just had to avail themselves of them.

A century or more after their founding, the congregations mentioned previously are in the process of reinventing themselves, using a sung liturgy as the inducement. Nothing else in their respective rituals has changed, sermons are still given and readings (though fewer than before) are still read. Yet the cycle of religious creativity has been marking time in these congregations for over a decade and gives evidence of remaining there for the foreseeable future. Neither emotion nor intellect predominates. Working in tandem, both elements so charge the atmosphere that worshipers seem to be *"standing" while "sitting"* (in the metaphorical sense; Epilogue . . . "Needed: Heart as Well as Mind"), alert and involved to the same degree whether attentively listening to a sermon or purposefully reciting prayer.

BEYOND THE MILLENNIUM

The lesson was first learned by our ancestors during their days of forced pyramid building. The oppressive stay in Egypt—a period roughly equal to our North American sojourn thus far—seemed to begin much more promisingly than the way it ended.

Legend relates that Father Jacob's final seventeen years, which he lived along the Nile, were the best years of his life. If so, things must have gone swimmingly for his progeny at first, yet many later commentators harbored doubts, *Rav* Nachman of Bratslav among them. According to his reading of the Exodus story, from the very beginning our Bible had referred to Egypt as "the earth's obscenity" (*ervat ha'arets*; Genesis 42). Nachman surmised that Scripture must provide a solution along with the puzzle: Jacob had earlier sent his ten remaining sons down to their brother Joseph with gifts of *zimrat ha'arets* (choice fruits of the land). Because *zimrah* (of which *zimrat* is the possessive form) also means "song"—sharing the root *z-m-r* with *zemirot*—Nachman concluded that Jacob's children survived Egyptian bondage by retaining their own musical tradition for study and prayer, the twin pillars of their spiritual life. That was the real purpose of Jacob's gift, to provide future generations with a key for preserving Israel's unique culture.

Ancient civilization progressed from hunting through sheepherding to farming, and as Rabbi Shlomo Riskin astutely notes, the Israelites were still at an intermediate stage when they left Egypt. In a soil-cultivating society far more advanced than their own, the erstwhile shepherd folk had to withstand temptations never imagined while raising cattle in their own hill country. Three meritorious deeds earned our ancestors their redemption, relates a midrash (rabbinic "search" for hidden textual meaning; *Bamidbar Raba* 13:19). They maintained their Israelite names, observed sexual propriety, and—equipped with the means to do so through Father Jacob's far-sighted resourcefulness—preserved Hebrew as the language in which worship and learning took place.

The first two of those praiseworthy accomplishments lie beyond the scope of this work. As to the last mentioned—preservation of Hebrew prayer—we must ask: at North American Jewry's quadricentennial in the year 2054, will it apply to the majority of us? True, we are pedaling through the *motions* of public worship as fast as we can, but is it still possible to cycle creatively while singing (or worse, speaking) God's song in a foreign tongue?

Procedures that have worked effectively in the past suggest an answer in Chapter 2: "A Few Ground Rules."

CHAPTER 2

A Few Ground Rules

The surfeit of instructions flings us from one discipline to another,
from immersion in the self to immersion in information . . .
How refreshingly different it would be if there were
no interruptions, no inclusions, no skipping of pages.
Martin Berkowitz,
"Making Religious Services Come Alive,"
Jewish Post & Opinion, 1995

*L*ike the compelling motif that inaugurates Beethoven's *Fifth Symphony* (1808), Jewish worship in the Grand Style came calling early on and has stayed with me ever since. Midday of the Yom Kippur following my Bar Mitzvah year, after chanting the Torah portion for a supplementary High Holy Day service some distance away, I was walking back to my home neighborhood. As I passed our community's largest Orthodox synagogue, its doors flew open and hundreds of worshipers rushed out, the women hastily removing bobby-pinned hair coverlets, and the men stuffing prayer shawls into velvet bags as they sped down the steps. Narrowly avoiding the stampede, I wondered what had caused it. Entry to services led by a cantor and choir during the High Holy Days was by ticket only, but with so many people having just left, I guessed that there were bound to be seats available and decided to take a chance.

OPEN TO ME THE PORTALS

Sure enough, the vestibule was unguarded, and as I passed through it into the sanctuary, a male choir struck up Psalms 24: Lift your heads, ye everlasting portals, that the King of Glory may enter. It was sheer coincidence, of course, but why argue with destiny on a day when one's fate presumably hangs in the balance. A white-robed cantor came striding down the aisle directly toward me, bearing the first of two Torah Scrolls, its silver ornaments gleaming, his song full-throttle, the floor beneath him vibrating. As the processional party completed its circuit back to the raised *Bimah* (platform) up front and returned both Scrolls to the *Aron*, massed congregational voices rose in a deeply moving version of *Eits Chayim Hee* (The Torah Is a Tree of Life). With the choir's basses furnishing dark harmonies below, the cantor's bright tenor spun a gossamer cadenza high above, the combined echoes ricocheting like bullets around the neo-Moorish sanctuary's vaulted ceiling.

I glanced up at the double-tiered gallery and noticed women dabbing at their noses with handkerchiefs, their eyes reddened from crying. Though undeniably stirring, the Torah recessional itself couldn't have inspired such a visible show of emotion, let alone a full exodus. It dawned on me that *Yizkor*, the Memorial Service held four times a year in Ashkenazic synagogues, had just concluded. That made an even greater impression, for in those days anyone with living parents usually left the synagogue before *Yizkor* commenced and returned when it was over. But the crowd I had scurried to avoid outside gave no sign of waiting around, evidently considering itself absolved of any additional religious obligations until the following Rosh Hashanah. Yet, wondrous to behold, every vacated seat was soon occupied for the *Musaf* (Additional) service by freeloaders like myself.

Just as well, I thought, for we newcomers would now fulfill the liturgical role of those who stood in the ancient Temple's courtyard during the solemn *Avodah* on Yom Kippur. While the Second Temple stood (516 B.C.E.–70 C.E.), every High Priest underwent this week-long ritual, which culminated in his entering the Holy of Holies and begging atonement for sins committed by himself, his tribe, and all Israel. I noticed that each time our cantor solemnly pronounced *hashem hanichbad vehanora*, "God's Revered and Awesome Name," while re-enacting the High Priest's three confessionals, many in the congregation joined him in kneeling and prostrating themselves until their foreheads touched the floor. It was the only time I had seen this done in the course of worship. The rapturous look on people's faces as they immediately rose to proclaim

> *baruch shem kevod malchuto le'olam va'ed*
> (blessed be His Name, Whose glorious
> kingdom is forever and ever)

was wondrous to behold. In ancient times pilgrims must have reacted similarly when, according to the Mishnah (*Tamid* 3:8; 6:2), they heard God's Name—as written—come forth from the mouth of the High Priest in purity and holiness.

In fact, every segment of the modern-day service brought with it a kaleidoscopic change of mood: undiluted awe (*Unetaneh Tokef*, "let us recount the solemnity of this day"); collective remorse (*Umipnei Chata'einu*, "because of our transgressions were we exiled"); abject sorrow (*Eileh Ezkerah*, "our martyrs we recall"); contrite repentance (*Ve'al Kulam*, "for all our sins, O God, forgive us"). At the very end, descendants of the priestly line (*kohanim*) performed the *duchan'n*. Shrouded in their gleaming white prayer shawls, they stood on the *Bimah* (called *duchan* in the Temple), soberly invoking God's blessing upon the entire congregation:

> the Lord bless you and keep you;
> the Lord make His countenance shine
> upon you and be gracious unto you;
> the Lord turn His countenance unto you
> and grant you peace (Numbers 6:24–26).

During those three hours of *Musaf*, I drifted in a sea of bodies swaying to an ever-varying poetic and musical imagery. I felt myself swept along by the current of heartfelt emotion, and apparently, so did everyone else. Our individual prayers somehow coalesced with those of the cantor, whose voice—simultaneously compelling and comforting—rode the crest of our collective wave onto the shores of God's mercy.

TRADITIONAL *DAVEN'N* DEFINED

I have never forgotten the experience. Nor, I imagine, does any Jew ever forget such an inner-directed spiritual exercise, which calls for worshipers—as much as their leader—to set the pace of prayer. Sociologist Samuel C. Heilman, who has written definitively on the reciprocal nature of synagogue prayer, emphasizes that a cantor can only sustain an already established devotional tone by reiterating the conclusion of each paragraph after worshipers have indicated that it is his turn. They signal him by a lessening of their vocal—or perhaps gestural—intensity, for *daven'n* involves the lips moving even if no sound emerges. Most often there is an accompanying drone, an undercurrent of prayer that an experienced cantor will catch on the wane and fling back like a Jai Alai player, accelerated by his own inventive energy. What flies between leader and pack are several hundred—or thousand—Hebrew words, depending on the particular service. The words require no introduction. After reciting them morning, noon, and night for two millennia, Jews—even if they are infrequent attenders—know certain foundational phrases as a mother knows her young. All that's needed is a *Minyan* of ten adults who choose one of their number to start them off; the rest has become second nature.

An age-old partnership between those praying and the one leading them *primus inter parem*—as a first among equals—enabled Jewish worship to survive intact up until quite recently. Its participants were familiar enough with the routine so that under less formal circumstances—say, that of a daily chapel service—almost any worshiper might also serve as cantor. In the synagogue of my own boyhood—Brooklyn's Young Israel of Borough Park—we youngsters never knew in advance who among the laymen might volunteer to lead prayer on a given Sabbath or Festival. Our only concern was that it be someone whose chanting elicited responses rousing enough for our piping trebles to blend in with the grown-ups' voices unobtrusively. The system worked—and still does in traditional settings—because the roles of producer and consumer are acknowledged by all parties. An individual is chosen to lead; everyone else follows. The leader opens and closes paragraphs, gauging his progress according to cues he receives from them. Individuals cue him so that he in turn may cue the group. To expedite matters, a comprehensive array of familiar signals has emerged, which worshipers traditionally acknowledge not only with unrestrained zeal but with the satisfaction that comes from fulfilling a religious obligation in timely fashion and in full measure (BT, Shabbat 119b).

Orthodox worship—including variants that go under the names chasidic ("pietist") and Sephardic (discussed in Chapters 6 and 7, respectively)—continues to elicit some 150 congregational responses every Sabbath, in addition to ongoing engagement in the *daven'n*. Conservative, Reconstructionist, and Reform services lessen the intensity of involvement by inserting an increasing number of English readings. This effectively sidesteps the easy give-and-take that always characterized Jewish worship, but in no way replaces it. Neither does periodically announced "congregational singing," which likewise bears little resemblance to the fluid prayer chant that used to swell organically into full-blown song when its moment ripened. Both of the new practices—readings carved in stone and singing on command—are self-conscious enough to stifle any initiative by worshipers. With so many built-in opportunities to utter the familiar prayer formulas *on their own* now denied the congregation, it should come as no surprise to anyone who has visited a North American synagogue lately that participation in worship often limits itself to slavish imitation of someone else's reading.

FROM OFFERINGS TO WORDS

The reluctance of today's synagogue-goers to initiate prayer without prior directives from the pulpit ignores a lesson learned during Israel's first exile in 586 B.C.E., when it had no choice but to approach God without ceremony. Hosea's earlier prophecy that instead of sacrificing bullocks, we would render *words* (the "fruit of our lips"; 14:3) was realized when a contingent of 42,000 Judean exiles returned from Babylonia. Not only did religious authorities restore systematic offerings in a newly rebuilt Temple, they democratized worship by instituting daily prayer services in all twenty-four districts of the land (Chapter I . . . "Worship in Classical Israel").

Earliest archaeological evidence of synagogue structures per se, existing anywhere in the Holy Land is from midway through the first century B.C.E. (Jericho; excavated in 1998 by Professor Ehud Netzer). Prior to then, an already-existent gathering spot such as the open area fronting upon a city's gates made do as a synagogue (from the Greek *synagein*, "to bring together"). There, prayers were offered at the exact times fixed for obligatory offerings at the Temple in Jerusalem (Mishnah *Ta'anit* 4:2). Absence of structures built exclusively to house synagogues did not preclude the holding of worship in public areas throughout the Judean hinterland in pre-Christian times. Mishnah, *Tamid* (2:1–4), is quite specific about the prayer service on prescribed fast days: where it was held (the town square); who led it (one whose house was full of children and devoid of sustenance); and what was recited (the Eighteen Daily Benedictions plus six supplementary ones from Psalms, I Kings, and Jeremiah).

As for regular morning and afternoon prayer gatherings in the outlying provinces, talmudist Solomon Zeitlin suggests that they duplicated all aspects of worship services held in Jerusalem, where, by the mid-first century of this era, some 400 synagogues thrived (JT, *Megillah* 3a; BT, *Ketubot* 105a). The Temple precinct itself housed a synagogue, that is, a hall that doubled as synagogue when it was not being used for its primary purpose: seat of the Great Sanhedrin (High Court of Justice). Known in the Mishnah as the Chamber of Hewn Stones (*lishkat hagazit*; *Tamid* 4:3), it is called "Solomon's Portico" in the New Testament (Acts 3:11). The Talmud gives eyewitness testimony concerning performance practice in this makeshift worship space (BT, *Sukkah* 53a; *Arachin* 11a). Levitical choristers, who sang several times a day over sacrifices in the Temple Courtyard, also participated in the *lishkat hagazit* rite. There, in addition to the Eighteen Benedictions mentioned previously, the Daily Liturgy included Scriptural excerpts (Exodus 20; Numbers 6, 15; Deuteronomy 6, 11) and prayers (*Emet Veyatsiv*, "true and certain is our obligation to love and obey God"). These were led by an appointed precentor, with the congregation and Levites joining in chanted responses (Mishnah, *Tamid* 5:1).

After national dispersal by the Romans late in the first century C.E., worship in the diaspora again restricted itself to prayer alone, just as it had 600 years before, during the Babylonian exile. This time around, the synagogue was recognized as a "temple-in-miniature" (*mikdash me'at*, after Ezekiel 11:16; BT, *Megillah* 29a) and its formal Order of Prayer—or *seder tefillah*—included an annual cycle of Scripture readings. Later, numerous liturgical poems would be added. The earliest of these, called *piyyutim* (from Greek *poietes*, "poetry"), arose in reaction to draconian laws issued by Emperor Justinian during the sixth century, which prohibited the community that survived in Judea from engaging in biblical or talmudic exposition. Instead, Scriptural and halachic material was surreptitiously introduced into the service through a new medium, laudatory hymns that taught Judaism's tenets in verse form: midrash through song. *Eil Adon*, "God, Lord of all Creation," a Sabbath Morning *piyyut* (singular of *piyyutim*) dating from the eighth century, is prototypical. In alphabetical acrostic it extolls God above all celestial beings and heavenly bodies: the two earthly luminaries as well as the five planets then known.

Penitential *selichot*, which appeared later on, begged forgiveness (*selichah*) for Israel's sins and were recited in the aftermath of national calamities. Originally, they came directly out of the Bible, beginning with Moses' plea on behalf of the Israelites, begging God not to consume them following their idolatry of the Golden Calf (Exodus 32: Lord, turn Thy fierce wrath and repent the evil against Thy people). Eventually, *selichot* grew into composed alphabetical acrostics (*Ashamnu*, "We Have Sinned," ninth century) and complete anthologies that were recited on fast days (*Kinot*, "Dirges for Tishah B'Av"; compiled from the tenth to the sixteenth centuries).

THE CANTOR AS SYNAGOGUE OVERSEER

As the liturgy grew in complexity, an official was appointed to supervise worship: the *chazan* ("cantor," in its original sense of *overseer* during the talmudic period; JT, *Yoma* 44a, *Megillah* 74d, *Berakhot* 9c). In addition, the need was felt for a competent "community surrogate in prayer," or *sheli'ach tsibbur*. The rationale for a prayer leader—who through his practiced recitation would absolve those worshipers not able to recite the statutory texts—appears in a compilation of early commentaries that were not included in the codified Mishnah: the *Tosefta* (*Rosh Hashanah* 2:18). Elsewhere (BT, *Ta'anit* 16a), the Talmud proper lists qualifications required of candidates for a *sheli'ach tsibbur*.

> Said Rabbi Judah bar Ilai: when they rise for prayer . . .
> they send up one who is modest and agreeable to the people,
> who knows how to chant and has a sweet voice;
> one who is well versed in the Scriptures . . .
> the Talmud . . . and all the prayers.

Masechet Soferim, a post-talmudic treatise on synagogue practice, documents that by the eighth century the prayer-leading function of *sheli'ach tsibbur* had merged with the supervisory role of *chazan*, creating an office very similar to that of the modern cantor (19:9; 11:4).

Rabbi Jacob ben Asher, a fourteenth-century codifier of Jewish law, delegated to the cantor a further duty: conveying God's words to worshipers through persuading and moralizing; that is, sermonizing (*Tur. Orach Chayim* 53). Salo Baron explains why, well into the modern era, cantors were asked to preach. "A congregation which had but one scholar would naturally entrust to such a 'messenger' the double task of leading in prayer and delivering the sermon." Communities that were able to support a rabbi in addition to the cantor would enjoy the services of a scholar who had no official connection with the synagogue, but whose principal duty was to interpret Jewish law. For most of the miniscule Jewish settlements in Europe, however, economic reality precluded engaging both religious functionaries. A *chazan/sheli'ach tsibbur* was always appointed first because communal worship could not proceed without him.

That is why cantors' duties were steadily expanded until by the sixteenth century they officiated at all the personal high moments of individuals' lives: birth, circumcision, marriage, and eulogizing the departed. When these functions transferred to the New World, the cantors who first performed them here were recognized as ministers of the Jewish faith (New York State Laws of 1684 and 1789) long before ordained rabbis arrived. Besides carrying out all the duties enumerated here, early American cantors were also expected to provide communal leadership and to decide religious questions. They performed all these religious functions on a *de facto* basis for almost 200 years. Yet it was not until the twentieth century that the cantor's legal status as one of *two* clergymen charged with leading worship in the Jewish religion was confirmed by a U.S. District Court (Washington, D.C.: Salkov Decision, 1966) and by the Internal Revenue Service (Special Ruling 78–301, 1978).

Up until the mid-1800s, cantors filling the ministerial role here did so in the absence of qualified rabbis, who refused to uproot themselves for an uncertain life in the American wild. Beyond that, a long-standing custom based on statements in the Talmud (Mishnah *Avot* 1:10: "despise the holding of high office;" BT, *Eiruvin* 13b: "he who pursues high status will find status fleeing from him") dictated that the rabbinical role avoid the formal status of an office. For that reason rabbis in European communities functioned essentially as teachers and religious arbiters. They commanded deference only by virtue of great learning, which they expounded publicly twice a year. Those occasions coincided with the afternoon hours in between worship services on Shabbat Hagadol and Shabbat Shuvah, the Sabbaths preceding Pesach (Passover) and Yom Kippur. Not until the early-nineteenth century were European rabbis thrust into the role of prayer leaders who also blessed the congregation and officiated at nuptial and burial ceremonies.

THE RABBI AS MINISTER

This development, limited at first to Western Europe, followed as an aftermath of the French Revolution, when Napoleon's armies carried forth its egalitarian Declaration of the Rights of Man. Many Jewish communities were emancipated and granted citizenship rights, and while the relative freedom lasted it engendered a widespread desire for change. Synagogue worship, the area most vulnerable to innovation, first underwent radical reform in the Westphalian town of Seesen, Germany. A small number of radical Reform rabbis in Western Europe exchanged their traditional juridical role for that of minister, "conducting" services in the manner of Christian clergymen. They drastically shortened the service and removed *piyyutim* and *selichot*, along with all references to the hope for a national restoration in Zion. When they also discontinued the chanting of prayer and Scripture, the radical Reformers stripped Jewish worship of its primary motive force. In a feeble attempt to replace it, they interspersed sporadic reading with a few hymns borrowed from Protestant usage, most notably "O Head, all Bruised and Wounded," the principal chorale of Johann Sebastian Bach's *Saint Matthew Passion.*

Such extreme bowdlerization of the service proved an exception even within Germany, where only a single congregation persisted in worshiping bareheaded and almost entirely in the vernacular: Berlin's *Reformgemeinde.* The liturgy in German *Liberale* (moderately Liberal, as opposed to the more radical Reform) synagogues—while slightly abbreviated when compared to its Orthodox counterpart—was sung almost entirely in Hebrew. It featured separate seating by gender, plus a Torah reading (known as cantillation) that covered the complete weekly *sidrah,* or "portion." Men wore hats and prayershawls, while a cantor—assisted by organ and mixed-or-boys' choir—led prayer. That anomalous blend of liberal thought and conservative practice held as a model in the German-speaking lands of Central Europe right up to the Second World War. This is evidenced by the *Einheitsgebetbuch,* the *Liberale* congregations' joint prayerbook (ed. I. Elbogen, C. Seligmann, and H. Vogelstein, 1929). Liberal practice, based on 1,000 years of cross-pollination with Christian worship in the Old World, would never accommodate the ritual incongruities that American Reform adopted once it had tasted New World religious freedom.

REFORM TAKES ROOT HERE

In the United States, no Jewish community had ever existed before a cluster of Sephardic refugees from religious persecution in South America arrived in the mid-seventeenth century and quickly established themselves (Chapter I ... "Early American/Jewish Worship: A Sephardic Monopoly"). After 1700 the Ashkenazic component increased, gradually leaving the earlier arrivers a proud but isolated minority who clung to an austere and measured rite that remains virtually unaltered to this day. Around 1825, the steadily ascendant *Ashkenazim* began to disassociate themselves from Sephardic synagogues and organize their own separate congregations. Orthodox custom still prevailed in both rites, but in another fifty years the young American republic—with its tolerance of varied religious sects—would provide fertile soil for a Reformation within Judaism. The prototypical substructure of most denominations in America at that time was congregationalism, a series of autonomous religious sects, each of which determined its own doctrine within the confines of local congregational units. This represented a fundamental departure from the well-organized European *kehillah,* accountable to a regnant Orthodoxy. Of all religions that thrived in the United States, Judaism was the least hierarchal. Freed from any central authority that might control the latitude of ritual change, it proved the most susceptible to rapid modernization.

During the late-nineteenth century, Reform attracted a majority of the quarter-million Jewish immigrants who arrived from German-speaking lands. Their primary goal was to become Americanized as rapidly as possible, and the Reform movement met that goal by offering a liberalized Judaism that would make it easier to throw off what many of the newcomers considered Old World superstitions. Founded as a national organization in 1873, the Union of American Hebrew Congregations (U.A.H.C.) adopted its so-called Pittsburgh Platform twelve years later, which sought to bring the liturgy "in accord with the postulates of reason" governing modern society.

Actually, the U.A.H.C.'s first *Union Hymnal* (Central Conference of American Rabbis, 1897) brought the liturgy more in accord with Protestantism, which had just begun preaching a gospel of social reform that seemed worthy of emulation. So did its hymn tunes. "O Praise the Lord" (page 5) quotes "I Know That My Redeemer Liveth" from the Christmas/Easter oratorio *Messiah,* and "Grateful Praises" (pages 158–159) echoes the Nativity carol "Hark! The Herald Angels Sing." At the same time, Reform rabbis in Louisville, Chicago, St. Louis, Baltimore, Philadelphia, Rochester, and Boston—some of them graduates of the Hebrew Union College in Cincinnati (established 1875)—began holding "Sabbath" services on Sunday. The rationale cited most often for this departure was a desire to increase attendance by having services coincide with the statutory day of rest in America.

REACTIONS TO RADICAL REFORM

As it entered its second half-century, American Reform began to backtrack. It had by then made its mark and could afford to reclaim selected elements of universal Jewish practice while still maintaining an unmistakably Liberal profile. Accordingly, the Columbus Platform of 1937 officially restored token observance of Sabbath and Festivals, along with a select few ceremonies and some use of Hebrew in the service. During that same period, Orthodoxy—which had organized in 1898 as the Union of Orthodox Jewish Congregations—stood pat on the right, opening up a vast middle ground of religious practice to a third stream: Conservative Judaism. This centrist movement, which saw radical change as a negative response to the gauntlet thrown by historical developments, had sprung up in Germany as a reaction to radical Reform. Rabbi Zacharias Frankel, an early moderate Reformer upon whose thinking Conservatism was based, withdrew from the radical camp in 1845 after it officially abandoned Hebrew as its language of prayer.

In 1854 Frankel founded a seminary in Breslau that trained rabbis in what he termed a Positive Historical approach of moderate change and retention of the liturgy in its original language. The main thrust of Frankel's argument went like this:

> If the historical Jewish genius has lent deep significance to its language, then contemporary disenchantment with its use is not an adequate reason for replacing it with the vernacular. That might be effected only when it no longer has significance for the Jewish people as a whole.

Since the people as a whole is in a state of constant flux, it is better to conserve traditions that are still vibrant. Reinterpret them if need be, but do not eliminate them.

Shortly thereafter, Frankel's attempt to conserve historical Judaism migrated to the United States, where it failed to stem the swelling tide of Jewish religious change. Conservatism's rabbinical school—named after Frankel's Jewish Theological Seminary—opened its doors in 1887, but attracted neither sufficient faculty nor students. Fifteen years later the school underwent complete reorganization under Dr. Solomon Schechter, and in 1913 Conservatism finally established itself on a national scale as the United Synagogue of America. By the 1920s affiliated congregations were generally following Traditional practice, modified by a variety of accommodations to modernity: sermons in English; mixed seating; a cantor, and professional choir (Chapter I . . . "Between the Wars"). No more than 10 percent of Conservative synagogues ever employed an organ to accompany services.

During the 1930s a left-wing offshoot of Conservatism, the Reconstructionist movement, advanced yet another prayer agenda. Founder Mordechai M. Kaplan took Reconstructionism's name from educator John Dewey's Pragmatist philosophy, which held that truth is not handed down once-for-all, but emerges through a process of fact finding in every generation. Believing it is "imperative that men break away from the habit of identifying the spiritual with the supernatural," Rabbi Kaplan reinterpreted the liturgy according to truths discerned by his own generation. Until Reconstructionism produced its own *Sabbath Prayer Book* in 1945 and *High Holiday Prayer Book* in 1948 (ed. Mordecai M. Kaplan, Eugene Kohn, and Ira Eisenstein), Kaplan's radical theories found expression in congregations reading silently from a traditional *Siddur* (prayerbook; plural: *Siddurim*) while rabbis recited aloud from English glosses explaining the liturgy's obsolescence.

FLUCTUATING ALLEGIANCES

From the 1950s on, American Jews had available four distinct worship approaches, among which Conservatism's middle-of-the-road adherence to historical norms in a modern setting drew a greater following than any other. Yet this potentially most successful of the movements suffered from a lack of self-definition. Its unclear demands in the area of personal observance at first attracted many who welcomed being able to write their own ticket of religious requirements. Eventually, though, the absence of clear directives translated into widespread malaise among Conservatism's lay constituency, especially its youth. In recent years, 50 percent of the Conservative youngsters polled by Jewish Theological Seminary Provost Jack Wertheimer thought that observance of *kashruth* (dietary laws) and marrying a Jew were "not important." Demographic studies had meanwhile shown Reform synagogues growing steadily in number, membership, and popular preference between 1975 and 1999, in almost direct proportion to the shrinkage of Conservative synagogues in the same three areas. Based on this evidence, it is reasonable to assume that a goodly number of new Reform affiliates came from Conservative ranks. No doubt some were motivated to join more affluent Reform congregations for the same reason advanced by their co-religionists in New York City a hundred years before. By their own admission at the time, relates historian Hyman B. Grinstein, it was in order to "occupy a position of greater respect amongst" their fellow citizens.

Another possible reason why upwardly mobile Conservative Jews were drawn to Reform was its continuing restoration of traditional Hebrew prayers led by a cantor. If that is so, the trigger for this exodus might have been Conservatism's unalloyed imitation during the 1970s and 1980s of a practice first instituted a century earlier by radical Reform: more and more prayers read in English (Chapter 5 . . . "Conservatism's 'Junket': Not for Everyone"). Worse, in an attempt to popularize the statutory Hebrew prayers that were left, Conservatism replaced chazanic chant with congregational mouthing of the most simplistic melodies, sung non-stop (Chapter 3 . . . "A True-to-Life Trip-Tik"). Unlike Reform, however, most Conservative worship offered nothing to support the singing, neither organ nor choir. In attempting to recast itself as a Liberal movement, Conservatism found itself unable to compete with Reform's more attractively packaged product.

LITURGICAL LIBERTIES

Since World War II, when it was jolted into action by the tragic events in Europe, Orthodoxy remains unique in preserving the liturgy intact. Moreover, its unexpected resurgence in recent decades has pre-empted claims by any of the other movements to represent normative Judaism. The trend is particularly evident at Ivy League colleges, where Jewish enrollment has achieved a critical mass. At the University of Pennsylvania, whose Jewish population amounted to 39 percent of its student body (7,000 out of 18,000) when I visited in 1999, Orthodox Shabbat services outdrew those of Conservatism by three to one and those of Reform by many times that.

As elsewhere, Orthodox services on campus are the only ones to be completely sung in their original language. Hebrew prayer in Reform, Reconstructionist, and even Conservative worship must often bear the weight of laborious rationalization or tendentious reinterpretation, neither of which allows the underlying text to speak for itself. In effect, synagogue-goers are being systematically distanced from their ancestral tongue (Chapter 3 . . . "How to Start Up Again"). Barely able to read Hebrew, they are now denied the opportunity even to hear an appreciable amount of it once a week. The overriding pattern of Jewish liturgical practice nowadays is a seemingly arbitrary skipping of pages—often hundreds at a time—which keeps everyone in a state of disorientation. A cast of players that has rehearsed the same script for thousands of years is now told to forget its lines and pay attention only to last-minute stage directions at every performance. "Somehow, [Judaism] fell into the capable but throttling hands of efficient but uncreative directors," writes Reform rabbi Norman B. Mirsky. "The time has come to free the actors, or else the audience will drift away."

The synagogue is not a theater, to be sure. Yet it remains the only stage upon which Jews may still practice the art of communal prayer. Like any art, true prayer doesn't preface, it simply proceeds. Would that today's worship began the same way. More often than not I have encountered officiants who greet their congregants in the mock-friendly manner of waiters introducing themselves to restaurant patrons: "Good Morning/Evening/*Shabbos*, ladies and gentlemen; my name is _____, and I'll be your rabbi for this service." They then compound the error by minutely analyzing every ritual before it is enacted. I have been equally dismayed to observe my cantorial colleagues introducing their own "selections" with all the annoying overkill of classical-music radio hosts. From a psychological standpoint it is arguable that both rabbis and cantors are defending their relatively recent role as conductors of a service rather than as front-rank leaders of a worshiping multitude. Their explaining every word and prefacing every act is tantamount to holding up a NOT GUILTY sign before the bar of history:

> Don't blame us for what's happening;
> we're doing something useful!

In reality, they are perpetuating a vicious circle: the more Hebraically illiterate a congregation, the greater the rabbinic rationale for further instruction. The more pulpit rhetoric, the less people respond, and so it goes.

In the distant past, religious authorities diligently tried to avoid any form of self-indulgence when leading prayer. The legendary talmudic sage of Roman times, Rabbi Akiva, thrashed about so extensively during his private devotions that students would later return and find him on the other side of the room. However, when serving as *sheli'ach tsibbur*, he would finish quickly, in order not to burden the community (*tircha detsibbura*; *Tosefta, Berakhot*, 3:7). During the Middle Ages, halachic authority Solomon ben Abraham Adret admonished cantors to take into consideration the strain upon congregants (*Responsa*, Part I:215), and biblical commentator David Kimchi compared those *chazanim* (plural of *chazan*) who enjoy the sound of their own voices to "the wicked of Israel who raise their voices against God" (Jeremiah 12:8). Cantors evidently had much to answer for in times past, but today they are no longer the only ones at fault. Rabbis, too, have forgotten the reproofs of their learned predecessors, along with admonitions of both the Bible (I Samuel 15:33),

> verbosity is the sin of idolatry

and Shakespeare (*Troilus and Cressida* 2:2),

'tis mad folly to make the service greater than the god.

Prayer and Scripture are being cut to the bone while the newly acquired moments overflow with increased chattiness. This seems to satisfy the desires of those attendees who prefer an unemotional, passionless rite unrelated in any way to their normal lives or daily activities. In compliance with that unspoken wish, the service has been made mechanical, therefore meaningless. Illustration: having the congregation rise on cue. Its purpose originally was to make a separation between the usual and the unusual, but the ups and downs have been so overdone that their effect is lost; people no longer know why they're standing (or sitting, for that matter). At one High Holy Day service that I attended in a suburb of Washington, D.C., the command "we *rise* as the Ark is *opened*" (at the Torah Scrolls' removal) was later contradicted by "the Ark is *opened*, yet we remain *seated* for *Berosh Hashanah*" (emotional turning point of the *Musaf* service and greatest ritual moment of the High Holy Days: *who shall live and who shall die*).

WORDS AND MUSIC

As it happens, Jewish prayer's hallmark—even at moments of impending doom—has historically been neither posture nor speech, but song. When the Jews of Blois, in Northern France, faced death in the year 1171, rather than renounce the religion of their fathers, they raised their voices in one last glory prayer to God. That hymn was identified by Rabbi Ephraim ben Jacob of Bonn, who chronicled the massacre, as *Aleinu* (Ours is to Praise the Lord), perhaps Judaism's clearest expression of faith. Even so, it is not the text of *Aleinu* but its haunting melody, still intoned on the High Holy Days, that arouses our souls and connects us with those sainted victims of a Medieval blood libel. The same is true of another text that we now have cause to sing with renewed dedication: *Ani Ma'amin* (I Believe with Perfect Faith in the Messiah's Coming). This next-to-last among the great twelfth-century philosopher Maimonides' *Thirteen Principles of Faith* was sung more recently by a martyred European Jewry. The six million who were annihilated live on in our collective memory whenever we sing their hallowed affirmation of trust in the Creator. *Aleinu* and *Ani Ma'amin* exemplify the way Jews have always prayed: through Hebrew words that ascend on wings of song (BT, *Arakhin* 11a).

While it is impossible to reach—let alone to sustain—that level of self-negation in ordinary worship, the principle of wedding words to music when placing ourselves in God's hands remains valid. Sacred music that, because it stands apart from secular trends, never becomes obsolete, enables us to approach God through heartfelt prayer. Sacred words, intended to connect the earthly with the Divine, enable God to approach us through moral instruction, wrote the anonymous tenth-century Italian/Jewish author of the *Josippon Chronicle*. In our own century a researcher into the aesthetic of Jewish worship, Cantor Adelle Nicholson, confirms that both our prayer and God's instruction are dependent upon the lyric art: "Flowing in time, music either launches text on its vibrations faster and deeper into the minds and hearts of those who hear it, or flies alone, released from the boundaries of text, bypassing the cognitive receptor in the brain, sending its powerful message straight to the soul."

That is so because music speaks to us on more primal—and therefore multiple—levels of meaning. It supersedes words. We frequently encounter moments during prayer that are pre-verbal; words cannot convey their impact. Only music, which psychoanalyst Theodore Reik called "the universal language of human emotion, the expression of the unexpressable," can articulate what we feel at such moments. Philosopher Hermann Cohen viewed religion (from the Latin *religare*, "to tie fast") as a binding together of individuals through reason. Since Jewish prayer is sung, it follows that the binding process in Judaism must take place by means of the musical sense. Cohen therefore argued that Judaism is a religion of reason articulated through the *sung* word.

Cohen's understanding of Jewish worship squares with an axiom central to Western culture ever since the Roman orator Cicero: Anything of importance must be expressed in words. Judaism has never had any quarrel with the efficacy of words, as the late doyen of American Orthodox rabbis Joseph B. Soloveitchik emphasized: "As long as ideas are bottled up in one's mind . . . they are unclear. Emotions, feelings, and thoughts are comprehended only after one has succeeded in expressing them in logically and grammatically constructed sentences."

From its inception Jewish communal worship has always taken great care to articulate thoughts precisely and in a fixed form, known as *keva*. But popular demand for sung prayer forced rabbinic authorities to relax the *keva* principle by permitting cantors to chant the statutory wordings, on condition they use preferred groupings of musical motifs that had evolved over many centuries. We recognize those motivic groupings as prayer modes (Chapter 1 . . . "Finding Common Liturgical Ground"; Chapter 4 . . . "Crossing a Boundary without Realizing It"). Their sanctioned use made room for the equally valid principle of *kavanah*, or self-expression within fixed form. Prayer modes lie beyond words, in a realm where the tension between governed regularity and mandated self-expression can play itself out. They adjudicate the claims of two polar opposites: the *obligation* to recite prescribed prayers and the *right* to concentrate idiosyncratically on one's own inner devotion. Through traditional *daven'n*, the hallowed vocal patterns have come down to us more or less intact, varying only according to our skill as worshipers and the inventiveness of those who lead us. Even heard fleetingly during our youth, whether at a grandparent's knee, in a house of mourning, or a catering hall, on recordings or films, the sound of Hebrew chant—unrestrained and free flowing—remains with us, never entirely forgotten. "We seem to have a collective unconscious memory," states Rabbi Nina Beth Cardin of the National Center for Jewish Healing, "which responds to the resonances from that heritage even if we may not consciously realize it."

And we are profoundly moved upon re-hearing it, no matter how many decades later. I acquired this insight in my first pulpit, Congregation Emanu-El of Philadelphia, where my predecessor, Pinchas Spiro, had instituted a program that taught B'nai-and-B'not Mitzvah to lead Weekday services. Spiro, Cantor Emeritus of Tifereth Israel Congregation in Des Moines as I write this, went on to do the same in Cleveland and Los Angeles for hundreds of adults and thousands more children during a career that spanned almost fifty years. His curriculum expanded to include the Preliminary sections of Sabbath-Festival-and-High Holy Day worship. He carried out this labor of love on the national level as well, through a Ba'al Tefillah Institute initiated by the Conservative Cantors Assembly, which distributes his teaching materials to anyone who requests them, lay men and women as well as professional clergy of any denomination. Spiro's pedagogical method trains people to lead prayer in a manner that invites animated congregational participation via the medium of chant. Each time a worshiping *Minyan* uses the same modes its parents and grandparents did, it recollects the piety and devotion of those earlier generations, whether or not its members "know" Hebrew in the conventional sense or have ever set foot in a synagogue. What counts is the strengthening of past ties through musical association.

WHAT HAPPENS WHEN WE INTERRUPT PRAYER

Prayer modes impart multigenerational overtones to every text sung in modern synagogues, meaningful allusions to other moments in our lives and the lives of our forebears over the course of two and a half millennia. Such passing musical references, ignored on any conscious level of awareness, are picked up by the scanning mechanism of our unconscious, where they join a host of inchoate feelings that lie buried deep within our psyches. Psychiatrist Carl A. Hammerschlag cautions that the unconscious mind will resist any attempt to address it directly. Therefore, chanted (read: *enchanted*) prayer "must approach the unconscious indirectly, even seductively," inviting those otherwise unutterable feelings to reveal themselves while enabling us to connect with them.

At that instant the present moment—and its flood of interpretive words— are temporarily suspended. Anything that deflects our attention back to prosaic surface details by focusing on a prayer's literal meaning or its page number or its liturgical significance, breaks the meaningful deep connections within us. Even in Aboriginal prayer, writes researcher C. M. Bowra, whenever "instruction has to be delivered . . . it weakens the instinctive impulse to creation . . . the thinking comes first and shapes the rite, and then the emotions follow in its wake with less than usual force." It is of no avail to rationalize that pulpit commentary may be the only guidance congregants receive during the course of a service; that is no longer true (Chapter 4 . . . "Keeping Worship Moving"). Even if it were true, on religious grounds alone the cost of such disruption would far outweigh any possible benefit. The reflexive Hebrew verb *hitpallel*, "to pray," connotes self-examination, a delving into our inner being rather than a preoccupation with the printed page. Whatever interferes with this emergent awareness of ourselves and our place in God's universe does not merely distract momentarily from worship, it stops it dead in its tracks.

Tuning into the Divine nowadays is, at best, a daunting prospect for most of us. In a world of sound bytes, photo opportunities, and titillated nerve endings, so much atmospheric static blocks the feeble signal of religious commitment that those who seek it are lucky to catch a few fleeting seconds once a week. How devastating, then, to have our own audio engineers—to whose care the job of locating God's elusive station has been entrusted—burst forth periodically with data concerning the equivalents of frequency count or megahertz range! A worship system that by the tacit approval of its lay leadership condones this sort of interruption makes it easier to understand why between 95 and 97 percent of North American Jews stay away from synagogues on a regular basis (Chapter 6 . . . "Bridging The Gap").

NON-JEWISH WORSHIP INFLUENCES

Another—more populous—religion might survive continuous pulpit palaver because that has been its historic norm. Protestant ministers *speak* Scripture to the congregation, which in turn speaks prayers to God. Musical participation by Protestant congregations takes the form of hymn singing, which stands light-years away from antiphonal *daven'n*. Attempts to supplant this pliant measure for measure with the rigidity of programmed chorales met with little success in Europe. On virgin American soil, where adherence to that sort of religious practice was associated with the leading Christian denomination and hence equated with model citizenship, a Protestantized Judaism took instant root. American Reform Judaism's founding father, Rabbi Isaac Mayer Wise (Chapter I ... "Competition Arrives, Tensions Increase"), led the way at Anshei Emeth Temple, Albany, in 1851 by abolishing chanted prayer and Scripture along with the office of *chazan*. Instead, he read the entire service.

His model: the Protestant Church format, described in the same year by a Japanese fisherman who had been shipwrecked off New England's coast. When the fisherman, John Manjiro, was eventually repatriated, the Shogunate government ordered him incarcerated as a spy. Notes of Manjiro's debriefing give a vivid impression of mid-nineteenth century religious practice in the United States.

> On each seventh day, called the *Shabasu*,
> they worship the One who made this world.
> There are many seats inside the temple.
> The one who presides stands on a high place
> holding his book. He asks those attending
> to open their books to certain pages.
> Then they all read together.
> Then they listen to his explanation.
> Then they all leave together.

The format of page announcements followed by rote reading and explanation originated in New England's Congregationalist churches during the seventeenth century. Now, over 300 years later, it has been adopted by Reform, Reconstructionist, and Conservative synagogues, which together represent almost nine-tenths of denominationally affiliated North American Jewry. With all the explanations and supplements our worship is largely at a standstill; we *pretend* to be at a loss without instruction, even though we have passed this way hundreds of times before. And so we plod through every alternative reading strewn in our path, dutifully, complacently, and often mindlessly. The best one can say about the bumper crop of spoken supplements tacked onto our liturgy was articulated long ago in the Talmud: he who adds, lessens (*kol hamosif gorei'a*; BT, *Sanhedrin* 29a). In this case the diminution goes beyond a body of hallowed texts, extending to the part of worship that perhaps antedates prayer itself: the attendant rituals that have evolved over time.

SYNAGOGUE RITUALS' FRAGILITY

There is something in people's psyches that gravitates toward action. Confirming God's Covenant at Sinai (Exodus 24:7), our people articulated this universal tendency by instinctively placing doing before hearing:

> *kol asher-diber adonai na'aseh venishma*
> "all that the Lord has spoken we will do and hear."

The Medieval *Sefer Hachinuch* (Book of Instruction) posited that man's intellectual and emotional life is influenced mainly by the things he does. In Judaism's view, deeds have always taken precedence over words: say little and do much (Mishnah, *Avot* 1:16).

Similarly, synagogue rituals—the myriad devotional acts that were not spelled out in prayerbooks until recent decades—comprise the most meaningful part of Jewish worship. In the view of cultural anthropologist Clifford Geertz, when rituals are *performed* during moments of "consecrated behavior" they open up vistas onto an imagined world that fuses with the world we live in. What is more, those sacralized moments have a decidedly beneficial effect on worshipers' mental health. Researchers at the Bowman Gray Medical School agree, based on a twelve-year study of religious involvement through participation in the rituals of prayer, as opposed to merely attending services and believing in the ethical principles of one's faith.

"To ritualize is to make oneself present," declares Tom F. Driver, a professor of theology at Union Theological Seminary. Indeed during the High Holy Days when we ritually alter the inevitability of our fate by loudly protesting

> *uteshuvah utefillah utzedakah ma'avirin et-ro'a hegezeirah*
> "the severity of the [Rosh Hashanah] decree can be averted
> [before it is sealed on Yom Kippur], through
> repentance, prayer, and charitable *deeds*,"

we are literally at one with the *sheli'ach tsibbur*. At that transcendent moment the synagogue becomes a Heavenly Court, before which the congregation stands in judgment. The *piyyut*'s poetic metaphor has passed into reality and we are terrified, until released by the realization that our destiny lies in our own hands, through behavior that is incumbent upon any Jew.

Even so, the enactment of any transformative ritual—including its requisite congregational response—can be corrupted by a breakdown of the conventions surrounding it. If a baseball catcher were to audibly call out each pitch instead of signaling for it silently, the game's pivotal drama would be destroyed. So, too, when a long-established ceremony of any kind—whether religious or secular—begins with talking instead of doing, with prompting in place of reflexive action, a mood of reverential anticipation that has been built up over centuries of common usage disappears beyond recall. That is why the English Victorians strove mightily not to let in daylight upon the magic surrounding events in which Royalty played a role. That particular convention is no longer upheld; in their zeal to know-and-tell all, the British press and populace have dispelled any semblance of mystique that may still cling to their monarchy. And we, in our eagerness to make the liturgy "relevant," have lowered our devotionals to the level of a course in remedial reading.

We have borrowed too many quirks of our larger culture and not enough of its good habits: playing to the camera rather than keeping our eye on the ball; pre-announcing the very opening words of our liturgy and then mouthing them by rote, because we assume that is the way religious feelings are expressed in English-speaking countries. But that is not how most North American or British churches actually begin a service. The entire congregation generally *sings* an opening hymn, stanza by stanza. Protestantism's prime medium of religious expression—reading—asserts itself only *after* the hymn has been sung. Nor are Protestants unique in commencing worship by singing rather than by speaking. So do inner-city ethnic Catholics, led by a deacon, before the priest takes over. Almost all religions rely on a variety of devices other than spoken words to mark their passage into the sanctified. Buddhist monks meditate via a chant so profound that it generates multiphonic overtones. Hindu Brahmans burn incense to the One before Whom All Worlds Recoil. Shinto priests use handclapping as a means of gaining the divine spirits' attention. Tao officiants sacrifice paper likenesses of the deities. Malaysian intermediaries between humans and the high god spin imaginary threads in the air, symbolizing ascent to heaven. Voodoo shamans juxtapose the shaking of rattles against a steady background of drumming. Native American medicine men pass around a ceremonial pipe and sing as they create healing paintings in the sand. Islamic *muezzins* rely upon a passionately delivered chant in summoning the faithful to prayer. So do *chazanim* in Traditional synagogues.

THE OLD SHALL BE RENEWED

If, for whatever sociologically dictated reasons, we sophisticated modern Jews feel compelled to single out one of our neighbor's religious customs for copying, let us take care also to note the manner of its performance. Readings are read, not described or introduced. By the same token, rituals are best enacted and not dissected. So are most events in our lives. We enter this world unannounced and we depart it the same way. Our deepest feelings come upon us without fanfare: love and kindness; duty and devotion. Why can't our religious observances proceed in similar fashion?

They can, and do, in a growing number of North American synagogues where a modest revival of almost-forgotten rituals has begun to spring up. During my many encounters with current practice I have never felt more in tune with a sacred moment than when Orthodox Rabbi Barry Freundel of Washington's Georgetown Synagogue raised a brimming *Kiddush* ("sanctification") cup and uttered a single formulaic word before intoning the wine-blessing: "*Savrai* ('By Your Leave')."

Like the crack of a pistol shot, 300 voices—male, female, young, and old— responded:

"*Lechayim*, 'To Life'!"

There it was: Franz Rosenzweig's *common gesture*; the supreme component of Judaism's liturgy.

Orthodox congregations are not the only ones to recycle former usages that were overlooked as we rushed to modernize. In Northern New Jersey's suburban communities, perhaps because of their proximity to the increased traditionalism of Manhattan's various rabbinical seminaries, I have watched worshipers in every movement—including Reform—gather up a corner of their prayer shawl (*tallit*) as the Torah is unrolled to several columns' width after being read. Wrapping the *tallit* fringes around their fingers, worshipers raise their arm toward the Scroll and salute its ceremonial elevation (*hagbahah*). As late as the 1980s, when most Reform temples discouraged even the *wearing* of a *tallit*, no one could have dreamed this would occur. Worshipers are also rediscovering the value of other spontaneously performed devotional acts. Witness the many who now cover their eyes as they fervently pronounce the final syllable—*echaaaaaaaaad*—of the *Shema* (Epilogue . . . "Renewing Liturgy through Its Performance").

I never anticipated seeing a Conservative synagogue that had previously oriented its cantorial podium toward the congregation suddenly encourage lay prayer leaders to again *daven* facing the Holy Ark. Nor would I have expected it to permit *kohanim* to *duchan*. Yet both customs have been reinstated at Philadelphia's Beth Zion-

Beth Israel, which formerly accompanied its Friday Evening services with an organ. Facing the Ark was at first limited to services held in the chapel, where young couples pursuing a more stringent program of observance predominated among the few regulars. Word about the Center City congregation that was receptive to Traditional practice soon spread, and young people began showing up for Kabbalat Shabbat in numbers sufficient to warrant moving the service into the Main Sanctuary. A Reader's table for the *sheli'ach tsibbur* was set up in the center aisle, facing the Ark, and an Oneg Shabbat was organized in the Library where worshipers—especially the unmarrieds—could socialize afterward for as long as they liked.

Many of the younger set also attend Festival services, and at their request *duchan'n* has been rescheduled in the late-morning Musaf service once during each holiday. To accommodate it meant restoring the *chazan*'s repetition of the *Amidah* (Standing Devotion, core of every service), and this practice carried over into Weekday services. The return of both customs, as well as recitation of the complete Grace after communal meals, has noticeably affected the congregation's worship. Like a butterfly let loose, it is once again on the wing. Just as encouraging is the fact that students at the nearby Reconstructionist Rabbinical College in suburban Wyncote, Pa., have wholeheartedly adopted the enthusiastic *Kiddush* repartee described here.

AND THE NEW SHALL BE SANCTIFIED

It is not the liturgy that stands in need of new rituals, but rather rites of passage for which until now there has been no prescribed liturgy. While Jewish boys are named at circumcision on the eighth day after birth, the naming of newborn girls—most commonly known as *Simchat Bat*—is so recent a ritual that communities refer to it by varying appellations and go about its enactment differently. One alternate designation—*Brit Benot Yisrael*—acknowledges the long-neglected Covenant that God made with Mother Sarah and, through her, with all Daughters of Israel who would follow (Genesis 21:12). In a comprehensive analysis of the influence that feminism has had upon the entire American Jewish community, sociologist Sylvia Barack Fishman affirms that under whatever nomenclature a Jewish daughter's birth is being marked, Orthodox synagogues have now joined the ranks of venues that host it.

The *Simchat Bat* that I watched Reconstructionist rabbi Linda Holtzman lead several years ago bore all the earmarks of a true ritual: sanctifying an event that had hitherto been taken for granted because it is so universal. The ceremony was an eye opener for me as well as for the tiny celebrant. After both parents offered introductory prayers, Rabbi Holtzman took the tiny infant in her arms as only a mother can.

We are now going to *awaken each of our newborn's five senses, one by one.* First, we welcome her into the family of Israel with the *sound* of her own name: Uphold this little one, O God, and let her name in Israel be _____ *bat* [daughter of] _____ and _____ . Just as she enters the world in health, so may she embark upon a life imbued with Torah, love, and righteousness.

Second, we ask Aunt _____ and Uncle _____ to stimulate their niece's sense of *sight* by lighting this candle in her honor.

Third, we invite _____ and _____ to present our celebrant with this toy and thereby activate her sense of *touch.*

Fourth, _____ and _____ will arouse her sensitivity to the beautiful *smell* of this freshly picked flower.

Finally, it is _____ and _____'s privilege to pronounce the blessing over this cup of wine and give their grandaughter her first *taste* of God's bounty.

The Awakening ritual concluded with *Mi Shebeirach*: May the One Who blessed our forebears Sarah, Rebeccah, Rachel, and Leah watch over this child. Then was heard the suddenly revelatory caroling of an old religious school favorite, *Heiveinu Shalom Aleichem*, "We Bid You Welcome." General wishes of *Mazal tov!* (Good luck!) affirmed the resourcefulness of contemporary Jewry in creating truly meaningful liturgical gestures from mundane raw material already at hand.

If we but allow it to happen, the proliferation of similarly charged moments within the more tightly structured framework of synagogue worship will one day remove the barriers between our past, present, and future. Without words, without speech, simply through performing timeless acts on our own, we shall not only glimpse but *partake* of the eternal: that which existed before we were born and will continue to exist after we are gone. In replicating the most meaningful events of our common history, time-honored rituals renew our ties to the Jewish folk as nothing else can. They operate far beyond the normal bounds of our daily life, yet they express our most intensely personal yearnings for meaning in a world that might otherwise appear chaotic.

THE PROBLEM WITH READINGS

Deepak Chopra, an endocrinologist who specializes in mind/body medicine, has written extensively on the universal danger of entropy, a dissipation of energy leading to chaos. The creative life force is in constant battle with entropy, as Chopra notes. "In physics, entropy is opposed by work, the orderly application

of energy; without work, energy dissipates." One of the easiest solutions to the
problem lies in giving people something constructive to do; in worship this means
engagement through ritual activity or *avodah* (with a small "a"), literally, "work."
It should not shock most readers to learn that rote readings do not fall under
the heading of work. Barely engaging either mind or body, they muster the lowest conceivable level of energy, hence are the least effective way to stimulate
people's interest.

'Tis the gift to be simple in our religious devotions, counsels the old Shaker
song, but it is decidedly not a benefaction to be treated as simpletons during
worship. That is what happens when prayer is confined to responsive readings.
Journalist Dan Rottenberg compared the phenomenon to "the earnest bleating
of a herd of sheep" he once heard outside his window at a French country inn.
"First the lead sheep would shout "Baaa'! Then the flock would repeat the leader's
incantation in unison . . . long, drawn-out baaas." It's an accurate depiction of
what currently transpires in many synagogues; the less sense the words make
(Chapter 8 . . . "Rethinking Some *Havurah* Strategies"), the more prating back
and forth.

THE PITFALL OF ANNOUNCEMENTS

Jewish congregations are not alone in succumbing to the current penchant for fir-
ing empty rounds of verbiage at one another. In order for priests to better com-
municate with their parishioners while reciting Mass, Catholic churches have turned
the altar around. The late Joseph Campbell, a lifelong Catholic and one of the
world's great authorities on mythology, took a dim view of the innovation: "It
looks like Julia Child giving a demonstration—all homey and cozy." Protestant
ministers, of course, have always spoken directly to their congregations. In trying
to follow suit, too many present-day rabbis and cantors have missed the mark and
wound up aping the mass-media habit of explaining what is about to take place.
The trouble with this is, it doesn't work. As Rousseau observed over 200 years
ago, anything pre-announced is guaranteed to disappoint.

Harold M. Schulweis, one of Conservative Judaism's most creative and out-
spoken pulpit rabbis, openly questions this unwarranted intrusion upon Jewish
worship.

> The way in which we conduct services is counter to everything I believe in. An illus-
> tration: "We're now going to have the meditative introspective prayer called the
> *Amidah,* pages twenty-one to twenty-seven." Having said "pages twenty-one to twenty-
> seven," I have *killed* it [compare: Prologue . . . "A Search for Precedents"].

Better not to announce readings—if read we must—or explain rituals. Instead, let each event unfold so that people can experience it fully and unfiltered.

THE WONDER OF SERMONS

The same holds true for worship's study portions. "A bad sermon provides an explanation," says Barbara Taylor, recently named to Baylor University's list of Twelve Greatest Christian Preachers. Taylor is quick to add, "but a good sermon provides an experience." One of the best I have ever heard was by the late Louis L. Sacks, then spiritual leader of Philadelphia's Conservative Ramat El Congregation. Rabbi Sacks, who boasted a stentorian delivery, was speaking on pollution in its many forms, including the fouling of our environment and the consequent dangers to our collective ecostructure and individual systems. He expounded on smoking and air pollution, on dumping medical waste and water pollution, on chemical fertilization and soil pollution. He advocated return to a simpler life closer to what nature intended, that is, devoid of artificial stimulation. He extolled the benefits of meditative thinking as opposed to mindless floundering, of sincere prayer versus grasping acquisition, mere curtain raisers for a ringing denunciation of the world's most pervasive poison: noise pollution.

His voice rose steadily as he recounted the evils of blaring radios, honking vehicles, drilling jackhammers, and roaring jets, all of which assault our eardrums and pulverize our psyches with their unbearable racket. Pausing just long enough to breathe, he bellowed, "WHAT WE NEED . . . IS PEACE AND QUIET!"

That was an experience.

A LOWERING OF STANDARDS

Today, in place of a single sermon during worship, we are subjected to five or six infomercials delivered at the most inappropriate times. One such inviolable moment is the *Amidah*, traditionally begun by taking three hesitant steps forward. Next come praisegiving, petitioning, acknowledgment, and periodic bowing, concluded by deferential leave-taking in the form of three steps backward. The *Amidah* was always recited softly enough to be inaudible even to oneself (BT, *Berakhot* 24b) just as the heavens and firmament declare God's glory soundlessly (Psalms 19:4–5):

> There is no speech
> nor are there words . . .
> yet their message goes out
> through all the earth.

For rabbis to announce anything before, during, or after this solemn prayer was considered sacrilegious. Lately, however, we subscribe to what Daniel Patrick Moynihan calls "defining deviancy down." The senator singled out American government officials' tendency to sanction what used to be deemed aberrant popular behavior when it is in their agencies' best interest to "redefine the problem as essentially normal and do little to reduce it." His observation also applies to contemporary synagogues, where the deviancy level of officiants rises year by year, as does the membership's tolerance of pulpit actions that were formerly considered unthinkable.

Cantors are no exception. They insert melodies to be sung aloud within what used to be considered the domain of congregational *daven'n*, and then raise stumbling blocks in the form of ill-considered musical arrangements that trip up anyone attempting to sing along. If repeated often enough, this habit of answering one's own question without allowing the other party to have a say leads to a chronic state of lassitude. Worshipers, after all, have come to *do* as much as to listen. Since there is no longer any victory to be gained by paying attention, they simply give up the fight along with all pretense at involvement.

Never before have Jewish worshipers sat back and let their *sheli'ach tsibbur* go it alone; they were too busy supplying the many timely responses built into every service. That abiding obligation—which includes responding or standing at appropriate times—hasn't changed, only people's perception of it as no longer necessary. How so? When congregants attempt to play their historical role in worship, they are often made to feel like interlopers. Answering *amein* to a blessing without the pulpit-generated preamble "and let us all say . . ." or rising for a *Kaddish* or an *Amidah* without waiting for the announced directive to do so, they are stared at as if having usurped rabbinic prerogative.

Actually, it's the other way around. Our leaders have overstepped their mandate, but we find it easier to continue imitating our Gentile neighbors rather than to reassert our own religious prerogatives. If rabbis want to read for us (we seem to be saying), let them. And if cantors want to pray on our behalf, more power to them since most of us are no longer able to decipher the language of our prayerbook. We ignore the fact that synagogue prayer has always constituted an implied partnership between the one delegated as leader and the ones being led. For this relationship to work it is essential that we hold up our end by responding on cue. If some worshipers have forgotten their standing assignment, rabbis and cantors should do more than simply issue instructions: *Re-train them by example.* The technique is routinely used by physical therapists to re-pattern blocked movements that the body remembers but can no longer perform without external assistance.

PRAYER THERAPY THAT WORKS

Back in 1975, Orthodox Rabbi Ephraim Z. Buchwald first spotted a dysfunctional-worshiper syndrome among newcomers to Lincoln Square Synagogue in New York, where he served as educational director. The rabbi commandeered an upstairs classroom, organized a service where beginners could learn to *daven*, and before long had initiated a National Jewish Outreach Program spread over 150 locations in the United States, Canada, Great Britain, and Israel. The Beginners Service that I attended at Lincoln Square twenty years later, still led by Rabbi Buchwald, was in fact an entry-level workshop that openly welcomed thoughtful probing about prayer, Scripture, halachah, anything. Some fifty people who kept coming and going all through the Sabbath Morning session's three absorbing hours fired questions—and answers—even before they were completely in or out the door. Men and women sat apart, the rabbi positioned at a net-like *mechitzah* between them just like a tennis referee, making tough instantaneous calls that often didn't fully satisfy either side.

Discussion of that week's *sidrah* included the case of two men engaged in a fight during which they collide with an expectant mother and inadvertently cause her to miscarry and lose the fetus (Exodus 21:22–23). The question then arose as to what constitutes a capital offense according to Jewish law. Rabbi Buchwald answered by spelling out the many rabbinic strictures that surround any death penalty: two sets of witnesses, one to warn the potential perpetrator of his or her contemplated act's illegality and consequences, another to witness the deed. He then explained that "an eye for an eye" meant compensatory payment (BT, *Bava Kamma* 83b–84a) and was never taken literally.

A clean-cut young man in his early thirties pointed out that the two pairs of witnesses really add up to three, since the second pair, who actually witness the murder, have an added obligation to warn the perpetrator and not stand idly by as murder is committed. An equally attractive young woman immediately challenged the rabbi, not over the point being discussed but about the fact that although the young man was apparently unmarried (with no wedding band visible to her discerning eye), he was wearing a *tallit*! Rabbi Buchwald assured the young woman that wearing a *tallit* was optional, even for a good catch like that particular bachelor, who (the rabbi added) happened to be an arbetrageur on Wall Street, as attested by his astute mathematical observation.

Taking the bait, another woman asked, "What about me; would I be permitted to wear a *tallit*, whether married or not [coyly introducing the possibility that she wasn't]?" The rabbi cleared up all lingering doubts by telling her she could wear a *tallit* even though unmarried, but inasmuch as doing so might be considered presumptuous, it was not a common practice among Orthodox women. "Then how come it's so common among the Conservative?" several women wanted to know all at once. A middle-aged man from the back of the room jumped in: "It's because they can afford it better!" At that the rabbi intervened and, pointing directly at the kibbitzer, smoothed any ruffled distaff feathers with the Solomonic comment "Now you know why _____ over there is still single!"

While learning to pray is the Beginners Service's stated objective, learning to *learn* is what it actually teaches people: about their religion and the way it expects men and women to interrelate with it and with each other. The Shabbat Morning liturgy—through which Rabbi Buchwald slowly walks his charges section by section, prayer by prayer, line by line, until they feel at home in it—is merely the centerpiece for a smorgasbord of socially slanted religious activities. The same learners—most of them actively seeking Jewish mates—mingle at post-service Shabbat luncheons, Holiday dance parties, a Model Seder, regular lectures, discussion groups, crash courses in Hebrew reading as well as Basic Judaism, and a Shabbat Across America program of Friday Night dinners hosted by congregations of all denominations, which, by its third year (1999), attracted almost 75,000 people. Over the past quarter-century hundreds of marriages have resulted from the various learners' courses, with many of the graduating couples continuing to attend together with their children. Often they will serve as volunteer leaders and teachers for the next generation of beginners.

WHAT SYNAGOGUES MUST DO NOW

Gentle patterning—in an intimate setting for learners—is what many of today's Jews need until their ritual skills become ingrained and they feel comfortable enough to approach God without benefit of intermediary. Worshipers who cannot read Hebrew must be systematically guided to a point where they can discern the musical echoes of their people's collective yesterdays in today's verbose services. For older folks, "the soul-stirring chants they were taught as children are never forgotten," wrote my own mentor Abba Yosef Weisgal (of blessed memory), a cantor who served his Baltimore congregation faithfully for fifty-two years. "Somewhere in their subconscious these beautiful songs have slept and, like the oncoming Spring, burst forth again." Just as their Gentile peers react upon hearing CDs of Gregorian chant even though they may not be churchgoers, Jewish youngsters with no religious school background relate instinctively to *daven'n* that is led with absolute conviction. At worst, they may see it as a means of preserving what critic Jon Pareles calls "ancient ways that may yet have something to teach." Their Gentile

counterparts have evidently come to view sacred chant as "a short cut to the solace and stability provided by a longstanding tradition," or they would not be buying
so many commercial recordings of it. In either case, words alone will not suffice,
for they cannot bring people to tears.

Spanish philosopher Miguel de Unamuno stated the case unequivocally
for Catholicism: "the holiest attribute of a temple is that it is a place where men
weep together." In Judaism, the synagogue stands in place of our Second Temple,
destroyed on Tishah B'Av in the year 70. "From that day on," taught Rabbi
Elazar (BT, *Berakhot* 32b), "the gates of prayer have been closed . . . but not the
gates of tears." An oft-quoted midrash (*Exodus Rabba* 38:4) has the Congregation of Israel complaining to God, "We are poor; we have no sacrifices to bring
before You." God replies, "I need only words." The people argue further, "We
know no words." But God silences them: "Weep and I will receive you as I did
your fathers."

Through what will future generations remember our present form of worship; through the timely platitudes that fill its prayerbooks, or through the timeless phrases that have ever told us what was, is, and ought to be? How wonderful
if we could regain our singing voices in prayer. Let it be via English poetization of
a *piyyut* or *selichah* that we chant to the old modal patterns, so long as we again show
the religious fervor that we have always shown before God. Almost a century ago
the brilliant physician-poet of Eastern European Jewish Enlightenment Saul
Tchernichowsky was so unnerved by murderous pogroms that erupted in Kishinev,
Bessarabia, that he could not bring himself to respond through his chosen medium of verse. After a year and a half, he finally penned the following open letter
to his editor, Dr Joseph Klausner.

> The life of every Jew should be a veritable song,
> in which order conquers chaos and life conquers death.
> But the realities of life—poverty, oppression and evil—
> convert this song of victory into a song of defeat.
> Against this fate we Jews must struggle.

We must reclaim the vital, almost defiant voice that Jews once mustered to
rail against the injustice of their situation. Outraged over the Blois community's
martyrdom, the twelfth-century liturgical poet Baruch of Mainz demanded of God:

> How could You let us be seized by fire?
> You, Who promised that "the House of Jacob

shall be a fire . . . and the House of Esau
shall be chaff" [Obadiah, Verse 18]!

With the dropping of that poetic gauntlet, our liturgy acquired a Jewish social conscience. If God could not be called to account when His innocent people were being decimated, of what value was their prayer?

One searches in vain for that characteristic blaze of righteous indignation—on behalf of other Jews—in our modern prayerbooks. Contemporary Jewish worship has declared poetic bankruptcy, partly because justified grievances like the previous one, with their accompanying demand for Divine retribution toward those responsible for the conflagration, have been erased from the liturgies of every movement except Orthodoxy (Chapter 3 . . . "Language: A Repository of Values"). Abba Kovner, a poet and World War II resistance fighter in the Vilna Ghetto, referred to the searing words of our liturgical poems as "a language of the living, which the dead will also hear and understand." They also provided an outlet through which antecedent generations could express their pent-up outrage over persecution. The ancient *piyyutim* that glorify God through mythically expanded Scriptural allusion, and more-recent *selichot* that decry calamity while eloquently beseeching Divine mercy in God's own words, used to be chanted by entire congregations in tones so elemental they practically superseded statutory prayer. Those powerfully moving hymns still bear—better than any other vehicle—all our folk memories, their triumphs as well as catastrophes. Unless we are again permitted to sing at least some of the immortal lyrics that tell Judaism's story—as did our grandparents and their grandparents before them—there is a strong possibility that as Tchernichowsky feared, "future generations will have no song."

How our various movements' most recent prayerbooks have attempted to forestall this eventuality is the burden of Chapter 3: "The Latest Road Maps."

CHAPTER 3

The Latest Road Maps

A [prayer] book will describe the notes to the music . . .
Just as, while a map is not a territory,
a map shows us how to get there,
so while the notes are not the music,
the notes tell us what to sing to re-create the sound.
                                        Jacob Neusner,
                            Judaism's Theological Voice, 1995

I once watched a young seminarian wait in line to greet the golden-voiced cantor Jacob Barkin after an especially well-sung concert. The student's emotional circuits were apparently so overloaded that when he finally stood facing Barkin, he could only blurt out: "*Chazan*, there are no words!" The cantor smiled and gently reassured him: "There are words, young man; you just have to find them." I believe a similar task faces Liberal prayerbook editors who feel most comfortable with English as primary vehicle of prayer, despite the rising tide of popular preference for restoring Hebrew to the service (see further on: "Rewriting Road Manuals to Accommodate Women Drivers"). In guarding their turf, prayerbook editors find themselves scrambling to find vernacular equivalents for Hebrew formulations that verbalize the average person's profoundest religious feelings. The prospect is Sisyphean; such itense self-scrutiny defies even private rumination and is certainly not conducive to public avowal. Moral stock-taking (*cheshbon hanefesh*) is not done on the floor of an Exchange but rather in the quiet places of one's soul. Words can help, like guideposts along a hidden trail, but only if they are positioned so as to reconcile the mindset of post-biblical Hebrew with the rhythms and usages of late-twentieth-century North American speech.

DETERMINING THE MOST INCLUSIVE ROUTE

The task would prove daunting enough without an added need to avoid sexually biased language, but it is no longer possible to ignore today's growing demand for gender-inclusive worship. Women have assumed an active leadership role not only in running and administering synagogues, but also in leading prayer and rewriting the liturgy. In 1994, for the first time, they formed part of the committee responsible for Reconstructionism's latest Sabbath and Festival prayerbook, *Kol Haneshamah* (ed. David A. Teutsch). Before that, Reform's *Gates of Prayer* (ed. Chaim Stern, 1975), Conservatism's *Siddur Sim Shalom* (ed. Jules Harlow, 1985) and Orthodoxy's *Art Scroll Siddur* (ed. Nosson Scherman and Meir Zlotowitz, 1984) were all produced by exclusively male committees. It was not until the 1990s that Reform and Conservative attitudes turned more gender-affirmative, out of deference to an unprecedented wave of initiative promulgated by knowledgeable women all across the religious spectrum.

NEGOTIATING A ROADBLOCK

Orthodoxy continues to prohibit women from leading mixed services, and a Vaad Harabanim (Rabbinical Council) in Queens, N.Y., has gone so far as to ban prayer led exclusively for and by women! Several members of the Vaad refused to go along with their more recalcitrant colleagues on this issue. One of them, who supervises a women's prayer group in his own synagogue, resigned in protest over the decision. Another, Rabbi Simcha Krauss, pleaded before his colleagues in the women's behalf. "People want something," he explained, "it's a quest for spirituality, a yearning to be closer to God, and if we can say yes, we should say yes." The Vaad turned a deaf ear to his argument.

Despite such setbacks, the Orthodox movement's most widely used current prayerbook continues to enrich synagogue going for both men and women. *Art Scroll Siddur* is the biggest boon to meaningful participation in Jewish worship since the first printed *Siddurim* appeared in Rome (under the imprimatur Soncino) over 500 years ago. Of all extant bilingual editions, it offers the most comprehensive assistance to lay people on any observance level. It is the first prayerbook to spell out when-what-where—and even how and why—one is expected to perform acts of devotion during prayer.

Some critics view all the bodily motions—bowing, stepping back, covering one's face—as overstress of prayerful attitudes at the expense of God praise. Reform liturgist Arnold Jacob Wolf categorizes such obsequious acts as "antiquarian . . . obscurantist . . . medieval . . . and reactionary." Evidently, the non-Orthodox types I have observed using *Art Scroll Siddur* at daily prayer services see things differently. The emptiness that they and many other modern Jews are beginning to discover at the core of their mundane existence is best filled through prayers of yearning. When accompanied by the gestures described previously, their prayer betokens the same submission with which one would approach a parent following long estrangement. In this respect *Art Scroll Siddur* has become the most convincing advocate of what was once considered normative Jewish worship.

As stated, Orthodoxy is far from approaching gender parity at present; the halachic fence that it has erected to prevent feminine participation in mixed prayer still stands. Within that restriction many an occasional breakaway *Minyan* will attempt to stretch Orthodox tolerance of egalitarianism to its absolute limits by encouraging women to prepare and deliver in-depth talks on the weekly *sidrah.* But as for allowing them to serve as community surrogates in prayer, the dictum that "a woman's voice is indecent [BT, *Berakhot* 24a; based on Song of Songs 2:14], for sweet is thy voice and comely thy countenance," retains its hold. Orthodox rabbis continue to categorize women leading communal worship as a sure source of sexual excitement. Thus, "when men sing and women join in, it is licentiousness; but when women sing and men join in, it is like fire raging in a field of flax [BT, *Sotah* 48a]!"

Orthodox feminists Susan Grossman and Rivkah Haut are firmly—if deferentially—opposed to that rabbinic position. In its place their wide-ranging anthology on women's role in the synagogue suggests a new working midrash based upon Psalms 45. At first glance a secular romance between a Hebrew king and a foreign princess, like the Song of Solomon it, too, may be interpreted allegorically as a covenantal relationship between God and Israel. In Grossman and Haut's reading, "God is waiting for the daughters of Israel to be brought into the inner courts of the palace [synagogue], asking them to leave the periphery [women's gallery] where they have remained for too long."

Writing on the same subject, Renee Rabinowitz Wagner maintains that the door leading into God's inner court will open to the key of knowledge. Her husband, Orthodox rabbi Stanley Wagner of Denver (now Emeritus), held no halachic objection to sermons by women. In fact, he welcomed them to the BMH Synagogue's pulpit on a regular basis, his one stipulation being that they build their talks upon authoritative rabbinic sources. Nor is the honor of being called to the Torah or the right to be counted in a *Minyan* that far off for Orthodox women, according to Blu Greenberg, a noted feminist lecturer and author. She regards women's cup of progress as half-full rather than half-empty and predicts that they will be recognized as *to'aniyot* (advocates; singular: *to'anit*) in courts of religious law in the not-too-distant future. A growing need to adjudicate halachic questions involving marital disputes prompted the Jerusalem-based Nishmat Center for Women's Studies to train Orthodox women as halachic consultants, or Poseks, in 1997. Two years later the first eight graduate scholars began answering questions primarily in the area of ritual purity, which determines the permissibility of conjugal relations at certain times.

The most pressing halachic issue at this moment is that of the *agunah* (literally, "anchored"; plural: *agunot*), whose husband has either deserted or refuses to grant her a *get* (rabbinically issued bill of divorce). In such cases the wife remains chained fast, unable to remarry. Regarding this issue, too, feminist pressure has lately produced minute cracks in Orthodoxy's heretofore monolithic refusal to budge. At the first international conference of Feminism and Orthodoxy (1997; renamed Orthodox Feminists, or EIDAH, in 1998, and spun off into the Jewish Orthodox Feminist Alliance, or JOFA, in 1999) Rabbi Emanuel Rackman, chancellor of Israel's Bar-Ilan University, reported on the formation of a *Bet Din Tzedek Leba'ayot Agunot*, "Duly Constituted Court for the Problems of Agunot." The *Bet Din* issues a legal brief based on acknowledged halachic precedent for every case adjudicated, and either annuls an *agunah*'s marriage or issues a specific type of divorce (*get zikui*) granted unilaterally without her husband's explicit consent. What is more, the children of a marriage dissolved in this way bear no stigma of illegitimacy. In its first three years, despite vociferous Ultra-Orthodox opposition, the Court freed almost 300 *agunot*.

A few months prior to the *Bet Din*'s founding, the Midtown Board of Kashrut in New York had sponsored a community-wide forum for the purpose of discussing both pre- and post-nuptial agreements to ensure that both parties will never use the *get* as a negotiating tool in divorce proceedings. A woman moderator led the discussion, held in a Modern Orthodox synagogue whose rabbi had lectured on "Gender Differences in Torah Study" just two nights before. Until the late 1990s, neither of those events could have transpired. Now, with the tacit understanding that change is inevitable, gender differences in Modern Orthodox prayer are being addressed as well.

REWRITING ROAD MANUALS TO
ACCOMMODATE WOMEN DRIVERS

If the door to ritual parity for women is now slightly ajar in Orthodoxy, it has stood wide open in the Reform movement since 1972, when Sally Preisand entered the rabbinate. Although that breakthrough occurred almost too late to affect *Gates of Prayer*, in preparation at the time and published shortly thereafter, Reform's prayerbook does go out of its way to avoid using masculine terminology exclusively when referring to humankind in general. Nevertheless, its English rendering of God remains uniformly male. Without exception, women Reform rabbis have attempted to skirt this dilemma by substituting "God" every time they encounter the words "He" or "His" as they read aloud.

Pushed to its absurd extreme, this strategy would reprogram the Torah recessional that appears in *Gates of Prayer* (page 446), from

> God's splendor covers heaven and earth.
> He is the strength of His people,
> Making glorious His faithful ones,
> Israel, a people close to Him

to the following gender-neutral gobbledygook.

> *God*'s splendor covers heaven and earth.
> *God* is the strength of *God*'s people,
> Making glorious *God*'s faithful ones,
> Israel, a people close to *God*.

Many male officiants prefer sticking to what is in the prayerbook. As the senior rabbi of one leading temple reportedly confided to his staff while deliberating a way out of the quandary: "The only consistency you can expect once you have opened the debate on God's gender, is inconsistency."

For years the Reform movement has been planning a completely revised prayerbook to appear shortly after the millennium. Its liturgical chairperson in 1992, Rabbi H. Leonard Poller, promised that along with more up-to-date English paraphrasing of Hebrew prayers in lieu of direct translation, Reform's twenty-first-century prayerbook would confront the issue of gender exclusivity. An interim *Gender Sensitive Prayerbook* (ed. Chaim Stern, 1992), formalized the "God"-for-"He/His" substitution, while emending Hebrew texts wherever feasible. Thus

> *ve'imoteinu*
> and our mothers

was attached to the standard invocation

eloheinu veilohei avoteinu
Our God and God of our fathers,

and Matriarchs Sarah, Rebeccah, Leah, and Rachel joined their respective partners Abraham, Isaac, and Jacob at every mention.

In 1993 the Central Conference of American Rabbis (C.C.A.R.) launched
a five-year project to study "The Role of Laity in Worship and the Development of Liturgy," chaired by Rabbi Peter Knobel and board member Daniel
Schechter of Beth Emet—The Free Synagogue in Evanston, Il. The project's
nine recommendations appear in a progress report by Rabbi Janet Marder, and
nowhere do they mention updating the liturgy or changing God's gender, as
previously advocated by C.C.A.R.'s Liturgical Committee. Rather do they suggest "prayer language which stresses inclusivity, . . . transliteration which aids
the worshiper, [and] a faithful translation of the Hebrew prayers." Such is the
desire within Reform ranks for attaining these three objectives that hardly a year
goes by without several congregations jumping the gun by issuing their own
customized prayer services.

The best of these off-print efforts for Shabbat morning is *Siddur T'feelat Shalom* (experimental edition, 1999), compiled by Rabbi Shelton J. Donnell of Temple
Beth Sholom in Santa Ana, Calif. *Matanat Shabbat* (1996), generated by the staff of
Temple Israel in St. Louis, stands right behind it in raising the level of congregational *kavanah* several notches. Both of these newly minted services are concise and
without preamble, invite participation by providing larger typeface, and create
translations that are truer to the original. They both transliterate the entire liturgy, and *Matanat Shabbat* places the transliteration directly opposite its Hebrew,
interlineally. *Siddur T'feelat Shalom* restores several texts that had been expunged,
including the lone Sabbath Morning *piyyut*, *Eil Adon* (Chapter 2 . . . "From Offerings to Words"). It also offers brief background information on essential sections,
as well as choreographic instructions like taking three steps forward to begin the
Amidah (Chapter 4 . . . "Keeping Worship Moving").

In addition, *Siddur T'feelat Shalom* seems to have intuited the significance of
Miriam's role in delineating the aesthetic parameters of Jewish worship (Chapter
1 . . . "Song at the Sea: Two Versions"). It credits her in a way that no other
prayerbook has ever done (my emphasis):

Moses *and Miriam* and the people of Israel
Sang this song to You with great joy.

The "song" was our people's first public prayer; Moses and Miriam served as its first prayer surrogates: *shelichei* (plural of *sheli'ach*) *tsibbur*. Since God Himself appointed them, their creative leadership efforts were prototypical of all that followed (Chapter I . . . "Ad Libitum—Versus Disciplined—Art").

Moses, whose *saraf* (bronze "serpent;" Numbers 21:5–9) would be considered a healing deity by Israelites for 500 years until Hezekiah dismantled it along with other forms of idol worship (2 Kings 18:4), initiated the Dionysian approach. Like the Greek fertility god's *vine*, which could bring either blessing or harm, Moses' reptilian effigy "cured" those who believed in it by symbolically coiling around them. Miriam's stance throughout her life remained more reserved, as when she waited patiently until certain that her infant brother would not drown in the Nile before taking action to assure his further safety (Exodus 2:4–8). At the Sea she again stood aside until her brother's passion had been spent, and then reworked his song for the ages along Apollonian lines. Just as the Olympian god of music was first to be identified with a *lyre*, Miriam was the first Hebrew prophet to take *timbrel* in hand while leading the people in worship.

One hopes that *Siddur T'feelat Shabbat*'s pioneering recognition of Miriam's liturgical legacy—as well as *Matanat Shabbat*'s use of gender-neutral terminology that stops short of absurdity—meets most feminist objections over the short term. During that grace period one might anticipate the following debate among members of the C.C.A.R.'s Prayerbook Commission, borrowing the wording of BT, *Bava Kamma*, "Primary Gate"; with my bracketed clarifications and humble apologies to the original talmudic discussants cited in the Mishnah and Gemara (exposition of laws set forth in the Mishnah).

Mishnah
If one left a "He" [referring to God] in the Gates of Prayer, and someone else came along and stumbled over it and broke the thread of common prayer,[the one who stumbled] is exempt. But if the one [who stumbled] was offended by it, the author [of the paragraph containing "He"] is liable to pay damages for the injury. If the stumble caused yet another one to slip and be hurt [by the lack of gender sensitivity], the author is doubly liable.

Gemara
Commented *Rav* Tzedek: If the one who stumbled did so deliberately [as in the case of a woman rabbi], in order to make the point that our sages of old were gender-insensitive, that person is liable.

Countered *Beth Din*: But lo! If the person [leading prayer] who stumbled did so unintentionally, it makes no difference whether it was a woman rabbi or not. That individual is exempt, and the one who left the "He" [over which another stumbled] is liable. If the former person left it deliberately, especially so if it was a male [namely, the prayerbook editor], then by an argument of *a fortiori* [*kal vachomer*] he is not only liable but must be politically corrected until he removes it.

ALTERING GOD'S GENDER: A SECOND OPINION

Rabbi Donna Berman of Hebrew Union College gives the reasoning behind this not-so-hypothetical position. "A male God . . . becomes a model, unconscious or otherwise, for our human relationships . . . man (suddenly not a generic term) rules over women, children, and the animal world." But not all women rabbis agree. The moment we address God as female, contends the Jewish Theological Seminary's Paula Reimers, through the metaphor of birth her own body is the universe. Inevitably, then, the deity is identified with nature and its inexorable process of killing or being killed, that is, death constantly making room for more life. According to this law of nature, there is no right or wrong, no moral basis for who hunts and who is hunted.

Rabbi Reimers's argument against feminizing God's gender rings true historically; the ancient *goddess* in fact represented violence incarnate. Tablets unearthed by anthropologist William Albright at Ras es-Shamrah on present-day Syria's northern coast describe the goddess riding naked astride a galloping horse and brandishing a weapon in her right hand as she "massacres mankind, young and old, from the sea-coast to the rising of the sun." Her worship rites invariably commemorated the death-and-rebirth cycle of nature, often in a spectacularly gruesome manner. Initiate priests of the Cybele Mystery Cult in third-century Rome, for example, would castrate themselves and offer their severed genitals to the goddess in re-enactment of her unfaithful lover Attis's death and resurrection. According to this school of thought, relates psychologist Edward C. Whitmont, man's role was to play the Dying God. He fought to the death with competing males and succeeded them as the goddess's child, then as her loving playmate, and ultimately as her sacrificial victim.

That mythic worldview has long since been superseded, despite the efforts of radical modern feminists to revive it. Monogamous marriage, the linchpin of human society, arose out of a need to accommodate certain biological realities. George Gilder, a senior fellow at Seattle's Discovery Institute, reasons that unless men can channel their natural urge to serve as providers through the role of family patriarch, they will dominate in other ways, as predators. Attacking the male sexual role by changing God's gender cuts across the grain of human experience. The

founding rabbi of ultra-egalitarian ALEPH—Alliance for Jewish Renewal—
Zalman Schachter-Shalomi, earlier in his career speculated on the consonance of
daven'n with Aramaic *davinun* ("from our fathers"). His conclusion: It is an incon-
trovertible fact "that in order to pray to God one has to identify with one's father
and address God as 'our God and God of our Fathers.'"

Altering our language of discourse with God would distort the study of Bible
and its singular commitment to Israel's upholding an eternal covenant with its
Creator and King (Isaiah 43:15). Beyond that, changing—or even neutralizing –
Divine appellation would negate our liturgy's stressing the moral authority of a
Heavenly Father. Nowadays such authority must often stand in place of a missing
earthly father, maintains Dr. Wade F. Horn, director of the National Fatherhood
Initiative, as the number of children being raised by single or divorced women in
our society now stands at almost one in two nationally and is rising rapidly. Assuming that half the children growing up in fatherless homes are boys, there exists
the real danger that over twelve million of them will have to worship a female figure in addition to the one they already have: their mother. "To develop healthfully,"
avers Jewish activist Dennis Prager, "a boy needs to separate from her, not bond
with another female figure; otherwise, he will spend his life expressing his mascu-
linity in ways that are destructive to women and men." Prager substantiates this
claim by citing the widely accepted statistic that 70 percent of the men currently
serving long-term sentences in American prisons for committing violent crimes
grew up without a father.

RECONFIGURING THE TERRAIN

Conservatism takes a more understated position on the gender question than does
Reform. The Jewish Theological Seminary began to ordain women rabbis a decade after Hebrew Union College, during the same year that its new Rabbinical
Assembly (R.A.) Prayerbook appeared. The original version of *Siddur Sim Shalom*
(1985) does retain God's masculine gender in its English translation, but this has
not led to anywhere near the schism that continues unabated in Reform. There
are two reasons why. Significantly fewer Conservative women have been ordained
as rabbis, approximately one-third the number, according to information given me
by the R.A. and C.C.A.R.. Second, while empirical evidence confirms a fair amount
of English readings—where the gender question might arise during the course of
Conservative services—they do not appear in the liturgy proper. Accessed through
a supplementary section at the back of the book, the readings draw attention away
from any gender emendations within the statutory texts proper. That is just as

well, because while "God of our Fathers" is consistently neutralized to "God of our Ancestors" in the original *Siddur Sim Shalom*, the Matriarchs are listed alongside their respective spouses only in a single Alternative *Amidah*.

This inconsistency is addressed in a spectacularly improved gender-sensitive edition of *Siddur Sim Shalom* (1998; editorial chair, Leonard S. Cahan), which, in an optional page to every *Amidah*, adds the Matriarchs in both Hebrew and English (page 115b):

> *elohei avraham, elohei yitzchak, veilohei ya'akov;*
> *elohei sarah, elohei rivkah, elohei rachel veilohei lei'ah.*
> God of Abraham, Isaac, and Jacob;
> Sarah, Rebecca, Rachel, and Leah.

The optional-page solution avoids forcing Conservative congregations that might be more Traditional into adopting a textual revision for which they are not ready. It also stops short of the lone *Amidah* wording in Reconstructionism's prayerbook *Kol Haneshamah*, which couples Matriarchs with Patriarchs (pages 294–295).

elohei avraham	*elohei sarah*	God of Abraham	God of Sarah
elohei yitschak	*elohei rivkah*	God of Isaac	God of Rebeccah
elohei ya'akov	*elohei rachel*	God of Jacob	God of Rachel
	veilohei lei'ah	and	God of Leah.

Let it be noted that despite the coupling, this wording does allow for all Patriarchs and Matriarchs to enjoy their own relationships with God, independently of their spouses.

Elsewhere, *Kol Haneshamah* moves beyond gender independence to a hermaphroditic Deity. Whenever the liturgy mentions *adonai*, usually rendered as "God," *Kol Haneshamah* treats the proper noun as a personal pronoun, alternately either feminine or masculine (my emphases).

> I shall exalt *her*, for *she* knows my name;
> *he* calls to me, I answer *him*.

This androgynous approach extends to worshipers as well, adjusting received terminology in the Hebrew text even when God is not mentioned. Rabbinic Judaism has traditionally accepted that since the time-dependent obligation of prayer fell only upon men who did not bear the responsibility of caring for young children at all hours, it is they who would bear the obligation of praying three times a day (Chapter 8 . . . "A View from the Right"). Hence, "I offer thanks" had always appeared as if spoken by a man discharging his obligation, *modeh ani*. *Kol Haneshamah* adds the feminine form of the verb: *modah ani*.

Of the four prayerbooks under scrutiny, only Orthodoxy's *Art Scroll Siddur* meets the needs of other groups in addition to the one for whom it is intended. Because it quotes so much halachah, *Art Scroll Siddur* is being used extensively by individuals who may not consider themselves Orthodox but are seeking to base their personal observance on broader knowledge. The detailed background information has given them much to mull over even when attending services of other denominations.

While Reform's *Gates of Prayer* is fairly effective for its own Liberal brand of worship, it could have been more so had it left Hebrew prayers intact and placed translations on each facing page, as did the Liberal *Einheitsgebetbuch* in prewar Central Europe (Chapter 2 . . . "The Rabbi as Minister"). At present, selected phrases of the Hebrew liturgy are cut and pasted into what is essentially a vernacular service on both pages. The only uninterrupted prayers are for "Reader" (i.e., rabbi); they appear in Roman-typed English and often run on for pages at a time. This allows no freedom of choice either for rabbi or congregation. Worshipers' italicized English lines amount to less than a sixth of the liturgy, plus an occasional Hebrew refrain, while the rabbi's lines represent over 80 percent of it. Such an arrangement assures that individual Reform congregations can never discover exactly what proportion of interaction works for them and in which language.

Reconstructionism's *Kol Haneshamah* follows Reform's lead in italicizing lines to be read by worshipers. It also duplicates the questionable format introduced in 1989 by *Oneg Shabbat*, a gender-free Friday Night prayerbook published by Conservative Congregation Neveh Shalom of Portland, Oregon (ed. Joshua Stampfer). *Oneg Shabbat* places translation, transliteration, commentary, and alternatives on equal footing with the liturgy, presenting five times more supplementary English than Hebrew on an average two-page spread. The Portland prayerbook's single service occupied 130 pages, seven times the average number for *Gates of Prayer*'s ten alternate services, three times the length of *Art Scroll Siddur*'s Friday Night liturgy, and twice that of the one in *Siddur Sim Shalom*. Only *Kol Haneshamah* outdoes it. By spreading the same service over 137 pages, it makes skipping (and frequent announcing) unavoidable.

One suspects that Reconstructionist worshipers would not have it any other way. The Statement of Principles that I was handed after a Shabbat Morning service in Congregation Adat Shalom of Bethesda, Md. (1992), summarizes the movement's attitude.

> In a world changing ever more quickly,
> it becomes increasingly important to . . .
> *reconstruct* Judaism in every generation.

The downside: just as physical reconstruction in a thoroughfare can seriously obstruct road traffic, liturgical reconstruction may delay consummation of prayer to the point of boredom. Too often I have encountered Reconstructionist services that were disjointed, lacking the clear progression that should characterize the religious exercises of any denomination: *purposeful beginning; rise to emotional heights; inspired conclusion* (Chapter 4 . . . "Authentic and Plagal Melodies"; Epilogue . . . "Needed: Heart as Well as Mind").

Reconstructionism's more lasting contribution to the renewal of Judaism in North America shows in the intimacy of Life Cycle events often held outside the synagogue, marriage being a parade example. It is now common for Reconstructionist families to collaborate over many months in planning and executing a home-made wedding *chupah* (canopy under which the bride and groom stand). This usually takes the form of a quilt whose squares have been decorated by individual relatives and friends of the couple. They may be hand-drawn scenes from the celebrants' childhood years or personal messages of love and blessing for their future together. Each scene or message is sewn into the fabric of that couple's story. After sheltering them during the marriage ceremony, it will hang permanently in the home they establish, providing fond reminiscences for a lifetime.

A TRUE-TO-LIFE TRIP-TIK

I have saved a closer analysis of Conservatism's 1985 *Siddur Sim Shalom* for last, not only because its unvaried typeface and skimpy Table of Contents make it the hardest to navigate and hence least effective, but because it is the prayerbook most reflective of its movement's problems. Sociologist Marshall Sklare locates Conservatism's greatest shortcoming in the centrist stance of the Jewish Theological Seminary's first chancellor, Dr. Solomon Schechter. Reasons Sklare: "Since most of Jewry at the time (1902) was observant . . . the Reformers could be accused of being secessionists . . . of not following the practices of [Schechter's] 'Catholic Israel.'" But when the immigrant generation underwent Americanization in the secular sense, and not—as Schechter hoped it would—through affiliation with his quasi-Orthodox brand of Judaism, it abandoned all pretense at observing religious commandments. For most of the twentieth century, Sklare notes, Jews who adhered to the Tradition were considered deviants, and the practices of Catholic Israel today feature outright Sabbath desecration and violation of the dietary laws.

In an effort to meet its constituents where they are, the Conservative rabbinate has gradually distanced itself from Orthodoxy. Each succeeding adjustment of religious requirements punted halachah a bit further downfield toward Liberalism: permitting driving to one's synagogue on Sabbath (1950); providing legally binding phraseology more protective of a bride's rights in the marriage document (*Ketubah*, 1953); ordaining women as rabbis (1985) and as cantors (1987). In point of fact, even before *Siddur Sim Shalom*'s appearance in 1985 many individual Conservative rabbis had altered the way prayer was handled in their congregations to a degree far beyond any textual emendations that the new prayerbook would put forth.

Prior to 1970 Conservative worship had steered a historically grounded course halfway between Orthodoxy and Reform. That is no longer the case, as has been noted by Eric Yoffie, president of the Union of American Hebrew Congregations: "Between the Orthodox mumbling a great many Hebrew words in a short time, and the Liberals rising and sitting and reading responsively, there isn't much!" Conservative synagogues have yet to recapture their golden mean of the post-War years: Hebrew chant as a matrix within which an occasional responsive reading floated in congenial suspension with much more frequent *spontaneous* song.

Conservative practice has since backed away from that centrist position and into a corner, where Liberal rising-sitting-reading on command butts up against a nonstop parody of Orthodoxy. True *daven'n* as a modus operandi would at least allow room for inventiveness, *à la* Dixieland jazz improvisation. In its Conservative spin, the prayer component of worship is no longer the cumulative result of many individuals' spontaneous efforts but instead the relentless muttering of musical doggerel cobbled together like childrens' mocking songs and sung by grown-ups who should know better. The words of Hector Berlioz are apt. Referring to nineteenth-century churchgoers who butchered the sacred songs of their faith with similar insouciance, the great Romantic composer suggested: "Tell me what you sing and I'll tell you what you hate!" Conservative regulars will deny the accusation, not realizing that their innate good sense gives the game away. Unsure that the musical pap they are repeating is meant to be enjoyable, they mumble it so half-heartedly that the impression given is one of grudging resentment toward the liturgy.

TOO MANY FORKS IN THE ROAD

Siddur Sim Shalom reflects that ambivalence. Unwilling to embrace mostly English prayer, which would exchange the ensign of Historical Judaism for that of high-tech America (since language is the bearer of culture), *Siddur Sim Shalom* presents an almost un-abridged—through significantly edited—liturgy hedged by a bounty of multiple-choice alternatives. At first glance, one would think that having at hand most of the text for various services might obviate the need to constantly skip around. In reality, things do not work out quite that way. Faced with three versions of a Weekday Evening *Amidah*, for example, even the most adventurous worshiper will be daunted by twelve pages of Traditional *Amidah* (210–222), four pages of Abridged *Amidah* (228–231), and four more pages of Alternative *Amidah* (231–235).

Anyone diligent enough to leaf past the Traditional *Amidah* plus an additional four pages of Reader's *Kaddish, Aleinu,* and Mourners' *Kaddish* in order to reach the Abridged version will be disappointed to find its thirteen middle blessings melted down into an unintelligable muddle. Maimonides (*Mishneh Torah* 2, Laws of Prayer 2:3) gives the definitive shortened form of blessings six, seven, and eight as three separate petitions:

#6—*lesolei'ach heyeh lanu*	"may You be a Forgiver towards us";
#7—*liheyot ge'ulim*	"may we be redeemed";
#8—*rachakeinu mimach'ov*	"distance us from pain."

Siddur Sim Shalom merges blessings number 6 and number 7 into *vetislach lanu liheyot ge'ulim,* an impossibly difficult Hebrew formulation ascribed to the third-century Babylonian teacher Samuel: "forgive us to be redeemed." This conundrum is then overriden by its English translation, "forgive us our sins; redeem us from our afflictions," which folds blessing number 8 into the batter, changes the meaning of all three blessings, and demonstrates that the left-hand page knoweth not what its right-hand doeth.

A LACK OF IMAGERY

Most prayer translations in *Siddur Sim Shalom* are clinically sterile enough to recall the Episcopal Church's *New Version* (ed. Charles Price, 1980) of its 1662 *Book Of*

Common Prayer. It, too, has been stripped of imagery and drained of evocation. In place of the old King James wording for Psalms 126:4

> turn again our captivity, O Lord,
> as the streams in the south

the New Episcopal Version has

> restore our fortunes, O Lord,
> like the watercourses of the Negev.

This, comments linguist Margaret Ann Doody, "irresistibly smacks of the desires of industrialists whose shares have collapsed."

Siddur Sim Shalom gracelessly flattens the same passage (Grace after Meals, page 754) by removing the cushioning "O":

> restore us, Lord.

And its next clause comes perilously close to Zionist fundraising jargon with the clumsy analogy

> as You return streams to Israel's desert soil.

Regarding poignancy of expression, even the bloodless New Episcopalian rendering keeps intact the Psalm's final verse

> He that goeth forth weeping . . .
> shall come again with rejoicing.

Siddur Sim Shalom takes the feel-good-all-over tack currently fashionable in Reform and Reconstructionist circles,

> A tearful man will plant in sadness . . .
> but he will come home in gladness,

and misses the point. Jewish exiles wept in Babylon as they planted cultural seeds that would bear fruit upon their return to the Judean homeland, but not because they were congenitally weepy!

The literate worshiper must wince at such awkward handling of cherished verses that have survived for centuries, not only in *Siddur Sim Shalom* but in the latest prayerbooks of all denominations. Earlier renderings—done in an age more attuned to the subtleties of language—gloried in their doublings and repetitions. With a series of slow cadences and a gradual build-up of clauses into a crescendo they achieved an effect far greater than the sum of their parts. Updates, in striving simultaneously for current relevance and scholarly preciseness, go out of their way to avoid the age-old metaphors that link us linguistically with our deepest feelings about existence. Had he lived long enough to evaluate these liturgical "improvements," philosopher Horace M. Kallen might have quoted his own dictum on leaving the original prayers intact. A descendant of the eleventh- to twelfth-century Kalonymos family of scholars who composed anguished *selichot* following the Crusaders' bloody rampages through Jewish communities along the Rhine, Kallen believed that "excellence names the peak we have reached when to move beyond it would be to deteriorate."

We move beyond our liturgy's peak of excellence whenever we mute its insistence on righteous behavior by Jews so that they may merit God's promise of ultimate recompense. *Siddur Sim Shalom* and *Art Scroll Siddur* both convey that message explicitly in Grace after Meals (pages 768–769/194–195, respectively).

> *Yir'u et-adonai, kedoshav,*
> *ki ein machsor lirei'av*
> Fear the Lord/*HASHEM*, O His holy ones,
> for then you will never suffer want.

Art Scroll Siddur is the most consistent in linking Heavenly reward with righteous behavior. To the passage from Psalms 126 discussed earlier—

> he who bears the measure of seeds
> walks along weeping but will return in exultation—

it attaches relevant commentary by the twelfth-century exegete Abraham ibn Ezra, to drive home the point. "The poor man carrying his precious seeds has reason to weep, fearing they may be lost," writes Ibn Ezra. God, seeing his plight, takes pity upon him and enables him to reap a bountiful crop. The "poor man" of the Psalm is Israel carrying its spiritual seeds through the long exile, afraid that its best efforts will be wasted. Reward for its sacrifice will likewise come from God, through bounty in the World to Come.

EMENDATION REPLACES TRANSLATION

Orthodoxy's point is that here, as always, the liturgy affirms both biblical and rabbinic consensus. Today's belief in an afterlife (the World to Come) is rooted in talmudic interpretation of three biblical texts (Isaiah 25:7–8; Isaiah 26:18–19; Daniel 12:1–3) that mention it explicitly. Reform, Reconstructionism, and Conservatism are troubled by our liturgy's inclusion of the Resurrection Doctrine, hence their respective prayerbooks decline to connect it with this Psalm of Return. Elsewhere, when the prayer text unequivocally identifies God as Reviver of the Dead (*mechayeh hameitim*), Liberal editors devise various ways of evading it. *Gates Of Prayer* alters the Hebrew to *mechayeh hakol* ("the source of life"; page 38). *Kol Haneshamah* forces it into the tautological *mechayeh kol chai* ("nurturing the life of every living thing"; page 299). *Siddur Sim Shalom* leaves the prayer wording intact, but attributes Divine power of revival not to God, but to His newly appointed surrogates (page 355; my emphasis): "Your great *mercies* give life to the dead."

None of these expedients satisfies Neil Gillman, prominent among a growing school of contemporary thinkers who are re-examining the relationship between soul and body in the light of philosophy's perennial mind/body duality. Ever since Descartes first posed the idea back in the seventeenth century—"I think, therefore I am"—corollary questions related to an afterlife have sprung up. Am I a body; and if not, can I theoretically survive the death of my body? Rabbi Gillman asserts that Judaism never fully accepted the Greek notion—found in Plato—that death marks the immortal soul's liberation from bodily existence. Traditional belief in a blissful paradise for the righteous is grounded in Maimonides, who expounded a coming together of body and soul (corporeal Resurrection) in the Days of the Messiah, followed by eternal life for the soul (spiritual immortality) in the World to Come. Accordingly, argues Gillman, when our liturgy asserts that God revives the dead, it is affirming God's ultimate power. "Replacing the original Hebrew [or] modifying the translation . . . deprives the worshiper of an encounter with the central themes of the classical tradition and the experience of struggling with their content."

Only *Art Scroll Siddur* translates *mechayeh hameitim* literally: "Who resuscitates the dead" (page 101), and reserves theological speculation for portions of the service devoted to study rather than prayer. Yet in its own way it, too, deputizes other concepts to represent the Deity. Whenever God's name—*adonai*—appears in the Hebrew, *Art Scroll Siddur*'s English rendering assumes the guise of another Hebrew equivalent, *HASHEM*. Its reasoning seems to be that "Lord," the usual English word for *adonai*, does not adequately convey Divine omnipotence. (*Adonai* is an archaic

Hebrew form of "my Lord," a pseudonym for the biblical Tetragrammaton, or four-lettered acronym Y-H-V-H that was pronounced only on Yom Kippur in ancient times by a High Priest (Chapter 2 . . . "Open to Me The Portals"). Apparently, other commonly used substitutions for "Lord" also fall short: the deliberately unfinished designations "L-rd" or "G-d" (sometimes "Lrd" or "Gd"), left that way in Orthodox publications to avoid inadvertent desecration should a book or periodical be dropped or damaged. *Art Scroll Siddur* has therefore elected to circumvent translation of the Holy Name altogether.

At present, Orthodox congregations rarely read English aloud. Except perhaps for the verses from Psalms and Ecclesiastes that serve as prelude to Yizkor (*Art Scroll Siddur*, page 810), they continue to perform their liturgy as received, in Hebrew. But for the many *ba'alei teshuvah* ("repentees," i.e., newcomers to Traditional practice) who cannot yet read Hebrew and must rely instead upon a line-by-line romanization of the liturgy, *Art Scroll's Transliterated Linear Siddur* (Seif Edition, 1998) will prove a blessing. While almost every prayerbook presents some transliteration, only *Art Scroll's* Seif Edition *romanizes the complete annual liturgy* and positions it directly opposite its Hebrew equivalent, line by line, so that learners can wean themselves from dependence upon it.

Although not intended as such, even *Art Scroll's* translation, which the editors claim "seeks a balance between the lofty beauty of the heavily nuanced text and a readily understood English," could occasionally be made to work as a fluid responsive reading. This becomes apparent if we compare the Orthodox and Reform treatments of *Baruch She'amar*, opening paragraph of the early-morning *Pesukei Dezimra* (Verses of Song) section, indenting and italicizing lines meant to be read by the congregation.

Art Scroll Siddur (page 59)
Blessed is He Who spoke,
And the world came into being,
Blessed is He.
Blessed is He Who maintains Creation,
Blessed is He
Who speaks and does.

Gates Of Prayer (page 290)
Blessed is the One who spoke,
And the world came to be.

Blessed is the Source of Creation.
Blessed is the One
Whose word is deed,
Whose thought is fact.

We perceive immediately that *Gates of Prayer*'s organization of the material is effective, as it ought to be if the overwhelming portion of a service consists of reading rather than singing. Still, *Art Scroll Siddur*'s wording is easily its equal in readability. If we set aside gender correctness, it is actually superior to that of any other recent prayerbook in communicative accuracy.

CHANGING THE RULES

While they may aim for a wide range of desirable ends, prayerbooks all bend the liturgy to make it coincide with their particular movement's agenda: social activism; respect of privacy; condemnation of bigotry, and so on. But despite the high-minded objective of striving to rectify perceived injustices of the past, historically hindsighted editing of prayers often succeeds only in reversing their intent. The blessing called *Gevurot* (God's Might), the varying treatments of whose ending—*mechayeh hameitim*—were discussed earlier, offers a prime example. It constitutes the second of three benedictions that initiate the *Amidah* and praises God Almighty for sustaining all living things. This is in accord with a rabbinical directive concerning prayer: "A person should always recount God's praises first, and only then offer supplication [BT, *Berakhot* 34a; derived from Deuteronomy 33 and Psalms 149]."

In one Reform version of *Gevurot* (*Gates of Prayer*, page 153) the reader's statement concerning God,

Your might . . . is everlasting,

prompts the following congregational response:

Help us to use our strength for good.

Question: if the spotlight is indeed on *God*'s might, how does *our* strength suddenly enter to usurp center stage? Reform's answer: through the door of social justice, surely an admirable ideal. To write us into the scene, however, Reform has

changed not only the standing rules of prayer but those of common-and-gram-
matical sense as well: human petition pre-empts Divine praise; subordinate clause
vies with its main subject.

There is nothing ethically wrong with employing petitionary prayer to help
rectify social wrongs. We even have a valid precedent for it: the eternal Jewish quest
for *tikkun olam*: fixing the torn fabric of this imperfect world. *Petition* certainly has its
place in the liturgy, either preceding or following *praise*. But it should never trespass
upon the territory of praise. A fervent plea for *tikkun olam* might appear in a private
meditation, such as the one prior to reciting Psalms (*Art Scroll Siddur*, page 979).

> Master of the Universe!
> Do not take us from this world
> before our time, so that we might
> fix that which we have destroyed.

Fixing this world clearly has no place among the opening laudations of an *Amidah*.
By placing it there, *Gates of Prayer* reveals its primary concern over realigning our
liturgy to fit the Reform movement's Liberal/Humanist program.

Thus, God's might becomes our strength, and God's sustaining all life transposes into our feeding the homeless. Latter-day prayerbook editors have been
emboldened into writing their own scripts. But unlike playwrites who must win
over audiences in order for their views to survive, prayerbook editors foist their
opinions upon captive audiences who have not necessarily bought tickets to that
specific show. Fairness alone would dictate that those who tinker with the liturgy
should make sure they don't destroy that which they have come to fix.

If Reform presumes merely to redistribute *some* of God's mighty attributes,
Reconstructionism directs *all* of our attention inward. Its alternative to the Gevurot
is actually a private meditation, complete with instructions (*Kol Haneshamah*, page 726).

> Think of a part of your present life . . . a relationship . . .
> that feels stagnant to you . . . it isn't growing . . .
> Now think of a part of your life that you have enlivened . . .
> allow yourself to feel gratitude and joy for that.

The Reconstructionist prayerbook further suggests that we assume "a comfortable *seated* position," which neatly capsizes the established practice of more than
two millennia to *stand* for the *Amidah*. It also ignores the traditional function of
Jewish worship and the purpose of a standing devotion within it: to acknowledge

an omnipotent power greater than ourselves. Granted, the potential for Godliness lies implanted within every human being, but ignoring God seems a dubious way to realize it.

It is as if today's adults have taken at face value the tongue-in-cheek prayer parodies that circulated during their adolescence. *Kol Haneshamah*'s good intentions were better realized by an anonymous 1940s take-off on one of the most widely sung synagogue hymns (*Adon Olam* "Eternal God"; Chapter 4 . . . "Authentic and Plagal Melodies").

> When I was small I went to *shul.*
> And every Friday night as a rule,
> Before going home we'd sing and hum
> That sweet melody—*Adon Olom.*
>
> It used to lift my spirits high,
> My childhood cares and troubles would fly,
> When things would go wrong I could find some
> New spirit in—*Adon Olom.*

The key to making yesterday's youngsters feel gratitude and joy lay in the phrase "*we'd* sing," which acknowledged that worship is a group-centered effort. Even when singing took the form of reciting along with the cantor in what yesterday's worshipers considered an undertone (Chapter 2 . . . "Traditional *Daven'n* Defined"), it was loud enough to be heard above the noise of vehicles passing in the street outside. Nowadays people are encouraged to plant themselves like Buddhas during a service and to disregard the constant interchange that always set Jewish worship apart from that of most other religions.

UNIVERSAL DISPLACES PARTICULAR

Why is historic Jewish practice no longer valid as our model? Why do modern prayerbooks attempt to funnel all humankind into prayers that were meant to commemorate events specific to our people? Why must they stress the unity of society at large and then urge divisiveness during a service: individuals sitting and meditating while the congregation stands and recites the *Amidah?* We dare not disrupt prayer any more often than we already do, even if there were justification for individuals to separate themselves from the mutually supportive sociodynamic of *daven'n.* But to what purpose? The chant of a practiced *sheli'ach tsibbur* offers a sufficiently free-flowing mantra within whose stream of musico-rhetorical ideas our own thoughts are free to come and go or to desist altogether, so that even empty moments can fill with the potential for pure awareness.

Sociologist Frida Kerner Furman half-jokingly urges Liberal Judaism to take the current rage for Relativism to its logical conclusion and openly declare: "This is the Torah which proclaims that humanity is one, even as God is One!" That liturgical shot would wing two theological birds at once: lower God to our level; and legitimize the wholesale removal of any reference to Jewish particularism from the service. The teaching that all are equal *before* God could then dovetail neatly with a new corollary: in its one-ness, humanity is equal *to* God.

LANGUAGE: A REPOSITORY OF VALUES

I do not mean to minimize the many impediments faced by any prayerbook editor attempting to make an ancestral generation's teachings pertinent to its modern counterparts. Beyond the difficulties of reconciling disparate value systems separated by twenty centuries, there exists a basic linguistic difference between the language of prayer and that of everyday speech in any era. Prayer terminology is always God-centered, and particularly so when functioning as petition:

Help us, O *God* of our salvation.

Colloquial parlance, being familiar, is *self*-centered almost by definition, even more so when asking a favor of another individual. In that case the Deity might be invoked solely as a means of emphasis:

For God's sake, help *me*, man!

Despite this difference, if we get the right words in the right order, as a writer/character muses in one of Tom Stoppard's plays, we can "nudge the world a little." One such well-ordered sequence of words has lasted for over a century. Appearing in Reform's original *Union Prayer Book* (1892), it translated the Messianic paragraph *Al Kein Nekaveh*, "We Therefore Hope in Thee," flanked by two laudations—*Aleinu* and *Kaddish*—that conclude every service. The rendering conveyed a message appropriate to an age that saw Reform Judaism take its place among many other socially conscious American religious denominations at the end of the nineteenth century. The original Reform wording (last appearing in the 1961 edition, page 306) continued to speak to worshipers through two twentieth-century conflagrations and a worldwide depression, all of which called for a bolstering of confidence in the future.

> May the time not be distant, O God, when Thy name
> shall be worshiped in all the earth, when unbelief
> shall disappear and error be no more . . .

This comforting formulation faithfully conveyed both meaning and word stresses of the Hebrew original, without losing verbal impact. A prayer in every sense and not merely a reading masquerading as *tefillah*, rabbis treated it as the closest thing to Scripture, rendering each word with a nobility of intonation usually reserved for the speeches of a Lincoln or a Churchill. That is exactly the way Swiss/Jewish composer Ernest Bloch set the text in his landmark *Sacred Service*, written during the Great Depression of the 1930s. True to what he observed during Reform worship at San Francisco's Temple Emanuel, which commissioned the service, Bloch stipulated that this passage be spoken in a highly inflected style of declamation known as *Sprechgesang* (speech/song).

Reform's felicitous translation of *Al Kein Nekaveh* lasted until the next prolonged period of widespread disillusionment, America's ill-fated military involvement in Southeast Asia, 1965–1975. When the Vietnam War ended, *Gates Of Prayer* (page 618) proceeded to rend asunder that which the *Union Prayer Book* had previously wrought.

> The day will come when all shall turn with trust to God,
> hearkening to His voice, bearing witness to His truth . . .

The new version avoids anything that smacks of value judgment, such as the negative terms *unbelief* and *error*. This please-everyone strategy also rejects "worshiping God's name" (perhaps out of fear it might offend agnostic members?). Belief, unbelief, and misbelief are therefore omitted in favor of a soothingly Polyannaish willingness to "trust" and "hearken" to God's voice. Where the old version spoke directly to God, the current one hides behind a disembodied third person that proclaims positive-sounding generalities to no one in particular. While leading a workshop on Liturgical Change for the Twenty-First Century, Rabbi Chaim Stern, who edited *Gates Of Prayer*, was asked why his committee members had replaced something that really worked. He attributed their failing to a perversity of human nature: "The really beautiful language was in *U.P.B.* [*Union Prayer Book*]; that's why they changed it!"

In 1985, Conservatism's *Siddur Sim Shalom* attempted to shed new light on the same passage (page 511).

> And so we hope in you, Lord our God,
> soon to see Your splendor sweeping idolatry away . . .

The attempt flounders both in its choice of words and in their grouping. Its metaphor is hopelessly mixed; we might picture God as the world's illuminator but hardly as its housekeeper. The rhythms are equally crossed: iambic meter clashing with trochaic; stress colliding with stress. When a congregation reads, unlike an orchestra it has no conductor to steer it past the rough spots. Prayer rearrangements that cannot be read at first glance should be discarded.

The Hebrew of our statutory liturgy, like the biblical poetry from which it stems, achieves a stateliness that is not easily matched in English translation. It was chosen "not just for the memorability of poetic language," insists Robert Alter, a noted Hebraist, "but also because . . . *parallelistic* verse offered a particularly effective way of imaginatively realizing inevitability." We have noted (in Psalms 126) how the promise of ultimate reward came couched in parallelism. Here too, in *Al Kein Nekaveh*, the consequences of moral transgression will follow without fail, surely as the consequent phrase of every verse follows its antecedent (*Daily Prayer Book*, tr. Philip Birnbaum, 1949, pages 135–136):

> *leha'avir gilulim min ha'arets*
> *veha'elilim karot yikareitun*
> Thou wilt remove the abominations from the earth,
> and heathendom will be utterly destroyed.

In lieu of such precious coin, minted by mishnaic redactors living geographically and chronologically closer to the biblical models than succeeding generations, many current rewrites of statutory Hebrew prayers follow Gresham's law in circulating liturgical currency of lesser value. They substitute pseudo-therapy and plodding banality, making sure to cite the buzz words currently in vogue: Justice, Truth, Love, and the politically correct Freedom for All People. These terms recur often enough to lose their impact, while most of the original prayers are relegated to a databank for possible future retrieval. This is what architects call "facadism," saving only the outer skin of historic structures while gutting them to provide space for activities that have little to do with the buildings' intended functions. I call it *liturgical taxidermy*.

VERNACULAR: A PRAYER MEANS, NOT AN END

I am not suggesting we revert to an exclusively Hebrew format. Surely, most modern Jews who strive to live simultaneously in Judaism and the modern world (to be *and* not to be) deserve devotional texts written in a language they can understand. Vernacular has played a significant role in our communal worship since the first rudimentary prayer meetings held by Judean exiles in Babylon during the sixth century B.C.E. were (presumably) dominated by Aramaic. An internationally spoken language along the Eastern Mediterranean littoral, Aramaic continued to occupy a prominent place in Jewish worship through the talmudic period, which ended 1,000 years later. Legal and mystical prayers composed in it are still recited today.

Similar foreignisms have entered our liturgy as Hebrew cognates, mimicking secular—even amorous—poetic models from other languages. Musicologist Abraham W. Binder cites one case. During the 1,200-year Spanish epoch,

> *muerame mi alma, ai muerame*
> Thou slayest me, O my beloved, thou slayest me,

became

> *meromi, al mah am rav homah*
> A people pine longingly for the One Who uplifts them.

Some of the Lord's songs on alien soil have always been sung in foreign tongues, prayers for the government of our Exilic host-countries at the very least. Let us use our current *Lingua Franca*—English—just as previous communities employed Greek, Arabic, Spanish, French, Italian, German, and Yiddish at various times, but in a proportion that does not drown our liturgical baby in its interpretive bathwater.

The 100-year battle to retain Hebrew as the acknowledged language of prayer in North American synagogues is still being fought, and the only unanswered question concerns how much of it shall remain and how much English commentary will surround that remainder. This is nothing new. During the Middle Ages what we refer to as *Siddurim*—prayerbook-prototypes—were really scholarly halachic discussions circulated by individual authorities like Amram ben Sheshna and Saadya ben Joseph, who headed the Babylonian academy at Sura in the ninth and tenth centuries, respectively. The early *Siddurim* resembled more a system of ritual law than a prayer collection; liturgical sections were reduced to bare acronymic headings and *shelichei tsibbur* were expected to know their full contents by heart. Yet there is a landmark turnabout between the way those handwritten reference manuals were used and the way modern prayerbooks are used. Medieval *chazanim* ignored the extensive legal material while chanting the indicated prayers from memory. Today's rabbis seem to ignore the Hebrew prayers while devoting all their energies to English glosses and alternatives instead.

HOW TO START UP AGAIN

The main drawback of a running pulpit monologue is that it usurps the purpose of *public* worship, a congregation's sole means of empowerment. One way to restore a sense of common purpose and mutual dependency is by spreading the burden of prayer among entire congregations rather than limiting it to the few who are appointed to lead. That type of worship innovation first occurred almost 2,600 years ago when the priestly rites were temporarily suspended during our people's exile in Babylon (Chapter 2 . . . "From Offerings to Words"). At that precarious junction, the permitting of communal prayer through Psalm offering "can be regarded as the wellspring of the synagogue," opines musicologist Reinhard Flender. There is every reason to believe that a similar opening-up of today's services will reactivate participation among a laity that has been expatriated from its liturgical heritage by synagogue professionals, the modern equivalent of a priestly cult.

It is not prayerbook editors who have deleted Hebrew on an unconscionable scale; that nineteenth-century horror story was rewritten with a happy ending, if one were to judge by the published material. More statutory prayers appear unabridged in contemporary Reform, Reconstructionist, and Conservative prayerbooks than in all the scholarly *Siddurim* of the Middle Ages combined. Not only that, but liturgical poems—which seemed well on their way out a generation ago—have increased in Reform's latest High Holy Day prayerbook, *Gates of Repentance*, by 50 percent over its predecessor, *Union Prayer Book Part II* (1953). Penitential pleas that had earlier fallen by the wayside—for example, *Ki Hineh Kachomer*, "As clay in the potter's hand"—reappear, along with a twelfth-century song of yearning for God by Judah Halevi (page 395).

> *Mi yitneini eved eloha oseini . . .*
> Were I Thy slave, O God Who made me,
> no other would I crave, with You alone to aid me,

perfectly suits the mood of *Minchah* on Yom Kippur afternoon: Atonement (at-one-ment) with our Creator.

Conservatism, too, has sought to fill the void left by its displacement of Medieval texts, through insertion of more recent *piyyutim*. One of the most effective new laudatory invocations—written by Hillel Zeitlin, a scholar of Jewish mysticism—appears in *Ma'ariv* for Rosh Hashanah (*Rabbinical Assembly Machzor*, ed. Jules Harlow, 1972, page 44).

> *Av gadol vekadosh, avi kol ba'ei olam* . . .
> Great and holy Father of all mankind,
> as You daily recreate the world, O Father,
> breathe spirit into me, Your child,
> that I too may live anew.

How fitting that Zeitlin's prayer of rebirth should be sung on Rosh Hashana Eve, the *Yahrzeit* (anniversary) of his martyr's death on the way to Treblinka in 1942.

Mi Yitneini, Av Gadol, and other inserted *piyyutim* have been set to the most exquisitely lyrical strains by contemporary composers. Worshipers respond in kind, humming along (until they learn the words) with a loving tenderness heretofore reserved for old standbys like *Avinu Malkeinu*. When poetic and musical imagery come together in this way, Jewish worship suddenly enters transcendent realms. The classically inspired Hebrew texts emerge as biblically contoured chants that charge the air with electricity just as surely as if a switch had been thrown.

A pity that it happens so rarely, for our rabbis have been too busy elevating what they do in English to canonical status. This self-indulgent policy only exacerbates what Leon Wieseltier, literary editor of the *New Republic*, terms

> a crisis of Jewish literacy in America that is
> unprecedented in Jewish history. The Jews
> of the United States are the first great Jewry
> in the history of the diaspora that believes
> it can receive, develop and transmit the
> Jewish tradition not in a Jewish language.
> For this, our historians will judge us severely.

In too many synagogues Hebrew liturgy has been reduced to a bare minimum of isolated fragments, stretching liturgical ties with our collective past almost to the breaking point (Chapter 2 . . . "Liturgical Liberties"). North American Jews now grope in vain for a common bond with their co-religionists elsewhere in the world, and especially in the Land of Israel where even Reform services rely mainly upon Hebrew.

LOOKING PAST OUR PRESENT TRAFFIC JAM

When synagogue officiants fail to connect with their own culture, they uncannily fulfill Friedrich Nietzsche's prophecy of modern alienation:

> and now the mythless man stands eternally hungry,
> surrounded by all past ages, and digs and grubs for roots.

If only our religious leaders would desist from uprooting what our ancestors planted, long enough to remember that at best their efforts will provide nothing more than menus—not the meal itself—and worshipers will end up eating the spiritual equivalent of cardboard. An anonymous Orthodox prayer editor attempted to fly in the face of this truism some years ago when air travel first became common. In reworking the traditional Wayfarers Prayer (*tefillat haderech*) for inclusion in the specially sealed kosher meals that airlines provide upon request, the editor for Wilton Foods deleted any reference to *listim* (bandits; *Art Scroll Siddur*, pages 222–223), reasoning that brigands would surely not attempt to hijack a jet plane moving at 500 miles an hour, 30,000 feet above the ground!

No matter how we reshuffle the liturgical deck, there is no way to guess at the different hands fate will deal us in each succeeding decade. We cannot assume that a prayer book stuffed with timely detail will ever keep pace with the culture shocks that every tomorrow has in store. During the 1960s Conservatism had misgivings about an *Amidah* passage in which God is asked to sound a Great *Shofar* (ram's horn) heralding *our* freedom. The R.A.'s Prayerbook Committee rewrote it to herald *man's* freedom (*Weekday Prayer Book*, ed. Gershon Hadas, 1961, page 58). In striving for universality, Conservatism managed to exclude women. Along came Reform a decade later and neutralized the request to read *proclaim freedom* (*Gates of Prayer*, page 41), thereby eliminating both men and women! Going by the book alone—albeit an updated edition which, in theologian David Hartman's words, "equates 'the now' with 'the good,' and 'the latest' with the important and valuable"—corresponds to driving with our eyes fixed upon the latest road maps. It is a mistake to assume that any *Siddur* can outrace history; such a shortsided approach will bring us no closer to our spiritual destination.

The highway to God leads directly from our heart, a road that Jewish worship has traveled passionately many times before, as recounted in Chapter 4: "Changing Lanes."

CHAPTER 4

Changing Lanes

At the beginning of the 1920s
the belief began to circulate that there were no longer
any absolutes of time and space . . .
in certain circumstances,
lengths appeared to contract and clocks to slow down.

Paul Johnson,
Modern Times, 1983

*A*s a teenager studying Fine Arts at the Cooper Union in New York City, I learned a great deal about architecture, painting, design, and sculpture. Most of it would not meld too well with my eventual career as a performer and teacher of sacred music, but one visual insight did stay with me:

there are no lines in nature;
objects take their shape from light.

The light plays upon objects, reflects back into space, and in turn changes the shape of their surrounding area. This phenomenon can be observed in late-fifteenth- and early-sixteenth-century Italian Renaissance paintings: in the smoky ambiguity of Leonardo's backgrounds and the tonal unity of Raphael's portraits. Among nineteenth-century French painters it is evident in the compelling everyday images of Daumier and particularly in the dappled-sunlight effects of Renoir. The "outlines" in these artists' compositions are really areas into which reflected light overflows from objects on either side.

FUZZING EDGES

My Life Painting instructor at Cooper Union, Sicilian-born Jon Corbino, employed an unforgettable method for reinforcing the no-lines-in-nature rule. Then at the height of his fame as a modern artist in the Old Style, Corbino evoked the haunting grandiloquence of seventeenth-century Baroque in every gesture. Almost fifty years later, the sound of his battle cry as he patroled the studio scrutinizing our neophyte efforts still rings in memory. If a clear image emerged on someone's easel, he would lunge forward, smudge it with his thumb, and growl "Fuzz those edges!"

Fuzzing its edges is not the only challenge currently facing art. William Rubin, long-time curator at New York's Museum of Modern Art, who in 1984 put together a landmark exhibit that compared Primitive artifacts with Modern painting and sculpture, had earlier spent many hours discussing his project with Pablo Picasso. In the exhibit's catalogue, Rubin recalls how Picasso told him exactly the opposite of what he expected. He had thought Picasso was drawn to primitive art because of its abstractness. But he found the eclectic Spanish master to be more impressed by its *magical* force and deeply concerned that Western art, relegated to museum galleries, was in danger of losing that elemental power.

Picasso's insight brings to mind a statement in the Book of Numbers (23:23) concerning God's people while they were still in their nascent stage of development: "neither is there any magic in Israel." The assessment seems chillingly prescient, for when modern Israelites gather in synagogues on this continent, their prayer seems entirely devoid of its acknowledged power to move and perhaps transform people (Chapter 2 . . . "Synagogue Rituals' Fragility"). The power failure is partially due to crossed signals within the domain of worship itself. My late colleague Yehuda Mandel, who had been chief cantor at Budapest's leading Orthodox synagogue—the Rombach—prior to World War II, once explained to me how Central European congregations observed an unwritten code of conduct, called *Lineale*. Everyone involved and everything that occurred in a service remained within an invisible—though clearly defined—*line* of demarcation. Be it liturgy, music, clergy, or congregation, no contributing element ever drew attention to itself by overstepping that unseen boundary during a service.

Nowadays, uncrossable lines of any kind within synagogue practice are unclear. The ambient glow of our surrounding North American space—emanating during the 1970s and 1980s from a narcissistic Me Generation, during the 1990s from a directionless Generation X, and at the millennium from a Generation Y that outstrips both of them in numbers and spending—has blurred former boundaries. After three decades of what artists call "negative space" shining a bright spotlight upon itself, our religious exercises can no longer generate enough inner radiance to reflect back upon their secular environment and influence its configuration in turn.

ENTERING DIFFERENT DIMENSIONS

Luckily for us, God often sends the cure even before the affliction. We now know there is a *continuum* between space and time, whose dividing lines can be so unclear that time appears to lengthen and space to contract. It all depends on one's point of view. Uninspired speakers routinely strike an audience as having gone on for hours, whereas in reality they may have been holding forth no more than three or four minutes. Feuding co-workers forced to share the same office are prone to view their room as miniscule, while in actual dimensions it may outstrip all others. Just so, in viewing the cosmos through a prism of Jewish worship, Rabbi Lawrence Hoffman defines time and space relatively, as "something of inherent value which we may or may not choose to recognize." He pinpoints worship as the discipline through which we condition ourselves to recognize "shape in time, and meaning in space." To restate Rabbi Hoffman's point in terms of my graphic analogy: if we choose to let it do so, worship can impart a sharper focus to space or time's outlines, which in their unrecognized state remain fuzzy.

The choice is ours to take an unoccupied room and designate it a synagogue, to appropriate an unscheduled hour and spend it in prayer. We might then fill that hour of synagogue prayer with sanctifying acts that enable us to re-experience other holy spaces and holy times that our forebears first inhabited. Dimensions coalesce, continents and centuries overlap, and once again we stand in Sinai's shadow or at Zion's gate. But how to enter that sanctified realm; how does one actually move from profane—to sacred—space and time?

Earlier in this century Albert Einstein and other theoretical physicists— notably, Werner Heisenberg—explained the essence of time as waves of probability and the nature of space as particles of infinitely pulsating energy. They were describing a quantum field of energy—our universe—in which molecules (since subdivided to the micro-level of photons, dions, mesons, quarks, and any number of other subatomic particles) move in all directions, through time as well as across space. With the right perspective, worshipers, too, should be able to cross dimensional barriers that were formerly considered impassable. The concept is not new to Eastern religious thought, where for centuries Buddhism has stressed that the boundary between sickness and health is nonexistent, and where interlocking black-and-white segments of the Taoist Yin/Yang circle each contain a sizeable dot of their opposite coloring. In a Western construct, crossing dimensional barriers would be somewhat like strolling along a giant endless ribbon, the twisted Mobius strip of mathematics. If we follow what appears to be its inner surface, when we emerge on its supposed exterior side, we will in fact have returned to the same spot where we started.

CROSSING A BOUNDARY WITHOUT REALIZING IT

Our passage from profane to sacred space and time can likewise be envisaged as an inside-out search; its goal is implicitly present—if unperceived—at the starting line. The passageway is akin to unclear distant objects in a painting, or to a melody's muted accompaniment, both of which may escape our notice at first glance or hearing. I am alluding to the *hum* of social conversation that normally fills the time between our arrival at synagogue and the start of services. Like an aural Mobius strip it can take our outward-bound energies and direct them inward, if we allow it to happen. Our problem is how to convert worship's humble backdrop—the randomness of our own small talk—into the purposeful murmur of prayer.

We can effect this conversion by keeping in mind two facts: (a) as stated, there is a continuum between time and space in the physical world; and (b) there is a parallel continuum between words and music in the world of prayer. Prayer words are located in space (on the printed page), while the music of prayer is located in time (as a progression of sounds). The *words remain rooted*, the *music moves constantly*. Jewish prayer thus constitutes a paradigm of the Dual Torah system that has been operative at least since early Pharisaic times (second century, B.C.E.): a synthesis of written and oral Law (Deuteronomy 17:11 and 32:7; BT, *Nedarim* 37b). In the world of physical existence, objects take shape according to the play of light as it moves across their surfaces. In the analogous realm of prayer, spatial and temporal components—words and music—reflect back upon and define each other.

Tractate *Berakhot* in both Talmuds (JT, 9:2; BT, 40b) refers to Statutory prayers as "the coin our sages minted" (*matbei'a shetav'u chachamim bivrakhot*). Applying a quantum overlay to that figure of speech might prove difficult; coins do not readily fly Heavenward. Yet I believe it is exactly what happens when liturgical words are wed to hallowed melodic patterns (Chapter 3 . . . "How to Start Up Again"). An age that claims to have seen UFOs descending from and ascending to the firmament is already reliving Jacob's dream of Divinely dispatched messengers shuttling between heaven and earth (Genesis 28). During worship, our messages to God travel on sound, as sacred words borne upon wings of song. They climb and descend in time-honored musical patterns—modes (Chapter 2 . . . "Words and Music")—that originated on windswept mountaintops in the Judean desert and were gradually modified through our people's prolonged contact with different cultures over the intervening millennia. Like Space Age rockets, modes of prayer always carry a payload when launched, in the shape of fixed liturgical texts. Just as with the Dual Torahs, a soaring oral tradition is anchored by its written counterpart.

Today's evolved prayer modes are a modern equivalent of Jacob's Ladder: their feet planted on earth; their head lifted toward Heaven. This image is reinforced by the Hebrew word for "ladder," *sulam*, which also translates as "musical mode." The numerical value of the letters that form *sulam* is the same as for those that make up the word *kol* or "voice": 136. According to the mystical discipline of *gematriah*, which derives hidden meanings from the numerical-value equivalents of Scriptural words, this is more than a coincidence. Verbal language here hints at the way musical language works, through vocal conduits by means of which Jewish worship has historically ascended the interdimensional continuum. Prayer modes are proven vehicles for quickening a congregation's devotional pulse and lifting it subliminally from profane—to sacred—space and time.

WHAT SCIENCE NOW CONFIRMS, RELIGION KNEW ALL ALONG

Thousands of years ago the Torah recognized that humankind is not basically sacral-minded; its concerns are largely materialistic, as illustrated by the Tower of Babel episode in Genesis, Chapter 11. The late Israeli biblical scholar Nechama Leibowitz commented with deep understanding on that tragic story of human overreach. Quoting from the Prophet Zephaniah (3:4), she argued that despite their innate drive to acquire ever greater wealth and power, people everywhere could still be led from the mundane to the spiritual through prayer:

> For then will I give to the people a pure language,
> that they may all call upon the name of the Lord.

The choice of a propitious mode of prayer—Zephaniah's "pure language"—to carry that universal call on high is left to the people. Scripture routinely omits musical details when delineating ritual observances, apparently because they were common knowledge. We may therefore infer its being a mode appropriate to the occasion.

Ecclesiastes (3:1) tells us there is a thing for every season, from which we learn to let every season do its own thing. In the case of prayer, although texts remain unchanged, just as minted coins retain their initial impression, musical modes vary with each season. Often in Traditional synagogue practice the words *baruch atah* (Blessed art Thou) are sung in one mode when they initiate a prayer and in a different mode when they conclude the same prayer. There is also a mode for opening worship and another for closing it, a mode of petition and a mode of praise, a mode of instruction and a mode of adoration, a mode of remembrance and a mode of renewal. Moreover, following the usage of many centuries, every mode changes seasonally as does the liturgy.

The more science discovers about the infinitely recurring—yet varying—patterns that make up our natural world, the more sense this mode-changing makes. Based on IBM physicist Richard Voss' comparative study of various musical as well as physical systems, we can safely state that synagogue prayer modes work best when poised about halfway between disorder and stability. Not surprisingly, the mathematical formula used to measure both musical and physical systems derives from close examination of nature. Computer experts use an almost identical equation to generate virtual images for a variety of random-yet-predictable natural phenomena, from the contour of a flowing river or the indentations along a coastline to the protruberances of a mountain range, all of which give the impression of changing shape according to the ongoing time of year, month, or day.

Could the reason our seasonally prescribed prayer modes work so well possibly be due to the fact that they reflect not only the profound meanings of certain Divinely inspired words, but also a harmony of natural elements that is likewise beyond our control? Ralph Waldo Emerson wrote that "every season yields its tribute of delight . . . nature always wears the colors of the spirit." Isn't it possible that when we utter specific words of religious import in a specific mode and at a specific season, through our worship we are spiritually reflecting the changing colors of nature? The season of early spring would seem to confirm that supposition.

At the full moon of every vernal equinox, Sephardic Jews who hale from Constantinople open the ritual portion of their Pesach Seder meal—

> *kadesh ur'chats, karpas yachats*
> (Order of the *Haggadah* or Passover "telling")—

in a musical mode identical to the one that Roman Catholics reserve for chanting their Easter Mass:

Deus Genitor alme, benignus nobis adesto
(God our Father, deal kindly with us).

Not only that, but if Easter Sunday should coincide with the first day of Pesach, yet a third group—*Ashkenazim* of German extraction—would be praying for *Tal* (Dew) in the same Spring-like mode of joyous anticipation. Casting the net for an even bigger catch, they would be asking God to

bless the seasonal sustenance
(*tal bo tevareich mazon*)

of a Middle Eastern land that He had promised to their distant progenitors. That these events, all of which unfold within the same annual time frame, should be so widely separated physically and yet so closely connected musically is surely not happenstance.

OPENING A WORSHIP SERVICE

No matter in which religious tradition a service takes place, its most critical season is always the opening, or *introit* (from Old French: "entrance"). An introit serves the same purpose as a poetic invocation: to give the impression of beginning in the midst of things. Homer's Goddess sang of Achille's anger ten years into the war against Ilion; Milton's Heavenly Muse justified God's ways to man only after Paradise had already been lost. An old chorale that Armenians sing at the foot of the altar while their priest is vested in the sacristy says it all: The best introits are deep and incomprehensible, *without beginning!* Von Ogden Vogt, a Protestant minister who prioritizes worship's dynamic aspect, describes the ideal introit as a confident, declarative exercise that captures attention and gets things going without anyone being aware of it.

That's exactly the way huge dance circles embracing hundreds of people mysteriously form in the plaza fronting Barcelona's cathedral every Sunday morning. The late historical novelist James A. Michener once attempted to pinpoint whatever common gesture served as introit for the so-called *sardana* dance.

One moment not a sign of dancing . . .
Within seconds a dozen purses, jackets,
walking sticks and coats were piled neatly
in [one] spot, and around them the Catalans,
strangers to one another, began their slow *sardana*.

He compared the process to ice suddenly forming crystals across the surface of water.

Getting people to pull spiritual oars together is a difficult task, especially at the moment when they are weighing anchor. In terms of a continuum they are still earthbound, pulled down by the same force of gravity that a first-stage rocket must overcome. The metaphor should tell us what is needed to get off the ground: a powerful force to lift our prayers into orbit, an expendable carrier. We need a throwaway text that is singular in its own right, not necessarily part of the service at hand but adaptable enough to set its tone.

The Galilean mystics of Safed debated this problem in the sixteenth century when Friday Evening worship began almost directly with *Barechu*, the Call to Prayer. For scholars of the mystical discipline known as Kabbalah ("that which is received"), immersed all week in speculation on the oneness of God, that was too abrupt a way to welcome the Creator's own day of rest. To provide a buffer, Rabbi Solomon Alkabetz composed the preamble, *Lecha Dodi* (Chapter 1 . . . "What Lies Immediately Ahead"). Alkabetz's nine-stanza pastiche of biblical quotes still did not meet the kabbalists' need for a more prolonged transition period, so it was prefaced with six additional Psalms (95–99; 29). In our century, the pace of life has so accelerated that we require yet another introit—a longer landing strip, as it were—before taxiing quietly up to the Sabbath gate.

And yet, whichever text we employ as an optimal introit will have to reckon with this chapter's introductory disclaimer concerning the absence of divisive outlines in nature as well as in art. An opening laudation ought to give the impression of being there *before* the beginning, like an armature waiting to receive the sculptor's clay. For that reason, any introit will work best when sung from *amidst* the congregation. Granted that before a service actually begins, worshipers still in the process of gathering do not resemble a congregation so much as a socializing group clustered at the rear of a room that purports to serve as a synagogue. Still, it is nowhere written that such a group must be called to order from a distant platform at the room's far end. In the chaotic conditions of Sinai's wilderness the Israelites' adversaries made their entrance from an unexpected direction, and recall what happened. As if shocked by the callous efficiency of their tactic, God warned our ancestors never to forget it: "Remember how Amalek met you on your way out of Egypt; he attacked your women and children from the tail end" (Deuteronomy 25:18).

The moral of the story for us: An *indirect* approach is the best way to commence prayer, just as the best way to access our subconscious *during* prayer is via the oblique effect of musical allusion (Chapter 2 . . . "What Happens When We

Interrupt Prayer"). Much the way a name just beyond recall is remembered once we concentrate on something else, a worship opening that catches us unaware is most effective. On High Holy Days, Traditionalist congregations know that the one chosen to lead *Musaf* will begin chanting its introit—*Hineni He'ani Mima'as*—from the rear of the synagogue, as if first entering. And although worshipers know full well that their *sheli'ach tsibbur* has been present in the synagogue all along, his suddenly offstage voice never fails to create a stir when it is heard quietly intoning

> here I stand, deficient in deeds and awed by Thee,
> yet I dare to come and plead on behalf of Thy people.

Those self-effacing words, sung with sincerity and conviction, establish a mood of profound devotion that lasts for hours.

Now picture a cantor and a rabbi following the same procedure on Friday evening prior to a Late service. The two would begin singing from amidst an unfocused multitude still gathering in the vestibule. Film buffs may be reminded of a scene from the 1940 movie *New Moon*, where an indentured servant in eighteenth-century New Orleans jogs a crew of sailors into crashing his master's party by leading them in a stirring march up from the waterfront into town. Just so, later arrivers would join our group as it filed into the Sanctuary, and the song would keep growing in volume. By the time everyone reached pews down front (no roped-off rear sections needed in this scenario), they would be fully primed for what is to come.

MUSIC TO GET THINGS GOING

Logically, such an unexpected physical entrance would be accompanied by equally oblique, or "indirect," music (musicologists call it *plagal*). This is not so far-fetched as you might imagine; the indirect musical opening is used with great success by other groups for other types of events, not necessarily religious. Melodies that inaugurate programs typically start from below their *tonic*, in Western music the note toward which they will eventually gravitate. The first three notes of France's national anthem, *La Marseillaise*, and the British Empire's *Rule Brittania* attack just that way:

> *France*, awake to glory;
> >Ye Sons of
> *Brit-ain* first, at Heav'n's command.
> >When

Once things have gotten underway, plagal melodies generally rise no higher than five or six notes (a *fifth* or *sixth*) above their tonic. Observe this in the "Hymn to Joy," which occurs midway through the final movement of Beethoven's *Ninth Symphony* (tr. Louis Untermeyer).

> *un-numbered*
> >be embraced,   millions,
> with this kiss to all the world.

The same is true of the next-to-last verse in popular composer Irving Berlin's unofficial national anthem:

> *God*
> >to the ocean white with foam,
> Bless America, my home sweet home.

These particular songs often serve to open secular rituals: military parades, political rallies, dedication ceremonies, sporting events, and so on. They function primarily as attention getters, bringing a crowd quickly to order so that proceedings can begin. So do four texts that have traditionally been used to great effect as Friday Night synagogue introits.

Shabbat Hamalkah	"We Gather to Welcome the Sabbath Queen";
Shalom Aleichem	"Peace Be unto You, O Ministering Angels";
Shehashalom Shelo	"Father of Peace, Grant us Thy Blessing";
Yedid Nefesh	"Beloved of the Soul, Compassionate Father."

Their most frequently sung melodies are uniformly plagal, starting from below the tonic and climbing no more than a fifth or sixth beyond it.

MUSIC TO WIND THINGS DOWN

In military terms, introits sung to plagal melodies will outflank their objective, just as Amalek outflanked our ancestors in the wilderness. The indirect approach works well as a means of engagement, but will not suffice when it comes time to wrap up either an encounter or a service. For that, we need music more reminiscent of modern-day Israel's 1956 Sinai campaign, a *direct* frontal assault that went under the code name "Armored Fist." Its purpose: to minimize casualties by bringing hostilities quickly to an end.

The State of Israel's strategy translates poetically into the lyrics of its national anthem, *Hatikvah* ("The Hope"; final verse):

> *ki rak im acharon hayehudi,*
> *gam acharit tikvateinu*
> so long as a single Jew remains alive,
> our hope for return to Zion will survive.

This is as direct a statement as was ever put into strophic form. It demands an equally "direct" melody (technical name: *authentic*), one that portrays the Jewish people setting forth undaunted on their seemingly endless journey.

The melody of *Hatikvah* does just that. It starts out step by step, rising five notes from its tonic:

                                        lei—vav
                              ba-
                    od
            -ol
    >Ko-

As its hope for eventual return to the Promised Land increases, so does its range, to a full octave (eight notes) above, twice:

    lo avdah tikvateinu;   *-atikvah sh'not alpayim.*

    >Od   *>Ha-*

MINOR AND MAJOR MODES

The melody of *Hatikvah* happens to be in a *minor*—or "sad"—sounding—mode. Why sad? For that matter, why is minor music's opposite—the *major* mode—considered to be "happy"-sounding? It goes back to the way humans—of any racial or religious descent—first learn to express their feelings by emitting appropriate sounds. When infants are hungry they cry, and their angry wail usually spans an acoustical space equal to the first three notes of the minor mode (a minor *third*). After infants are fed, their satisfied cooing generally expands to cover the slightly wider three-note interval by which a major mode is defined (a major third). Adults unconsciously carry memories of those first oral needs and gratifications into their

singing of prayers. In Freudian terms supplications are expressions of pain, usually associated with sadness; hence we offer petition in the minor (crying) mode.
Laudations, which reflect pleasure, are connected with happiness; that is why, when
giving thanks we employ the major (cooing) mode.

Regrettably, the minor mode has played an overly prominent—though often justified—role in our devotions; over the centuries Jewish existence has been
anything but serene. Some 150 years ago Herman Melville unknowingly gave voice
to the trepidation Jews often feel during intervals of smooth sailing.

> Would to God the blessed calms would last.
> But the mingled . . . threads of life
> are woven by warp and woof:
> calms crossed by storms;
> a storm for every calm.

As squalls of intolerance pursued and overtook us in every safe haven, the modes
of our prayer shifted accordingly.

The Jewish folk's tempestuous—often harrowing—past is accurately mirrored by the State of Israel's national hymn, which alternates between anguished
sigh and rebellious shout. Yet despite its somber mood, *Hatikvah*—like the people
it represents—manages to defy the pain of adversity. Its melody climbs as high
as most voices are capable before returning home, filled with hope. Its octave
range from lower-to-upper tonic is typical of an authentic (direct) melody in a
minor (sad) mode.

Is there meaning to a melody like *Hatikvah* and if so, asks composer Aaron
Copland, "Can you state in so many words what the meaning is?" His reply is a
qualified "No." Although listeners unquestionably experience emotional reactions
to certain tone progressions, it is hard to pigeonhole those feelings beyond the
broad-spectrum categories of happy or sad. Readers can easily prove to themselves
how perception of music varies when the spaces (commonly called *intervals*) between notes of a melody are widened to accommodate a major mode or narrowed
to fit a minor mode. To test this, try singing the opening two lines of *Hatikvah* in
a major mode by widening its intervals. Take the first two phrases of *Hatikvah* (*kol
od baleivav penimah, nefesh yehudi homiyah*) and fit them to the major-mode folk melody
which we know as

> Twinkle, Twinkle Little Star,
> how I wonder what you are!

Notice how your frown turns into a smile halfway through. Now go back to the nursery rhyme's words; sing them to *Hatikvah*'s minor-mode melody and watch your smile fade.

AUTHENTIC AND PLAGAL MELODIES

Whether a song conforms to the major or minor mode does not really determine its effectiveness as an opening or closing hymn. What counts is whether its music moves plagally or authentically. Melodies like *La Marseillaise* and *Rule Britannia*, both of which advance *indirectly* from a fourth below to a fifth above the tonic, work best as *openers*. For that reason two plagal settings—despite being in the minor mode—have caught on as introits for Sabbath morning in Reform, Reconstructionist, and some Conservative synagogues (Orthodox services never deviate from the statutory *Birkot Hashachar*—or Morning Blessings—as opening invocation). The first introit—

> *Ashreinu, mah tov chelkeinu*
> Happy are we, goodly our portion—

uses a syncopated dance tune for its text, which appears shortly after *Birkot Hashachar*. The second introit—

> *Halleluyah! halelu eil bekodsho*
> Praise God in His holy dwelling—

quotes a lilting folk tune for Psalms 150, toward the end of *Pesukei Dezimra*. Both airs are unpretentious and provide live ammunition for the service's opening salvo. As a result, they prove sure-fire winners first thing in the morning when early birds need the encouragement of a small victory. In addition, both melodies' low-pitched spriteliness quickens the spirit of those stalwarts who have arrived in time to warm up without embarrassment. Confront the same diligent worshipers first thing with a direct and wide-ranging tune like *Eits Chayim Hee*, which demands real effort because it paraphrases the octave leaps of *Hatikvah*, and they will quickly fade. Yet *Eits Chayim Hee* succeeds famously as a curtain closer for the Ark a bit later (Chapter 2 . . . "Open to Me the Portals"). It's a matter of choosing the right form of melody for the right spot. A high riser, *Eits Chayim Hee* is the perfect stage setter for what normally carries a service to its peak of inspiration: the *rabbi's sermon*.

Worship ideally opens with a diversionary tactic that overcomes inertia as it subtly reminds us who we are in relation to God. Two-thirds of the way through, worship's impetus climaxes like a thunderstorm whose fury has gradually mounted and now erupts in full force. Then it quickly abates, gathering energy for one final affirmation of our faith.

In this, a service's parabola also replicates the curve of human experience. "It is the pattern of many illnesses to develop slowly towards a 'crisis'," notes composer and musical theoretician Ernst Toch, "after which recession and reaction set in quickly." The same is true of *La Marseillaise*, the plagal opening anthem par excellence (see earlier . . . "Music to Get Things Going"). Its smaller semi-climaxes

> your children, wives and grandsires hoary,
> behold their tears and hear their cries

drive ever upward, forming what Toch calls a "wave" which finally breaks at

> to arms, to arms ye brave,
> the avenging sword unsheathe.

This occurs exactly two/thirds of the way through the song's 28 measures, at numbers 19 through 22. Thereafter, its climactic wave rides the surf resolutely shoreward:

> March on, march on, all hearts resolved
> on victory or death!

I unpack several of worship's smaller semi-climaxes in Chapter 5 . . . ("Palatial Bldg, Fabulous Meetng Facilty, Heavnly Apntmnts, Avalbl Wkend Only"). For now, suffice it to characterize them as preliminary bouts to a main event: the sermon. This synagogue practice originated 600 years ago (Chapter 2 . . . "The Cantor as Synagogue Overseer"), and has grown steadily more important as the rabbinical role in public worship inexorably came to synchronize with that of Christian clergyman. A sermon is part and parcel of ecclesiastical function, but it also fits the profile of Jewish worship surprisingly well, as an exegetical summit whose cresting provides a natural sequel to the cantillated Scripture that preceded it. Descent from the mountain follows as denouement leading to the final hymn.

Music that gets right to the point in a ringing statement and sends us on our way exhilarated and reassured—i.e., an *authentic* melody—is most effective for a *closing* anthem. *Hatikvah*, with its outgoing octave jumps, would do nicely if it were not already appropriated as a standard opening hymn for nonreligious events. Two other direct melodies in the minor mode are frequently sung at service endings, both of which sound like variations on the theme of *Hatikvah*. The first is for an eleventh-century text, *Adon Olam*, "Eternal God," whose standard hymn tune dates from 1904. Like the melody of *Hatikvah*, it rises an octave in defiance (at *ve'im ruchi* . . . "I place my life in God's hands without fear").

The other well-known closing hymn that also holds out hope for our future through its authentic melody is for the fourteenth-century text *Yigdal* (O Praise the Living God). The celebrated Anglo/Jewish singer Meyer Leoni composed a tune for it in 1760, and its popularity quickly spread even among non-Jewish Londoners who had occasion to frequent the Duke's Place Synagogue where Leoni served as chorister. Pioneering Jewish musicologist Abraham Zvi Idelsohn looked into its origins and found that an early Methodist Revivalist minister—Thomas Olivers—had adapted Leoni's *Yigdal* tune to his own text, *The God of Abraham Praise*. Olivers's hymn appeared in 1772 and, reports Idelsohn, "became so popular that it had to be published in eight editions in two years, reaching its zenith in 1799." It appears in hymnals of various Protestant denominations to this day, and the reason for its longevity is the same as that for *Adon Olam*. Both melodies help bring worship to an optimistic conclusion despite their sad-sounding mode. Their forthrightness perfectly suits the comforting imagery of their hymnody—"trust in the living God, for He is eternal"—and reinforces the feeling of a community having reached harbor safely.

KEEPING WORSHIP MOVING

Sandwiched in between a Sabbath Morning service's opening and closing are other sections that evoke moods of their own: praise God, then ask for sustenance (*Amidah*); honor the scroll in formal procession, then read from it aloud (Torah); genuflect before the Eternal, then rise to recall those mortals who have gone before (*Aleinu*). Each of these sequential acts provides a regular ebb and flow that suits what the heart feels as well as what the mind senses. Whenever we interrupt this devotional rhythm, proceedings inevitably bog down and inertia sets in. The tallest hurdle we face in worship is that of maintaining *momentum*. A mood may develop gradually but it dissipates in a millisecond (Chapter 2 . . . "Synagogue Rituals' Fragility"). The Talmud therefore cautions us not to interrupt a benediction once it has begun, not even to greet the long-awaited arrival of the prophet Elijah (BT, *Berakhot* 3a; 29a).

As for the endless informational time-outs that intrude upon actual prayer nowadays, given a viable alternative they need not be perpetuated. Certainly, the lame

excuse of guiding a ritually inept congregation will no longer hold up. At the Reform movement's 1997 Biennial, a 7:00 A.M. service titled "Bowing, Bending, and
Rising: Learning the Choreography of the Prayer Service," organized by Rabbi Daniel
Freelander, was filled to capacity and overflowed into an adjoining hall. No longer
will the lay delegates who participated have to rely on pulpit instructions during
worship. And should they forget, help is available in the Orthodox *Art Scroll Siddur*—
preferred by many young Conservative worshipers as well—which indicates every
conceivable ritual act along the way (Chapter 3 . . . "Negotiating a Roadblock").

If consulting an Orthodox *Siddur* is perceived as a forsaking of Reform "and
return to the movement [their] parents and grandparents turned away from," as
Richard N. Levy, president of the C.C.A.R. at the time of this writing suggests,
there are other alternatives. Philadelphia's P'nai Or Religious Fellowship, connected
with the Reconstructionist movement, pioneered in producing a *Siddur* that included
pictograph symbols directing users when to bend the knee, bow the head, even
join in singing. Heeding the guidelines and instructions offered in *Or Chadash* (ed.
Leila Berner and Burt Jacobson, 1989) or the most recent edition of Conservatism's
Siddur Sim Shalom (for Shabbat and Festivals, 1998) will do just as well in keeping
intrusive announcements to a bare minimum.

Another strategy would be for officiants to carefully plan each service so as
to avoid skipping within sections. Knowledgeable readers might raise a valid objection: traditional services that follow the consecutive pagination of a comprehensive *Siddur* still occasionally require people to take notice when a number of
pages should be skipped, as in the case of a special *Amidah* for Festival or Rosh
Chodesh. Yet even in those rare instances, noninvasive help that stops short of
outright interruption is available. Orthodox congregations Beth T'filoh in Baltimore and B'nai Torah in Indianapolis (to name but two that I am personally aware
of) have for years utilized liturgical "scoreboards," built into the front part of their
sanctuaries. Moving numbers track the exact page at any given moment. When
asked whether the signs violate a halachic prohibition against creating something
new on Sabbath or Festival, Rabbi Ronald Gray of B'nai Torah explained that the
numbers are already imprinted on the rollers; rotation merely uncovers them.

ENLISTING THE LITURGY'S BUILT-IN
MOTIVATIONAL DEVICES

Even with all the help available, worshipers will not plunge ahead on their own
without assurance that whoever is quarterbacking the service is not about to switch
signals at the line of scrimmage. People in every denomination, including Ortho-

dox, are acting gun-shy. But it need not be so, the means for turning things around are in place. Each device we enlist to indicate page numbers unobtrusively—and each set of instructions we publish to assist worshipers quietly—will work only if those who lead services follow the game plan.

Jewish worship, which is articulated through speech and song, always does best when offering assistance along the way through a *nonauditory* medium. Otherwise, prayer must constantly halt in order for announcements to be heard, and that is precisely where services are at their most vulnerable. For the sake of audibility while worship is in progress, any interjected information has no choice but to override the collective voice of a congregation, which sixteenth-century poet Saadiah Longo likened to the voice of God Himself: *kol hamon kekol shaddai* (*Seder Zemanim*). Shouting is counterproductive under any circumstances, and especially during prayer, where a sensitive writer like Ralph Ellison might justly characterize it as "an assault upon the temples of the ear." That applies no matter who is doing the shouting. Chicago's Traditionalist Loop Synagogue, which appeared to be functioning without benefit of professional clergy at the time that I visited, provides a case in point. During Purim services, several lay regulars took it upon themselves to play "rabbi" by competing in volume with the massed voices of worshipers. In this contest the rotating masters of ceremony had an unfair advantage: overloud amplification that—like Jonah's great whale—swallowed the *Megillah* reading along with its accompanying *gregers* (Yiddish: "noise-makers") used to obliterate every mention of the villain Haman's name.

In the ritualistic performance of opera, which is also primarily sound-oriented, English captions of what is being sung now project above most prosceniums. Subtitles involve people continually in the action by letting them follow rapid stage dialogue in their own language. Synagogal Torah reading—which demands complete concentration on an equally swift narrative—can likewise be arranged to stimulate active congregational involvement.

The U.A.H.C. recently asked every one of its congregations to train a cadre of members in reading from the Scroll of Law. Its Music Commission organized local workshops and issued study packages in preparation for two-day regional seminars held on the East and West coasts. This represented a natural first step toward fulfilling the liturgical invocation "give honor to the Torah," *tenu chavod latorah*. The next step would be to actively involve not only the few who cantillate from the Scroll, but also the many who listen to it being cantillated. If the language of Scripture remains unintelligible, it is as if God has left a message on our voicemail: "Hi! This is Me. I called today, but you were out." Many centuries ago the Prophet Isaiah (50:2) recorded that message in Bible-speak: Why, when I came, was no one there; why, when I called, would none respond?

In order for us to be there when God calls, we might consider resurrecting an ancient procedure first introduced by the Scribe Ezra not long after the missed connection just mentioned: interweaving translation with cantillation. As reported in the Talmud (Mishnah *Megillah* 4:4; *Tosefta, Megillah* 3:20) the translating was accomplished after each complete line had been read, and in a language that everyone understood. Nowadays, effective pulpit rabbis like Albert L. Lewis (now Emeritus) and his successor Stephen C. Lindemann of Temple Beth Sholom in Cherry Hill, N.J., best impart understanding by dividing their Torah "translation" or teaching into a series of interrelated *forums* involving the congregation. Each exchange of views opens with the rabbi posing a leading question—having to do with moral problems raised by current events—which elicits answers whose implications are then measured against ethical principles set forth in that week's *sidrah*. The Q and A sessions are generally spaced between every second or third Torah portion, and the amount of informed excitement they generate far exceeds anything triggered by even the most eloquent discourse.

Another effective motivational technique would be to have Scriptural episodes that are inherently confrontational re-enacted dramatically by two or more people. Conservative rabbis Cathy L. Felix and Elliot S. Schoenberg suggest that talented congregants might write a brief skit concerning the confrontational theme and perform it as a lead-in to the sermon. "For example," they write, "a skit about a wife nagging her husband [viz., Mother Sarah, urging Father Abraham to banish the concubine Hagar and her son Ishmael; Genesis 21] . . . leads into a sermon called 'Five Things Men Should Know about Women.'"

Or a Scriptural scene might be *cantillated in English* by using the signs printed in every Bible to indicate word grouping and voice inflection, just as they are in Hebrew. Until now, this dramatic device has figured prominently only in Shavuot Confirmation cantatas; it is time to let everyone in on the secret. Example: if Deuteronomy, Chapters 27 and 28, were done this way, the Israelite tribes stationed half on Mount Gerizim and half on Mount Ebal in the Sinai Wilderness could be personified by congregants seated on opposite sides of the sanctuary. One side would cantillate the series of curses to which the other side would answer "Amen." For the series of blessings they would reverse roles. This antiphonal type of involvement would also do wonders to raise the energy level of English readings, aver Rabbis Felix and Schoenberg, because it moves the fulcrum of worship from pulpit back to pew.

Here are a few more biblical situations that lend themselves exceptionally well to re-enactment by lay people.

Abraham's Binding of Isaac upon Mount Moriah
(Genesis 22),

Jacob-and-Esau's dispute over their birthright and paternal blessing
(Genesis 27),

Joseph's revelation to his desperate and unsuspecting brothers
(Genesis 45),

Korach's rebellion against the Divine authority of Moses and Aaron
(Numbers 16),

Balaam's she-ass solemnly protesting her master's unwarranted abuse
(Numbers 22).

USING THE TORAH-BLESSING MODE CREATIVELY

The last-mentioned episode was dramatically brought to life for me in a San Francisco synagogue some time ago. The rabbi—a former stand-up comedian, as I later discovered—cleverly wove the traditional chant for calling up an *Aliyah* (Torah honoree) into his patter describing the special occasion.

> *Ya'amod* . . . we call up our distinguished member Mr. . . . er . . . Ginsberg son of . . . er . . . Ginsberg [the rabbi had apparently misplaced a card bearing both Hebrew first names] now come forward who is observing the anniversary of his Bar Mitzvah in this very synagogue on this very day, sixty years ago, *Chazak* . . . may his strength increase . . . let's hear it for him!

Amidst decidedly unsynagogal applause the 73-year-old celebrant came slowly forward, ascended the *Bimah*, and stood there, silent. The rabbi pointed to a card bearing the Torah Blessings printed in extra-large type. Ginsberg said nothing.

The rabbi (figuring the gentleman was embarrassed over his understandably rusty Hebrew) pointed to the first word in English transliteration; still silence on Ginsberg's part. The rabbi (by now suspecting that Ginsberg's English comprehension had weakened as well) prompted him by spelling it out: B-O-R-C-H-U. He even sang it in transliteration: *Bor-chew* [accenting the second syllable, as in Hebrew]," to which Ginsberg responded in the same Torah Blessing mode: "*Gezundheit!*"

The rabbi gave Ginsberg a look that, if it could kill, would have felled him on the spot, but confined his venom to a chanted retort (so his congregation—largely invitees of the honoree—would imagine it was all part of some septuagenarian Bar Mitzvah ritual): "I see your blessings have gotten better"; to which

Ginsberg replied in kind, "I see your hearing has gotten worse!" Whereupon the rabbi, without missing a beat, turned to the open Scroll and began reading aloud—first in Hebrew and then in English—a passage about the heathen prophet Balaam mistreating his long-suffering beast of burden. Not wishing to offend the fair sex's sensibilities, he altered the animal's gender to suit his subject and concluded with

> *vayiftach adonai et-pi ha'aton*
> the Lord caused to open—
> the mouth of the *jackass.*

Pointing with one hand in the open Scroll and with the other at Ginsberg he ordered: "Kiss here!"

STUDYING THE ORAL TORAH

That punch line carried a real impact, delivered in the musico/rhetorical declamation reserved for calling people up to the Torah. When "Torah" in its broader meaning expands from written Scripture into an enduring Oral tradition preserved by the Talmud, Codes, and Commentaries, it is still transmitted through chant. Abraham Cahan, editor of the *Jewish Daily Forward* for almost a half-century, described the melody to which Orthodox seminarians pore over rabbinic texts: "When intoning the Talmud you live in two distinct worlds at once . . . while your mind is absorbing the meaning of the words you utter, the melody in which you utter them tells your heart a tale of its own." The melody for studying Talmud is really a modal pattern that keeps repeating, with variations, as in the chant for *Mah Nishtanah* ("Why is this night different?") taught to very young children prior to the Seder on Passover Eve. Known as the *Study* mode, it has attained unparalleled efficiency at conveying textual meaning, whether before sizeable audiences or in the semiprivacy of a *chevruta*, where two Talmud students go head to head as they test opposing arguments certain to crop up in the next day's lecture.

HOW *DAVEN'N* WORKS IN WEEKDAY SERVICES

Ashkenazic synagogues use a related chant, even more ancient than the Study mode, for reciting the *Birkot Hashachar* that opens Weekday Morning services. Envision the scene at a traditional *Minyan*. It is early, somewhere between 6:00 and 8:00 A.M., as people straggle into a chapel, sleepy-eyed and hungry. Some of them don only a *tallit*, some also bind *tefillin* (leather phylacteries) on their bicep and forehead. Others choose to do without either, but almost all are in their own private universe, mourning the death of a close relative by attending services daily and—despite their great personal loss—reciting a *Kaddish* that praises God and affirms His dominion over the world that He alone created (Chapter I . . . "Finding Common Liturgical Ground"; Epilogue. . . "A Foretaste of Eternity"). Slowly, bench neighbors turn to one another. Group activity begins to surface: a bit of current events; a snippet of gossiping; both antithetical to prayer.

How are worshipers galvanized under those workaday circumstances? Not by an announcement or by community singing, certainly not with an entrance of robed officiants heading an introit processional. Weekday prayer begins when someone—usually a lay person acting as *sheli'ach tsibbur*—starts to chant the opening blessings in rapid fashion using a simple Weekday mode that, in the estimation of musicologist Eric Werner, dates back to the days of our Second Temple.

> Blessed art Thou, O Lord, Eternal Sovereign, Who hast given
> the mind understanding to distinguish between day and night.

That simple ritual act of acknowledging the Creator automatically elicits responses from those attending: *Baruch hu uvaruch shemo* (Blessed be God's Name); *Amein* (Amen); and somehow, without fanfare, the entire group's prayer is aloft like a first-stage rocket.

The musical mode that fuels this launching is hardly distinguishable from the one in which Roman Catholics sing their Scriptural Antiphon for the Vespers (Evensong) service, *Vota mea Domini* (Psalms 116).

> I will pay my vows unto God
> in the presence of all His people,
> in the courts of God's house,
> in thy midst, O Jerusalem.

Early Christians evidently learned it from former Levitical choristers who survived in exile after the calamity of 70 C.E.; their tombs are still identifiable in Roman catacombs (Chapter I . . . "Worship in the Middle Ages"). Later, several Church Fathers would indirectly confirm the impression made by Hebrew Psalm singing, among them the seventh-century contemporary of Pope Gregory I, Isidore of Seville. He wrote, "In the primitive church the singer made his voice resound by so moderate an inflection that he was closer to declamation than to singing." This observation gives a clue to synagogue prayer at the time. Jewish communities throughout the diaspora continued to sing their statutory texts in a way that had earlier been refined by 1,000 years of Temple usage. Isidore was describing "logogenic," or word-based singing, called *psalmody* by musicologists and *daven'n* by Ashkenazic Jews (Chapter 2 . . . "Traditional *Daven'n* Defined").

Organized Jewish worship was always led by a chief musician, starting with King David's appointee, Asaph the Levite, who ministered before the Ark (1 Chronicles 16:7) and later presided in Solomon's Temple (2 Chronicles 5:12). "Who is the "leading singer" in today's open society?" asks Virgil C. Funk, president of the National Association of Pastoral Musicians. If houses of worship are to survive, asserts Reverend Funk, today's leading singer must be the assemblage of worshipers. But that raises the even harder question of how to delegate worship. If we assign too *much* to the assemblage, the service becomes a singalong. If worshipers have too *little* to do, they quickly looses interest. Responsorial psalmody, with the precentor initiating and the congregation concluding every verse, maintains a fragile balance between performance and participation. That is why it so rooted itself in Jewish religious practice early on that not even the special motifs later prescribed for cantillating Scripture (Chapter 5 . . . "Music for Taste-Testing Biblical Portions") could dislodge it.

A PRAGMATIC APPROACH TO INTRODUCING MELODIES

After Isidore of Seville's era it took another 1,300 years to unhinge psalmodic chanting from a crucial passage of the *Aleinu* prayer that explains why Jews bow only to God—

> *shehu noteh shamayim veyosed arets . . .*
> for He stretched forth the heavens
> and laid the foundations of earth—

and replace it with the melody from a children's nursery rhyme

> The Teensy Weensy Spider
> went up the water spout
> down came the rain and
> washed the spider out . . .

not once, but six times, counting repeats and sequences.

The congregational version—which soon caught on in North American synagogues of every persuasion—stemmed from a group of singalong melodies that counselors at the Conservative Ramah summer camps set to liturgical texts during the 1960s. Known as Ramah songs, they were based unmistakably upon American folk and popular music, many of them becoming modern prayer staples. Yet to some authorities within the Conservative movement they represented musical parody, or worse. The late Samuel Rosenbaum, executive vice president of the Cantors Assembly for almost forty years, declared, "If we must have new finger-snapping jump tunes we do not need to make icons out of those . . . free-wheeling tunes from Ramah which, especially in their early years, were meant to attract youngsters to prayer in a summer camp environment at any cost and in any way."

Such a purist stance ignores two realities. To begin with, the popularization of *shehu noteh shamayim* was not a departure from traditional practice. If anything, it enhanced it, inducing congregations to sing a passage that had theretofore been ignored in the rush to recite Mourner's *Kaddish*. Second, tunes that were originally considered "foreign" have occupied a permanent spot in Jewish worship at least since the twelfth century. Melodies of indigenous song types from various lands of Jewish settlement have been so thoroughly absorbed into our received repertoire that they are no longer recognizable as an Arabic *Muwasha*, Spanish *Villencico*, French *Virelai*, German *Minnegesang*, Italian *Bergamasca*, Austrian *Laendler*, Polish *Mazurka*, Russian *Troika*, Hungarian *Zigeunerlied*, or Rumanian *Hora*.

Why shouldn't the typical American song type—deriving from the poignant spirituals of black Africans brought here as slaves—establish a foothold in the contemporary synagogue liturgy after three and a half centuries? The way we now sing *shehu noteh shamayim* sounds very much like *That Old Time Religion*, first sung by the Fisk University Jubilee Singers at Revival meetings over 100 years ago:

> oh it was good enough for Moses,
> and it's good enough for me!

Moreover, its melody happens to mesh seamlessly with the prayer chant that precedes and follows it. As if cut from the same modal cloth, it typifies American folk-and-popular elements that coincide—or are made to coincide—with historical synagogue usage.

For the Jewish lineage of the *shehu noteh shamayim* melody reaches back a lot further than Negro spirituals. It finds precedent not just in North American culture but in countless individuals' memories of attending synagogue from their earliest childhood. Folk wisdom always draws from the well of tradition, and here again it proves itself the peer of book learning. This passage—which many of us enjoy singing above all others—merely places into metered time a Torah cantillation motif known for at least a millennium by its pattern-indicating symbol: *telisha gedolah.*

ARE WE HAVING FUN YET?

Our adaptation of the *telisha gedolah* motif, however, goes beyond what is customary when deriving prayer chant from older Scripture reading. We have additionally redeployed the Hebrew prayer's stress patterns to conform with colloquial speech rhythms that surround us every day of our lives. Paradoxically, the self-confident Americanized version serves to bolster our sense of Jewish identity within the larger environment, in several ways. Sung in Hebrew, it tells us *who* we are. By combining a quote from Isaiah (51:13) with an American folk tune, it reminds us *where* we are. It conforms to Jewish religious norms by echoing a musical motif prominent in Scripture reading. It also involves us actively in prayer, with a rare sense of joy. Finally, it provides a worship moment that we anticipate with secret pleasure, reminiscent of when we were children in an assembly hall, mangling the lyrics of our school alma mater and getting away with it. According to some, this may not be praying by the rules, but it surely is fun.

Another example of musical adaptation from common American usage is the phrase that children recognize as "singing Polly Wolly Doodle all the day." It crops up in the official *Marines' Hymn*, the wintertime *Jingle Bells*, the peace-seeking *Where Have all the Flowers Gone*, the inspirational *Bridge over Troubled Water* and the anti-war *Born in the U.S.A.*, just to name a few instances. Yet it also echoes the Ashkenazic Torah cantillation motifs *pazer* and *zarka*, used for centuries to recite Psalms 93 on Friday night:

adonai malach . . . bal timot

The combined theme of these two motifs recirculates in the most popular current melodies for two other Friday Night prayers:

> *Veshamru*   (commandment to keep the Sabbath);
> *Shalom Rav*   (prayer for peace).

Moreover, *Veshamru* introduces a "shuffled tempo" by delaying every other eighth note just a fraction, in the style of 1930s Swing music ("every little breeze seems to whisper *Louise"*). *Shalom Rav*, on the other hand, uses a 1950s Peacenik technique, the "pushed beat"; anticipating certain eighth notes ahead of time and holding them through the actual beat (*"the answer, my friend, is blowin' in the wind"*). Combining these two performance practices yields a syncopated rhythm akin to folk/rock which—like speech—"contradicts the rhythms of the body," claims author and critic Anthony Burgess. "An honest musical setting of speech fights against regularity of accent," he elaborates, "always a little ahead of the regular beats of the heart." Thus a wondrously reflective Beatles' lyric will embroider its own fanciful design around an insistent and pulsating rhythm.

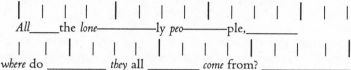

THE HALF-A-LOAF RATIONALE

The trick in worship is not to lose our balance if canonized texts are occasionally sung to seemingly off-beat settings. In the case of every adaptation that takes root, a branch of currently flourishing popular music grafts itself onto the sturdy trunk of ancient prayer modality and revitalizes its timeless words just as surely as oxygen-rich blood energizes our tired bodies. Yet an overdose of oxygen can cause light-headedness, just as raucously belting out an entire paragraph can lead to frivolity. Liturgical considerations ought to moderate the extent of exuberant display before it crosses over into unacceptability. Like a dab of highlight in painting, one emotional outburst goes a long way in prayer. A single Ramah phrase—or popular adaptation—sung with abandon will suffice to balance several pages of psalmodic phrases that preceded it, if it is followed by more chant. That is why congregations sensitive not only to the needs of worshipers but also to the intent of prayers they are reciting will surround the prismatic colors of *shehu noteh shamayim* with the earth palette of psalmodic *daven'n*. They will precede the shuffled tempo of *Veshamru* by solemnly reciting *Hashkiveinu* ("Cause us to lie down in peace and awaken unto life"); they will follow the pushed beat of *Shalom Rav* with the hush of Silent Devotion ("May my words and thoughts be acceptable before Thee").

Staunch Traditionalists will have to tolerate this sort of musical lane changing until a younger generation of synagogue-goers becomes reattuned to our liturgy's historic sound: sinuous psalmodic chant alternating between cantor and congregation. During this characteristic dialogue cantors retrace the footsteps of precentors in the Second Temple's *lishkat hagazit* (Chapter 2 . . . "From Offerings to Words"), while congregants reprise the role of Levitical choristers. I make no mention here of rabbinical function because today's pulpit rabbis—by a strange twist of fate— have assumed the original supervisory role of the *chazan* during mishnaic times (Chapter 2 . . . "The Cantor as Synagogue Overseer"). The core element that has otherwise remained constant over all the centuries is a non-stop synergy between *sheli'ach tsibbur* and those *daven'n* along.

GUILT FEELINGS EXPRESSED THROUGH RELIGIOUS MUSIC

Another key feature that has always permeated Judaism's seasonally shifting liturgy is uneasy fluctuation between joy and sadness. At moments of greatest happiness our liturgy seems to pull tight against the reins of unchecked celebration; at weddings, cries of *Mazal Tov!* mingle with the crack of a glass being shattered in mournful remembrance of national calamities past. So, too, when we gather as families to recount the Passover redemption in springtime, our sense of national fulfillment is diminished by the humane recollection that Pharaoh's charioteers were simultaneously drowning in the sea. Following an ancient custom on Seder night (BT, *Megillah* 10b) we deliberately spill wine—to forestall any gloating over the horrors suffered by *all* Egyptians—as we enumerate the Ten Plagues.

A month earlier in our religious calendar, Purim rejoicing turns correspondingly self-conscious when we read about the plight of our forebears dwelling in Persia during the fifth century B.C.E. Threatened with mass murder at the instigation of Haman, the king's minister, they were granted royal permission to take up arms at the eleventh hour. Because in defending themselves, they slew hundreds of their tormentors in self-defense, the pertinent verses (Esther 9:6–7) are rushed through in one breath, so as not to draw listeners' attention to the highly justified retaliation. (But, of course, this hurried treatment—just as does the deliberate Passover wine spilling—guarantees precisely the opposite result.)

In the dead of winter, three months earlier still, Chanukah candles seem to flicker at mention of "the slaughter which God has prepared for the blaspheming foe" (in the hymn *Maoz Tsur*, "Rock of Ages"; Chapter 5 . . . "Seasonal Borrowings"). Modern prayerbooks unfailingly substitute a more euphemistic rendering of that verse: "furious they assailed us, but Your arm availed us." While replaying our people's greatest victories, we insist on wearing the hair shirt of penitents. We will rewrite history in order to deny ourselves any semblance of satisfaction over having been allowed to triumph once in a while.

Whenever Judaism's collective superego fills us with remorse in this way, we have learned to placate our guilt through prayer. On Sabbath we legitimize the self-serving desire for redemption by singing our concluding prayer in the hope-filled *Hatikvah* mode. The two hymns previously discussed in this chapter—*Adon Olam* and *Yigdal*—both fit this category (see earlier: "Authentic and Plagal Melodies"). Still, notes *American Jewish Year Book* editor David Singer, at times even that will not suffice. Though fully "immersed in the pleasures of American life," we are unable to shake a "sense of otherness." I would suggest this is especially true around the High Holy Days, a period of self-examination when feelings of not belonging might bubble to the surface. Coupled with a seasonally induced desire to repent moral shortcomings, our cultural malaise finds expression in the quint-essential prayer of Atonement, *Kol Nidre* (All Vows), which asks God to forgive our unfulfilled personal commitments to Him. Its signature motif—in a plagal/minor mode—is unmistakable. Starting from below, its melody rises slightly above the tonic note before descending, as in the phrase *haba aleinu* (referring to rash vows we are liable to make between now and Yom Kippur "to come").

```
                  ba-
               a-                        a-
(tonic ___)            a-                      lei-
                    a-          a-
                         a
     >ha-                                            nu
```

IT'S NOT JUST US

The Forgiveness motif likewise initiates other essential prayer melodies: Israel and Samuel Goldfarb's congregational *Shalom Aleichem* (one of the four Friday Night introits mentioned earlier: "Music to Get Things Started") and Sol Zim's responsive *Ledor Vador* ("All Generations Recount Thy Greatness"). The obvious question arises, why should a motif associated with Atonement also accompany texts that greet ministering angels and laud the holy God? According to musicologist Deryck Cooke, who assigns an entire lexicon of feelings to various note combinations, this particular configuration "conveys a powerful outburst of painful emotion, which does not protest further, but falls back into acceptance of grief." The painful emotion (despair over our plight) is followed by brief protest (in the form of prayer), and ultimate acceptance (of God's judgement). I cannot think of a better way to recapitulate the mood evoked by Judaism's Day of Atonement or, for that matter, Christianity's Passion story. Perhaps that is why the same musical phrase asks forgiveness of sin in

Bach's *Saint John Passion* ("rest in peace, O Holy Redeemer"),
Handel's and Haydn's *Te Deum* celebrations ("keep us this day without sin"),

and

Mozart's and Verdi's *Masses of Requiem* ("their souls release to
                                              realms of peace").

If there is any validity to the notion of a Judeo/Christian tradition shared by both cultures, it may lie in the nonverbal domain of tonal figures, which speak to us more succinctly than words. The sequence of notes under discussion—with its anguished rise from the deep and momentary breaking of the surface before sinking back to its fated level—tone-paints "a feeling of continuing sorrow," avers Deryck Cooke. That would explain its appearance in Christian liturgies that hinge on the concept of original sin; expiation through a Savior's death is prerequisite to salvation. Persistent feelings of sorrow might likewise explain why we Jews quote the phrase in *Kol Nidre*: to ask forgiveness of transgressions between ourselves and God. But again, what is there to forgive when we are observing Shabbat—not Yom Kippur—and singing God's praises; why must pain so often intrude upon our moments of supreme pleasure?

A month before he died, I put the same question—in different words—to my 92-year-old father, Hyman W. Levine. A businessman all his life, in his retirement he had reluctantly agreed to lead Preliminary services for his synagogue. He told me it was in self-defense; the other pensioners who attempted to *daven Birkot Hashachar* and *Pesukei Dezimra* did so *ohn tam* (Yiddish: "without taste"). Their ineptitude was barely tolerable during weekdays, but totally unsupportable on Sabbath mornings. Recalling (or thinking he recalled) the mode he had heard as a boy in Suwalki, Poland, my father stepped into the breech as Designated *Davener*. Now, at my request, he gave me a sample of his dimly remembered chant for the *Amidah* repetition of Shabbat morning, which to my ear sounded just like a rearrangement of the music for *Kol Nidre*. I told him so.

"The reason is . . ." replied my father in the same ritual sing-song he had employed for answering the Four Seder Questions during my childhood, "that under the Tsar, every *Shabbos* was like Yom Kippur. And when I came here as a teenager and had to support your grandparents, life was still a struggle. So why should I change the way I *daven?*" The ancient Babylonian academies of Sura and Pumbedita would have concurred: he follows his ancestral custom (BT, *Sabbath* 35). But what is *our* excuse for reverting to a mode of Forgiveness when we should be offering thanks to God, Who enabled our parents or grandparents to settle here and ensure a better life for their posterity?

WHY THE FORGIVENESS MODE PERSISTS

There are two reasons. The first was suggested 200 years ago by Reb Israel, the Maggid (preacher) of Koznitz, whose main focus was on the idea of Redemption. Unable to accept that the entire world was devoid of morally upright individuals, whenever he recited the benediction Redeemer of Israel—which occurs in both morning and evening prayer—he would silently add:

> *Ribono Shel Olam*
> [Master of the Universe],
> I beg You to redeem Israel;
> and if You do not want to do that,
> then at least redeem the Gentiles!

The implication can only be that Israel is as yet unworthy of Redemption. It must first undergo the experience of *teshuvah* (repentance), which, along with acknowledgment of having sinned and showing remorse and resolving never to repeat the transgression, includes asking forgiveness.

The second reason has to do with a previous generation of North American Jews' perceived helplessness while millions of their European brethren perished during World War II. An immense burden of *guilt* over their inability to prevent what we now realize was beyond their control continued to trouble our parents and grandparents even after a Jewish State was established in 1948 as refuge for those who survived. Not until the triumphant events of June 5–10, 1967—when Israel overcame both isolation by its hostile neighbors and abandonment by its supposed allies—did the cloud of self-implication finally lift. Just before it did, 1960s Jews seemed to be reliving the despair of the late 1930s and early 1940s, only this time they no longer felt themselves helpless. Jacob Neusner calls attention to the fact that "diaspora Jewry responded en masse . . . and the outcome was completely different; at last the painful memories and the guilt could be laid to rest."

The Six Day War's outcome partially answered an unspoken question that still haunts us: Why did God allow the Holocaust to happen? We will never understand why *they* were singled out to die; but the fact is that *we* were spared. That in itself would seem to vindicate the Bible's strategy of dividing the Jewish people into two camps when danger loomed: "if the one camp is smitten, the camp that is left shall escape" (Genesis 32:8–9). In place of self-recrimination, the miraculous victory of 1967 suggested a new equation that explains our status as survivors through no apparent merit of our own: national Exile through Holocaust; followed by national Redemption through Israel. In any given crisis *some* of the Jewish people will always survive, and this time it was our turn. We not only remained unscathed, we have prospered in order to underwrite God's ultimate plan for the Saving Remnant of European Jewry. The plan is alluded to in a new version of *Al Hanisim* ("For God's Miracles"), a prayer that had previously been recited only on Chanukah and Purim. Conservatism adapted it for *Yom Ha'atsma'ut* (Israel Independence Day; my emphases).

> In the days of world war and destruction,
> *six million* of our people were brutally slain . . .
> Then . . . scattered *remnants* sought refuge in
> the Land of our Fathers . . . You, O Lord . . .
> wrought deliverance to your people *Israel.*

Through their untiring efforts to sustain that deliverance by supporting the State of Israel financially, politically, and in countless other ways, North America's six million Jews (counting Canada) tangibly demonstrate the Divine purpose for which they have been spared.

Reform makes a like connection between the death camps of Poland and a new life for survivors in their own land. During the Passover Seder, its *New Union Haggadah* (ed. Herbert Bronstein, 1975) sets aside a *Fifth* Cup of Redemption and asks participants to hallow it with these incantatory words.

> It is still dark as we pour this cup, but light dawns over Zion . . .
> Passing . . . out of the *fiery furnace* seared in body and soul,
> Reborn in self-redemption . . . The people of *Israel lives!*

Reconstructionism flatly rejects the concept of supernatural miracles performed in our behalf. Yet its latest prayerbook presents an excerpted memoir of Holocaust survivors, "In Germany at the End of World War II," that allows those involved to state the case in their own words.

June 3, 1945—Here we are, the first few comrades,
sitting on a truck that is taking us *from Buchenwald*
. . . from the barracks, the watchtower, the SS quarters
. . . We are all determined to follow this road to
a place of our own . . . This road must take us to *Palestine.*

While Orthodoxy firmly believes that God performed miracles for our ancestors in the days of Judah Maccabee, the son of Mattathias, and also in the days
of Queen Esther, the daughter of Avichayil, it has not standardized a liturgy for
the modern-day miracle of *Yom Ha'atsma'ut.* The jury is still out on whether we, "as
mere humans, [can] identify our exact location in the grand plan of Redemption,"
states Yeshiva University's President, Rabbi Norman Lamm. Even the widely recited prayer *Avinu Shebashamayim, Tsur Yisrael Vego'alo* ("Father in Heaven, Israel's Rock
and Its Redeemer"), which refers to the establishment of a Third Jewish Com-
monwealth as "our Redemption's first flowering," may be presumptuous, according to this understanding of a Messianic Era that can only come unawares
(BT, *Sanhedrin* 97a). Nevertheless, in a comprehensive anthology of essays, editors Bernhard Rosenberg and Fred Heuman present a consensus of leading Orthodox rabbinic thought that does link our people's inestimable loss during the
Holocaust—ever so tenuously—with the headiness engendered by Israel's victory
in its War of Independence (1948–49). I would summarize the correlation that
many of the learned contributors imply between Exile and Redemption in our own
day, as follows.

There is no radical explanation as to why
God permitted the Holocaust to take place
. . . yet we must take consolation in the fact
that *the six million who were martyred*
"gave" the Jewish people back its Land.

No wonder we prefer hearing the mode of Forgiveness even in prayers that
proclaim God's greatness. In a very real sense, the State of Israel—through its
perseverance in the face of heavy odds—has redeemed not only the surviving
European remnant but North American Jewry as well. That is why we are to be
forgiven for overindulging our collective sense of relief, even at the cost of lump-
ing petition—and contrition—with praise. Night and day we exclaim before the
Creator

mi chamocha ba'eilim, adonai . . .
"who is like You . . . revered in praises"!

And we clothe our laudation in sackcloth and ashes: Penitential music sung on the Eve of Atonement:

veyeira'eh kippureinu ad arev
may our forgiveness arrive at nightfall.

In effect, we have obliterated the boundaries that formerly marked off different sections of the liturgy.

MIXED MODES ARE "IN"

The lesson my art instructor taught many years ago—that there are no clear-cut delineations in our universe—has been borne out as much in worship as in painting. It has since acquired a corollary in synagogue song: barriers of any kind no longer exist in our prayer modes. We may now safely change tonal lanes without causing the sky to fall or placing our firstborn in danger of Heavenly retribution.

When singing prayers in a specific mode during a specific season, it is all right if we err in applying music of Forgiveness to words of Praise, either through a surfeit of emotion or a lack of awareness. Still we are deeply stirred, and often shaken, by the resulting mismatch. One shudders to think of the cosmic ramifications if every synagogue in North America got the combination right, all at the same moment. For now, the various national movements are each content to possess a fragment of the whole, which they prize as if it were chipped from the long-lost tablets that God inscribed for Moses (Deuteronomy 10:4)

The way each movement singularly displays and celebrates its Sabbath treasure is revealed by Chapter 5: "Castles in Time."

CHAPTER 5

Castles in Time

I'd love to open a spiritual store called Eternal Life.
Clients would come in and . . . our specially trained
Travel agents would prescribe an itinerary . . .
I would recommend the 52-week stress-management
Shabbat program which allows you to travel
to your spiritual goal in a virtual reality machine.
     Moshe Waldoks,
       "At the Shabbat Synaplex Mall," *Kerem*, 1994

Rabbi Joshua ben Hananya ranked highly among the so-called Vineyard of Scholars who perpetuated talmudic learning in the ancient coastal-plain town of Yavneh immediately after Jerusalem's fall to Rome (BT, *Gittin* 56b; *Tosefta, Berakhot* 2:6). As his people's emissary he had frequent occasion to visit the Imperial City and mingle with members of its ruling class. Once, when a dignitary who had visited Judea asked him why the dishes served in his country on Friday nights emitted such an appetizing aroma, Rabbi Joshua replied: "It is because we put a special spice in it, called Sabbath." "Will you let me have some of your Sabbath-spice," inquired the Roman. "I cannot, Your Excellency," answered Rabbi Joshua, "for if you want to savor the Sabbath, first you must keep it, as God has commanded [BT, *Shabbat* 119a]."

THE ORIGINAL SABBATH MANDATE

Evidently a man of great tact, Rabbi Joshua chose not to add that God had actually issued a *double* commandment concerning the Sabbath. Exodus 31:16 states "the children of Israel shall *keep* the Sabbath," as Joshua correctly noted. The sequel to that statement, "to *make* the Sabbath a perpetual covenant," was extraneous to his point, but is central to ours.

A DAY OF REST FOR TODAY

Observing a weekly day of inactivity in our highly mobile society is difficult enough; finding something constructive with which to fill its prohibition-laden hours is doubly challenging. Heaven knows we have tried; fifty years ago our rabbis were futilely touting Shabbat as a self-help cure for workaday stress. Unfortunately, explains Jenna Weissman Joselit in an unblinking survey of early-twentieth-century American Jewish culture, all such efforts at getting us to regularly observe Shabbat "fell on deaf ears; American Jews steadfastly preferred the occasional, the 'once in a while' approach to modern Jewish living." This despite the fact that even devout Christians admire the Jewish Sabbath. Huston Smith, a leading scholar of comparative religion, openly confesses envying Jews (including his own son-in-law) their septimal night-and-day of recuperative rest, something he feels has been utterly lost in Christianity.

The truth of the matter is that very few modern Jews undergo the weekly spiritual R & R of which Huston Smith speaks so covetously. But those who do keep the Sabbath every week seem to acquire an ennoblement of soul (*neshamah yeteirah*; BT, *Beitsah* 16a) that lasts from its inception to its conclusion. The joy they feel increases geometrically through communal prayer with other like-minded individuals, since it connects them in spirit not only with those present but with all who have ever observed the Sabbath in similar fashion. Only good can accrue from the harmonious interaction that ensues among the worshiping group's members as together they transcend specificity of moment and place. Research shows that each of their bodies responds to the stimulus of communal prayer by producing its own inner relaxants, known as endorphins. Dr. Herbert Benson of Harvard Medical School associates this innate biochemical response, involving "the body's decreased respiratory rate, heart rate and blood pressure," specifically with "the traditional rocking and chanting during Hebrew prayers." In sum, *daven'n* would seem to qualify as a prime relaxant.

But it may not be unique in that regard. Other salutary pastimes whose benefits might rival those of collective worship could also be awaiting discovery. Let me mention one that would appear germane: children's seemingly mindless viewing of garden-variety TV (as opposed to violent programming). That it puts young viewers at ease is clear to anyone who has ever attempted to intrude upon the trance-like state that ensues. Nor has it been shown that children remain anything but alert and reactive throughout, argue investigative journalists Stephen Seplow and Jonathan Storm, who compiled a book-length report on how television has redefined our lives. Though maddening to parents, the deeply meditative condition of children absorbed in TV watching could be an ideal stage-setter for creative endeavors. Far from inducing apathy as has been claimed, screen gazing for hours at a stretch could prove the ultimate stimulant for childhood's most ultimately fruitful activity: daydreaming. That is precisely when youngsters are at their creative peak.

So are adults, whose abstracted musings while woolgathering often lead to moments of concrete inspiration. That is why a similar case can be made for outwardly lethargic, seemingly disinterested synagogue attendees going through the regimented motions that typify a good deal of today's Sabbath services (Chapter 2 . . . "Non-Jewish Worship Influences"). Congregants' lips might move automatically on command, but in the private world of their still-active imaginations, civilization's next great scientific discovery or cultural breakthrough may be silently germinating.

THE REAL SIGNIFICANCE OF SABBATH

Setting aside any benefits derived from attending Sabbath services, the Day of Rest itself would seem to offer a boon to health, a stepping off the treadmill of endless striving, onto the terra firma of simple acceptance. Yet it is not feasible to treat Shabbat as nothing more than a protracted meditation in the manner of Far Eastern religious disciplines. The notion of quietly watching the world go by without reacting for a period of twenty-four hours strikes most of us instant achievers in the West as a colossal waste of time. Writer Mary Gordon elaborates. "It is as if we suffer from a new disease: Parasabbath, fear of the Sabbath . . . 'you look rested' is considered an insult, an accusation of laziness."

Despite the wrong turn that early-twentieth-century American rabbis took in trying to sell Shabbat as a relaxation panacea, it appears they were actually headed in the right direction all along. One of their pre-eminent thinkers, Abraham Joshua Heschel, re-examined the qualitative essence of Sabbath and found that unlike Pilgrimage Festivals—Pesach, Shavuot, and Sukkot—which coincide with physical phenomena like rain or dew or harvest, Shabbat does not depend on space and the things it contains. "It is not the thing that lends significance to the moment," observed Heschel, "but rather the sanctified moment that permeates all things with its aura." Sabbath is the sanctifying moment par excellence, for which Jews built a splendid liturgy, a *Castle in Time*. In contrast to that, other religions were constructing spatially defined cathedrals (from the Latin for "chair," a seat of ecclesiastical authority) or mosques (from Old Spanish *mezquita*, after Arabic *masjid*, "a sacred place for prostrating oneself") in which to celebrate their holy days.

Judaism's devotional constructs—Time Castles—are built upon liturgies that developed after the destruction of its Castle in Space, the Holy Temple that stood in Jerusalem until the first century of this era. (Chapter 2 . . . "From Offerings to Words"). Some Time Castles are frequented no more than once or twice a year; those limited to High Holy Day visitations admit penitents only on Rosh Hashanah and Yom Kippur. Festival Castles fare somewhat better, those of Orthodox and Conservative persuasion receiving pilgrims on six holy days during the milder seasons of spring and fall. But there is no doubt that for almost 2,000 years Sabbath morning's Castle has remained the most popular year-round destination for Jews. Erected to commemorate Creation's seventh day—when God paused to reflect on the world He had made—the Sabbath Morning Castle reflects a liturgical world divided into seven sections rather than days.

> I—Humans—praising in "Preliminary Blessings and Verses of Song"
>   (*Birkot Hashachar/Pesukei Dezimra*)
> 2—God—teaching "Judaism's Credo and Accompanying Benedictions"
>   (*Shema/Uvirkoteha*)
> 3—Humans—praying in "Standing Devotion #1"
>   (*Amidat Shacharit*)
> 4—God—teaching "Weekly Scripture"
>   (*K'ri'at Hatorah*)
> 5—Humans—teaching "Weekly Scripture"
>   (*Devar Torah*)
> 6—Humans—praying in "Standing Devotion #2"
>   (*Amidat Musaf*)
> 7—Humans—praising in "Hymns of Glory"
>   (*Shirei Kavod*)

The liturgical blueprint for Sabbath Morning adheres to an architectural design first set forth in the Torah: juxtaposing devotion with instruction; interspersing our own ephemeral words with the eternal Word of God. The certainty that offering glory hymns stands shoulder to shoulder with quoting Scripture is a foundation stone upon which our Sabbath liturgy rests. It also provides a rationale for the mandate concerning Sabbath having been given in two parts. Whenever Israelites perform a special Order of Prayers for the Sabbath, they are moving beyond merely *keeping* the day of rest. biblical commentator Benno Jacob sees it as fulfilling the second part of God's instruction in Exodus 31, namely, to *make* the Sabbath, an imperative found nowhere else, not even in the Ten Commandments (Exodus 20:2–14; Deuteronomy 5:6–18).

HOW THE SABBATH MORNING LITURGY EVOLVED

During biblical times the Sabbath respite afforded parents an opportunity to re-acquaint themselves and their children with ancestral teachings, to retire from the six-day marathon of hand-to-mouth existence and consider what it all meant. In that sense the Day of Rest offered a foretaste of the World to Come (Chapter 3 . . . "Emendation Replaces Translation"). Sabbath provided the weekly opportunity for a summing-up of life, a preview of Judgment Day, pictured in subsequent Jewish folklore as one long, all-embracing conversation with God, during which individuals would experience both Heaven and Hell. As a result, the custom developed of gathering on Shabbat to converse with those who were considered closest to God: holy men. While the First Temple stood (ca. 950–586 B.C.E.), families made special pilgrimages to sit at the feet of learned seers and listen to words of wisdom. Abraham ibn Ezra infers this custom from the biblical incident (2 Kings, Chapter 4), in which a Shunamite man, seeing his wife prepare to set out seeking help from the Prophet Elisha, demands to know:

> Wherefore wilt thou go to see him today;
> it is neither New Moon nor Sabbath?

Eventually, formal prayer was appended to unstructured Sabbath learning. The rationale: people felt that simply listening to God's words did not suffice. They needed to weave those words into prayers that implied a quid pro quo relationship with God. Here is one patterned after the promise spelled out in Deuteronomy 11:13–21, contingent upon Israel's acceptance of God's suzerainty.

> O Lord our God, we have observed Thy commandments,
> inscribed them on our doorposts and taught them to our children;
> now do Thou ensure rain for the land in its proper time,
> and prolong our days and the days of our children upon the earth.

Combined, the two consecrated activities of learning and worship not only distanced Sabbath from any kinship with the daily routine of earning one's bread, they introduced a positive aspect to the weekly prohibition against work. They also imparted to the keeping and making of Sabbath a limited *spatial* dimension, a

> *place* where man can . . . re-equip himself for the
> battle with the elements of our mundane existence,

in Nechama Leibowitz's view. Liturgist Ovadiah Camhy develops this spatial aspect a bit more vividly. He perceives the Sabbath place built by Jewish commitment to Sabbath observance as an actual structure,

> a great turreted *castle* whose peaks
> climb toward heaven in spirited prayer.

Leibowitz's re-equipping place and Camhy's turreted castle provide just the structural metaphor we need to compare Sabbath services as they unfold today in North American synagogues of varying denominations. To appreciate our survey's full capability in virtual-reality terms, readers might realign their mental search engines until the third dimension of Abraham Heschel's Castle in Time comes up like a Web site. That will help fine-tune the image for which we are searching: a sanctified moment made visible, whose home page we may visit at leisure. Narrated as a Time travelogue, our weekly quest readily lends itself to evaluation on the basis of either having reached or fallen short of a spiritual goal. Liturgy sheds some of its mystery when browsed as a Sabbath Castle containing priceless furnishings that have accumulated over many centuries. It is easier to speak in the real estate jargon of "rooms" and "wall hangings" than in the liturgical terminology of petitionary subsections and benedictory coteries.

PALATIAL BLDG, FABULOUS MEETNG FACILTY, HEAVNLY APNTMNTS, AVALBL WKENDS ONLY

Envision, therefore, a Time Castle consisting of seven halls, every hall corresponding to a section of the Sabbath Morning liturgy. Castle halls are divided unevenly according to their functions, like Books of the Pentateuch. Genesis and Numbers narrate the story of ancient Israel's peregrinations while four of the Sabbath Castle's seven halls accommodate the narrative of modern Israel's prayer. Exodus, Leviticus, and Deuteronomy legislate, just as the other three Castle halls (starred below*) furnish areas for studying God's Law as set forth in the Torah.

I—VESTIBULE	=	*BIRKOT HASHACHAR / PESUKEI DEZIMRA*
		(Preliminary Blessings Verses of Song)
2—THRONE ROOM*	=	*SHEMA / UVIRKOTEHA*
		(Credo and Accompanying Benedictions)
3—ROYAL CHAMBER	=	*AMIDAT SHACHARIT*
		(Standing Devotion #1)
4—DINING ROOM*	=	*KERI'AT HATORAH*
		(Weekly Scripture, read)
5—REFECTORY*	=	*DEVAR TORAH*
		(Weekly Scripture, taught)
6—GUEST CHAMBER	=	*AMIDAT MUSAF*
		(Standing Devotion #2)
7—GRAND BALLROOM	=	*SHIREI KAVOD*
		(Hymns of Glory)

NATIONAL MOVEMENTS AS TIME-TRAVEL AGENCIES

Imaging a Castle in Time underscores how solidly the Sabbath Morning liturgy is built, for it has withstood the ravages of earlier—less tolerant—environments and the radical innovations of its most recent visiting groups, called movements nowadays. Years ago, when theological as well as ritual lines were more clearly drawn, a revealing anecdote made the rounds of North American Jewry.

Question: What difference is there between the Orthodox, Conservative, Reform, and Reconstructionist movements?

Answer: It has to do with the way they pray:
The Orthodox say: *Tateh in Himmel* (Yiddish for "Our Heavenly Father").
The Conservatives say: *Avinu Shebashamayim* (its Hebrew equivalent).
The Reform say: *Our Father, Which Art in Heaven*.
The Reconstructionists simply announce: *To Whom It May Concern* . . .

Today the two outer movements mentioned here—Orthodox and Reconstructionist—still differ recognizably in their approaches to God, but formerly bold delineations between the two inner ones—Conservative and Reform—are less pronounced. Still, all four movements maintain enough variance between them so that when any one of them arranges a weekly visit to the Sabbath Castle, it is able to offer an appreciably dissimilar program. The situation is analogous to four competing Time-travel agencies, each running its own customized tour to the same Sabbath Morning attraction, in every North American city containing a sizable Jewish population.

Depending on their category—Luxury, Deluxe, First Class, or Budget—tour itineraries differ chiefly in the specific Castle halls they avoid in order not to overstep time limits. To make the halls they do visit appear more attractive, the agencies' local representatives have developed a host of innovative activities called rituals; the fewer rooms visited, the more time available for ritual activities. Some branches of the more old-fashioned agencies choose to ignore any limit on tour duration, hewing to a pre-World War II European convention of remaining inside the Time Castle for between three and four hours at a stretch. But no matter how extended or how brief, every Sabbath tour concludes with a light repast, called *Kiddush* after the sanctifying wine blessing that inaugurates it.

ORTHODOXY'S "GRAND SAFARI"

The industry's longest and most inclusive First Class jaunt, Grand Safari, schedules stops in every Castle hall. This necessitates certain adjustments in order to provide even minimal flexibility within a jam-packed schedule. Entering every room with a full contingent would mean running well past the normal midday hour for a requisite second Sabbath meal (*Kitzur Shulchan Aruch*, 77:13–16), so Safari gets underway with a bare minimum at 8:30 A.M. At a brisk pace it traverses the Vestibule's Preliminary Blessings and Verses of Song, the Throne Room's Credo and Accompanying Benedictions, the Royal Chamber's Standing Devotion #1, and about half of the Dining Room's Scripture Reading. Somewhere between 10 and 11 o'clock, late arrivals begin to slow it down. By then every tour place is occupied, so Safari has no choice but to proceed more deliberately through the remaining three halls, led in musical Hebrew commentary by a *chazan* guide. Well-versed in Medieval minstrelsy, this cantorial functionary employs a kind of *semi-sung* delivery reminiscent of Chaucer's Prioress:

> ful wel she song the service divyne ;
> entuned in hir nose ful semely.

THE *CHAZAN* AS TRAVEL GUIDE

Orthodox *chazan* guides further entune their song by infusing it with a *quavering* vocal quality, a fluctuation that sounds almost like crying. When attempting to convey to tour groups even a microfraction of the Lord of All Castles' greatness, guides' voices will often tremble naturally of their own accord. Perhaps to disguise this involuntary quaver, *chazan* guides have used the tremulous technique as a matter of course for the better part of two millennia. When combined with the added richness of singing, it helps induce a heightened state of consciousness in both listeners and performers.

The Talmud, a Baedeker of law and legend that covers Castles and every other aspect of Time travel, has for centuries been studied with a chant that enables each student to remember and repeat it for others (BT, *Sanhedrin* 99a–b). The Talmud also ordains that holy Scripture be read with melody (BT, *Megillah* 32a). These rulings, dating from the first and second centuries of our era, were not lost on Church Father St. Jerome, who lived in Bethlehem some 300 years later. Musicologist Hanoch Avenary cites Jerome's report of Palestinian Jews "rolling up—by memory—the books of prophecy of Moses [as] they chant the Divine commands." Avenary's comparative study of Hebrew, Syrian, and Greek liturgical traditions reveals that Hebrew prayer chants effectively parallel the entire evolution of Christian plainsong, the basic ritual chant of both the Eastern (Orthodox) and Western (Catholic) church rites. For centuries, synagogue *chazanim* and church cantors in both rites featured the same quavering-voice technique, which by mid-sixteenth century conflicted with the new polyphonic (multi-voiced) style in which Catholic Masses were being composed. When choristers all sang their individual parts simultaneously with a tremulous vocal quality, the result proved too muddy for the Council of Trent, which in 1564 banned what it called *tremula voce*.

Hardly affected by the protocol of Christian cathedrals, *chazan* guides continued resorting to a *tremula voce* when reciting long sections of mandatory commentary from official Sabbath Time Castle guidebooks. Called *Siddurim*, the guidebooks are distributed to Castle visitors so they can engage in lively "confrontation" with their *chazan* guide, explains Avenary. The guide seems to "bend" his portion of the dialogue, adding multi-toned trills to certain words by way of underscoring them. However, the visitors' half of the dialogue must be kept simple because of an overriding need to move along and not dwell unduly on any one Castle area. The contour of this continuing repartee imitates the parallelistic structure of Psalm texts quoted in the *Siddurim*. Psalms express a given idea in two different ways, pausing midway as if posing a question, and then supplying an answer. Any guidebook chant that follows the contour of such texts is therefore termed *psalmodic*. When performed as responsive dialogue on reciting tones (Chapter 1 . . . "Finding Common Liturgical Ground"), psalmody is the musical fulfillment of a Mishnaic dictum concerning teaching: pose the question according to subject, and give the answer according to rule (*Avot* 5:10). The guide's queries are broad, that is, musically evocative. The group's replies are brief and to the point.

MUSICALLY EMBELLISHED COMMENTARY

There is another reason why guides have traditionally embellished their chanted commentary. Prior to the advent of electronic amplification, European Castle halls were limited in size. But they made up for that with ornate decoration, and the guides spun their song in a fashion that matched the elaborate décor. In addition to bending and trilling the vocal line, they tossed in roulades of notes—*coloratura*—toward the ends of phrases. The coloratura flowed rapidly and cleanly because there was no echo in the tiny rooms. Gilded moldings and embroidered curtains absorbed sound, unlike the stone walls of Medieval Castles, which reinforced it and gave rise to long reciting tones (Chapter 1 . . . "Finding Common Liturgical Ground"). In those small plastered chambers guides found it necessary to enrich their singing by tossing out notes fast enough to disguise the lack of natural reverberation.

The same principle applies to singing outdoors, as in the original Time Castle situated within the precinct of ancient Jerusalem's Temple just before it was destroyed. When the Temple's Levitic guides were sent as captives to Rome late in the first century (Chapter 4 . . . "How *Daven'n* Works in Weekday Services"), they took that early version of ornamental commentary with them into exile. Over time, their perfectly poised chant, punctuated by melodic flourishes at the midway pause and final cadence of every verse, was adopted by the early Church along with the psalmodic texts that were sung to it. The Christianized version of Levitic psalmody, which initially replicated its distinct parallelistic scheme, later sprouted ornate exclamatory *Alleluias* (fifth–tenth centuries) along with melodically and textually intricate *Tropes* (tenth–twelfth centuries) that were many times longer than the balanced phrases to which they were appended.

Song embellishment flowered even more spectacularly in the eighteenth-century Baroque era. Architectural historian Michael Forsyth describes the theaters in which a brilliant secular style known as *Bel Canto* (Beautiful Song) blossomed.

Filled with sound-absorptive, elaborately costumed
spectators and heavy drapery . . . with a short
reverberation time tending toward "open air" conditions,
the Italian opera house had characteristically clear, intimate
acoustics which allowed the rich ornamentation of Baroque
arias to be revealed to splendid effect.

In view of these historical precedents, critic Michael Scott is of the opinion that ornamental effects "are not mere singer's vanity . . . but part of a basic vocal grammar as old as—perhaps older than—music itself."

In the context of guides singing commentary as they chaperone visitors through the Sabbath Time Castle, ornate declamation never fails to move visitors, for it perfectly complements the blend of biblical, mishnaic, and Medieval Hebrew in which its message is delivered. Especially during the Guest Chamber's Standing Devotion #2 (*Amidat Musaf*), Orthodox *chazan* guides go to great lengths extolling the virtues of several intricately carved Oriental furnishings. Outstanding among these is a complex tapestry called *Kedushat Musaf* (Additional Glorification), woven secretly by Judean craftsmen living under a harsh sixth-century Byzantine-Christian occupation. One singularly hateful decree banned entry to the Throne Room, which contained the original manuscript of *Shema Yisrael*, Israel's Declaration of Interdependence with God. This did not sit too well with the Judean community's religious leaders, who determined to reposition the Credo late enough in Castle itineraries so that government agents, tailing every group of weekly Time travelers, would be thrown off the trail. They hit upon the idea of building an additional hall modeled after the Royal Chamber, a Guest Chamber where the secret police would not think of looking after having searched five prior rooms. Guest Chamber decor replicated the *Kedushah* tapestry that had shown so well during the Royal Chamber's Standing Devotion #1, with one improvement. The prohibited Credo motif was woven surreptitiously into its design, lending it such luster that it came to acquire the Hebrew name for that "additional" sheen: *Musaf*.

KEDUSHAT MUSAF: A DEPARTURE POINT

The embattled Judean community was thrilled to view a substitute copy of the Interdependence Declaration more intricately adorned than its Throne Room original, especially one created under such conspiratorial circumstances. Since then, the Guest Chamber has been a favorite of Orthodox tourists. In tribute to its heroic past, *Kedushat Musaf* receives royal treatment on every Grand Safari; *chazan* guides rhapsodize over it so expansively that visitors frequently steal furtive glances at their watches. Realizing how late the hour, a venturesome few invariably slip away before the tapestry viewing ends, forgoing the Grand Ballroom's Glory Hymns and complimentary *Kiddush* repast rather than skimp on their restorative Shabbat afternoon nap.

Premature departures of this sort have plagued Orthodox tours for years, nor are they always viewed with equanimity by the Castle staff. On one memorable Safari for which I enrolled as a high school student drawn by the beautiful singing, I noticed a number of visitors slipping away before the *chazan* guide had ended his remarks on the significance of *Kedushat Musaf*. As they tried to leave via the Guest Chamber's rear exit, sounds other than the tour group's normal *ooh*s and *aah*s were heard. Someone shouted "Stop!" Loud noises emanated from a melee between the would-be escapees and a contingent of guards who were grappling with them, cries of "let me out," cloth ripping, wood splintering. We stared in disbelief at one unfortunate who had tried unsuccessfully to run the blockade. He staggered under the weight of a heavy oaken door that he had managed to pull off its hinges, while next to him stood a guard holding a sleeve he had torn from the man's jacket while trying to restrain him. We were shocked; all I could think of were stories I had heard concerning older Time Castles in Eastern Europe. Many years later the tales were confirmed in a memoir by one of the last Golden Age *chazan* guides (Chapter I ... "The American Century of Jewish Worship Revisited"), Hungarian-born Samuel Vigoda. It seems the leading synagogues in cities like Vilna and Warsaw, which boasted heavy concentrations of Jewish residents, indulged in the common practice of overselling places on every tour. This routinely led to hordes of irate ticket holders congregating outside the buildings, sometimes breaking down doors in an effort to gain admission. By way of contrast, North American Time travelers are so sporadic in their attendance on Sabbaths when no Bar or Bat Mitzvah is scheduled that the Castle guards' main concern is to prevent anyone from leaving, by means of force if necessary.

REFORM'S "HIGHLIGHTS" PACKAGE

Reform's Gates of Leisure agency offers a luxury Castle tour, Highlights of East and West, which starts at the more realistic hour of 10:30 and runs till somewhere between noon and 12:30. Like Orthodoxy's Grand Safari, it, too, hurries through the Vestibule's Blessings and Verses, as well as the Throne Room's Credo. It then decelerates and, since the later Guest Chamber stop was inserted to elaborate upon much of what had already been viewed earlier, Highlights concentrates instead on a single Standing Devotion in the Royal Chamber. Unlike Orthodox tourists who are familiar enough with Castle routine to require little or no assistance, less extensively Time-traveled Reform visitors seem to relish periodic prompting along the route. To expedite matters, a guide staff—consisting of one *chazan* and several rabbis—explains every item in two languages, one Eastern (Hebrew) and one Western (English). East—West Highlights makes only a perfunctory stop for the Dining Room's Scripture reading, taking no more than three hasty nibbles out of a biblical feast intended to nourish at least seven. Limiting biblical intake to three portions allows for a more leisurely tasting of Scriptural recipes—known as commandments—in the Refectory, which houses an ornately fronted *Ark*. For the State of Israel's poet laureate, Yehuda Amichai, the Ark recalls something elemental and threatening.

> In a dark womb shaped like a synagogue dome,
> round, ancient cave of prayer, the open Ark
> blinding, like an interrogation, a third degree.
> "Do you confess? Do you confess?"

THE ARK AS CULINARY FIXTURE

North American Time Castles generally take a lighter tack toward the Ark, treating it more like the gingerbread oven of *Hansel and Gretel* fame, as they vie with one another in commissioning ever more stagy (and sometimes ominous-looking) shapes. An artist who created one such conversation piece for a Time Castle in the Canyonlands of America's Southwest attempted to avoid cliche by shaping it like a cloud-covered mountain. A brochure handed to my tour group as it entered, explained that the lower part of the Ark's surface was left unfinished to signify the difficulty encountered in all spiritual beginnings. The difficulty gradually eases, as shown by a smoother-textured middle section, and the absence of a visible top hints at limitless future possibilities.

The spiritual journey traced so graphically by that Ark's varied surface textures corresponded exactly to "The Successive Stages of Creativity" (Chapter I) that any work of art undergoes: roughness; refinement; and reinterpretation ad infinitum. That alone should have qualified it for registration as a national landmark of Time Castle furnishings. Unfortunately, the artist fabricated his protuberant creation out of blackened cast iron and fitted it with a single massive door that, when opened, exposed a dimly lit, cavernous interior. This left me and my fellow Time travelers guessing exactly what the Ark was supposed to represent.

The concensus of that prizeless contest was a foregone conclusion, since the Canyonlands Ark's form—like that of the Ark in every other Time Castle—follows its function: a place to heat and test the Sacred Recipes about to be transmitted in the Dining Room.

B'NEI / B'NOT MITZVAH AS SOUS CHEFS

Castle Arks also serve as Refectory backdrops for several innovative Reform procedures. During one standard ritual, the rabbi guide conveys private instructions to young Sous Chefs, who are then elevated to the status of B'nei/ B'not Mitzvah, that is, bound by the same rules as adult Time travelers. Other tourists, too polite to eavesdrop, wait patiently for a signal that the special instructions have been concluded. That signal is the rabbi's salute, in which she or he raises both arms high above the youngsters' heads while invoking a Culinary Benediction that asks God to bless their every flavorful effort and allow it to rise like yeast, threefold. The rabbi's lofty salute evidently commemorates how ancient priestly guides, the original Chefs who had mastered Sacred Recipes, would raise their arms above their heads while blessing patrons of the Jerusalem Temple's Refectory (Mishnah, *Sotah* 7:6). That might explain why Reform's Highlights brochure mostly refers to its tour venue as a temple, whereas other Time-travel agencies alternate between that designation and "synagogue."

Ancillary Highlights rituals involve parents or grandparents of the Sous Chefs either handing them the Torah Scroll of Sacred Recipes or draping them with the silken *Cordon Bleu* -striped *tallit* sash. Everyone then rushes through the Grand Ballroom where they wash down miniature rolls of challah bread with jigger-sized plastic cups of sweet wine or grape juice. Reboarding their tour bus, they head off to a post-Highlight luncheon at the latest "in" restaurant or country club.

Many anecdotes surround the youthful Sous Chefs, who customarily respond aloud to their rabbi guide's whispered colloquy and yeasty blessing. The cleverest response I ever witnessed involved a Bat Mitzvah at Philadelphia's Main Line Reform Temple. Closing the Ark door, she turned to address our tour. She told us how her parents had taken her to Israel the previous summer instead of to the nearby Jersey Shore, which would have been her first choice. As it turned out, their limousine driver had fortuitously scheduled a stopover at the Dead Sea. The soon-to-be Bat Mitzvah learned that it was the lowest spot on earth, its dense atmosphere so efficient at filtering sunlight that a quick and easy tan was guaranteed without burning. Even its sulphurous mud was said to have a rejuvenating effect when rubbed onto one's face.

Peering out at the Refectory ringed by our sea of faces, the child touched her cheeks and asked, *"So tell me, do I look any younger?"*

CONSERVATISM'S "JUNKET": NOT FOR EVERYONE

Conservatism's Time travel agency, Seminary Rambles, has tried to publicize its supposedly deluxe Junket for Everyone in recent years, with mixed success. The agency produces annual brochures and regularly takes out full-page ads in the *New York Times*, but many of those who sign up complain they were not given what had been promised. The problem stems from a basic misconception of what Seminary Rambles actually represents. Its business expanded mightily after the Second World War when it started providing a more upscale version of Orthodoxy's Grand Safari, at the time rated no higher than three Stars of David. Junket for Everyone immediately attracted war-weary ex-servicemen and their brides anxious to raise families in the suburban areas where Rambles had set up branch offices. At the height of its success Junket fielded a superbly equipped cadre of Hebraically fluent rabbi-and-*chazan* guides, who showed enough of every Castle hall to satisfy their socially mobile, mostly upgraded-Orthodox clientele. In some cases the Conservative tour leaders added enough hymn singing by a mixed chorus with organ accompaniment to make even Reform clients (suburbanites since before the war) feel at home.

During the 1970s, Junket's rabbinical guides began appropriating chazanic commentary and offering it as English reading instead of Hebrew chanting. This deprived younger visitors of their principal exposure to the Holy Tongue: texts sung from *Siddurim* during Castle visitations. In addition, the deviation from past procedure greatly upset Traditionalist patrons of long standing. To appease them (and to economize in the process), Seminary Rambles eliminated choir and organ from most tours, which only succeeded in alienating Liberal affiliates used to background music. In a misguided effort at further Liberalization, Junket's rabbinical guides continued to trim their cantorial colleagues' duties, eliminating the chanting-aloud of both Standing Devotions—*Shacharit* and *Musaf*—in the Royal and Guest Chambers in order to accommodate still more commentary in the vernacular. All of this was evidently motivated by a desire to imitate nineteenth-century guides on Reform's East–West Highlights package who had copied the solo techniques of Protestant ministers and read everything from a prepared script. Contemporary Conservative Time travel apparently forgot that many of those earlier expeditions had failed to accomplish their spiritual objective, and that part of Reform travel's increased popularity in the late twentieth century has been due to its rabbis and cantors sharing equal responsibility while on guide duty, each in their own unique way.

TO SHARE OR NOT TO SHARE

Equal parcelling-out of Highlights tour duties is by now so ingrained that often it takes an expert to tell whether a particular Reform guide was trained as a rabbi or as a cantor. In 1990 my wife and I took part in a sparsely attended Sabbath Morning pilgrimage sponsored by New Orleans' Touro Synagogue. Our lone companions were a dozen Religious-school students, members of the synagogue's Confirmation class, yet the robed officiant shepherded us through every Castle hall just as if the tour were oversubscribed. He did not miss a note, chanting all the expected commentary in a rich bass-baritone that sounded somewhat strained, as if it were scaling unaccustomed heights of rhetoric. A good description would be to imagine *The Flight of the Bumble Bee* burped on a tuba. Not until afterward, when we thanked him for his strenuous efforts in making the trip such a vivid experience, did we realize he was rabbinically ordained. It seemed the regular *chazan* guide, who possessed a tenor voice, had been called out of town because of family illness. The rabbi quickly stepped in and covered for his absent colleague, not even bothering to have the organist transpose into lower keys.

TALES FROM "JUNKETS" PAST

Despite Conservatism's disinterest in cultivating a similar *esprit de corps* among its professionals, it must be stated that Junket for Everyone still garners a respectable crowd most weeks. Truth to tell, a goodly portion of that crowd remains woefully ignorant of the role it is expected to play while on tour. An incident that I observed as a choir member some forty years ago in the Refectory of Baltimore's Old Chizuk Amuno Synagogue (now Beth Am) on Eutaw Place attained notoriety in this regard. The father of one Sous Chef was honored with opening the Ark. Never having performed the ritual before, he gave its tasseled Donor curtain such a violent tug that it came in contact with a row of exposed light bulbs inside. The curtain, called *parochet*, happened to be one of the Refectory's most treasured appointments, bearing the embroidered names of an agency founder and his wife. Shortly afterward, while Divine recipes from the Scroll were being read aloud, the *parochet* started to smolder. At first no one noticed. During the threefold Culinary Benediction, however, it suddenly ignited, filling the Refectory with dense smoke. At that instant our rabbi guide dropped his upraised arms and—Moses-like—

issued an Eleventh Commandment to his Castle elders: "Thou shalt call the nearest Fire Department."

After the blaze had been extinguished, one elegantly dressed matron wearing a crucifix turned to the Bar Mitzvah's mother seated next to her in the first row of invited guests and loudly gushed, "*How quaint, my dear, I didn't realize you people still burned incense!*"

Another Junket proved serendipitous for George Exoo, a nonpracticing Unitarian Universalist minister whose reviews of Castle-Mosque-and-Cathedral tours were aired regularly over Pittsburgh's NPR station WQED. One time, on special assignment to Milwaukee, he joined a Sabbath Morning exploratory contingent under the auspices of Conservative congregation Beth El-Ner Tamid. Later he described the experience.

> Not a minute of the two-hundred and forty bored me.
> . . . I thought to myself, as time and again
> the congregation broke into melodious
> spiritual song, "these folks sing like Methodists."

Reverend Exoo found nothing conservative about his fellow Junketers when it came to hospitality either; from opening prayers to punch and pastry afterward, they made him feel at home.

RECONSTRUCTIONISM'S BUDGET BARGAIN

For those favoring a do-it-yourself Budget format, Basic Adventure, modestly priced, makes a lot of sense. Reconstructionist Time travelers, who delight in being involved with the planning of their itinerary, frequently hold a briefing session with their guide at the agency office one hour prior to departure. The session does not so much determine the rooms to be visited as the manner in which they will be shown. For instance, when any other agency's contingent arrives at the Royal Chamber, a guide normally emphasizes the oversize dimensions of its Kingly three-poster, which memorializes Abraham, Isaac, and Jacob, the three Patriarchs who first devised rudimentary Standing Devotions (based on episodes in the Book of Genesis: 19, v. 27; 24, v. 63; 28, v. 11). This happened long before scheduled Castle circuits were available and it enabled individuals to offer simple private prayer at fixed times: morning, afternoon, and evening. Reconstructionists feel that the Royal Bed's provenance has been misrepresented and that the sacred dormer is actually a *Queen*-size four-poster, with each post referring to a Matriarch: Sarah,

Rebecca, Leah, and Rachel; wives of the three Patriarchs. (Jacob, the third Patriarch, had sheepishly accepted a second wife rather than argue with his father-in-law, a cattleman from Twin Rivers, Mesopotamia, which accounts for the extra spouse; Genesis 29.) All of this is thrashed out at the briefing session or, if that is not feasible, during the ADVENTURE itself.

THE FEMININE TOUCH

In the Refectory where Scriptural Recipes are tasted, Reconstructionists prefer being served the culinary creations of a female—rather than the usual male—chef. Some think this is because the founding of Reconstructionism's Rabbinical Guides' College in 1968 happened to coincide with the rise of militant feminism among Jewish women. Others, like Tikva Frymer-Kensky, former director of the College's Biblical Civilization and Homemaking department, extol as "the archetypal female occupation . . . the transformation of natural substances not immediately beneficial to humanity [into] products essential to human well-being." Just as women have historically been entrusted with transforming indigestable grains into life-giving bread, female rabbi guides are by nature ideally equipped to tenderly guide their charges through the process of converting Torah recipes into ethical everyday living.

CARRYING A FULL LOAD

Female participants in the no-frills Basic Adventure also do not mind lending a helping hand should their rabbinical tour leader falter in the Refectory. When that occurs, her sister travellers—would-be guides at heart—stand ready to offer catering hints that have been taste tested during previous Castle visits. So much helpful advice was tried out over the years that by the late 1980s every Reconstructionist Castle had to issue its own collection of proven recipes in loose-leaf folders. Often the contributed ideas had been photocopied from other agencies' published *Siddurim*. In 1994, Reconstructionist headquarters finally updated its own Sabbath and Festival *Siddur*, and guides thought they had in a single sourcebook as many tempting dishes as they would ever need. However, the new cookbook omitted mention of one dish that was a perennial favorite of veteran tourists: the Guest Chamber and its glowing *Kedushat Musaf* tapestry. This omission prompted the Mother of all Reconstructionist Castles, New York's Sociey for the Advancement of Judaism, to use a Conservative *Siddur* containing the Guest Chamber dialogue in tandem with its own agency's new *Siddur*. The two volumes—plus a weighty

Bible (called *Chumash*), brochures, and newsletters distributed weekly—add up to a significant handful for visitors.

TOT SHABBAT EVERY SHABBAT

To burden them even further, Basic Adventure welcomes so many young children aboard that many of its excursions seem to be geared for baby-sitters and their charges. Before booking space, prospective clients should be aware that dress code, touring procedure, and running commentary are decidedly casual on these excursions. While visiting a Castle located on the Reconstructionist Rabbinical College's campus, my group and I were asked to seat ourselves around the floor of the Vestibule and to greet those situated next to us on either side. The rabbi guide then regaled us with a medley of children's classics set to Sabbath Morning lyrics, accompanying herself on a guitar. Noticing that the youngsters present took no active part, I inquired why, and learned it was because each Religious School class visits the Castle only once a semester. The children never become familiar enough with the touring routine to join in. But their parents, who habitually chaperone every one of their offspring on separate outings for each grade during the year, have learned the songs by heart and sing them with unaffected enthusiasm. The impression is one of adults spinning fairy tales to a juvenile audience.

THE DEVAR TORAH: A PREPARATION OF DIVINE RECIPES

Appropriate background music accompanies visits to most halls in the Sabbath Morning Castle. An exception is the Refectory, where Scriptural preparations are demonstrated. It provides no atmospheric sound due to the intense concentration needed for absorbing the Master Chef Moses' 613 Divine Recipes. These are prepared by every rabbi guide in a uniquely personal way, calculated to leave a lasting impression on tourists. Since there are so many repeat visitors, the Scripture-preparation talk or Devar Torah (also called sermon) must be done differently every week. Some weeks the Devar Torah turns out so different that it surprises even the one delivering it. Not for nothing are rabbi guides called spiritual leaders. Ever resourceful, they must be on their toes particularly during this part of the tour, for even the best-made talks oft go astray when fate intervenes.

In the long-ago days before air conditioning became a commonplace, I shared the podium as *chazan* guide with a rabbi who was short-statured but long-winded. He always wrote out every step of his demonstration in longhand, an average presentation covering anywhere from fifteen to twenty pages. In warm weather, with the Castle windows open, occasional breezes would waft over the heads of our appreciative group. Once in a while the breezes would waft my rabbi's handwritten pages off our stand and onto the floor. He would bend down and, being vertically deprived, was able to pick them up and continue speaking without breaking stride. What he did break was his train of thought, since the order in which he retrieved his pages did not always match the sequence in which they had fallen.

The puzzling thing was that our audience never seemed to notice. So mellifluous was his speech and so full-blown his rhetoric that everything he said seemed perfectly sound to his nodding listeners, whether or not it was sufficiently cooked or needed further seasoning. He must have been aware of the effect his words had upon them. Once, when asked why he did not permit mixed seating on a professedly Modern Orthodox tour, he replied, "I have no objection to men and women sitting together [when Time traveling], but at the thought that during my talk they might be *sleeping* together, I draw the line."

TRAVEL MUSIC

At the sermon's conclusion, guests (presumably awake by then) file out of the Castle's Refectory to the next hall, whether it be for the Guest Chamber's *Amidat Musaf* on Orthodox and Conservative tours or directly to the Grand Ballroom's Hymns of Glory on Reconstructionist and Reform excursions. To expedite an orderly exit, Reform's Highlights will sometimes provide an anthem related to the sermon's theme. The anthem—like music heard in other Castle halls—has come to be identified with its own brand of mood music or mode.

MUSIC FOR ADMIRING THE CREDO AND STANDING DEVOTION

As an illustration, music sung or played during the Throne Room's Credo and Royal Chamber's Standing Devotion #1 fares very well in arousing patrons' interest. It features an exotic musical mode named *Ahavah Rabah* (Abounding Love), which is linked with the petitioning of Royal favor and therefore considered a *supplicatory* mode. The mode flourished in ancient Judea but was prohibited by Jerusalem's internationally celebrated Time travel agency, Temple Trails. This was because foreign visitors from Phoenicia, who first introduced it to Judea, played *Ahavah Rabah* music on a double-barreled flute during their orgiastic mountain retreats, run by the R-rated tour operator Baal Cults, Inc. When Temple Trails suffered a hostile takeover by the militant Titus Flavius's Roman Archway Walks, most Israelite clients left on an extended Middle Eastern journey. Centuries later their descendants heard the same mode while trekking through Asia Minor and connected it with tales told to them by tribal elders. Perennial wanderers by then, the former Judeans welcomed it as an old friend from the distant past. Wherever they migrated, they taught it to Sabbath Castle guides, particularly in the Balkans, Hungary, Rumania, the Ukraine, and Southern Poland. During the twentieth century, when lights went out in Sabbath Castles throughout Europe, the *Ahavah Rabah* mode featured in both Throne Room and Royal Chamber found a new home in North America.

MUSIC FOR TASTE-TESTING BIBLICAL PORTIONS

Dining Room music-to-scroll-by is sung by a special guide known as *ba'al kri'ah* (Scripture reader). While he or she nibbles at the seven weekly Torah portions, visitors silently make their own selections from the *Chumash* menu. The melody for reading Torah portions builds from tiny fragments of a few notes each, all the fragments connecting through a cantillation half-sung and half-spoken. At times cantillation resembles the staccato spiel of an auctioneer, cadencing in a melifluously drawn out inflection. This is especially true of passages that list Sacred Recipe ingredients and detailed instructions on how to incorporate them.

> Scoop out a handful of choice flour and frankincense . . .
> place it in the oven and bake it into unleavened cakes . . .
> break it into little bits and . . . pour oil on it (Leviticus 2:2–6).

At other times Torah reading seems closer to the florid effusiveness of a *chazan* guide. This happens when a *ba'al kri'ah* dramatically announces Daily Specials like the Ten Command-mints that were first served to ancestors of today's Castle tourists around 1350 B.C.E. (Before the Castle Era). The Torah-reading mode is more majestic than *Ahavah Rabah*, in order to praise what is being offered rather than dwell on personal wants of the listeners. A *laudatory* mode, it is named *Adonai Malach* (The Lord Reigns) and bespeaks optimism; in Robert Browning's words:

> God's in His heaven,
> All's right with the world!

It was not by chance that the Pepsi Cola Company selected a popular version of this bright, upbeat mode (*It's a Small World, after All*) to accompany its theme exhibit at the New York World's Fair of 1964–65. Musically trained visitors will recognize it as a major mode (Chapter 4 . . . "Minor and Major Modes"), while other listeners might simply enjoy its happy sound.

MUSIC FOR TRANSMITTING PROPHETIC DIRECTIONS

One area of the Dining Room—designated the Prophets' Corner—is reserved for Sous Chefs who have undertaken to practice diligently until they are able to replicate the speech/song of a *ba'al kri'ah*, but in a more sombre minor mode better suited to reading a *Haftarah* (prophetic lesson) about the perils of remaining permanently attached to lower links on the spiritual food chain. The ancient Hebrew prophets used to lead crowded open-air pilgrimages during which people were constantly getting lost spiritually. In order to focus their charges' attention on the right path in life, prophets developed a schoolmasterly way of warning them about the lurking danger of taking wrong turns. The prophetic way of singing out moral instructions has come down to us as *Magen Avot* (Shield of our Forebears), a *didactic* mode.

> Thus saith the Lord: stand ye in the roads and look;
> ask for the ancient paths and see which is best;
> walk upon it, and ye shall find rest for your souls [Jeremiah 6:16].

MUSIC FOR VIEWING THE *KEDUSHAT MUSAF* TAPESTRY

There is a moment during many Orthodox and Conservative Castle tours when the three principal prayer modes—*Adonai Malach, Ahavah Rabah,* and *Magen Avot*—are heard one after the other, in musical references often reworked from secular sources. This occurs in the Guest Chamber, where visitors stand facing the *Kedushat Musaf* tapestry and learn about its significance. The *chazan* guide's musical explanation might begin in laudatory (*Adonai Malach*) fashion, quoting some sublime air from French *Opéra Comique* for the words

> *hamakdishim shimcha bakodesh*
> seraphim sanctify God's name in holiness.

Next a supplicatory (*Ahavah Rabah*) mood sets in, perhaps through the melody of a sprightly Yiddish folksong at

> *kevodo malei olam*
> God's glory fills the universe.

The guide's final paraphrase, in a didactic (*Magen Avot*) vein, might be borrowed from a modern Israeli pastoral ballad, to teach that

> *mimekomo hu yifen berachamim*
> God will turn to His people in mercy.

No matter the specific tunes that are incorporated, they are invariably familiar enough for voyagers to join the guide's commentary in an impromptu chorus that frames the ancient *Kedushah* with its own tapestry of sound.

This is always the pinnacle of Orthodoxy's Grand Safari—and frequently also of Conservatism's Junket for Everyone—when visitors finally get into the Sabbath spirit and a supernal light seems to illuminate the Guest Chamber. Reform's Highlights of East and West and Reconstructionism's Basic Adventure omit this hall entirely, having presented essentially the same attraction as part of their Royal Chamber exhibit three halls earlier. Reform's version is a bit abridged, displaying a tableau of both *Kedushah* tapestries (*Shacharit* and *Musaf*) intertwined. Like its separate prototypes, the composite tapestry displays angels on high and God turning to His people, but in altered sequence and less detail. The guide's music is more classically conceived and tourists listen to it in polite silence, joining in only at the intervening responses (Isaiah 6:13, Ezekiel 3:12, Psalms 146:10). Despite the minimal involvement of its clientele, Reform's tableau can provide a moving experience when guided by an accomplished cantor backed by choral responses and organ accompaniment (assuming the tour in question is part of a Luxury package).

HYMN SINGING IN THE GRAND BALLROOM

If travel in general is broadening, excursions to the Sabbath Castle are doubly so. For after passing through its halls and learning who they are and from whence they came, Time travelers enter the glittering Grand Ballroom to determine at last where they are headed. The wonder is deepened even more so, contends Abraham Idelsohn, for those who had never before seen its interior. Had they merely visited the Castle on a weekday, without qualified guidance, and "suddenly stepped into its bewildering splendor without first having passed through the corridors, they would never be able to feel its glory fully."

Accordingly, the most beautiful wall hangings and genuinely uplifting lyrical strains are reserved for this seventh hall. Best of all, here tours may compensate for displays not seen or heard earlier because they were located in rooms that their particular itinerary happened to omit. An example: before entering the Grand Ballroom, any Sabbath tour has the option of making a brief side trip back to the Refectory, opening the Ark and joining in the thirteenth-century Glory Hymn (*Shir Hakavod*; Chapter 6 . . . "Going One-on-One with God") by Rabbi Judah of Regensburg.

> *An'im zemirot veshirim e'erog*
> *ki eilecha nafshi ta'arog*
> Sweet songs I conceive and chants do I weave,
> for unto Thee alone my soul shall cleave.

The Glory Hymn's most popular melody is set to the Time-travel rhythm
| DUM da da DUM - | DUM da da DUM - |
which derives from Throne Room protocol for the Jewish New Year. During their annual tour on the second morning of Rosh Hashanah, Orthodox High Holy Day Castle visitors sing an even older glory hymn,

> *Eder vahod etein betsivyon,*
> *shevach e'eroch beniv vehigayon*
> homage and adoration
> I offer in garlanded praise,

to the same rhythm and essentially the same tune as *An'im Zemirot*.

The ominous drumbeat rhythm of *Eder Vahod's* melody—essentially a March to the Scaffold—traces back to a grim episode during the seventeenth century. University of Freiburg historian Walter Salmen recounts its likely provenance. When Vienna's Jews were expelled by Emperor Leopold I in 1670 and not even the Pope's intervention could ameliorate their fate, witnesses reported hearing them drum themselves out of town to the rhythm | DUM da da DUM - |. Professor Salmen does not identify the specific selection that accompanied their departure, but a good guess would be Psalms 114, whose words fit both rhythm and circumstance.

Be -		TSET yis- ra -	EL mi- mits—	RA - -	YIM -	
"When		IS - rael de-	PART-ed from	E - gypt's	LAND -	
(-		DUM da da	DUM da da	DUM da da	DUM -	)

My hunch is that the actual *Betset Yisrael* melody with which Jews bade farewell to the city they had earlier dubbed "Bloody" (*Ir Hadamim*; after a 1421 expulsion) appears among fifty Psalm settings by the Italian Baroque composer Benedetto Marcello. For eleven of the settings Marcello borrowed well-known synagogue tunes, the one for Psalms 114 sharing its rhythmic tattoo with both *Eder Vahod* and *An'im Zemirot*. The same rhythm accompanies many other prayers sung during Castle tours by *Ashkenazim*, most notably at the Vernal and Autumnal Festival exhibits for *Tal* ("Dew," on the first day of Pesach; Chapter 4 . . . "What Science Confirms, Religion Knew All Along") and *Geshem* ("Rain," on Sh'mini Atseret, the eighth day of Sukkot).

SEASONAL BORROWINGS

When commemorating liturgical events that occur but once a year, it is common practice to borrow masterworks from neighboring Time Castles in order to display them in the Grand Ballroom. Whenever a borrowed treasure is on display, guides refer to it directly in their closing remarks. In the event their loan request has been denied, they will still find subtle ways of hinting at the sought-after object. One expedient is to apply its melody—normally associated with the upcoming holiday—to that Sabbath's regular concluding hymn. Groups invariably light up when singing *Adon Olam* or *Yigdal* to the majestic Seder tune *Adir Hu*, "Mighty God," during the eight days of Pesach or the celebratory post-*Megillah* tune *Shoshanat Ya'akov*, "Jacob Rejoiced," on the Sabbath preceding Purim. Sabbath Morning tours during December generally borrow *Maoz Tsur*, the centerpiece of seasonal Chanukah exhibits, which usually rests in a less-frequented Castle whose visiting hours are restricted to eight consecutive early-winter evenings. This majestic paean lends itself exceptionally well to any number of Castle commentaries sung on the Sabbath(s) of Chanukah, its lofty melody being particularly suitable for a closing anthem, as are its lyrics in Solomon Solis-Cohen's translation.

> Mighty, praised beyond compare,
> Rock of my salvation,
> Build again my House of Pray'r
> For Thy habitation!

> Haste my restoration: let a ransomed nation
> Joyful sing
> To its King
> Psalms of dedication.

THE AFTERGLOW OF GROUP TIME TRAVEL

Whatever the holy day that occasioned our individual pilgrimages, by journey's end we share the feeling of having arrived together at a common destination. Renewed in spirit by all we saw and heard in the preceding halls, we are uplifted even further by the exalted lyricism of that final glory hymn, so redolent with familial associations and vivid memories of childhood. We emerge from our Time Castle reassured that—despite the temptations of modern life—at least for a few meaningfully spent hours we have apparently not strayed beyond recall from the path laid out long ago by our Patriarchs and Matriarchs. Yet even the most regular worshipers among us—who never miss a weekly trip—cannot help but wonder if our route to the Sabbath Castle is the only one, or have other parties fanned out into parts of the forest so remote that they are no longer in sight?

The mystical journey taken by one of those divergent but still highly visible expeditions occupies Chapter 6: "Melodies in Space."

CHAPTER 6

Melodies in Space

How may we compare the earthly Palace of Song
with its Heavenly counterpart?
To a pair of stringed instruments vastly different in size.
The smaller one below is set in vibration,
and it resonates immediately in the larger one above.

> Jacob Joseph of Polnoye,
> *Toledot Ya'akov Yosef*, 1780

*S*everal decades back, when New York's Jewish Museum exhibited a comprehensive collection of ritual objects from around the world, one room stood out especially. It contained exquisitely illuminated, partially unrolled *Megillot*, the handles of whose wooden staves had been decorated in lovingly carved floral relief. Every scroll hung at eye level, supported almost imperceptibly by clear lucite brackets set on the gallery walls. One pair of brackets remained empty—with a small card affixed where the scroll should have been—explaining that the missing *Megillah* was out on temporary loan. I had just finished reading the card's miniscule print when two fashionably dressed women stopped to admire the brackets. "What won't they think of next?" said one of them without bothering to don the bejewelled reading glasses that stylishly adorned her neck. "Plastic rollers make a lot of sense when wood is so expensive!"

YOU CAN'T TELL A SCROLL BY ITS COVER

Like the two women admiring empty holders, a large segment of religiously non-affiliated North American Jews has traded its books for bookends. Strangers to synagogues are often so taken with its ceremonial props that they mistake trappings for content and end up venerating objects. Those who only occasionally attend Sabbath Morning worship might deem the varicolored prayer shawl placed upon a Bar or Bat Mitzvah celebrant's slender young shoulders, or the richly mantled and regally crowned Scroll of Law, as *objets d'art*. Yet a steadfastly observant minority values both *tallit* and Sefer Torah even more so, not so much for their intrinsic worth as for the higher use to which they are put in daily prayer and study. That still leaves too many Jewish families who regard the fringed garment and handwritten parchment as museum pieces to be gingerly handed from grandparents to parents to children when celebrating life-cycle milestones during their infrequent synagogue visitations.

WHAT HITLER COULDN'T DESTROY

I would like to contrast that sort of passing nod to tradition with an older form of Jewish piety: celebrating the sacred *moment* and not the things encountered during that moment. It is practiced by a group of fiercely competitive chasidic sects named after towns in Hungary, Poland, Russia, Rumania, and Czechoslovakia, where they were founded. The sects—Satmar, Bobover, Lubavitcher, Belzer, Gerer, Vizhnitzer, Munkaczer, Bratslaver, Modzhitzer, Klausenberger, Skverer, and Stoliner (in descending order of size)—were all but obliterated during the Holocaust. Worldwide, *chasidim* now total less than 800,000, where before the Nazi slaughter over three million had thrived in Eastern Europe alone. The residue of those millions defies definition as a movement, since until recently *chasidim* would only frequent synagogues loyal to their sect's own spiritual Master. The latter, called rebbe ("rabbi" or "teacher," in Yiddish), was originally referred to as a *tzaddik*, meaning one who has stood the test of righteousness and is, therefore, a proven leader. His dutiful followers have always been known as *chasidim*, or devout ones (singular: *chasid*).

Chasidim believe in going the extra mile where observance is concerned; ideally, a chasid is one who says, "What is mine is yours and what is yours is yours" (Mishnah, *Avot* 5:13). *Chasidim* are easy to spot, for they insist on retaining the garb their antecedents wore hundreds of years ago: the bewigged women in ultramodest long-sleeved frocks; the bearded menfolk all in black and affecting earlocks (Yiddish: *payes*). Ever since chasidic survivors of the Holocaust arrived here in significant numbers shortly after the Second World War, their influence upon nominally mitnagdic (anti-chasidic) Orthodoxy has been pervasive. At first *chasidim* served mainly as a reminder of what had been lost—the life piously lived without expectation of earthly reward. In time their example would provide the impetus if not for a revival of that life style, then at least the opportunity to observe it at close hand and understand what motivates it.

The closer contact has influenced both parties, comments Jewish Establishment gadfly J. J. Goldberg in an article on the amazing proliferation of Lubavitcher *shluchim* (outreach workers) these days. Goldberg notes that of between 35,000 to 45,000 Lubavitchers worldwide, perhaps a third together with their families "now live outside the cloistered framework of the traditional chasidic community, interacting daily with non-Orthodox Jews . . . as rabbis in congregations whose members mostly drive to services on Saturday." By maintaining their own strict code of personal observance while serving nonobservant congregations with cheerfulness and irresistable goodwill, the *shluchim* are slowly but surely "taking the place once occupied by Modern Orthodox rabbis." This development sends the most hopeful signal for future reconciliation not merely of Orthodoxy with the other national movements but ultimately within the infinitely graded spectrum of Rightwing Orthodoxy itself.

At present the only thing one can state with certainty is that mainstream Orthodoxy has lately chosen to become more than a little chasidified. The currently surging Orthodox birthrate still lags behind chasidism's incredible doubling of population every fifteen years, as projected by a chronicler of the movement, Robert Eisenberg. But it confirms the urgency with which Orthodox families in general have determined to emulate their chasidic neighbors in denying Hitler what he most sought: the posthumous victory of eliminating all future Jewish generations. Professor Haym Soloveitchik of Yeshiva University imparts an additional spin to the merging of chasidic and mitnagdic lifestyles: joint retrenchment against the pervasive secularism of our society. In this match made by necessity, both parties must concede a bit on externals: "*Chasidim* have adopted the mode of talmudic study and . . . in turn, the *mitnagdim* have adopted some dress of the *chasidim*." Well put, for nowadays it is hard to distinguish by prayerbook or apparel alone whether those participating in a Traditional *Minyan* or poring over a talmudic tractate owe allegiance to one camp or the other.

THE WAY OF THE MYSTIC

The most distant forerunner of today's *chasidim* was Rabbi Akiva ben Yosef, lone survivor among a group of second-century talmudic sages who "entered the orchard" of speculation concerning God's nature (JT, *Chagigah* 14b). The others "gazed and died . . . suffered madness . . . abandoned the faith," while Akiva emerged unscathed and was able to assimilate the mystical revelations. In his mind's eye he rode a chariot (*merkavah*), envisioned 700 years earlier down to its last detail by the Prophet Ezekiel, directly to God's Glory Throne. (The Sephardic liturgy for Yom Kippur Eve still includes a *selichah* calling for *elohei hamerkavah* "God of the Chariot," to answer us.) Sometime during the thirteenth century, Spanish kabbalist Moses ben Shemtov de Leon formalized *merkavah* mysticism into a seminal work: the *Zohar*, or Book of Splendor. It revolves around Rabbi Akiva's disciple, Simeon bar Yochai, who wanders in quest of *Ein Sof* (The Endless One). Along the way Simeon and his companions stop at ten Heavenly Spheres (*sefirot*) named after progressively ascendant attributes of *Ein Sof*. The *sefirot* commence with

10—*Shechinah* (Presence).

9—*Yesod* (Foundation), and culminate with

8—*Hod* (Splendor),

7—*Netsach* (Eternity),

6—*Tiferet* (Beauty),

5—*Gevurah* (Power),

4—*Chesed* (Love),

3—*Binah* (Understanding),

2—*Chochmah* (Wisdom),

>1—*Ayin* (Nothingness), ascend through

Simeon's upward-leading path was lit by a dark flame: the light that was present at the Creation. Growing in radiance, it gradually assumed the form of a Heavenly Palace, from which *Ein Sof*'s Presence had previously departed. The sixteenth-century kabbalistic seeker into the mysteries of Creation, Isaac Luria of Safed, offered a rationale for this departure. *Ein Sof* had at first vacated a region within Himself, creating an empty space, the chaotic void of Genesis, called *tohu vavohu*. *Ein Sof* filled the void with vessels to contain the outwardly radiating Divine light. When the light proved too penetrating for its containing vessels, they shattered, scattering sparks through the universe.

Daniel C. Matt, a twentieth-century reconciler of Jewish mysticism with modern cosmology, posits a scientific rationale for the Lurianic light. The energy-generating Big Bang that gave birth to the universe some fifteen billion years ago was followed by "300,000 years of cooling [during which] matter and radiation had decoupled, and the universe turned transparent. This was the moment of 'let there be light'!" According to Matt, the broken vessels of Kabbalah, unable to contain God's Divine light, parallel the broken symmetry of an expanding and cooling universe whose fundamental forces have fractured to permit the creation of matter and energy. If the sparks of scattered light could be reunited, if the universe's temperature could again be raised sufficiently, we might *restore* the perfect world that existed "In the Beginning/Before the Big Bang."

Chasidim, the keepers of kabbalistic flame in our day, call that conscious act of restoration: *tikkun*. They believe they are following a preordained cosmic path, stopping only to gather up scattered sparks of the Divine light along their route. They view the process as one of restoration for themselves as well; like the Divine sparks, they have been widely scattered. In eighteenth-century Central Poland the Great Maggid (preacher), Dov Baer of Mezhirech, taught that during prayer Jews ought not to think of their own personal needs. Rather should they plead that the *Shechinah*—understood by students of Kabbalah as the feminine component of Divinity—might be redeemed from exile. This will come about only if they do the will of their Father in Heaven, living righteously and performing charitable acts, which will enable them to retrieve the scattered sparks. As a result of their collective effort over time and through space, the *Shechinah* will return permanently to Her Heavenly Palace. That would set the stage for Israel to eventuality merit its own final Redemption, which can come only from God.

A foreshadowing of that epiphany occurs every Friday evening at sunset when *chasidim* recite the mystical passage *Kegavna* (*Zohar III*: 135a–b) just prior to beginning the *Maariv* service proper.

> As for the *Shechinah*, the six weekdays are but preparation
> for Her . . . With Sabbath's arrival, the Glory Throne is prepared
> for the Heavenly King, and the *Shechinah* is in perfect union
> with God . . . Illumined by the supernal light, the principalities of
> severity and lords of judgement flee from Her, And no other
> power reigns beside Her in all the worlds . . . The holy people are
> invested with new souls . . . for now is the time to commence prayer.
> That is precisely when the moment of truth arrives for *chasidim*.

WORDLESS SONG

Chasidic prayer is predicated on the belief that certain halls in the Heavenly Palace open only to song. Uri of Strelisk, an eighteenth-century *tzaddik* known for his ecstatic devotion, left a timeless piece of advice on how the average person might circumvent this difficulty. "Among the Heavenly Palace's halls," he said, "the one that opens only to music is the smallest." But anyone who sincerely wishes to approach the *Ribono Shel Olam* need only enter that one room and it is enough. Ever since, chasidic doctrine has conceded to music an *a priori* role in worship, to the point of rendering words superfluous. Reknowned teacher Shneur Zalman of Liady instructed his disciples that the soul speaks through melody, whereas words only serve to interrupt its emotional outpouring. *Chasidim* therefore consider the swiftest and surest means of approaching God to be songs without words, that is, *nigunim* (singular: *nigun*).

Israeli philosopher Rivka Schatz is of the opinion that our words in fact have no influence upon *Ein Sof*; it is rather His influence upon us that matters. Like the second-century *merkavah* mystics and sixteenth-century kabbalists before them, today's *chasidim* are aware of this human limitation, striving always to negate their ego in order to achieve closeness with the Endless One. They prepare the way for that eventuality by sending forth *nigunim* into space as conduits leading upward through the four *olamim* (worlds) that God established for humankind at the time of Creation.

> 4—Spirit (*Atsilut*, world of Emanation)
> 3—Mind (*Beri'ah*, world of Creation)
> 2—Heart (*Yetsirah*, world of Formation)
> >1— Body (*Asiyah*, world of Action)

Starting as random tunes in the corporeal world (*Asiyah*), *nigunim* assume a devotional contour (*Yetsirah*) more suited to serving God, through the creative thought (*Beri'ah*) of individuals who thereby experience an indescribable uplift of spirit (*Atsilut*).

By originating in the world of Action and moving upward to that of Emanation, *nigunim* in effect reverse a creative process by which the fruits of human endeavor usually emanate.

> >1—Impulse (spirit)
> 2—Thought (mind)
> 3—Shape (heart)
> 4—Form (body)

That reversal of direction is enormously significant, because it presupposes familiarity with a creative process common to all art (Chapter 1 . . . "The Successive Stages of Creativity"). "To know the stages of the creative process," wrote Gershon Scholem, the dedicated scholar who singlehandedly legitimized the academic pursuit of Jewish mysticism, "is also to know the stages of one's own return to the root of all existence." Quest of that spiritual knowledge is what drives *chasidim* Heavenward like a moth to flame.

REDEEMED MELODIES

Chasidim will go to any lengths in their set task of attaining oneness with God. They set no limits on the choice of prayer melodies, because whatever seems foreign to our ears may in reality be only temporarily estranged from an earlier Hebraic origin. That includes tunes borrowed from Church usage, which are considered fair game for retrieval. Musicology does concede the possibility—however remote—that such tunes might retain a spark of the melodic fires ignited thousands of years ago in the Second Jerusalem Temple. *Chasidim* believe that still-glowing embers from those soul-searing melodies have never been extinguished. "It is the task of the *tzaddik* to return the wandering sparks of the sweet tunes to their original source of holiness," writes historian Abraham Kahana. How so? When the holy strains were carried into exile, early Christians—out of a desire to authenticate their offshoot religion—incorporated them into the Church's evolving liturgy. That is how echoes of pre-Christian Judean song may have come to reverberate 1,000 years later in European cathedrals as solemn Gregorian chants. Conceivably, surviving snippets of those ancient Judeo/Christian chants resurfaced in the eighteenth-century piping of shepherds or the gamboling of peasants or the blaring of military bands, all of which reflect the influence of religious hymnody. In the poverty-ridden lands of Eastern Europe, discerning *chasidim* then singled out the errant snatches of tune from among myriad others encountered on their wanderings (Chapter I . . . "When Rite Was Considered Wrong in the Past").

Like Israelites exiled in their far-flung diaspora, the melodic sparks found themselves a long way from home, awaiting redemption. They were essentially twice-borrowed: once by the early Church fathers from Judaism's Temple psalmody (Chapter 4 . . . "How *Daven'n* Works in Weekday Services"), and back again by the early *chasidim* from Christianity's medieval plainchant-become-modern-folksong (Chapter 5 . . . "The *Chazan* as Travel Guide"). By this reasoning the early *chasidim* were acting as redeemers of their distant kinsmen's property that had been relinquished under duress, restoring it to the descendants of its rightful owners under the Law of Redemption in Leviticus 25. The melodic sparks' homeward journey to their Heavenly Palace of Song—or its earthly counterpart, the synagogue—after so many centuries of dispersal, might seem endless. Nevertheless, as if laid out by the Celestial Stationmaster Himself, the tracks that those sparks have been following in modern times just happen to lie along the Main Line of chasidism's musical rail system.

THE WAY OF THE CHASID

The line's rolling stock consists of *nigunim*, mostly without words, but sometimes set to verses from Scripture or *Siddur*. The *nigunim* are of two polar types: *d'veikut* ("clinging"), and *rikud* ("dance"). Meditative *d'veikut nigunim* like *Avinu Malkeinu* (with which most readers are presumably familiar; Chapter 1 . . . "The Century Wanes") originated in Lithuania and White Russia, where worship followed the lead of a rigorously intellectual rabbinate that frowned upon emotional display. Lively *rikud nigunim* of the *Havah Nagilah* (Let Us Rejoice) variety proliferated elsewhere: in Rumania, Hungary, and Southern Russia, where chasidic rebbes promulgated a style more openly expressive of the biblical precept to rejoice on one's holy days (Deuteronomy 16:14). Yet *Avinu Malkeinu* and *Havah Nagilah* were both forged from the same exotic-sounding Middle Eastern prayer mode, *Ahavah Rabah* (Chapter 5 . . . "Music for Admiring the Credo and Standing Devotion"). The difference in their individual moods arises from the way each *nigun* is performed: *Avinu Malkeinu* tenderly, with devotion; *Havah Nagilah* wildly, with abandon. A *d'veikut nigun* is typically soulful, full of yearning. As it climbs through the higher *olamim* in slow and sustained tempo, every angel, seraph, and cherub maintains respectful silence. A *rikud nigun*, in contrast, conveys the antithesis of silence as it rises. Filled with joy, it gathers both volume and momentum until it cannot be ignored by the Endless One and His Heavenly host of gatekeepers.

With or without words, both *nigun* types traverse psychological—as opposed to chronological and geographical—time and space. They telescope millennia and hemispheres for those who choose to go their route, negating the concepts of early/late as well as near/far. Worshiping via *nigunim* instead of English readings might strike modern Jews uninitiated in the ways of chasidism as primitive and not up to the effusive verbosity normally associated with contemporary religious practice. But chasidism and its *nigunim* are operating in an earlier frame of reference, one much closer to our world's Creation almost 6000 years ago, according to the reckoning of Judaism's perpetual timetable. Over two millennia after scattering a part of the Divine light through space, *Ein Sof* had His people resettle in a plentifully stocked Egypt to avoid the famine that had overtaken them in Canaan. Hundreds of years later He led them out of bondage in that North African land and revealed Himself to them on a remote peninsula leading to Asia Minor. *Chasidim* get to relive that redemptive experience through the magic of *nigunim*, both tender and wild.

A gale-force wind from the East causes mighty waters to part, providing a dry and passable track bed. Passengers on this psychological train seem to follow a Divinely laid out interaquatic route along the Nile Delta as lightning illuminates their path toward a remote, cloud-shrouded mountain peak. There in the wilderness they receive—and formally accept—a commanding list of ten do's and don'ts that will reshape human thought and alter the course of history. According to a statement reiterated in Deuteronomy (5:3; 29:13), the list of universal commands by which Israel agreed to abide remains as valid for our generation as it was for those who departed Egypt, crossed the Sea of Reeds, and stood at Sinai. That we are living over thirty-three centuries after the Israelites' original journey makes no difference to *chasidim*; with Ecclesiastes, they believe "that which has been is that which shall be" (1:9).

MULTIDIMENSIONAL WORSHIP

Although the chronological length of chasidic worship on Shabbat morning is identical to that of any Orthodox service (about three hours), chasidism fills the time frame somewhat differently. It provides *safety valves* throughout the service, which allow both *nigunim* and worshipers room to move. *Chasidim* are known to regularly burst forth in song and dance at various portions of the liturgy, reinforcing their already intense devotion through seemingly extemporaneous—though precisely controlled—gestures. The vocal and bodily motions afford them more than one perspective on prayer, something that affiliates of other denominations never really experience. Educator Steven Lorch writes of "breathing-time" within Orthodox *daven'n*, "filled with improvisational material . . . so that the ambiguities . . . of the music may be taken in before one is pushed into new sections and their multiple meanings." He compares the effect that such revelatory moments have on worshipers' perception of reality to the ancient Greeks' first use of single-point perspective in art, ca. 500 B.C.E. If Lorch's analogy is valid, we might gauge the geometrically increased perspectives that *chasidim* gain—through exuberant dance as well as song—to be on a par with the multiple architectural and sculptural, harmonies achieved by the Acropolis of Athens in the Age of Pericles.

While contemporary synagogues frown upon improvisation of any kind during services, in the past a certain amount of license had been freely granted those trying to forge a mystical link between the earthly Palace of Song and its Heavenly counterpart. During the mishnaic period (roughly 200 B.C.E.–200 C.E.), individual discovery of alternate prayer wording was actually judged noteworthy. One sage, Rabbi Simeon, urged his disciples never to settle on any one version exclusively: Make not thy prayer a fixed form (*Pirke Avot* 2:18). Simeon's reasoning: not all roads lead automatically to *Ein Sof*; individuals must try every avenue, never despairing of reaching their goal. Those who truly seek Him believe that

God Himself depends upon such diligent pathfinding. That is because the End-less One cannot return to the place from which He withdrew at the time of Cre-ation until enough Israelites from every remote area of Jewish settlement have passed through the earthly Palace of Song's seven liturgical halls—on the same seventh day—and marveled at the treasures they contain and sincerely expressed their desire to serve none but the One Who Created Such Wonders.

Until then, whenever a new prayer path is discovered, *chasidim* are free to traverse it in a variety of ways. Psalms 29:2 advises: worship God through the *adorn-ment* of holiness (*hishtachavu ladonai behadrat kodesh*; later transmuted into the rabbinic principle of *hidur mitzvah*: always exceeding the required measure in fulfilling a commandment; BT, *Bava Kamma* 9a–b). This would suggest that it is permissable—even desirable—to upgrade one's synagogue-going experience; if not to Luxury Class, then at least to Deluxe. From all accounts, Judeans living during the first century did follow that precept until the Second Temple's gilded doors closed for the last time and they were forced to relocate on short notice throughout the an-cient Near East. Rabbi Morton Green describes the plight of those suddenly dis-placed persons once their formerly decorous approach to God was no longer fea-sible. "In exile their aesthetic sense became atrophied . . . they were forced to forsake the beautiful for the necessary, in order to survive." Yet the chasidic descendants of those exiled Judeans have never stopped advocating the *adornment* of holiness. It was given to other Classical cultures to discover the holiness of *beauty*, while post-exilic Israel had no choice but to concentrate on revealing the beauty of *holiness* through whatever means were available to it.

Word of law rather than sense of intuition would thenceforth govern the banished Israelites' existence. They lived within the bounds of minute rules de-signed to ensure their endurance as a cohesive folk by curtailing individuality. Only after dutifully walking circuitous paths (*ma'aglei tsedek*) laid out by Almighty God could an Israelite worshiper aspire to an easing of those restrictions and permit ripples of inspiration to overrun the brim of his or her assigned vessel. I once heard the late Rabbi Jacob Agus lead a learning session on the 23rd Psalm at a house of mourning, during which he noted that "the metaphor of 'overflow'—*kosi revayah*—in this poem of Figurative Transformation signifies one's homecoming, an indica-tion that the individual has merited a place-setting—or *cup*—at God's table." Rabbi Agus's transcendent explication recalled an old Digger proverb, quoted by Ruth Benedict in her landmark anthropological study of Native Americans:

> In the beginning, God gave to every people a cup of clay;
> and from this cup they drank their life.

Like Israelites, the American Indians suddenly find themselves in cultural exile; their cup—like their culture—is now broken. Post-Holocaust *chasidim* are living in the shadow of a similar debacle and have been diligently trying to retrieve the spilled contents of their broken vessels as they pursue a mystical road back to God.

POST-WORSHIP: WHEN *NIGUNIM* HOLD SWAY

In upholding their end of the Covenant that God made with our forebears, *chasidim* scrupulously fulfill one particular clause scripted by the Great Assembly (*kenesset hagedolah*) first convened in Jerusalem over 2,300 years ago. The Assembly's Resolution on Statutory Prayer—*matbei'a shetav'u chachamim bivrakhot* (Chapter 4 . . . "Crossing a Boundary without Realizing It")—remains stamped onto the coin of Jewish worship in perpetuity, setting forth words to be uttered at every service. The prayer words serve a double purpose; they are noble enough to satisfy the One at Whom they are directed, yet they are familiar enough to discourage any but the most daringly innovative pioneers from essaying imaginative end runs on their own. *Chasidim* tread a singularly fine line between reciting the prescribed words and going beyond them to attain levels of ecstacy, by periodically interpolating *nigunim*; only after the words have been uttered can *nigunim* hold sway. Nowadays, such ecstatic moments are better suited to the less rigidly structured aftermath of formal services: during the immediate post-worship refreshment (*Kiddush*); at the Third Sabbath Meal toward evening (*Se'udah Sh'lishit*); and at a final nighttime reunion meant to prolong the day's glow of otherworldliness by regally ushering out Queen Sabbath (*Melaveh Malkah*).

All three festive gatherings foster spur-of-the moment *nigun* singing. The reassembled party sits around a table (Yiddish: *tisch*), running through one tune after another as the mood strikes. A *nigun* starts slowly and repeats over and over, climbing a half-step at each succeeding chorus until the pitch grows too high for comfort. Suddenly it drops an octave so that the process can begin all over again. Finally, after one of those many crescendos, the *nigun* diminishes and gives way to its successor. Without a professional cantor to steer them safely through the numberless repetitions, participants' voices often sound raucous. Their performance, which Israeli musicologist Uri Sharvit characterizes as *geschrigen*, "shouted," (rather than sung), makes up in noise what it lacks in finesse. One loose parallel might be early American "shape note" singing, a system of sight-reading by means of four successive note symbols, each differently shaped. The symbols formed a movable musical template that could theoretically cover the entire melodic range of a hymn. To hide wrong notes, the standard level of volume was triple *forte*, unless someone was able to sing louder.

GOING ONE-ON-ONE WITH GOD

A similar goodnatured abandon permeates the shouting and table-pounding that is considered normal when *chasidim* perform joyful *rikud nigunim*, especially those reserved for the *tisch* at celebratory occasions. The particular Sabbath or Holiday's course of prayer having been run, individuals now have a chance to play the role of song leader for family and friends. They do so completely devoid of self-consciousness, for they recall the reassuring words inscribed by Judah of Regensburg in his compilation for the pious, *Seifer chasidim* (thirteenth century; 2: 8–9).

> You should never say, "my voice is not agreeable" . . . there is nothing
> that induces a person to love the Creator and to enjoy His love in
> return more than the [average] voice raised in an extended tune . . .
> Only the intention and devotion of the singer count.

Judah's idea was revolutionary in its day: consider the Holy One, Blessed Be He, a personal friend! He immortalized his daring attitude in *Shir Hakavod* (Chapter 5 . . . "Hymn Singing in the Grand Ballroom"), a glory hymn that offhandedly tells God,

> Nod Your head should my prayer prove acceptable
> *uvevirchati tena'ana li rosh.*

Shir Hakavod is often led by a young child, whose innocence proclaims the hymn's spiritual purity. Its candor set a standard for every succeeding *tzaddik* and rebbe, down to the twentieth-century guitar-strumming rabbi/troubador Shlomo Carlebach, who created hundreds of songs that were equally ingenuous. In the 1950s Carlebach perfected his motivational techniques by entertaining at a type of Orthodox singalong called *kumzits* (from the Yiddish for "come, sit") wherever New York teenagers were likely to gather: in synagogues; community centers; and Catskill Mountain resorts. A decade later he moved to the West Coast and began reaching out to Jewish dropouts and drug addicts in San Francisco's Haight-Ashbury district. At a House of Love and Prayer, which he founded, he taught irresistable tunes like *The Whole World Is Waiting to Sing the Song of Shabbos*, and once the song was learned he would slip in compelling challenges like "the whole world is waiting for Jews to be Jews." Little by little he brought hundreds of young runaways back into the fold.

BRIDGING THE GAP

Like Judah of Regensburg before him, Shlomo of Carlebach conceived hymns and wove chants intended to bridge the gap between earthly and Heavenly Palaces of Song. The rationale was that only once did *Ein Sof* suspend His own decree (the heavens are unto God while the earth is given to humankind; Psalms 115:16) and meet mortals halfway, via the act of Revelation. Since then it has been humankind's neverending task to try and scale God's domain in turn, through song. Every day, in the words of an anonymously authored Atonement prayer (*Ya'aleh*),

> our entreaty has risen at dusk,
> and our cries have ascended at dawn.

Yet, taught Rabbi Carlebach, at nightfall we are still earthbound. He couched the moral of this lesson in the language of a chasidic parable.

> Reb Elimelech of Lizensk dreamed of rebuilding the Heavenly bridge over which God had traveled to Sinai, and in his dream he beheld millions of people working on it. He asked the angels: "This is a very narrow bridge, why can't a few people build it?" He was told: Everyone is asked for just one brick.

The bridge is not finished because too many individuals have yet to supply a brick. A 1990 National Population Survey found that only 41 percent of America's 5.5 million Core Jewish Population belonged to synagogues, and of those, a mere 11 percent worshiped every week. In 1993 and 1997, further polling indicated that the number of synagogue affiliates may possibly have shrunk to 25 percent. Even if we accept the earlier number and add a similar proportion from Canada's 360,000 Jews, we find a bit over a quarter-million regularly attending synagogues in North America. *Four-and-a-half percent* of those who identify themselves as Jews by Religion hardly provide enough bricks to extend a span heavenward. Until many more people climb aboard every Sabbath (by contrast, the number of attendees on High Holy Days is thirteen times greater: 1.33 million), our narrow bridge to God will remain incomplete.

THE PULL OF MYSTICISM

Poet Rodger Kamenetz believes that the mystical stream of Judaism, which until very recently had been relegated to the status of a minority report by affiliates of the national movements, can speed completion of that bridge. He quotes the late and widely revered Lubavitcher Rebbe, Menachem Mendel Schneerson, on what Jewish rationalists have been missing.

> There are great treasures in the soul. There's faith, there's love,
> there's awe, there's wisdom. All these treasures you can dig.
> But if you don't know where to dig, you dig up mud—Freud—
> or you dig up stones—Adler. But if you want to get to the gold,
> which is the awe before God, and the silver, which is love,
> and the diamonds, which are the faith, then you have to find
> the geologist of the soul who tells you where to dig.

What's needed are more caring experts on mining these internal gems, and if rabbis and cantors across the board won't—or can't—fill the void, young Jews will keep on gravitating toward empathetic figures like the Rebbe or his disciples who, by opening wide the door of prayer, allow valid reasons for remaining Jewish to enter their souls.

Rabbi David Aaron, dean of the Israelight Institute in Jerusalem, is one of those disciples. "If you are the Creator," he asks, "why put Adam and Eve in the Garden of Eden, knowing that they will sin?" His answer: "Because unless you've been in Paradise you will never recognize what it is that you're looking for." He likens Jewish souls to the broken vessels of Lurianic Kabbalah, looking to be repaired. We hope for re-connection with the light of Divine goodness, which we've already experienced—in the metaphysical sense—if only for a millisecond. The Divine "goodness" is nothing less than God's Presence, for which all of us hunger and without which we are empty vessels.

ITS DETRACTORS, TOO, FALL UNDER MYSTICISM'S SPELL

The good news is that thousands of Jews who do not normally think of themselves as chasidic have become enamored with at least one element of the mystical discipline: *nigunim*. Through them, synagogue-goers in every movement are now being exposed to the deep and lasting influence of chasidism without even realizing it. Cantors are enlivening Torah processionals with *rikud nigunim*, while rabbis are larding their sermons with classic tales about *tzaddikim* far-enough removed in time to have acquired a patina of saintliness.

How ironic that the spiritual heirs of yesterday's truculent mitnagdic authorities should today dip thirstily into Judaism's ever-running mystical stream.

Any worship approach that pricks the hide of conventional practice is bound to draw blood, and chasidism proved no exception. Four times during the eighteenth century, Rabbi Elijah ben Solomon of Vilna, the acknowledged religous leader (*Gaon*) of intellectually minded Lithuanian Jewry, excommunicated all *chasidim*. Mystical writings were burned and the religious teachings they contained were ridiculed, just as they had been under the last Babylonian *Ge'onim* (plural of *Gaon*) during the tenth and eleventh centuries. The mutual animosity had in fact already been repaid in kind by chasidism's Book of Splendor. Through a sardonic play on words, the *Zohar* (on Exodus 1:14) reinterpreted biblical embitterment of Israel's life by the Egyptians to forecast persecution of *chasidim* by the established rabbinate of its own day.

Harsh slavery (*ba'avodah kashah*) hints at *da kushya*, "scholarly obfuscation."
With mortar (*bechomer*) means *bekal vachomer*, "by tortuous reasoning."
With bricks (*bilveinim*) implies *belibun hilcheta*, "through arcane hair-splitting."

Paradoxically, even the sainted Rabbi Akiva had entertained antirabbinic views in his youth. When, after a lifetime of diligent study he emerged as the leading talmudic genius of his generation, Akiva confessed that while still an illiterate shepherd, he had said: "I would that I had a scholar before me, for I would maul him like an ass." His disciples protested: "Rabbi, say 'like a dog'!" Akiva answered them: "At the time I preferred the former, which bites and breaks the bones, while the latter only bites but does not break the bones [BT, *Pesachim* 49b]." This freely offered admission survived rabbinic censorship only because it underscored the point made even more emphatically in a preceding discussion: scholars are praiseworthy, while the unlearned are contemptible. So, too, do many of today's Liberal rabbis make use of chasidic teachings when it suits them, while continuing to fulminate against *chasidim* collectively at every opportunity.

In point of fact, notes sociologist Charles Liebman, "*Chasidim* retain little that makes them doctrinally unique," and their mode of worship no longer shocks people as it once did. When the first modern chasidic teacher Israel Baal Shem Tov (Master of the Good Name) sent his disciples off on solo meditations in every direction 250 years ago, one could observe them climbing lonely mountain paths, skygazing, or wandering along forest trails listening to the song of birds. But no matter how intently they meditated, their own limited imaginations could carry them only so far. When Rabbi Israel died in 1760, the descendants of his disciples no longer knew which path to climb or which trail to wander, and were forced to gather in groups once again. By then they had forgotten the accepted rules of praying with a community. When left alone, they continued to sing without words, and when forced to comply with established synagogue protocol, they did so only grudgingly. To critics of their deportment it did not matter that *chasidim* acted no differently in their own informal prayer room (*shtibl*), where no eyebrows were raised at individuals walking about or rocking back and forth in corners, sometimes mumbling or whispering, othertimes groaning or sighing.

A few perceptive observers looked beyond the off-putting facade of chasidic nonconformity and discovered an almost childlike innocence—coupled with an earnest love of God and fellow beings—at its core. In September of 1901 a young Reform rabbi, Judah Leon Magnes, left his San Francisco home to study in Berlin. While there he often *davened* in a *shtibl*, and in a letter to his parents he lovingly described the religious fervor of its worshipers.

> Prayers are made simply to allow them to express in words—in voice—that feeling called religious which is within them . . . [They] delight in singing out of tune and making [their] voice last longest . . . I have seen Orthodox services before, but never one in which I took so much interest and felt so much pride.

Rabbi Magnes, who would later serve as founding chancellor of the Hebrew University in Jerusalem, never felt more at home than when in the company of *chasidim*.

SOME STILL FEEL THREATENED BY *CHASIDIM*

Today not all North American Jews relate as positively to *chasidim*; many resent the intrusion of these intransigent pietists into their comfortably materialistic world. Pundits have attempted to rationalize the animosity of otherwise tolerant individuals toward this particular segment of their co-religionists. "We come from a history of persecution," reasons humorist Jackie Mason, "and are always struggling to be accepted by proving that we're not Jewish." Part of that effort to belong is dressing like everybody else—which *chasidim* certainly do not—and that is one reason why more assimilated types resent them.

What Mason and other well-meaning apologists may not realize is that *chasidim*—along with the rest of Polish Jewry—*were* attempting to look like everybody else back in the sixteenth century when they first started wearing long gabardine caftans and hats set off by wide fur brims. Alfred Rubens, a former chairman of the London Jewish Museum, notes that caftans and fur-trimmed hats were the two most identifiable features of Polish and Russian national dress ever since Medieval times. However, when Poland's Jews tried to follow suit, government authorities predictably moved the goalposts. Historian Simon Dubnow records the reaction of deputies to the Piotrkov Diet of 1538. They immediately issued a new constitution that severely restricted what Jews could wear, and from then on Polish Jewry's habitual costume lagged woefully behind the times. Two centuries later, when most of Catholic Poland had adopted Western European dress, Jews still retained the former caftan and fur hat. With Enlightenment—late in the nineteenth century—Polish and Russian Jewry finally adopted modern dress, except for several million *chasidim* who still retained the outmoded raiment of their early Masters.

The fact that they still do so upsets some Jews who will accept chasidic attire only as a fashion statement. Linda Nochlin, a professor of Modern Art at New York University, labels herself "open, rational, literary, politically and culturally left," and files *chasidim* under "Jewish in the wrong way: retrograde, uncultivated, narrow, rule-ridden and authoritarian." Yet when the French couturier Jean Paul Gaultier showed a self-styled "Chasidic" collection for both sexes in the fall of 1993, Professor Nochlin viewed the wave-making event quite positively. Why? Because Gaultier's stunningly beautiful models in male drag effectively skewered Orthodox Judaism's insistence on separating the sexes. Nonetheless, even Nochlin would draw the line if male models were to sport Semitic-looking noses in addition to their artificial *payes*. That would be "too Jewish."

I believe the target here is not Orthodox Judaism per se, but chasidism, the irrepressible remnant of a once-flourishing majority of Eastern European Jewry who refuse to play the assimilation game. To *chasidim*, the issue of gender separation in public pales beside what they consider the life-and-death need for total separation from a God-less society. When a Liberal Jew strolls down Main Street, he remains anonymous. But when a chasid appears in his distinctive regalia, he and everyone else knows exactly which ethnic group he represents, and to which self-segregated minority within that group he belongs. *Chasidim* boast the courage that comes from an internalized faith and Christians respect them for it. But their audacious appearance alerts their Americanized co-religionists to the unnerving realization that were it not for the grace of garb, they, too, would stand out as "different."

CHASIDIC *NIGUNIM* RESCUE JEWISH WORSHIP

Truth to tell, *chasidim* kept pretty much to themselves until their ranks were decimated less than halfway through the twentieth century. But a generation later, by an unlikely coincidence the example of their undilutedly ethnic practices would prove a godsend to North American synagogue practice, which had run out of ideas. It started when a Tel Aviv theatrical troupe semi-staged an hour-long medley of chasidic *nigunim* that had been supplied with vernacular lyrics. The song genre was invented late in the eighteenth century by Yitzchok Isaac of Kalev, who so loved the pastoral ballads of his native Hungary that he would adjust their words and melodies to sound more Jewish.

> An ode in the wild woods, to a far-away rose [*Ros, Ros*]

became

> a plea to the *Sh'chineh* [Yiddish pronunciation] so far away,
> to let the Exile end this day [*Sh'chineh, Sh'chineh*].

During its adaptation, the wistful Hungarian folk melody was rewritten in a mode normally used for studying Talmud (Chapter 4 . . . "Studying the Oral Torah"). Israeli composer Dan Almagor borrowed the *Tzaddik* of Kalev's Judaized version, along with a dozen other fervently devotional dialogues with God cast from the same mold. He strung them together as a series of dramatic tableaus emanating from a chasidic tale by Israel of Ruzhin.

> Master of the universe!
> We do not know the place in the forest
> where previous generations went,
> and we are therefore unable to kindle the flame
> as they once did.
> Nor do we recall the prayer they recited,
> and we have also forgotten the tune they sang.
> We know only one thing, and it must suffice:
> that *There Was Once a Chasid* . . .

The dramatic technique of wedding *nigunim*-with-words to interspersed narrative proved so effective that amateur Jewish theatrical companies began staging productions of *There Was Once a Chasid* in synagogue auditoriums all over North America. Cantors quickly appropriated the underlying idea, enlivening their congregational repertoire with chasidic bits and pieces. But they soon realized that tired old chasidic standbys like *Vetaher Libeinu* (Purify Our Hearts) were not sufficiently upbeat for regular use, so they commissioned new ones composed to modern folk-rock rhythms. Israeli songwriters, eager to supply the mushrooming demand, complied with a complete repertoire of neo-chasidic *nigunim* over the next two decades. Recordings and sheet music of annual Chasidic Festivals sold briskly all over the world, but especially well in the United States and Canada. They were followed by live performances featuring several generations of young Israeli artists who unknowingly helped pay off countless sponsoring congregations' mortgages through benefit concerts. Very quickly, cantors discovered that some of their formerly jaded parishioners were spontaneously singing along with the new refrains. Chasidic-style tunes were the catalyst; they gave contemporary Jewish worship a boost of adrenaline that would last for another quarter-century.

OVERDOING IT

Even Reform worshipers suddenly felt an urge to join in the singing. But after a lifetime of prayer through English readings they were ill equipped to do so, a fact alluded to in a songster "conceived as the musical component of the U. A. H. C. Religious School Curriculum." One of its songs, *The People in My Synagogue*, succinctly describes Reform worship as previously understood by the congregation (my italics).

> Oh, the *Rabbi* leads us all in prayer . . .
> Oh, the Cantor sings our songs.

Now, however, it suddenly became the *cantor* who was expected to lead in prayer, and Reform worshipers hadn't a clue as to how they should follow. Latter-day *nigunim* came wedded to unfamiliar Hebrew words long since excised from the *U.P.B.* (Chapter 3 . . . "Language: A Repository of Values"). Moreover, Israeli rock-style *nigunim* demanded energetic participation that was far removed from organ-accompanied hymn singing. To circumvent the difficulty, an alternate means of lay involvement was introduced: mass handclapping.

It quickly spread to all the national movements and, in a strange turnabout, the only worship now distinguished by a lack of clapping is chasidic. A visit to almost any other type of service—including Modern Orthodox—is liable to include not only rhythmic applause but also stomping of feet and grabbing of shoulders, particularly in the uninhibited atmosphere of Southern California. I once wandered into a Friday Night Conservative "happening" in suburban Los Angeles, which bore an eerie resemblance to the Solidarity Service envisioned some sixty years earlier by novelist Aldous Huxley.

Men and women . . . ready to be made one,
to lose their separate identities in a larger being.
The first Solidarity Hymn was a brief haunting melody,
repeated plangently to a pulsing rhythmic accompaniment,
and visceral in its effect . . . Ultimately the participants form
a dancing circle with hands on the preceding person's hips,
shouting in unison and beating the insistant refrain . . .
Individuals, inspired, shout out solos.

All of these elements were present, plus *rhythmic applause* that an electronic organ reinforced until the hip-hugging circle snaked its way out of the sanctuary and into the adjoining auditorium where a roaming accordion took over.

Handclapping and other newly introduced group activities have since grown commonplace at sporting events in America. Whenever there is a lull in action on the playing field—which occurs at every break for TV commercials—a hired mascot cajoles the crowd into performing en masse. If we were to zoom in on individual sports fans during any one of those artificially created intervals, ignoring the frenetic surface activity, we might detect boredom and a bit more besides. It is reminiscent of the criticism that critic John Podhoretz levels against contemporary theater. Podhoretz singles out the prompting that performers now freely engage in onstage, and compares audience reaction to the anger we all felt as children towards "the irritating fellow at summer camp who demanded that everybody on the bus clap to or sing along with "Michael, Row the Boat Ashore." The result can only be described as forced and unnatural, a desperate release of tension that has built up in perfectly justified reaction to the meaninglessness of what audiences are witnessing. The same holds true for synagogues. Whenever officiants sense the need for an infusion of energy, they resort to the worship equivalent of a Wave rolling around ballpark grandstands. At the slightest pretext they decree a makeshift "standing devotion" (Chapter 2 . . . "Liturgical Liberties"), implemented to the cool beat of a *nigun* made in Israel.

THE CANDLE FLICKERS

Many of the Israeli imports took root on their own, some filling a tangible need. Nurit Hirsch's *Oseh Shalom* (May the One Who establishes peace on high send peace unto us on earth) garnered First Prize at the initial Chasidic Festival held in 1969. Congregations welcomed it as a soulful refrain that provided a congregational ending for either the *Amidah* or Readers *Kaddish*, both of which conclude with its words. Despite the fact that it builds to a dance-like climax in the stirring manner of Russian folk songs, over the course of time *Oseh Shalom* has lost its freshness and acquired the very predictability it was intended to overcome.

Oseh Shalom typifies neo-chasidic tunes that have gone stale. Along with a dozen others, it still manages to work on a purely mechanical level, artificially pumping up enthusiasm when a group's attention wavers. But the scattered sparks of light that Chasidic Festival hits once helped gather now retreat before their inevitable approach; worshipers comply indifferently, out of a sense of dutiful obligation. Given no other genuine and readily available alternative, the one-time novelties have assumed a harsh pedantry and dry routinism reminiscent of the four-square refrains they supplanted. This is partially because like a leaf under glass, *nigunim* fade when held fast between bar lines on a page. *Chasidim* were alchemists, able to transform mundane material into inspired musical miniatures. When *mitnagdim* try to duplicate chasidic technique on a mass scale, the result is more like a replay of *The Sorcerer's Apprentice*: magic that has been overly watered.

Nevertheless, once the tsunami of neo-*nigunim* began to engulf synagogues with pulsating waves of rock-inspired rhythm, a significant portion of the earlier congregational repertoire disappeared. Now, after so many years of being sung on demand to syncopated finger snapping, the latest tunes prove no more effective than the old ones. This is particularly true of those that attempt to encompass lengthy paragraphs. If the traditional melodies—based on prayer modes—were felt to be too drawn out, their replacements are so percussively offbeat that people can barely enunciate the syncopated torrent of syllables. The early *chasidim* first did away with words for a different reason; their intent was to "break the vessels" imposed by a set rubric of prayer, to move beyond a fixed formula into the higher spheres of God's Presence. Their fervidly sung *nigunim* functioned as musical bridges between heaven and earth, melodies in space, by means of which they tried to ascend as many of the ten *sefirot* leading to *Ein Sof* as they were able.

Yet at best, *nigunim* offered no more than a potential means of realizing the Psalmist's recurrent dream (27:4)

> one thing only have I desired . . .
> to behold the graciousness of God
> and to visit His Heavenly Palace,

they were never viewed as an end in themselves. But our religious leaders have failed to understand this; their ill-conceived abuse of *nigunim* for the sake of retaining control over worship has led to utter boredom. Worshipers are generally boxed into singing every section of every service to the same pounding beat, even though a third of all chasidic *nigunim*—including the latest ones—are neither foot stompers nor table bangers. With all the current interest in relaxation as a stress reducer, we might anticipate hearing at least one meditative *d'veikut nigun* during a typical service. Sadly, this hasn't come about.

Even likely candidates for reflective treatment—*Adonai, Sefatai Tiftach* (Eternal God, Open Thou My Lips), normally whispered as a private invocation prior to the *Amidah*) and *Al Shloshah Devarim* (The World Stands on Three Pillars), meant to be reverently sung while the Torah Scroll is dressed—are bounced into boop-a-doop rhythms better suited to the lyrics of a Broadway musical (*I'd like to coo with my baby tonight*) or a campfire-cookout singalong (*I Been Wukkin' on de Railroad*). It is regrettable that our appointed religious functionaries continue to distort what should have been the single greatest influence upon contemporary synagogue practice. It is scandalous that we still allow them to do so. In any other field an immediate protest would be in order, or else consumers would quickly turn to alternate sources of supply.

REKINDLING THE FLAME

A few actually did, in rare instances when a choice was available. From the mid 1960s to the mid 1980s the membership of Beth Abraham Congregation in Dayton benefited from one such viable alternative. It arrived in the form of a 100–voice Youth Chorale whose founder and director, Cantor Jerome B. Kopmar, commissioned twenty-nine oratorio-length works of Jewish music that have since become classics, mostly for the liturgy and many on chasidic themes. A onetime classmate of mine at the Jewish Theological Seminary in New York, Jerry Kopmar was inspired by our instructor in Ensemble Singing—conductor Siegfried Landau—to involve children in synagogue life by having them perform choral music. Jerry called it "teaching *Yiddishkeit* through the back door," a modest endeavor that engaged between 300 and 400 families over the years and perhaps twice as many youngsters. Open to everyone, it offered the most all-consuming Jewish youth activity in his community and lasted well into the participants' later relationship to synagogues as adults. They learned the meaning of total commitment to a cause, just as their parents did in flocking willingly to synagogue whenever the Chorale assisted in leading services. Prayer became an important part of the youngsters' lives; the hours they spent in *shul* on Shabbat morning were the best hours of their week. They reciprocated by faithfully attending whatever number of rehearsals was required for each performance. In 1982, at the age of seventy-eight, the famous operatic tenor Jan Peerce appeared with them in his last concert. Afterward he referred to that evening as perhaps the most fulfilling of his entire career, and to the children as true professionals.

So they were. While mastering a wide range of music commissioned especially for them, without even realizing it the modern-day Levitical apprentices acquired liturgical skills that their parents had forgotten. Worship was made so beautiful and so fulfilling, they would always want to be a part of it. Admittedly, this success story was one of a kind and enjoyed a lifespan of only two decades. Its residual effect has been incalculable, however, particularly in the area of chasidic *nigunim*, that portion of the Chorale's repertoire that remains most accessible to youth choirs in other synagogues. There is a real magic to *nigunim* sung by children in arrangements written expressly for their voices, specifically the medley entitled *Rejoice and Sing*, which B'nai Abraham's Chorale recorded in the mid-seventies. Its eight *nigunim*, dramatically varied in mode and tempo, have since metamorphosed through Jewish communities like the melodies in Isaac Leib Peretz's chasidic tales: they "have many souls, may live and may die, and even be resurrected."

Nigunim also figure in a more recent success story. Shortly after Shlomo Carlebach died suddenly in 1994, Cantor Elliot Kranzler of the Riverdale N.Y., Hebrew Institute determined to teach his congregants the melodies that Carlebach had recorded for what was to be his final album, *Shabbos in Shomayim* "Sabbath in Heaven" (Jerusalem: Noam Productions, 1995). It took Kranzler three years of spoon-feeding the *nigunim*, one by one, until he had layered in a completely new Kabbalat Shabbat service. The 800 men, women, and children who now flock to it every Friday at sundown—many of them belonging to other synagogues—exemplify the attempts being made by creative individuals within every movement to revive the liturgy. In this case involvement-through-song originated with the cantor of a Modern Orthodox congregation whose rabbi, Avraham Weiss, subscribes to the dictum there is nothing unholy; there is only the holy and the not yet holy.

The Riverdale Kabbalat Shabbat substantiates this claim. As an entire congregation works out intricate harmonies and dance steps to accompany the eight introductory Psalms and the nine stanzas of *Lecha Dodi*, the *nigunim* themselves undergo sacralization. When I asked what prompted him singlehandedly to implement this renaissance, Elli Kranzler told me, "I had to do it, *tefillah* is too important to be abandoned."

WHAT'S IN A NAME

We learn from Velvel Pasternak, who pioneered in compiling anthologies of *nigunim*, that while unrestrained word repetition is a distinguishing feature of chasidic sing-

ing, it does not carry over into chasidic worship. If that applies to the ritually formulated words without which no service can proceed, it is doubly true of *God's
Name*, which *may not be repeated in prayer* (*Shulchan Aruch: Orach Chayim* 5). The prohibition was never honored by Reform musicians, many of whom chanced to be
Gentiles unaware of its existence, and is now increasingly ignored by Conservative
and even Orthodox cantors who strive mightily to quote Chasidic Festival hits
exactly as popularized by the generally nonobservant Israeli artists who recorded
them. Repeating God's name under the guise of faithfully reproducing the latest
nigunim has become American Jewish worship's way of painting the flag in nontra-
ditional colors. When artist Jasper Johns hit upon the latter idea in 1954, people
wondered whether he was disrespecting the national icon or appropriating it as a
"ready-made" familiar object. Some saw Old Glory inaccurately reproduced;
others perceived a meticulously crafted graphic image. Just so, 1990s liturgical die-
hards view neo-chasidic songs' repetitive mention of the Holy Name (e.g., in *Shema
Yisrael*) as a desecration which trustworthy synagogue composers—including
Salomone Rossi, the noblest of them all—unfailingly managed to avoid (Chapter
I . . . "Seventeenth- and Eighteenth-Century Sephardic Ascendancy"). Those guilty
of the offense, if pressed, would defend it as the lighthearted application of Pop
Art treatment to hidebound religious convention.

WHEN SPARKS FLY

This is especially lamentable, because the emotional power of *nigunim* lies in their
very repetition—at increasingly accelerated tempos—until participants begin to
dance as well as sing. To build this mood of excitement, *nigunim* cannot avoid re-
using words—with the substitution of *HASHEM* for God's written Name (Chapter 3 . . . "Emendation Replaces Translation")—and for the most part not during
worship. On Sabbath day, *chasidim* indulge in that kind of abandon—exhausting
themselves through the strenuous exertion of simultaneous song and dance—only
after the various services have ended. At *Kiddush, Se'udah Sh'lishit,* and *Melaveh Malkah,*
through the medium of *tisch nigunim* sung to *zemirot* texts penned by the great kabbalist
Isaac Luria himself, *chasidim* are finally able to attain a state of ecstacy.

All three communal Sabbath meals evoke fond reminiscences of the liturgy
through their seamless procession of *zemirot,* but do not replicate actual prayer. In
the fourteenth century, Rabbi Jacob ben Asher equated each of the three Sabbath
worship services with a specific Shabbat in history (*Tur: Orach Chayim* 292). Friday Night Maariv represents Shabbat Bereishit, the very first Sabbath following
Creation (Genesis I:31–2:3). Saturday Morning *Shacharit* symbolizes the Shabbat

on which Revelation is thought to have occurred (BT, *Shabbat* 87b). Saturday Evening *Minchah* anticipates the time of Redemption, an era depicted as *yom shekulo shabbat,* "eternal Sabbath" (Grace after Meals; *Art Scroll Siddur,* page 194). The *zemirot* sung at meals following each of these services carry their individual themes forward in a mood that is nostalgic and expansive, allowing ample opportunity for partaking in both bodily and spiritual nourishment.

Franz Rosenzweig ascribed particular importance to *Se'udah Sh'lishit,* the Third Meal of Sabbath proper, and *Melaveh Malkah,* the optional extra meal that follows *Havdalah* long after Sabbath's official end. Rosenzweig characterized them as "culminating feasts . . . through which the community is reborn to active life." The *zemirot*-texts sung at those two meals tell us how this comes about.

> *BEMOTSA'EI YOM MENUCHAH,*
> *shelach tishbi lene'enachah*
> As the holy day of Sabbath departs,
> let Messiah's harbinger gladden our hearts;
>
> *yishlach et podeinu,*
> *ELOHIM YIS'ADEINU*
> let our exile end,
> our Redeemer send;
>
> *padah Adonai et Ya'akov,*
> *AL-TIRA AVDI YA'AKOV*
> Redemption is near,
> My people, do not fear.

End-of-Sabbath *zemirot* provide timeless moments that the Creation songs of Friday night and the Revelation hymns of Saturday afternoon can only anticipate; they convert eternity into today.

The interval after *Se'udah Sh'lishit* is especially trying for *chasidim,* reluctant to part with *Sh'chineh* and *Shabbes,* the twin feminine polarities of their religious world. "Under night's darkening cover," wrote the Yiddish novelist Sholom Asch, "a struggle takes place in each soul between the festive and the workaday . . . *chasidim* cling desperately to Sabbath as to a mother's apron." And so they delay her departure with *Melaveh Malkah*—which is not really a meal but a farewell party—and can therefore be arranged loosely enough to last well into the night. By then they will have made the unavoidable transition from sacred to profane, thanks to a bit more food, drink, and singing. The *nigunim* chosen for Saturday night are sent upward like flares from a lifeboat, released from whatever tonal restraints had previously held them fast. Mystical, God-intoxicated hymns in which can be heard wind and storm as well as the lilting rhythm of a waltz, they artfully transport us to spheres far beyond the actual moment or immediate scene. Their aim? That of all religious song: to bring from background to foreground in our awareness the joy and wonder of this world and an abiding love for all God's creatures.

IF YOU ARE GIVEN A LEMON . . . MAKE LEMONADE

Rav Nachman of Bratslav often pondered the spiritual rebirth that every Jew may potentially undergo—just as *chasidim* do—by the time Sabbath departs. He carried his concern a step further, believing that individuals of every creed should collect all that is beautiful, holy and pure in this world, for those qualities correspond to ideals within everyone's soul. From what they collect, each person is able to construct his or her own private Palace of Sacred Song, which they may visit once a week at the very least. Their individual structures—ephemeral at best—represent equally elusive fragments of a universal song shared by every other human being. When all the notes of that song eventually fall into place, that is, when all humankind will have attained a higher level of spirituality, it will recognize individually and collectively that a part of itself has returned to its Eternal source.

"Life and its many problems wear a person down," Nachman conceded, "and with each defeat one finds it harder to rebound." Still, he maintained, the Psalmist (104:33) urges us on:

> *ashirah ladonai bechayai*
> I sing to the Lord while I live.

Nachman understood that the first part of this verse would not repeat itself literally in the second half

> *azamrah leilohai be'odi*
> I sing to God while I still am.

There had to be some distinction between the two clauses, a meaning deeper than their otherwise identical parallelism. The answer lay in *bechayai* and *be'odi*, the final words of each half-verse, which he interpreted as follows.

Ashirah ladonai bechayai
I sing to the Lord *while in the prime of my life,*
azamrah leilohai be'odi
and beyond that I praise God *with whatever is left of me.*

Though buffeted by circumstance, we persevere with whatever remains of our inborn optimism: that single note of God's eternal melody that we are duty-bound to send soaring into space. It is the lone common gesture left to us in an age of liturgical dumbing-down. We may have forgotten how to *daven*, and a good deal of our congregational make-work exists only to justify all the page turning. Yet if by some miracle even one moment of unmistakably moving prayer has been left intact during a service, we must treat it as if the entire universe hangs upon our singing that phrase with the proper intent.

Another substantial part of world Jewry continues to excel at this, as related in Chapter 7: "A State of Mind."

CHAPTER 7

A State of Mind

Tell me, Marrano, brother mine,
Where have you set your Seder table?
__Deep in a cave, in a chamber,
__There I have set my Seder table.
Tell me, Marrano, what will happen
When they hear your voice?
__When the tormentors find me,
__ I shall go down singing!
      Abraham Reisen,
      "Zog Maran,"
      Epizodn fun Main Lebn, 1929

$\mathcal{N}$umerous cultures hark back with reverence to a distant past before recorded history began. Australian Aborigines refer to it as the *dream time,* their most fruitful and fulfilling period, in the estimation of anthropologist Robert Brain. The late Nobel Laureate Octavio Paz assigned equally high creative marks to Meso-American Indians' year-end observances, which transform time into a dream-like state of legendary proportions. Sara Horowitz, director of Jewish Studies at the University of Delaware, locates the Jewish people's longing for a mythical past in the first three chapters of Genesis. She characterizes the account of humankind's beginnings in Genesis 1–3 as "dream time, a time like no other time . . . an impossible harmony toward which we strive as best we can in our own lives."

SEPHARDIC DREAM TIME

Jews have historically seen themselves as living somewhere between the perfection that was at the beginning and the perfection that will recur at the end of days. But one Jewish subgroup has recalibrated Eden forward in time to correspond with the tenth to twelfth centuries, and transposed it westward in space to Moorish Spain. Among that subgroup, called *Sephardim* (Chapter 1 . . . "Worship in the

Middle Ages"), dreams endured until quite recently of again traversing the bleached-white plazas of Malaga, of re-entering flower-bedecked habitations in Cordoba, of once more inhaling the fragrance of Granada's orange blossoms or negotiating tenebrous stairways in the cobbled lanes of Gerona.

SEPHARDIC REAL TIME

Descendants of Medieval Spanish Jewry were able to sustain this yearning for a return to the pre-Expulsion paradise of their forebears only by overlooking the periodic encroachment of religious persecution upon their accomplished ancestors' fabled garden. Throughout 900 years of Jewish settlement in the Iberian peninsula, mistreatment by rulers of other faiths was the norm. At regular intervals during the early Christian period, the lengthy Islamic interregnum and the final Christian reconquest, Spanish—and later Portuguese—Jews faced exile or death if they refused to forsake Judaism. Those were their only options in the early-seventh century under Visigothic kings, in the mid-twelfth century under fanatical Almohad princes, and again in the late-fourteenth to late-fifteenth centuries under Catholic monarchs.

That final stretch of unabated persecution reached a climax in the bloody riots of 1391, 1413, and 1456, after which most of Spain's once-proud Jewish population was left destitute. There resulted a massive rush to abandon the faith rather than perish, perhaps half of the *Sephardim* officially embracing Christianity out of desperation. Of the so-called *conversos* (converted ones), a small number continued to practice Judaism as best they could, in secret. But even for the valiant few who attempted to uphold both religions simultaneously—the new one openly, the old one clandestinely—such a perilous subterfuge could not succeed beyond a generation or two. Cut off from rabbinic texts or teaching, the covert Jews' only access to Mosaic Law would have been through the Bible, which was forbidden to laity under sixteenth-century Catholicism. The obsessive fear of being reported to the Inquisition by one's domestic servant over so innocuous a practice as laying out fresh table linen on Friday nights became unbearable. Inevitably, the grandchildren of those who had submitted to baptism would break all connections with a reviled Jewish heritage that they were forced to mime, imperfectly at best, in terrified privacy but never allowed to live publicly.

Moreover, Israeli historian Benzion Netanyahu disputes the cherished myth of *converso* martyrdom on the altar of Judaism even prior to 1391. In uncovering the roots of Spanish-Catholic animosity toward Jews he finds more cause to label the majority of earlier converts as "conscious assimilationists who wished to merge with Christian society," a goal in which they succeeded spectacularly right up to the mid-fifteenth century. Their rapid ascent to the highest positions in Spanish society, including the royal court, incurred an almost insane jealousy on the part of clerics who had converted the New Christians to Catholicism. Among the incensed churchmen were a number of apostate Jews who now turned against their former coreligionists and—invoking the racist pretext of *limpieza de sangre* (purity of blood) as bogus justification—raised a canard over the *conversos'* inherited guilt for the death of Jesus some 1,400 years before. It then became a theological imperative for the Church to condemn New Christians en masse as secret Judaizers. Branded as Marranos ("swine"; derived from Arabic *mujarram*, or "prohibited," referring to the pork that former Jews ate to demonstrate their fealty), they were removed from their high estate and kept apart from Jews as well as Old Christians.

Benjamin R. Gampel, another researcher into the pre-Expulsion period, portrays the Marranos as "an unassimilable avalanche . . . living in two worlds, lighting Shabbat candles while crossing themselves, fasting on Yom Kippur and observing Christmas, holding a Seder in secret and openly observing Lent." Yet those *Sephardim* who remained loyal Jews were less fortunate still, compelled to live in separate quarters of towns even as their means of livelihood was systematically removed. By 1478, as Ferdinand of Aragon and Isabella of Castile prepared for accession to the thrones of their respective kingdoms, many once-powerful Jewish communities had been completely decimated. Just as Spanish Jewry appeared to have sunk to its lowest estate, the royal heirs apparent approved the institution of a special "Holy Office" within the Church. Its first act was to unleash an unrelenting Inquisition in areas formerly under Moorish control, to which the desperate Jewish population had fled. Inquisitor-general Tomas de Torquemada, himself partially of Jewish descent, suspected all *conversos* of remaining in contact with their unconverted Jewish brethren, whom he categorically accused of trying in every manner to subvert the New Christians' holy Catholic faith. Between 1480 and 1492 he condemned to death over 13,000 *conversos* and supervised the torture of another 20,000 into confession of their misdeeds and reacceptance by the Church.

Still not sated, Torquemada demanded a summary expulsion, the one sure way of avoiding further Judaizing. The king and queen swiftly concurred. In their edict of March 31, 1492, they ordered that every last Jew depart from their kingdoms within four months, "never ever" to return (red-lettered in Spanish by the rarely used unconditional negative *siempre jamas*). Given the prolonged reign of terror endured by those who had remained faithful, contends Sephardic scholar Jose Faur: "when 100,000 [some estimate as many as 250,000] Jews left in 1492, the question we should ask is not how come so many had converted during the previous century but rather, how come so many had remained loyal?" In all, Jews had constituted a mere 10 percent of the population of fifteenth-century Spain, but their influence endured. Over a century after the *Sephardim* were expelled, Ladino (Judeo/Spanish) terminology would still be used to describe the hapless fictional knight-errant Don Quixote as *uno desmazalado* (i.e., lacking *mazal*, Hebrew for "luck").

THE PORTUGUESE EXPERIENCE

In 1497, the derogatory term *Marrano* took on an added meaning. To commemorate his betrothal to Ferdinand and Isabella's daughter, King Manuel I of Portugal entrapped the Jews of his kingdom—including many of the thousands who had fled from Spain—in Lisbon on the pretext of allowing them to leave. Instead, he forcibly converted them at one stroke. Because Portuguese Jews did not accept Christianity of their own volition but through coercion (*fazer na marra* in Portuguese, hence *Marrano*) they would stubbornly guard their old traditions in private. It was just as well they did, for nine years after their forced conversion, systematic persecution climaxed with the Lisbon massacre in which 3,000 New Christians lost their lives.

In 1531 Manuel's successor, John III, instituted an Inquisitional tribunal, after which the Marranos' days in Portugal were numbered. By 1578 most of the self-designated *anusim* ("coerced," in Hebrew) had migrated to Holland, where the Inquisition followed them. It was not until Spain's Armada suffered decisive defeat by the English in 1588 that Catholic influence over the Netherlands was finally broken and the Portuguese-descended Marranos, now Dutch nationalists, were able to reclaim a religious heritage they had never renounced.

IBERIAN TRIUMPHALISM IN A SEPHARDIC DIASPORA

In addition to the Netherlands, outcasts from Spain had meanwhile resettled eastward along the Mediterranean Basin where they simply overwhelmed already-established Jewish communities. The pattern of instant hegemony obtained in every country where Sephardic exiles landed; they considered themselves a caste above the settled population in whose midst they were forced to live. Nor did the claim lack substance. Notable leaders of Sephardic Jewry's dream time—Hasdai ibn Shaprut, Samuel Hanagid, Judah Halevi, Moses Maimonides, Moses Nachmanides, Hasdai Crescas, Isaac Abarbanel, and many others—had served as physicians, ministers of state and financial advisers to kings. They also functioned as learned religious authorities to their own people, bequeathing to posterity entire libraries of biblical exegesis grounded in neo-Greek philosophy, halachic responsa based upon natural science, and versified liturgy that rivaled the finest in Arabic poetry.

Out of deference to the great achievements of those scholar/statesmen, the title *chacham* (Wise Man) has always been conferred only upon Sephardic rabbis who were ripe in both years and wisdom. During the 1980s I heard a pertinent anecdote concerning the latter-day ramifications of this custom in Israel. An attractive young woman boards a bus in Jerusalem and finds only two seats unoccupied, one next to an Ashkenazic rabbi and the other next to a Sephardic rabbi. The Ashkenazic rabbi immediately signals her not even to attempt sitting next to him (Heaven forbid). Mortified, she backs away and remains standing. The Sephardic rabbi then beckons to her and with a knowing smile says: "Come sit near me, my daughter; he's only a *rav*, but I'm a *chacham!*"

REDUCED TO A FOOTNOTE IN NORTH AMERICA

The story may derive from an actual incident in Israel, the majority of whose population now stems from Sephardic communities throughout the Middle East that flourished up until Israel's War of Independence. In the United States and Canada, however, Jews of Sephardic descent constitute a dwindling minority-within-a-minority, a bit over 200,000 in all, according to Rabbi Herbert Dobrinsky, an organizer of Yeshiva University's Sephardic Studies Program. That is slightly more than the percentage of Core Jewish Populations in the United States and Canada who regularly attend synagogue services on Sabbath morning (4.5 percent; Chapter 6 . . . "Bridging the Gap"). If we apply the same ratio to North America's *Sephardim*, perhaps 13,500 might be worshiping on any given Sabbath.

There are two mitigating factors that might serve to augment the previous figure: Sephardic worship is conducted under strict Orthodox guidelines (despite being viewed in some Fundamentalist quarters as not quite up to par because its liturgy is worded and pronounced differently), and Orthodox services are generally better attended than any others. Secondly, as Indian-born Sephardic journalist Rahel Musleah reports, "in the past 20 years the number of Sephardic synagogues [in America] has doubled from 50 to 100, not including small Minyanim that are housed within larger Ashkenazic congregations." Therefore, we can safely add 20 percent to our weekly estimate, which would yield a figure of 16,200, or 6 percent of the regular attendees. Even based on that probability, Sephardic identity in the West must ground itself elsewhere than upon a ratings game. If assimilation worries all Jews, it positively terrifies those of Sephardic lineage because every child who intermarries—not with a non-Jew but with an Ashkenazi, as is most frequently the case—further hastens the disappearance of their culture. The current operative term for describing a multicultural society like ours is "salad bowl." Instead of dissolving into a common stew, as the obsolete Melting Pot metaphor dictated, exotic populations that now enter any developed country all struggle to retain their crisply defined individuality. Sephardic Jewry, with its own unique flavor, is but one of many self-assertive ingredients being tossed together, and that is why the Israeli anecdote about its salty spiritual leadership applies to North American *Sephardim* as well.

SEPHARDIC AND ASHKENAZIC SELF-IMAGERY

It has been said that the greatest distance between people of different persuasions is not space but custom. Distinguishing traits vary even within the same ethnic group, especially if segments of it were dispersed geographically over a considerable period. During the past five centuries *Sephardim* have presumably been asking the same self-defining questions as *Ashkenazim*. One of the prime ways to find out if their answers differ and if so—to what extent—is by examining each branch's folk tales, ballads that narrate the exploits of early heroes who appeared shortly after their dream time. The way an ethnic group envisions its ancestors—through stories passed from generation to generation—is a good indicator of the way it sees itself.

As to how many ancestral figures might suffice for a recognizable family likeness, the Bible offers a recondite clue. Shortly before his death on Moab's heights overlooking the Promised Land of Canaan, Moses charged every Israelite to accept God's Covenant, "from the one who chops your wood to the one who draws your water" (Deuteronomy 29:10). Rabbi Simeon J. Maslin observes that these two occupations were singled out because they encompassed all generations of Jews, from first to last. The first Jew, Abraham, *chopped wood* for an altar upon which he was to sacrifice his son (Genesis 22:3). The last Jew (according to this modern midrash) is Elijah, because he will usher in an era when all flesh acknowledges God, thereby nullifying the need to differentiate between Jew and non-Jew. And Elijah *drew water*—also for an altar—whose Divine fire vanquished the priests of Baal (I Kings 18:34).

Let us now see if God spoke differently to the Bible's first and last Jews in Sephardic versus Ashkenazic folk tradition. To flesh out an otherwise skeletal portrait, we include: Terach's wife, who was the mother of Abraham; the remaining two Patriarchs, Isaac and Jacob; three of the four Matriarchs, Sarah, Rebecca, and Rachel; a host of angels on high; Jacob's older twin, Esau; several lost sheep from the flock of Israel; the Prophet Isaiah in his preaching mode; a worldful of infants at the end of days; and a poor Jew and Jewess in Russo-Poland, all of whom figure along with our heroes in the mythical tales.

ABRAHAM

During the night before a baby boy's circumcision, Sephardic women sing to its mother—in Ladino—of the pre-childbirth travail endured by *La Mujer de Terach*.

> *The Wife of Terach* was pregnant,
> each day she grew more pale.
> Not knowing what to do,
> she wandered the streets.
> She suffered pain,
> she wanted to give birth.

But before she could do so, her son Abraham already sat signing his name and studying in the *ishiba* (Ladino for yeshivah).

Ashkenazim find less to celebrate and more to complain about concerning Abraham. Like many Russian/Jewish folk prayers, *Abram Batka Nash* shifts back and forth between Yiddish, Ukranian, and Hebrew.

> *Abraham Our Dear Father,*
> why don't you go, why don't you pray
> that God should wake us,
> that God should take us
> to our own land: *le'artseinu nashu.*

No longer a newborn, Abraham has grown old, to the point where Eastern European Jewry must prod him into fulfilling his progenitorial duties.

ISAAC

Sephardic congregations sing a sublimely moving *piyyut*—*Et Sha'arei Ratson Lehipatei'ach* (written by Judah Samuel Abbas, twelfth century)—in which Abraham's son Isaac appears as a youth of superhuman courage. Bound upon the altar, he instructs his aged father:

> Take my ashes and tell Mother Sarah,
> "this is what remains of the lone son
> born to you in your advanced years,
> who offered himself up to the knife and the flame."

The lad's fortitude moves angels on high to plead his cause until God relents, promising forever to *Open the Gates of Mercy* for Isaac's descendants on the anniversary of that fateful day, Rosh Hashanah.

God seems to work His will differently through the Ashkenazic figure of Isaac, who is pictured not as a juvenile hero but as a muddle-headed codger. *Yitzchok Ovinu Farhert Zaine Bonim*, a poetic reworking of Genesis 37, transfers the imagined action to a Jewish hamlet in nineteenth-century Russia.

> The grey-bearded Patriarch has eaten his midday Sabbath meal,
> recited Grace, and now dodders about the house in his silken robe.
> Humming an earnest tune his father had sung to him,
> *Father Isaac Quizzes His Sons* on the weekly *sidrah*.

In his declining years Isaac has gone blind as well, and so it falls upon his wife, Rebecca, to orchestrate the transfer of a Divinely promised birthright to their younger son Jacob, later renamed Israel.

JACOB

The younger son stars as pastoral hero of a Sephardic Friday Night *zemirah*. A pastiche of biblical quotations, *Yedidi Ro'i Mekimi* interweaves both given names with the Eternal People's redemption.

> O Jacob, re-establish God's altar,
> Let Zion no longer weep;
> Let Israel no more falter,
> Let Rachel return to her sheep!

The *Beloved Shepherd and Upholder* gathers every stray—including the body of his beloved Rachel, who died in childbirth on the way to what is now Bethlehem—and returns them to the flock called by his God-given name: Children of Israel.

But again, *Ashkenazim* find less to celebrate about Jacob; in fact the *maggidischer moshel* (preacher's parable) *Osso Boiker* portrays him as downright irresponsible.

One Saturday night Jacob sets out on a journey,
but falls asleep when a violent storm rages.
Upon awaking he hears the voice of God
pronouncing words of judgement that
paraphrase Isaiah's prophecy [21:12],
"*Morning Has Come* and so has night,
but you, Yankele, have slept through both!"

Yankele (diminutive of "Jacob" in Yiddish, used here in a mocking vein) is more
a lost sheep than a shepherd; when Redemption finally docks, he misses the boat.

GRANDEES AND THE REST OF US

How to explain the pale, almost bloodless hues in which *Ashkenazim* painted their
forebears except as a reflection of their own perceived helplessness. We know from
events of the past century that the 2.5 million Eastern European Jews who fled to
North America wanted nothing more than to escape their bitter existence. Yet
while this mass exodus was going on, an even greater number continued to linger
at home, debating legalistic minutiae until it was too late. And all the while, they
were unpretentiously projecting an Ashkenazic self-image on the smallest screen
imaginable, singing of earthly—rather than heavenly—heroes who seem much more
frail and subservient than their vigorous, self-reliant Sephardic counterparts. In
the wintry confines of frigid Russia, Father Abraham could only pray for his children; Isaac could not manage even that without help, and Jacob proved a total
disaster.

Such was not the case with *Sephardim*, whose ebullient outlook enabled them
to stare down adversities of the greatest magnitude. They left Spain reluctantly,
each family taking along the keys to its old home, passing them from father to son
in the hope of returning someday. I had always considered this account to be a
fanciful legend until viewing photographs taken by Edward Serotta of a 500–year-
old set of house keys in Sarajevo, whose Sephardic community dates from shortly
after the Spanish Expulsion. Sephardic liturgical ballads reflect this inbred optimism; they depict the Patriarchs—and themselves—as aristocrats basking in the
sunny Mediterranean clime. That is where Abraham set a precocious pattern of
learning for all future generations of Jews, where Isaac pleaded successfully before
God on their behalf and where someday, Jacob would lead the wandering flock
safely back to its homeland.

ELIJAH

This divergence between Sephardic and Ashkenazic folk imagery persists through the last Jew alluded to in Deuteronomy. Elijah is associated in the collective Jewish subconscious with Sabbath's departure, Motsa'ei Shabbat. Traditionalists in both camps believe that on a Saturday night at the end of days, the prophet will reappear as herald, with the long-awaited Messiah—heir to the throne of David—in tow. Until then, since Elijah did not die (2 Kings 2:11), he wanders the earth in various guises, rectifying wrongs. The Sephardic Cradle song *Esta Noche Es Alevada* pictures him at his apocalyptic best, maintaining constant vigil during the final Motsa'ei Shabbat of history.

> Standing guard through *This Luminous Night*,
> the prophet watches over every infant wight.

In an exalted vision, Elijah singlehandedly upholds God's covenantal promise to assure the future of His people as witness to the nations.

Ashkenazim from Russia/Poland portrayed Elijah quite differently, usually in the secondary role of messenger. In the ballad *A Maiseleh* (*A Tale*), the seer functions mainly as a conduit through which Divine intercession might arrive for a typically impoverished couple, if they are wise enough to accept it.

> One Sabbath Eve before dusk a stranger appears
> at their hovel and they willingly share with him
> what little they possess. The following evening
> he departs after reciting *Havdalah*, leaving
> behind the equivalent of a small fortune.

But they quickly squander it down to the last *zloty* (Polish for "gold" coin), and retribution follows just as swiftly: the milk curdles; the wine sours; the couple is left penniless, as before.

THE PICTURE IS CHANGING

Perhaps because of the grinding poverty they had endured for so long, *Ashkenazim* really didn't anticipate riches. Certainly, during its sweatshop stage the immigrants' passage from benighted Eastern Europe to the Golden Land could justifiably be classified as a progression from rags to rags! That evaluation underwent drastic revision upward by the time the Eastern Europeans had been in America for 100 years and their billionaire great-grandchildren routinely made up almost a quarter of the *Fortune 500* list and just under 50 percent of the top *Art & Antiques* collectors. Social commentator Jean Baer states: "Where money and high achievement count, Jews are now counted among the elite." Nor do Sephardic—as opposed to Ashkenazic—origins matter any longer. In the face of rampant marriage out of the faith, we can only assume that such Old World distinctions, along with other folkways that are gradually disappearing will make way for a multiform New World Judaism whose own unifying traditions and self-defining myths are only now being determined.

 Sephardim constitute an important part of that emergent Judaism, for as history has shown, their traditions do not disappear without a desperate struggle. Herbert Dobrinsky assures us that "there are many corridors which lead to the Heavenly Palace." In actuality, only a pittance of the corridors in North America's earthly Palaces of Song echo to the footsteps of Sephardic worshipers on any given Sabbath. Yet the influence of those particular synagogue-goers far exceeds their numbers. Their prayer covers the same liturgical ground as that of Ashkenazic Orthodox services. But it does so in even greater detail and with procedural variations having to do mainly with the pace of their *daven'n* (*tefillah*, in Sephardic terminology), the physical layout of their synagogue (*esnoga*, in the Amsterdam/London *Minhag*) and their treatment of Thanksgiving Psalms (universally referred to as *Hallel*).

THE PACE OF SEPHARDIC *TEFILLAH*

Instead of opening and closing paragraphs that congregants then complete in an undertone, Sephardic *chazanim* chant every word of the liturgy in a meticulously enunciated Hebrew akin to the Israeli usage of an earlier, more literary-minded generation of settlers bent on reclaiming the ancestral language. This by itself substantially lengthens the duration of every service. In addition, lay volunteers who customarily lead the *Birkot Hashachar* and *Pesukei Dezimra* sections do so inexpertly, and therefore haltingly. Not only that, but if ten adult males are not yet present, the volunteers have standing instructions to further slow things down as long as necessary until a quorum is reached and the *Shacharit* proper—with its Call to Prayer—can begin officially. Even after an appointed *chazan* has taken over, the tempo does not quicken appreciably. Sephardic worshipers all join in reciting key phrases aloud at pre-arranged passages, which allows the *chazan* a few seconds of respite. He then backtracks to gain momentum—much like a broad jumper—and reiterates the group's already-rendered formula before leaping ahead. When repeated often enough, this echoed response retards forward motion sufficiently to dissuade habitual attendees from ever arriving promptly.

The languid pace decelerates even more at Torah reading time, since Sephardic *esnogas* are laid out with an eye toward accommodating an elaborate and stately ceremonial. Where *Ashkenazim* fill the synagogue completely with seating, *Sephardim* leave an entire central area bare, flanked by facing rows of benches along either side. This arrangement provides space for an impressively deliberate ceremonial in which a Torah Scroll is removed from the Ark (*Heichal*) and borne the full length of the hall, accompanied by a full retinue of synagogue officials, before being unrolled and read aloud from a ballustraded platform (*Teivah*) at the opposite end. Eastern *Sephardim* stemming from North Africa, the Levant, and the Balkans differ in this particular from their Western or Spanish/Portuguese cousin. The Easterners often read from an upright-standing Scroll encased in precious metal or wood, while Westerners read from a soft-covered Scroll laid flat upon the table. Both traditions defer with great courtesy, however, to those called up by their "Good Name" (*ya'amod hashem hatov . . .*) for an *Aliyah* honor. At that moment, younger members of the honoree's family also rise and stand in place throughout the interval their elder remains at the *Teivah*.

THE SEPHARDIC *ESNOGA*'S FLOOR PLAN

The Spanish/Portuguese *esnoga*'s cleared central space actually reflects an austere seventeenth-century floor plan that originated in Amsterdam, "a product of the Protestant Baroque style: straightforward, reticent, and staid in contrast to the more exuberant Jesuit Baroque," notes architectural historian Rachel Wischnitzer. Dutch Reformed ministers used to walk the full length of their church's nave (central aisle) at the commencement and conclusion of every Sunday service, singing and greeting, in order to provide tangible evidence of unity with their congregations. They consciously played the part of spiritual pastors, concerned about the flocks put in their charge. Pointedly solicitous clerical behavior of this sort contrasted starkly with the aloofness of Catholic priests whose prime obligation of office, according to a compendium on Church practice at the time, was to "sing the divine office with devotion." In addition to maintaining a separatist and celibate lifestyle, Catholic priests would enter and exit from the sacristy (very front) of their cathedrals when officiating, never mingling with worshipers. The name "Protestant" arose partly from protest against this hierarchal Catholic procedure. The Dutch ministers' ceremonial promenades—which offered the opportunity for social intercourse with the congregation along the way—were eventually adopted by clerics of every religious denomination in North America.

SEPHARDIC AND ASHKENAZIC TORAH SERVICES

The ritual of synagogue Torah reading includes parading a scroll from the Ark to a reading table beforehand, and returning it to its place afterward. What distinguishes Sephardic removal and replacement of the Scroll is its unhurried tempo, regulated by a repertoire of carefully preserved melodies, all sung with great dignity and restraint. Non-Sephardic practice is quite different. Simply put, every other service—with the exception of Reform, which at one point (Wuerttemburg, 1838) actually discontinued the Torah processional—seems to degenerate at this juncture into a parody of Dutch reformed practice: greeting, but without the singing. The few Ashkenazic worshipers who attempt to join in their cantor's processional hymn are outvoted by a noisy majority seizing upon the interlude as a chance to circulate among acquaintances. Those in the procession—officers of the congregation and youngsters celebrating their Bar or Bat Mitzvah—take their cue from the rabbi, who follows directly behind a Scroll bearer and personally greets everyone within hailing distance. Handshakes soon give way to exchanges of "Good Shabbos," hugs, kisses, pleasantries, and uninhibited laughter. At each pause for personal greeting, the gap widens between Scroll bearer and those supposedly following in close formation. When the Scroll finally reaches the *Bimah* unaccompanied by its retinue (in flagrant violation of universal Jewish practice), there ensues a five-minute free-for-all devoid of any pretense at prayer, while the processional's main body works its way through a socializing crowd that by now has totally forgotten what higher purpose brought it together in the first place.

This could never happen in Western Sephardic worship where the Scroll bearer, *chazan*, *rav*, and synagogue officials remain fully visible from every vantage point as they proceed deliberately up or down the cleared central space. Spanish/Portuguese Torah ceremonials in particular demand a perfectly straight and evenly spaced row, whose members engage in a considerable amount of formal bowing from the waist before disbanding. Under those conditions worshipers have no choice but to remain in place, refrain from conversation and slowly sing the sustained hymn tunes. (A lessening in formality coupled with a quickening of tempo would transform the Western Sephardic Torah processional into a model for all others.)

HALLEL TUNES

Just before the Torah service, special prayers are recited on some half-dozen occasions during the year when Shabbat happens to coincide with Rosh Chodesh or any of the three Pilgrimage Festivals or when it falls on Chanukah. This special liturgical section is named *Hallel* (praise) after the six Thanksgiving Psalms (113–118) that it encompasses. Expectations formerly ran high on such occasions, especially following the Second World War, when Ashkenazic cantors would outdo themselves with at least one ambitious setting of a *Hallel* Psalm text. What is more, Modern Orthodox synagogues at that time would in fact encourage the assemblage to break ranks and be seated—in the midst of *Hallel*, which is always recited standing—whenever a cantor and choir embarked on one of those lengthy musical arrangements. I mention this fact not to point out an isolated divergence from halachah but to underscore the ease with which those who were stationed on the *Bimah* cued worshipers. In an era less dependent upon spoken directives, rabbis simply sat—or rose—when it was appropriate to do so, and everyone else did likewise.

More recently, as familiarity with the Sephardic *Hallel* repertoire increased, other traditions have have been borrowing from it. For it is truly unique; its effulgent tunes at their best (see on Psalm 118, a bit later) conveying a sense of serene and joyful well-being. True, the *nigunim* that *chasidim* typically sing at festive gatherings (Chapter 6 . . . "The Way of the Chasid") might also lend themselves to performance in synagogues of other persuasions, but not as easily. If the tunes chosen should happen to be of the lively *rikud-nigun* variety—joyously sung and often danced as well—they would require more time (and space) in which to generate a frenzied climax than the amount available in less demonstrative traditions. And alternatively, if highly introspective *dveikut nigunim* were featured, they would leave little impression on the current up-tempo world of modern Jewish worship. Synagogue practice always mirrors its larger environment—in our case, a planet tilting precipitously toward Hard Rock—which cannot easily adjust its axis to show a softer underside. Sephardic *Hallel* melodies seem to orbit the equator of that cultural dilemma; as radiant hymns of praise they never go out of fashion.

Psalms 118: *Hodu Ladonai*, "give thanks to the Lord for He is good," will highlight the clear-cut differences between chasidic and Sephardic *Hallel* styles. When *chasidim* stemming from Modzitz—near Lublin in Central Poland—sing the Psalm, they do it to a rather fast-paced tune. Swaying and dipping, they punctuate every break in the melody with interjections set to the particular filler syllables (*bi-dee bi-dee bom*) preferred by their sect. Chasidic *Hallel nigunim* thus tend toward the isotonic: explosions of energy without resistance. By way of contrast, worshipers who follow the Amsterdam/London *Minhag* render *Hodu Ladonai* in a sustained and well-balanced manner best understood as isometric, an equality of opposing forces held in tension until released.

Sephardic Thanksgiving Psalms' sedate performance style is grounded in the power of praise words to concretize what they proclaim. In studying Navajo Indian prayer, University of Colorado anthropologist Sam Gill determined that in order for such words to bear a potentially transcendent meaning, they must "enlist a performance style in transforming [themselves] into meaning-giving messages." In this respect Sephardic *Hallel* recitation is extremely effective, especially when an utterance such as *va'anachnu nevarech yah*, "we bless the Lord" (Psalms 115:18), is immediately converted into the act it describes: *halleluyah*, "praise the Lord!" Sephardic group-singing's performance style at times resembles loosely measured chant, which allows worshipers the split second needed to make a connection between word and deed. Its lack of rigorously measured rhythm transposes it into a timeless, otherworldly dimension where syllables seem to float semi-detached from the words they form. At other times, during passages clearly defined by an imposed meter, the deliberate rate of enunciation is so tightly controlled that listeners experience the same net effect: they feel themselves disembodied, an aggregation of minute particles and waves churning through the quantum foam that comprises our universe.

Many contemporary synagogue-goers have no patience for such ultra-protracted rendering of the *Hallel*. Yet those who submit to its discipline are rewarded with a sense of inner peace and fulfillment as through few other means. This might explain why melodies from the Sephardic *Hallel* repertoire are routinely played as processionals accompanying non-Sephardic marriage rites. Family and friends who gather to celebrate nuptials are tied to one another by common descent and aspiration, and are in no hurry to relinquish even one joyous moment from the occasion. The sustained fervor of anthems like *Hodu Ladonai* gives voice to their common consciousness and helps transform the union of two young people into a galactic event.

EARLY SEPHARDIC SETTLEMENT IN NORTH AMERICA

We have seen that shortly after their expulsion from the Iberian Peninsula, standard bearers of Sephardic religious practice seized the tiller and set full sail while their Ashkenazic counterparts remained stranded on alien shores (earlier: "Grandees

and the Rest of Us"). Once Inquisitorial flames no longer burned with any fre-
quency, Sephardic worship continued to chart much the same graph, with peaks
rising in Mantua, Venice, and Amsterdam. Another blip shows up along North
America's Atlantic shore, generated by twenty-three Dutch refugees of Portuguese/
Sephardic derivation who arrived penniless in 1654. Over the next 150 years,
progeny of those legendary twenty-three would build and sustain synagogues in
New York (Shearith Israel, 1655), Newport (Jeshuath Israel, 1658), Savannah
(Mikveh Israel, 1735), Philadelphia (Mikveh Israel, 1747), Charleston (Beth
Elohim, 1749), Montreal (Shearith Israel, 1768), and Richmond (Beth Shalom,
1789). And then the Sephardic worship chart flattens out.

We know from historian Malcolm Stern that during the Colonial era
America's *Sephardim* were prolific on a biblical scale, with some couples rearing
up to twenty offspring. But even during that initial growth spurt, more than 15
percent of the Sephardic unions recorded by Stern were intermarriages with non-
Jews, and the percentage increased dramatically in succeeding generations. Still,
as Stephen Birmingham—Boswell of American Jewry's rich and famous—reminds us, for *Sephardim* this was an age replete with legendary figures. He writes
of the "Revolutionary heroes David and Esther Hays [who] slipped through
enemy lines to feed starving American troops." In addition, magnanimous fin-
anciers like Haym Solomon and Harmon Hendricks voluntarily contributed
enough money to tide the rebellious new republic over its Revolution of 1776
and Maritime War of 1812.

Early American *Sephardim* did business with the founding names of American commerce: Clinton, Franklin, Livingston, Schuyler, Van Courtland, Van Wyck,
Sears, Barron, and Rutgers. One Sephardi (Moses Seixas) gave George Washington the rhetorical wording for his First Inaugural letter to the Jewish community
proclaiming the United States "a government which to bigotry gives no sanction,
to persecution no assistance." Another (Uriah P. Levy) fought anti-Semitism in
the U.S. Navy for half a century and rose to the rank of commodore. The
Confederacy's secretary of state (Judah P. Benjamin) was Sephardic, as was the
justice (Benjamin N. Cardozo) who succeeded Oliver Wendell Holmes on the
Supreme Court bench. A Sephardic poetess (Emma Lazarus) composed the ex-
hortation "give me your tired, your poor . ." which appears on the Statue of
Liberty's pedestal, and a Sephardic Suffragette (Annie Nathan Meyer) founded
Barnard College for Women. But despite their rise to national prominence in the
absence of persecution—or perhaps because of its absence—America's most successful *Sephardim* elected to play the role of reverse *conversos*, outwardly professing
Judaism while awaiting the first opportunity to escape from it.

THE WEALTHIEST INTERMARRY

Sephardic businessmen were pioneers in civic philanthropy, though mostly for non-Jewish causes. Judah Touro of New Orleans, who as a young man converted to Episcopalianism, ran true to form. At his death in 1854 he left half his personal estate—almost a million dollars—to every imaginable charity, almost all of them Gentile. Of that half, only 1.5 percent was bequeathed to fourteen synagogues around the country, which still bear his name (Chapter 5 . . . "To Share or Not to Share"). Many *Sephardim* who did keep the faith saw their children make socially advantageous marriages and immediately abandon Judaism. Indeed, intermarried descendants of the original *Sephardim* would eventually swell the ranks of American society's most distinguished families: Rockefeller, De Lancey, Livingston, Goodwin, Stevenson, Ingersoll, Lodge, Tiffany, Van Renssalaer, and Hopkins. Among later generations who chose to remain in the fold, Judaism would hardly be observed. Worship was replaced by veneration of faded old family portraits, and ancestral escutcheons remained the only connection with one's Jewish roots.

OTHERS PLOD ON

That is why history records nothing further of Sephardic ascendancy in the New World throughout the nineteenth and twentieth centuries. Neither may we infer anything noteworthy transpiring during religious services held by the original families, if present-day practice is a true barometer. Sephardic ritual in Colonial America "emphasized simple 'readings' of the cantor in slow, measured voice and tempo," informs historian Peter Wiernik. And in those slow, measured readings lay the seeds of the Western Sephardic synagogue's ultimate decline in this country, for they allowed no break in the relentless monotony of three-and-a-half hour Sabbath services. A weekday Sephardic-style *Minyan* morning and evening continues to remain problematical for the same reason.

EASTERN *SEPHARDIM* JOIN THEM

The founding Sephardic community—descended from poets, philosophers, physicians and judges—was in fact on the verge of disappearing when others arrived whose ancestors had been "tailors and shoemakers" (as pious New Christians referred to their former co-religionists) in Spain. The newcomers had lived quietly in Arab lands until the present century, observing their cherished religion with ever more fervency and superstition as penance for the sins that (they imagined)

must have led to their antecedents' mass expulsion. In the early 1900s they began
to emigrate here from Greece and Turkey, and could not believe what they saw.
The reports they sent home, aglow with descriptions of Jewish prosperity in the
New World, led more emigres to venture forth. Those in turn would eventually
be augmented tenfold by their still darker-skinned and more primitive-appearing
cousins from the Levant, Balkans, and North Africa, spurred by the Turkish Revolution following World War I. They all gravitated toward the stately Spanish/
Portuguese synagogues built a half-century before in North America, but not to
the point of overwhelming them, as has occurred elsewhere.

Beginning in the 1960s, for example, a quarter-million *Sephardim* from Morocco, Tunis, Algeria, and Egypt inundated the 180,000 Jews who remained in
France after the Holocaust. Worship, until then Ashkenazic in a grandly operatic style, could not cope. The result today is a strange bird neither airborne nor
edible. Futilely striving to satisfy both traditions at once, a *chazan* leading services in the ornate neo-Romanesque edifice on Paris's Rue de la Victoire emits
a cacophany that would feel more at home in the Casbah of Tangier. Unlike
Central European Ashkenazic Jews in nineteenth-century America, who backed off
to organize their own preferred type of service when confronted with Amsterdam/
London ritual, twentieth-century North African *Sephardim* have simply taken over
existent Ashkenazic houses of worship in France. The North Africans were accustomed to a highly informal manner of praying. In Morocco, the synagogue
had often consisted of a single room tacked onto the home of a wealthy individual. Functionaries subsisted on honors auctions held during the *tefillah*, and
decorum waned in direct proportion to the length of proceedings. Worship often
gave the impression of being an adjunct activity to greeting friends and enjoying
a good laugh. It is easy to see why that type of prayer appears as misplaced in
Paris's Rothschild Synagogue as chasidic *daven'n* would be in New York's Reform Temple Emanuel.

Sephardic worship as practiced in North Africa and the Levant is equally
far removed from the stately *Minhag* that first arrived in the New World via Portuguese-descended Dutch refugees. For 350 years, if a non-*Sephardi* vied for
the position of minister in any of the Western Sephardic synagogues—as did
Westphalian-born scholar Isaac Leeser (later to become American Jewry's first
national leader) at Philadelphia's Mikveh Israel in 1829—he first had to demonstrate a mastery of the proudly unchanging Western rite. Mikveh Israel's present
order of service does not deviate appreciably from that established by Gershom
Mendes Seixas, the "patriot rabbi" who fled from New York in the 1770s. (Seixas
earned the sobriquet while still a *chazan*-minister at New York's Congregation

Shearith Israel, by removing the plaque that bore a perpetual blessing for the welfare of Britain's King George III).

BOTH BRANCHES MEET IN PHILADELPHIA

Even today, *Sephardim* of Eastern derivation who join established Western Sephardic synagogues in North America must adjust to the prevailing practice. It is much less animated than they would prefer; Sephardic *chazanim* trained in London—current seat of the World Sephardi Federation—are reserved almost to the level of inertia, and their stoic self-containment is contagious. Only in the unlikely event that one of their own is asked to lead prayer do Eastern *Sephardim* show signs of life at a Spanish/Portuguese service. On one such occasion that I had the good fortune to observe, the father of a Bar Mitzvah celebrant invited Moroccan-born *chazan* Jo Amar to officiate in Philadelphia's Mikveh Israel. The family had emigrated from Iraq in the late 1970s, and of necessity joined the only Sephardic congregation in the area. After nearly two decades they were celebrating the last child's religious coming-of-age, to which several hundred guests had flown in from all over Europe and Israel.

The visitors' spoken Hebrew was impeccable, unlike their demeanor in synagogue. Some of the men at first refused to wear prayer shawls, but when persuaded by the *parnas*, they sullenly flipped the silken *tallit* over their head upside-down and inside-out. A few of the women carried shopping bags full of hard candies into the sanctuary. But instead of lobbing the wrapped sweets gently for children to retrieve, they fired them like musket shot at everyone called to the Torah. When requested to desist until all honorees had descended from the *teivah*, the ladies promptly redoubled their salvo.

Chazan Amar chanted the *Shacharit* and *Musaf* sections as he customarily does, from the heart and with a magnificent native musicality, the Easterners joining in loudly and clearly. Mikveh Israel regulars seemed to appreciate this generous display of vocal fervor but politely demurred at every cue that was not exactly in sync with their own unvarying custom. They finally came alive during the Torah recessional, conducted by the minister of Mikveh Israel, Rabbi Albert E. Gabbai. Then it was the guests' turn to maintain silence and gape as the Torah bearer, *rav*, *parnas*, and trustees filed toward the *Heichal* at an incredibly deliberate rate of one half-step every five seconds. The accompanying hymn—*Mizmor Ledavid* (Ascribe Glory to God; Psalms 29)—perfectly matched this slow-motion advance in its languid tempo, while giving the home team a chance to demonstrate some of the exquisite forbearance that characterizes Spanish/Portuguese *tefillah*. Compared to Ashkenazic—or even Eastern Sephardic—worship appears so maddeningly cautious that scholar Hanoch Avenary felt compelled to issue the following caveat.

> Traditional Amsterdam-Sephardic song as it is intoned . . .
> today makes a deep but somewhat strange impression
> on the listener. One is tempted to say that it is Oriental
> music misunderstood . . . and nevertheless performed
> in a naive faithfulness.

SUDDENLY EVERYONE WANTS TO BE SEPHARDIC

Despite this warning, a small but dedicated segment of contemporary Jewry has been steadily shifting its allegiance from Ashkenazic to Sephardic worship. After five centuries of divergence, our salad-bowl society has mixed the descendants of both traditions so thoroughly that it is now possible to mirror the early *conversos'* shadow existence in reverse image. Instead of New Christians lighting Sabbath candles in a subterranean chamber, Marrano-descended Old Christians are today joining Sephardic congregations and immediately evoking ancestral memories that resist classification as either imagined or real. For who among us can say with certainty how often their family tree has been uprooted from one locale and transplanted into another since the late-fifteenth century?

As early as 1818 the Reform Temple of Hamburg, Germany, engaged a Sephardic cantor and continued to do so until 1873. "The Reform Jews of Hamburg perceived the Sephardic rendition of *piyyutim* as a valid substitute for, or addition to the German chorales," observes Edwin Seroussi, a professor of musicology at Bar Ilan University. The Sephardic psalmodic style of alternating musico/rhetorical question and answer between *sheli'ach tsibbur* and congregation evidently appealed to the early European Reformers, as did the clarity and dignity of Hebrew prayer when enunciated in the Sephardic dialect. The Hamburg Temple retained Sephardic prayer pronunciation up until the First World War. Its sister congregation, the *Reformgemeinde* of Berlin, continued to sing with a Sephardic accent the few Hebrew responses left in its radically shortened liturgy until 1942, when the community was dissolved.

Jews on both sides of the Atlantic were not alone in identifying with the branch of biblical Israel that had borne golden fruit in Spain and Portugal during the Middle Ages. First-rank Gentile writers like George Eliot and James Joyce constructed highly regarded works of fiction around quasi-"Spanish" characters

(Daniel Deronda; Leopold Bloom) who lived in nineteenth-century London and twentieth-century Dublin. Real-life heroes descended from *Sephardim* cropped up as well. Bernard Baruch, financial adviser to five presidents of the United States, was always thought to be of assimilated German-Jewish lineage. Yet at the end of his long life he too played the Sephardic trump card, claiming descent from "a rabbinical family . . . of Portuguese-Spanish origin." Moreover, he took great pride in the fact that his ancestral roots stretched back to pre-expulsion Spain. So did the foremost contemporary Argentine poet, critic, essayist, and short-story writer Jorge Luis Borges. Out of a certainty that *converso* blood coursed through his veins, he unearthed historical evidence pointing to a Catalan origin for his family—Borges Asevedo—during the kabbalist epoch in thirteenth- to fifteenth-century Gerona. When questioned about the lack of more recent documented linkage with his mystically minded Sephardic ancestors, Borges replied:

> like Felix Mendelssohn's *Songs*,
> my Jewishness is *Without Words*.

This is the diametric opposite of an attitude taken by current-day Spaniards who maintain that their pure Christian lineage is untainted by Semitic blood. It turns out they are frequently mistaken. Victor Perera, a Sephardic journalist from Guatemala, documents the fact that his direct ancestors lived in Spain as early as the fourteenth century. His thirty-five-year search for distant relatives in present-day Spain led him to numerous practicing Catholics—including a Church official—who had no idea of their ancestors' Jewish past.

How could it be otherwise? The several hundred thousand Sephardic Jews who underwent baptism in the century prior to 1492 would by now number several *million* Spanish Christians among their unsuspecting progeny. Those myriad offspring of *conversos* for the most part remain ignorant of their Jewish past until it is pointed out to them, and then they deny it. They differ in that respect from the hundreds of North American non-Jews who, as soon as they discover their geneological ties to a lost Sephardic heritage, eagerly embrace it. Filmmaker Patricia Giniger Snyder documents the tortuous path of return taken by Hispanic-American Catholics living in Colorado and New Mexico after realizing they were the descendants of Marranos. How else to explain families who, in Snyder's words,

> never ate pork, or meat and milk at the same meal,
> celebrated the harvest by building a structure of branches
> and leaves . . . and would hold a private marriage ceremony

under a canopy after the Church mass. Once a year
they would disappear into the rural fields . . . to ask God
forgiveness for the sins committed the previous year.

Other puzzling family rituals consisted of cleaning the kitchen cabinets every spring right before Holy Week. Tables were covered and families ate a flat cracker-like bread called *grutas*. Boys were circumcised by a doctor when they were eight days old, and cemetery headstones were often engraved with either a six-pointed star, seven-branched candelabra, or the Hebrew letter *shin* (for *shadai*, "the Almighty"). Whoever butchered sheep recited a blessing beforehand and removed the sciatic nerve afterward (a time-consuming procedure perfomed by hardly any kosher butchers today). "It is not an exaggeration," remarks Rabbi Joseph P. Weinberg, "to say that all of Northern New Mexico eats kosher meat but no one knows why." Now the descendants of those secret Jews can recognize the rituals for what they really were, ancestral practices hazily perceived through the scrim of sixteenth-century Marrano existence in the New World.

Historian Martin A. Cohen, who researched the tragic story of one such Marrano family—the Carvajals—discovered a previously overlooked connection between the Conquistadors of New Spain (as Mexico was then called) and early American settlers north of the border. Among General Cortes's army were quite a few Spaniards of Jewish ancestry, one of whom—Hernando Alonso—was burned at the stake by the Mexican Inquisition for secretly Judaizing. "In the two-and-a-half centuries of its existence, the Inquisition in New Spain . . . sent over 100 alleged Judaizers to their death," writes Cohen, and "put scores of others to flight." The most common route to safety taken by those who fled was up through Texas and into New Mexico.

THE GAMES HISTORY PLAYS

Since 1992, the quincentennial anniversary of Sephardic dispersal, descendants of those secret Jews have been converting back to their ancestral faith not only in the Southwest, but throughout the United States, many of them even before they knew the truth. It is as if medieval Sepharad—with its interwoven memories of Golden Age accomplishment alongside blood-red Inquisition—has inhabited their psyche all along. Perhaps theologian Arthur Green is right: "the God we call Y-H-W-H is really not a noun at all, but a form of the verb "to be" that has been arrested in motion." In like fashion, maybe our collective folk memory of Sephardic culture is less a state of mind and more a continuing process—a becoming—for us, just as it once connoted a very real place for those who called it home.

Twelfth-century Andalusian philosopher/poet Judah Halevi once exclaimed in awe and wonder:

> Lord, where shall I find You . . .
> The sphere of heaven cannot contain You;
> How much less the halls of the Palace.

Little did Judah know how accurately he was describing our contemporary synagogues—earthly Palaces of song—on any given Sabbath morning. How bittersweet if the 6 percent of loyal synagogue attendees who are his spiritual heirs (see earlier: "Reduced to a Footnote in North America") should prove a saving remnant for the other 94 percent, many of whom are presently anesthetized by worship less authentically Jewish than that practiced unknowingly by Christian descendants of Marranos for 500 years.

Even a cursory glance reveals that much of our Americanized Ashkenazic ritual has turned into a caricature of its surrounding neo-Roman culture. In place of liturgy—serving God—many of the religious exercises currently in vogue offer nothing but *panem et circenses*—the bread of ostentatious edifices and the circuses of pseudo-ceremonies. As a result, small groups of Ashkenazic-descended North American Jews have lately banded together in search of a more authentic and less pretentious prayer experience, closer to the way they imagine their great-grandparents worshiped in Eastern Europe.

The continuing struggles and lasting influence of those closely knit groups are examined in Chapter 8: "Sacred Circles."

CHAPTER 8

Sacred Circles

There is a group that finds it as difficult to live with
the synagogue as to live without it . . . If you belong
to [it] you probably want to be lightly touched by
something you don't quite understand but know
is very powerful . . . You need the synagogue to
help you along. How are you going to grow in a
synagogue full of good people with slightly shriveled
souls who seem to love responsive readings?
Richard J. Israel,
"How to Survive Your Synagogue,"
The Second Jewish Catalogue, 1976

*H*ow wonderful if every Jew disappointed by what transpires in today's synagogues could stand on a walker pad facing a virtual reality simulator, don a head-
set, press a menu item marked "Shabbat," and, with a *whooosh* accompanied by
spiraling bands of color, zoom into a receding funnel that led to the sanctified
place where Sabbath morning's liturgy is ideally enacted. In on-line lingo that place
is designated as Cyberia, a computer-generated space where the frontier between
hallucination and reality dissolves. There the liturgy would be virtually sung by
Israel's Sweet Psalmist, bytes of Torah would issue from the Lawgiver's lips, and
high-density images of *Kiddush* wine would pour forth from the Creator's own cellar,
closely guarded since the world's Creation. Unfortunately, such an eschatological
on-line worship experience is not only unrealistic in the literal sense, as a personal
objective it is beyond realization. That is because prayer and study carry far greater
weight when offered in a group, a *Kitah*—or more familiarly, a *Havurah*—as advocated in both Talmuds (JT, *Nedarim* 40a; BT, *Berakhot* 63b).

The group also plays an indispensable role in Franz Rosenzweig's theological scheme of things. We gain the kingdom of God only when we gather "in as-
semblies' (*bemak'halot*; Sabbath, Festival, and High Holy Day *Shacharit*) and praise
God unto eternity. Our collective prayer then rises to a universal plane, "our souls

in reciprocal union with all the world." Death is nullified as Israel—having reaffirmed its covenant with the Creator as an eternal people—attains the everlasting redemption to which other nations still aspire.

TRANSFORMING THE WORLD ON A SMALL SCALE

Israel's archetypal assembly encompassed "all the Congregation" (*kol-adat benei-yisrael*; Leviticus 19:2) whom God commanded to lead holy lives as they entered the Sinai wilderness. For most of us latter-day Israelites wandering through private deserts of our own devising, the concept of Congregational Israel is too large to fathom. We can more easily relate to Jacob Neusner's metaphoric Circle of the Sacred, a small group that we are free to join on any given Sabbath, and thereby transform the world. Unlike a virtual corridor in Cyberspace, the Circle— or *Havurah*—does not serve as a pass-through. Instead, ritual acts performed in common by those who comprise a *Havurah* somehow change the ordinary into the consecrated, both within and without its confines. An intimate group ritually oriented in this way constitutes a miniature Congregation of Israel as it meanders through the various sections of Sabbath morning's liturgy, guided largely by its own inclination.

Havurot (plural of *Havurah*) are generally much smaller than synagogues, North American Jewry's worship environment of choice. Where a synagogue might include several hundred in its weekly exercises, most *Havurot* accommodate no more than twenty to fifty in their prayer gatherings. Since *Havurot* employ no ordained clergy, different individuals accept responsibility for leading various sections of the service. While they do not claim to have attained parity with professional rabbis or cantors, *Havurah* members carry on gamely. Through wrestling with the difficult task of being at times performers and at times audience, they share the best motivation of all. Bernard Reisman, founding director of Brandeis University's Communal Studies program and the first scholar to analyze *Havurot* in depth, elucidates.

> *Communitas* [Latin: community] is achieved through
> desire to maintain approval of one's peers . . . serving
> as models and teachers for one another.

Each volunteering member teaches his or her peers by leading rituals, evoking responses at all the right moments, leading the processions, and reciting the words, enlivening the present by recreating the past.

The rituals of Shabbat morning cannot be enacted by one person alone. University of Minnesota anthropologist Riv-Ellen Prell, who closely observed a *Havurah Minyan* for three years during the early 1970s, confirms that rituals are ideally performed in community. At the same time she calls attention to the uniqueness of *Havurot* among prayer communities. Their family-like intimacy supplies "the arena where the worshiper's convictions or doubts are transformed into religious action in order to create his or her own Judaism." Such opportunities for private soul searching coupled with group camaraderie are all too rare in the hyperstructured world of North American Jewish worship.

GIVING JEWISH LIFE A MODERN SPIN

Because *Havurah* populations are tiny in comparison with those of synagogues, the feeling of kinship that they engender is much greater. People choose *Havurot* in order to participate and not from a sense of duty or social obligation, as frequently happens when they attend synagogue services as invited friends or associates of a family celebrating some life cycle event. In *Havurot*, the distribution of privileges as well as obligations is not limited to a guest list. Nor are proceedings divorced from the participants' everyday life; they are what give that life meaning. Active involvement with others upon whom they depend and who depend on them begets an awareness of mutual purpose: the *renewal of Judaism*.

Why renewal? Because very few *Havurah* members hew to a strict Orthodox regimen in their personal observance. They are mainly middle-of-the-roaders disillusioned with the pretentious chauvinism of Jewish worship as defined solely by denominational affiliation. As the new millennium commences, synagogue movements are guarding their territorial prerogatives with a zeal reminiscent of 1870s-style American factionalism when widespread Jewish exposure to New World religious choices began in earnest. In a remarkable essay on the four generations that have defined American Jewry thus far, Lawrence Hoffman notes that at the time, every denomination—Jewish or Gentile—viewed itself as a religion in its own right. In the late-nineteenth century there were only two types of Jewish service: Orthodox or Reform. By the eve of World War I, a toned-down version of Orthodox worship was available in the form of Conservatism, and prior to World War II a further diluted ritual presented itself as Reconstructionism (Chapter 2 . . . "Reactions to Radical Reform").

During the postwar years North American Jews erected hundreds of suburban school-and-synagogue buildings to which they drove their children but hardly ever entered themselves. In place of worship they substituted membership; simply belonging to a congregation became the most convenient form of identification for a rising suburban Jewish middle class. To be sure, certain modifications patterned after Protestant usage accrued to the worship services that 1950s Jews no longer attended. Their European-born grandparents—the "defining" immigrant generation of North American Jewry in Rabbi Hoffman's time line—had been opposed to similar modifications as too radical a reform of the tradition they brought with them. The children of that generation, who came to maturity on North American soil at the century's turn, welcomed innovation as being in tune with their surrounding culture. The car-pooling grandchildren, born during the 1920s into an already-Americanized synagogue, could only view the reforms as accepted practice.

The grandchildren's offspring, some of whom would go on to found *Havurot*, looked a bit further back and found that only the labels of contemporary Jewish worship innovations had changed but not their content. The introduction of family seating, enforced decorum, spoken prayer in English, vestigal Scripture reading, shortened services, alteration of statutory texts to reflect the prevailing intellectual climate, and the near-elimination of prayer chant had been advanced as planks in the Reform movement's original platform (Chapter 2 . . . "Reform Takes Root Here"). Religious moderates of the defining generation rejected them, but their spiritual descendants living in the changed world of the 1990s embraced every last one. Today all of those changes fall within mainstream Conservative practice, in reaction to which *Havurot* sprang up over a generation ago.

Havurot claim that latter-day Conservatism's cleaned-pressed-and-altered version of the old immigrant religion is unacceptable to them, yet the Judaism that these Sacred Circles practice together once a week likewise passes traditional procedures through a modern filter. What distinguishes *Havurot* from Conservative synagogues is their acknowledgement of the deep-seated aversion that individuals in our culture have to organized religion. This trait moved the nineteenth-century French observer Alexis de Tocqueville to remark that Americans, living as they do in a true democracy, "are unmoved by ceremonial observances, and are disposed to attach only a secondary importance to the details of public worship." *Havurot*— the most democratic form of worship that Jewry anywhere has yet devised—are no exception. Generally content to sketch their itinerary in barest outline, they encourage group members to fill in their own details along the trail. Like frontier societies, *Havurot* see themselves as an aggregation of rugged individualists clearing uncharted paths. They are therefore entitled—in fact, obliged—to circle their wagons against the danger of societal incursions.

Their self-reliance in ritual matters supports the conclusion reached by sociologist Robert Bellah, who headed a University of California research team that spent seven years studying the phenomenon of American individualism.

> Once religion is disestablished, it tends to become
> part of the "private sphere" . . . this suggests the logical
> possibility of over 220 million American religions
> [as of 1980], one for each of us.

Some *Havurot* retain the complete liturgy for *Shacharit* and *Musaf*; others recite only those texts that have become familiar through chasidic-style singing. Still others concentrate on a handful of refrains, chanting slowly and with eyes closed like Buddhist monks, retreating to the "pool of quiet" within themselves while perched serenely upon cushions arranged in concentric circles.

In short, *Havurah* members are committed to their religion, but not as it was practiced by earlier generations. Their religious stance confirms historian Arthur Hertzberg's judgment that American Jews have always harbored "a conscious anti-European streak" as they strove "to give their Jewishness the aroma of the religious tradition . . . but on the condition that they could decide what they wanted to keep and remember." Like their fellow Jews, *Havurah*-goers seek a group feeling, but they attain it through concensus rather than coercion. Each independent unit sets its own criteria for picking and choosing elements of the statutory *sidrei tefillah*, rather than accepting an imposed order of service *in toto*.

RADICAL BEGINNINGS AND PHILOSOPHICAL UNDERPINNINGS

When *Havurot* first emerged, the Jewish Establishment regarded them as dissident organizations. Several of the *Havurah* founders barged into a national fundraising meeting of Jewish Federations and threatened to disrupt it unless their views were heard on where the money should be spent. In addition, many had taken an active part in New Left demonstrations that violently protested American military action in Vietnam. But the young protesters who were about to start *Havurot* broke with their radical colleagues when the latter turned to openly denouncing Israel—newly victorious in the Six Day war of 1967—as an imperialist oppressor of native-born Palestinians.

Havurahniks voted against this doubly unfounded accusation with their feet. Once having made their point, however, they steered clear of the Middle East minefield and headed toward problems closer to home. In fact, they rejected the very cornerstone of their generation's adversarial stance: its unconnectedness. Havurahniks were primarily interested in reasserting loyalty to both Jews and Judaism while seeking viable options to entrenched religious institutions. To further that search they formed their own counterculture, a Jewish one that blended elements from several sources into a unique religious outlook.

At first, its prime mover was the growing nostalgia among American Jews for the close-knit community life that their grandparents had lived in the backwater *shtetls* (small towns) of Eastern Europe. A previously published anthropological analysis of that culture by Mark Zborowski and Elizabeth Herzog appeared in paperback early during the 1960s. It defined the *shtetl*'s universe as "a planned whole, designed and governed by the Almighty, who created it from original chaos . . . a complex whole, but basically . . . characterized by order, reason and purpose." The *shtetl* model held promise of systematic personal re-engagement for disaffected modern Jews living in an impersonal society that seemed to share little of their concern for the survival of minority cultures.

Broadway playwrite Joseph Stein was among those who read Zborowski and Herzog's account, and he determined to share their real-life depiction of the *shtetl*, warts and all. A collection of tales by humorist Sholem Aleichem ("the Jewish Mark Twain") provided Stein with a cast of lead characters: Tevya, a turn-of-the-century dairyman; his wife, Golda; five eligible daughters; and their various suitors. As the younger generation marries and moves away or is lost to assimilation and political extremism, the older one is uprooted by a pogrom. *Shtetl* society disintegrates before the reader's eyes, never having entered the modern age.

A screen adaptation of the Tevya stories, starring the legendary actor Maurice Schwartz, had appeared in 1939, but it appealed only to a Yiddish-speaking audience. Playwrite Stein's expertise was in live theater, and he envisioned an English-language musical treatment that would retain the film's bucolic *mise en scène*. To give the stage production a unifying theme, he borrowed Russian/Jewish painter Marc Chagall's signature motif: a street musician (*klezmer*; Yiddish contraction of the Hebrew *k'lei zemer*, "musical instruments") fiddling from a middle distance rooftop while two lovers embrace in the foreground. Songwriter Sheldon Harnick fleshed out the concept with a series of vignettes that captured the essence of chasidic God-dialogues (Chapter 6 . . . "Chasidic Nigunim Rescue Jewish Worship") through the simplicity of their lyrics. Composer Jerry Bock's musical score skillfully blended Russian and Jewish folksong to reveal an interconnectedness among all of these elements. The collaborative effort proved an instant hit from its opening in 1964. It began with an unforgettable tableau called "Tradition," without which the lives of *shtetl* Jews would have been as shaky as a *Fiddler on the Roof!*

The *Havurah* founders agreed. They were familiar with French writer Andre Schwarz-Bart's Goncourt Prize-winning novel about the millions who "turned from *Luftmenschen* into *Luft*" during the Holocaust. Schwartz-Bart's protagonist, Ernie

Levy, represents the final link in a familial chain that had for centuries supplied one of the legendary *Lamed Vav* (BT, *Sukkah* 45b), thirty-six righteous ones without whose collective virtue "the sufferings of mankind would poison even the souls of the newborn, and humanity would suffocate with a single cry." Despite knowing they are both destined to perish in Auschwitz, Ernie weds his beloved Golda (who coincidentally bears the same name as Tevya's wife in *Fiddler*). During their hastily organized wedding a fiddle player—clad in black prayer shawl—pirouettes and turns, his music ascending like smoke in the sky as he accompanies a nuptial dirge that memorializes every young *shtetl* couple murdered by the Nazis.

> The great seas cannot quench love
> and the rivers cannot drown it ____
> Oi vei _____ Oi vei vei _____

Havurah founders were also familiar with Rabbi Abraham Joshua Heschel's exquisitely poetic summation of *shtetl* life, which appeared in pocket format at around the same time. Heschel was convinced that the Jewish people had come into its own in Eastern Europe, not like a guest living in someone else's house, but openly and without reservation. "A world has vanished," he wrote, and the next generation would be "either the last Jews, or those who will hand over the . . . legacy of ages." Members of North American Jewry's next generation conceived of *Havurot* as their vehicle for renewing that age-old legacy amidst a culture that had Constitutionally disestablished religion.

The mid 1960s marked the passing of another Jewish thinker who had revived interest in the vanished world of Eastern Europe by collecting and retelling tales of chasidic Masters in a half-dozen volumes published over a span of forty-two years. Martin Buber first encountered the intense interpersonal spirituality of chasidism as a boy in Austrian Galicia, and he would return to it again and again in search of source material for his own philosophical system. I-Thou is built upon relationships, good or bad; indeed, if someone straightforwardly hates, s/he is nearer to relation than a person without either hate or love. In the chasidic conviction that any ordinary Jew can approach God directly, Buber found living proof of his theory. And in the "little societies" that were were steadily reclaiming the Land of Israel, he saw hope "for the emergence of a structurally new society . . . in mankind's struggle for self-renewal."

Buber's visions—at once utopian and homespun—dovetailed handily with the *Havurah* program: independent, self-reliant circles of committed individuals bent on re-establishing their connection with Judaism. *Havurot* also claimed a historical precedent: communes that had flourished along the Dead Sea in the wake of Syrian/Greek persecution twenty-one centuries before. Those ancient cultic settlements had worshiped according to their own rite but continued to send offerings of grain and produce to the Jerusalem Temple. So, too, many of the *Havurot* continued to evolve their own form of worship even as they eventually affiliated with synagogues.

THE DANGERS OF GOING MAINSTREAM

Twentieth-century *Havurah* members grew up in an atmosphere of social upheaval. Their parents had passed through the fires of a Great Depression and Second World War and were permanently conditioned to embrace conformity for the sake of maintaining stability, or simply to survive. But once unemployment and the Axis powers were licked, perceptions changed. "By the '60s," writes social critic Shelby Steele, "this self-sacrificing and honor-bound generation found itself identified with America's deepest national shames: racism, sexism, militarism." It was against this perceived exploitation that the postwar Baby Boomers rebelled.

A flood of them suddenly going off to attend universities gave a further boost to independent thinking. Living far from their parents' ingrained acquiescence to government policy right or wrong, many Jewish undergraduates discovered surrogate families of fellow idealists in *Havurot*. Journalist Shelley Kapner Rosenberg quotes Rabbi Arthur Green, one of the earliest *Havurah* founders, who depicts his comrades-in-arms as "true pioneers spearheading an ongoing spiritual quest . . . seeking in the *Havurah* the context, knowledge, and atmosphere that would enrich this search." Green himself would at one stage of his academic career assume the deanship of Reconstructionism's Rabbinical College, drawing a neat parallel to the common progression of *Havurot* in this country. Initially, they disparaged all manifestations of institutionalized Judaim, especially synagogues. But as their children reached Hebrew School age, most Havurahniks signed on as dues-paying members.

Students of comparative religion will discern a universal pattern at work here: yesterday's sect has become today's religion. Jakob Petuchowski frames it in terms of traditional Jewish prayer: "one generation's *kavanah* is another's *keva*" (Chapter 2 . . . "Words and Music"). An inherent danger lies hidden in this adage, particularly for some of the older *Havurot* that have undergone expansion: what starts out as intensified religiosity can quickly congeal into institutionalized fustiness.

Methodism offers an object lesson. In 1729 it was founded within the Anglican Church as a "religion of the disinherited," relates sociologist Will Herberg, "fervent, emotional and personal." It quickly moved overseas and spread along the American frontier. After the Great Awakening of 1734 and the Great Revival of 1795 it had outpaced every other Protestant denomination. By 1850 it counted almost 1.5 million members, including over 200,000 Negro slaves, who brought with them a slew of rugged Gospel songs in which testy Old Testament stubborness was still very much evident.

> Standing by a purpose true,
> Heeding God's command,
> Honor them, the faithful few,
> All hail to Daniel's Band!
>
> Dare to be a Daniel!
> Dare to stand alone!
> Dare to have a purpose firm,
> Dare to make it known.

Based on the classic separatist stand in defense of their religion taken by four captive Judean youths in Babylon (Daniel 1), this no-holds-barred Gospel song typified many that had been sung in Southern Methodist churches since before 1820. Half a century later, when the Civil War ended and newly emancipated blacks left to form their own Colored Church, much of the earlier fervor left along with them. The Negroes' African-derived, syncopated, overlapping call-and-response style of worship was no longer welcome in a denomination that had become comfortable with its success. *Daniel's Band*—stalking through the land in defiant recall of Christianity's roots—never entered Methodism's official hymnal.

This is clear evidence of an inner contradiction endemic to every religion: pious fervor leads to hard work which results in prosperity, which induces a love of things as they are and ends in an aversion to change. Procedural rigidity replaces the natural fluidity and ease of worship that distinguished a movement's springtime. In Wesleyan terms, the outer form of religion might remain but its inner spirit has vanished. In the words of Shneur Zalman, founder of CHaBaD (for *CHochmah—Binah—Dei'ah*; "Wisdom—Understanding—Knowledge"), the scholarly branch of chasidism: "if riches increase among Jews and they prosper, they become estranged from God." By this measure, the more-established *Havurot* may espouse—but aren't always up to practicing—an old-time religion.

HAVUROT AND BILINGUAL/TRANSLITERATED PRAYER

Be that as it may, readers old enough to recall the compartmentalized American synagogues of 1968—a watershed year for anti-establishment activism—will appreciate just how profound have been the influences of *Havurot* upon other movements. Simultaneous prayer in Hebrew and English, introduced by West Coast *Havurot* in the early 1970s, was quickly snapped up by Reform and reissued as alternating bilingual prayer, at least in its printed form. Overnight, almost every English paragraph in the new Reform prayerbook found itself in lock-step with a Hebrew partner. To accommodate this sudden infusion of traditional liturgical texts, many Reform Congregations had to officially reinstate the office of cantor after a long stretch of unofficial banishment.

That reprieve of Judaism's sacred singer came too quickly upon the heels of liturgical change for most synagogue musicians to recall the example of their nineteenth-century predecessor Louis Lewandowski, chief choral master in the Berlin Jewish community from 1876 until his death in 1894. Lewandowski had hit upon the idea of selectively alternating Hebrew and vernacular text—German, at the time—within the same prayer as a free-flowing *cantabile* that fell somewhere between metered song and fluid recitative. Written for cantor, choir, and congregation, his *Deutsche Kedushah* proved so appealing that although intended only for *Neilah*, the concluding service of Yom Kippur, it was soon featured in Sabbath and Festival services at German synagogues of every stripe, including Orthodox.

During the twentieth century, two American synagogue composers would follow Lewandowsky's lead, over fifty years apart: Edward Stark (*Let Us Adore*, 1911); and Arthur Yolkoff (*Tov Lehodot*, 1966). Their approach differed from the attempts of most composers to fit prayerbook wordings to popular song settings, adding their own Hebrew lyrics, which often proved grammatically and accentually suspect. A partial listing of rhythmic subheadings chosen by the latter group tells it all: "Mariachi"; "Reggae"; "Soft Shoe"; "Calypso"; "Funky"; "Bouncy"; and so on. Other, more "serious" composers put forth bilingual choral arrangements for cantor and choir that proved far too complex for congregational participation. In aggregate, the efforts of both popular and serious composers produced a number of works that merit a serious hearing, but not in the context of communal prayer. To my knowledge, Stark and Yolkoff were unique in adapting motifs from biblical cantillation and—using the standard prayer texts—weaving them into balanced psalmodic recitative that alternates between Hebrew and English. It is true bilingual *daven'n*.

The other viable alternative to that workable option in the face of endemic Jewish illiteracy is to print *every prayer in Roman type* for those who cannot read Hebrew. In 1998 Rabbi David Wolpe of Sinai Temple in Los Angeles decided to pursue that course. He offered monthly services—aimed at unaffiliated young singles—that provided the entire Friday Night liturgy transliterated in a booklet, along with the congregation's regular *Siddur*, the *Sabbath and Festival Prayer Book* (ed. Morris Silverman, 1946). The target group came in droves. Lisa Schiffman, founder of the Clickon Judaism Web site, dubs them Generation J, "fragmented Jews . . . in a kind of limbo . . . suspended between young adulthood and middle age, between Judaism and atheism, between a desire to believe in religion and a personal history of skepticism."

They bought into a musical service composed by the gifted Craig Taubman in a variety of twentieth-century styles ranging from 1940s Blues and 1960s film scores to 1980s neo-chasidic hits, all backed by a rockin' band of twelve musicians playing half-again as many instruments. Recorded on a CD by Sweet Louise Productions (Sherman Oaks, 1993), *Friday Night Live*'s moods alternate between joyous and pensive. The melodies, catchy enough to be sung at first hearing, derive from themes that sound familiar because they straddle both Scriptural cantillation and American folksong (Chapter 4 . . . "A Pragmatic Approach to Introducing New Melodies")." The concluding hymn, *Yigdal*, for example, quotes Torah, *Haftarah*, Lamentations, and Ecclesiastes motifs that closely parallel phrases from the pre-Civil War era: *Follow the Drinkin' Gourd*; and *Wayfaring Stranger*. Rhythms throughout are so infectious that prayers are danced both during the service and afterwards at an Oneg Shabbat. There are no readings, only one ten-minute learning session taught by Rabbi Wolpe. All of these user-friendly elements, including being able to sing the Hebrew words, played a part in attracting between 1,600 and 1,700 enthusiastic participants each month throughout the service's first year.

Our national movements have inexplicably dropped the ball on either alternative. Apart from Sinai Temple's Friday Night booklet, the commercially produced *Transliterated Linear* editon of *Art Scroll Siddur* and locally circulated Sabbath Morning pamphlets *Siddur T'feelat Shalom* and *Matanat Shabbat* (Chapter 3 . . . "Rewriting Road Manuals to Accommodate Women Drivers"), the official *Siddurim* provide no systematic romanization of the Hebrew prayers. Nor do they allow for chanting in Hebrew and English, a logical next step in North American Jewry's cyclical turn toward re-engagement in worship (Chapter 1 . . . "The Ground Shifts"). Meeting people where they are is also being accomplished through the efforts of individual cantors like Faith Steinsnyder, who prefers the bilingual approach. At a Yom Kippur Afternoon and Memorial service that I attended in 1997, her normally reticent Reform congregants chanted *Let Us Adore/Va'anachnu Kor'im* (And So We Kneel)—bilingually—with the fervor of Havurahniks, and followed that with a convincing English *daven'n* of *The Lord Is My Shepherd* (Psalms 23). This type of resourcefulness, inspired by earlier composers as well as the original *Havurot*, is fueling Reform's gradual return to the religious center. In 1999, for the very first time it affirmed the principle of "Mitzvot, sacred obligations," which Orthodoxy has long treated as mandatory biblical commandments between God and humankind.

HAVUROT AND LITURGICAL DECONSTRUCTION

From the beginning, *Havurot* encountered difficulties with the traditional *Siddur's* seemingly archaic, often anthropomorphic imagery. At the time a battle raged in the academic world over the way language was to be understood. *Havurah* members, on average of a higher literary acumen than run-of-the-mill synagogue-goers, were strengthened in their objections to the old prayer wordings by a revolutionary new critical reading of classic literary texts. It had developed from a series of lectures given early in the century by Swiss linguist Ferdinand de Saussure, in which he observed that the connection between a verbal "sign" and what it signified is arbitrary. Saussure's lectures were published in translation shortly before *Havurot* began to function. Almost simultaneously, French anthropologist Claude Lévi-Strauss applied the same theory—by then named Structuralism—to mythology in general. According to Lévi-Strauss, mythic tales of all cultures contain a message other than the one that might immediately be inferred from their narrative surface. *Havurot* paid attention, and by the 1970s many were setting aside separate areas for well-researched analysis and comparative evaluation of Hebrew prayer. Weekly sessions—during prearranged breaks from prayer—always featured lively discussion of how particular wordings had originated and how they might be rephrased in modern terminology, given the new understanding of ancient metaphor and its central place in Jewish worship.

Reconstructionist and Conservative rabbis soon copied the *Havurah* discussion-group model, albeit in an application that was tangential to its original intent. Without institutionalizing either a separate room or specific time slot, they incorporated the idea as an opportunity for impromptu lecturing, no matter what the prayer of moment during a service. The *Havurah* example of airing personal doubts was taken as license to dissect the liturgy, using Structuralist methodology. A healthy synagogal interchange of worshipers' uppermost prayer concerns was converted de facto into Instruction through *Deconstruction*.

Deconstructionism is defined by Laurence Lerner, a professor of literature at Sussex University, England, as "the form of criticism which sets out to analyse . . . a particular work . . . of literature so as to reveal its ideological basis." The assumption of ideological bias underlying every text—secular or sacred—falls into line with a prevailing academic willingness to view written truths as relative and written facts as simply social constructs engineered by an unacknowledged power structure. From that position it is but a small step—for anyone so inclined—to dip into the barrel of historical hindsight and tar Judaism's statutory liturgy with the brush of colonialism, racism, sexism, and so on.

HAVUROT AND GENDER INCLUSIVENESS

Among innovations that have worked, *Havurot* may claim credit for the increasing number of women who are currently serving as rabbis and cantors in three of the four national movements. Almost from their inception *Havurot* acknowledged that all worshipers could choose to wear the same ritual accoutrements: yarmulke and *tallit. Havurot* also made it plain that women as well as men were welcome to serve as cantors or rabbis. Through experience, *Havurot* learned how to accommodate women's different physical capabilities. The fledgling prayer leaders pioneered in displaying a smaller and lighter-weight Torah Scroll that either sex could lift and display comfortably.

In turn, the challenge of sudden engagement after a lifetime of ritual passivity encouraged women to delve into the history and traditions surrounding every synagogue appurtenance. Feminist author Letty Cottin Pogrebin elaborates: "They were aiming for not just equality as women with men but as *Jews with Jews*." They studied the terminologies and delivery techniques that men had practiced exclusively for twenty centuries, adopting them to their own feminine persona and sensibilities. Without changing the time-honored Hebrew wording, *Havurah* women added a parallel English commentary that captured the wonder they felt in assuming leadership roles. Their interpretive remarks also expressed a certain uneasiness about the tradition that had excluded them for so long. Riv-Ellen Prell cites one penetrating excerpt from a Los Angeles-based *Havurah*'s first Creative Women's Service.

> A pause in our service.
> Time to take the Torah out of the ark.
> It's an unfamiliar pause for me.

Usually I sit and watch my men friends approach the ark,
touch the Torah, hold the Torah.
Can I lift her?
Will I know how to hold her?

How do I relate to the Torah,
I who have never been close to her?
The Torah is the central symbol of Judaism,
but I've hardly read from her.
The Torah is the central symbol of Judaism,
but I've hardly held her.

Back in 1968 the notion of leadership roles for women in synagogue worship was unthinkable. Then the intimacy and intensity of *Havurah* services made its participants aware that the needs of half the membership were not being addressed. That heightened awareness thrust *Havurot* into the forefront of egalitarian initiative, where they were quickly joined by Jewish feminists of every persuasion. Supplementary readings in the latest Reconstructionist, Reform, and Conservative prayerbooks owe much of their language to the battles regularly fought in *Havurot* over finding a gender-neutral appellation for the God of our fathers and mothers.

A VIEW FROM THE RIGHT

Orthodox feminists have observed these inner struggles of *Havurot* as spectators from the sidelines, but with great interest nevertheless. Their conclusion: when the time comes for them to take the liturgical playing field they will have to set their own ground rules. Not for them the self-conscious role playing whereby men and women enjoy equal opportunity to display their ignorance whenever called upon to fill even such transparently contrived assignments as reading an English translation of the Torah Blessings (which every child knows by heart) immediately after they had been chanted in Hebrew by a teenager. Yet even this elementary exercise is muffed often enough to reinforce the charge that egalitarianism is nothing more than gimmickry when people intuit that artificiality is afoot and that unpreparedness is acceptable.

Lack of rudimentary Jewish knowledge is anathema to the growing ranks of Orthodox women who have completed advanced study programs for select scholars at all-female institutes in Jerusalem (MaTan, Midreshet Lindenbaum, She'arim

College, and Nishmat) or New York (Drisha). The degreed women have become as halachically knowledgable as many male rabbis, and their hard-won expertise more than qualifies them to arrange and lead a *Minyan* for women only. In fact, since the mid-1970s, Orthodox women have been worshiping in their own prayer groups for the first time in 700 years (Chapter 1 . . . "Where We Stand in the Cycle"). Supported by a Women's Tefillah Network that coordinates over 100 such groups worldwide, the number of participants has increased to approximately 20,000. Many of the same women attend an annual Conference of Orthodox Feminists that the Network organizes in New York. By its second year, 1998, of forty-one sessions on the Conference's agenda, thirteen—almost a third—devoted themselves to halachic questions involving women and *tefillah*.

After having led prayer, read from the Torah, and expounded upon it at their own *Minyan*, Orthodox feminists like Blu Greenberg no longer hold back when attending synagogue services along with their husbands and families, even though they are seated separately. Greenberg sees signs of this everywhere; women are now singing out with full voices, even reciting *Kaddish* along with the menfolk. She predicts an imminent convergence of two other recent phenomena, both of which emanate from solutions first essayed in the *Havurah* movement a generation ago and both of which are unstoppable by any other means. In her view, the reality of women increasingly serving as rabbis in Liberal movements (Chapter 3 . . . "Reconfiguring the Terrain") and the reality of more and more Orthodox women engaging in higher Jewish learning are about to collide.

As if to prove the point, early in 1998 two Modern Orthodox New York congregations, Lincoln Square Synagogue and the Hebrew Institute of Riverdale, independently took the radical step of training and then engaging a woman as "congregational intern." Both interns taught adult classes, made hospital visitations, mentored Bat Mitzvah candidates, counseled other women on spiritual matters, and delivered monthly sermons. One difference: Lincoln Square's first intern, Julie Stern Joseph, gave her talks in a downstairs ballroom, following services. Riverdale's inaugural intern, Sharona Margolin Halickman, delivered her sermons during services, from a pulpit accessed by twin staircases from the men's and women's sections. Officials at both synagogues denied that by having their pioneering interns perform what are normally considered rabbinic duties, they were preparing the way for Orthodox women rabbis. Yet by giving them the specific title of "intern," they implied a process of becoming. If the next step is not imminent, it is now at least an arguable possibility in Orthodox circles.

Historical precedent tends to reinforce this contention. The groundswell for women's ordination began back in the year 1903 when Henrietta Szold—who would later found both the Hadassah movement and Youth Aliyah—studied at the Jewish Theological Seminary in New York, an exclusively rabbinic school at the time. By 1921 Martha Newuark—the daughter of faculty member Professor David Neumark—was enrolled as a rabbinical student at Hebrew Union College in Cincinnati. In 1935 several women enrolled at the Jewish Institute of Religion in New York, among them Irma Leventhal, granddaughter of Orthodox rabbi Bernard Leventhal, who had served the Philadelphia community for forty years. In neither case was the time ripe. In 1926 the C.C.A.R. overruled a faculty vote to ordain Ms. Neumark, and, states historian Pamela Nadell, "the 1930s candidates were all women of rabbinical families, who would not stray from the fold."

Historian Leon A. Jick reminds us that "in rabbinics, change emerges from below and is then 'proclaimed' from on high." So it was with Reform and Conservative ordination of women in the 1970s and 1980s, and eventually so will it be with Orthodoxy. In forward-looking Orthodox synagogues like Manhattan's Kehillath Jacob and others, *gabba'im* (lay officials) are already bringing the Torah to women during Shabbat Morning services, inviting them to respectfully touch a *Siddur* to the Scroll in the same manner as men. It seems inevitable that before long we shall also see Orthodox women being invited to expound upon the Torah, as full-fledged rabbis.

To keep the halachic kettle simmering until that transpires, Blu Greenberg raises an immediate objection to one aspect of the Orthodox stricture against women functioning as cantors for mixed congregations (Chapter 3 . . . "Negotiating a Roadblock"). The ban states that any person who does not have a specific religious obligation cannot fulfill that obligation for others (BT, *Rosh Hashanah* 30a; *Menachot* 43a). Women are thus exempted from positive precepts that must be performed at fixed times, like praying three times a day at the appointed hours. Thrice-daily prayer is based on the biblical verse (Psalms 55:18) "evening and morning and afternoon I will pray incessantly," which women cannot fulfill because of an overriding obligation to care for their children. They are therefore ineligible to lead others in a formal service at those—or any other—times.

Greenberg notes the ambiguity of this position, since both the Talmud (BT, *Berakhot* 20a) and Maimonides (*Mishneh Torah* 2: Laws of Prayer 1:1–2) state categorically, as she puts it: "No set times are given in the Torah but rather were formulated subsequently by the rabbis. The . . . original commandment cannot be considered time-limited, so women are obligated [to pray]." If so, a woman could be allowed an exemption from obligatory prayer during her childbearing years, say, until the youngest reaches age 13 when it is responsible for observing mitzvot on its own. Then, as one who is again obligated to pray in a quorum (*tefillah betsibbur;*

Megillah 23b), a woman could enable every other person present to fulfill their obligation, either through her participation in the *Minyan* or—if she is capable—by her leadership of it as *sheli'ach* (feminine: *shelichat*) *tsibbur*.

A HUNDRED OF YOU SHALL DRIVE TEN THOUSAND

If all these developments did not arise directly as a result of *Havurah* ferment, they have certainly shadowed the movement's rise to an uncanny degree. It is only fitting that *Havurot* should have functioned as catalysts for Orthodox women's gains, since they were thereby repaying a withdrawal made on account some decades earlier. When *Havurah* leaders first cast about for role models in the late 1960s, they copied the warmth of feeling within Orthodoxy, together with its intense commitment to Judaism. They sought to create the same supportive atmosphere in a non-Orthodox community, to recapture—even in part—a religious way of life that the vast majority of American Jews had forsaken.

Havurot excavated their own channel to a meaningful renewal of Jewish worship, one that managed to avoid both the shallow-water shoals of Reform's facile rhetoric and the deeper—but nonetheless divisive—undertow of Orthodoxy's exclusivist stance. They treated all comers as equals without having to endure close religious scrutiny, giving them full access to both participatory and leadership roles in a daring move that was new to synagogue practice anywhere. They also discontinued the counterproductive division of labor that had previously rendered congregants inert and had converted rabbis and cantors into overbearing pitchmen for a product that few were buying. The payoff on that long shot proved most rewarding for other movements that followed suit, leaving *Havurot* to trail in their numerical wakes, far behind as before.

As of this writing, the National *Havurah* Committee estimates there are some 300 *Havurot* across the United States and Canada, averaging thirty-five adults each. If two-thirds of those 10,500 people showed up on any given Sabbath, weekly attendance would total 7,000. But at least half the regular attendees now count themselves as part of the movement with which their sponsoring synagogue is affiliated. In Encino California, for instance, eighty-five individual *Havurot* affiliate with a single Conservative congregation, Valley Beth Shalom. Many rows of seats in the main sanctuary are habitually occupied by *Havurah* members throughout the year, including Shabbat mornings, which correspondingly reduces attendance at their respective *Havurot*. If the same split-attendance pattern repeats itself elsewhere, *Havurot* cater exclusively to perhaps 3,500 people, 1.3 percent of North American Jewry's regular weekly worshipers.

MAKING PEOPLE FEEL AT HOME

Being so few in number themselves, *Havurah* members are extremely tolerant of other minorities. They welcome individuals leading alternative lifestyles who, when they first join, are still grasping at all sorts of tenuous ties to Judaism while weighted down by an overwhelming ignorance of its religious practice. Through being accepted without question into a close-knit community, by publicly sharing that community's doubts while privately praying words that they may or may not believe, many former strangers to their own heritage experience a feeling of homecoming. Marginal Jews often find in the *Havurah* a road back as well as an avenue for moving on. Performance is the key. Those who have managed to survive for years in a spiritual vacuum bring a fresh meaning to their sudden involvement with rituals, especially inclusive ones that reach out to encompass an entire congregation.

Michael and Sharon Strassfeld, whose three-volume guide to traditional practice for modern Jews reflects much of *Havurah* thinking, highlight one such communal gesture.

> At the Upper West Side *Minyan* in New York, the custom has arisen to pass the Torah from person to person after it is removed from the Ark, with great celebration and joy . . . One Shabbat, a visitor who had never seen the custom before, broke down and wept as he received the Torah and passed it on. He explained later that, on the infrequent occasions he had been to synagogue since his Bar Mitzvah, he had refused all honors offered to him because he had forgotten many of the rituals and was afraid to shame himself by making mistakes.

The Torah-passing custom was derived from a *Shacharit* prayer: They all accept the rule of Heaven, one from the other (*vechulam mekablim aleihem ol malchut shamayim zeh mizeh*). Its imaginative way of involving people is quintessentially "Havurah." Every Sacred Circle produces its own interpretation of the Jewish life our great-grandparents lived in Europe, continually trying to identify its salient components and conflate them into novel forms adapted to current circumstances.

Owing to the *Havurah*'s manageable size, its *shelichei tsibbur* have no problem being heard without the aid of amplification. This establishes an immediate rapport between them and their peers, for the sound of their voice does not emerge electronically from physically disassociated wall-or-ceiling speakers. Orthodox *Minhag* precludes the use of amplification, but the indirect "canned" sound that one routinely encounters in Reform, Conservative, and Reconstructionist services creates instant subliminal alienation among worshipers who find themselves surrounded—sometimes blasted—by disembodied voices. Control over their environment slips away, Sabbath calm retreats before weekday-like bombast, and the pervasive anomie of society at large takes over. Human beings relate better to the "echoeless, yet strangely compelling" *live* sound of other human beings (in novelist Jack Finney's words) than to mechanically boosted approximations of that sound. Amplification in synagogues, although sometimes justified by the sheer size of a room, is merely one more link in the chain that binds us to our outer-directed environment. Mechanization has so deprived us of personal choice in our daily routines that chronic indifference results. One way for people to extricate themselves from this societal torpor is via weekly involvement with like-minded folks who are committed to each other's survival as Jews. In that micro-universe, there is no place for microphones and the abuses they engender.

RETHINKING SOME *HAVURAH* STRATEGIES

The *Havurah* movement's boldest moves have swum—against the current—into the mainstream of contemporary Jewish worship. But along the way they have inevitably lost strength. Like salmon who survive all obstacles and finally return to their natal lake, exhausted, some of the best *Havurah* ideas retain barely enough strength to spawn progeny when transplanted to the inhospitable environments of Establishment synagogues. Recall the stratagem of setting aside study time to work through problematic wording or phraseology in traditional worship formulas. In too many cases it is being manipulated as a club with which to bludgeon Hebrew prayer.

Not content with that sort of slow death, New York University historian Norman F. Cantor would administer a merciful coup de grace. He calls for immediately jettisoning 80 percent of the liturgy, to be rewritten by a select group of Jewish creative spirits from the fields of music, poetry, the novel, theater, film, and television. Half the sermons in a given year would be delivered by an academic or learned lay person, one-quarter of whom would be women, and one-quarter under the age of fifty.

I second Professor Cantor's demand for rewriting liturgical translations; not 80 percent, but certainly a few of the more questionable passages. If, as Reform's *Gates of Prayer* proclaims, "*separate and APART is God*" (page 318; my emphasis), how is it possible that "*we UNITE with Him*" (page 224)? Reconstructionism's *Kol Haneshamah* has "*the voice of THE ANNOINTER making the desert writhe, of ENERGY giving pangs to the wastelands of Kadesh*" (page 38), a metonym whose paired attributes are far-fetched enough to shake all meaning out of Psalms 29. In place of "*open MY lips that my mouth may declare Your glory,*" Conservatism's *Siddur Sim Shalom* substitutes "*open

YOUR lips within me, Lord" (page 800), a figure of speech that beggars the worshiper's imagination.

Even Orthodoxy's *Art Scroll Siddur* lapses occasionally into business-like terminology, as in the paragraph following *Shema Yisrael. "You shall love . . . God . . . with all your RESOURCES"* (page 93) blunts the edge of our subconsciously remembered "with all your MIGHT," uttered by an aged Rabbi Akiva at the point of martyrdom (BT, *Berakhot* 61b).

That brings us to the crux of what any liturgical translation must provide in order to qualify for use during worship: a faithful approximation of the original's *poetic imagery.* In previous generations when synagogue-goers were more familiar with the age-old wording, there was no need for prayerbooks to differentiate between poetic and prose passages. The paragraphs all looked alike, yet people treated the versified sections as poetry, reacting instinctively to their rhymes and rhythms. Even the finest English translations—rewritten by "Jewish creative spirits," as Professor Cantor would have it—cannot approach the Classical Hebrew's loftiness of spirit or depth of feeling. The most we might hope for is a graceful vernacular approximation that would work in tandem with the original formulations.

If we are ever to reclaim Judaism's indigenous form of prayer—chant moving back and forth between *sheli'ach tsibbur* and congregation—we cannot avoid the interim step of alternating English with Hebrew in certain parts of the liturgy. Many Reform congregations are almost there without realizing it, trolling the Deuteronomic prayer mentioned previously—*Thou shalt love the Lord thy God*— in a modulated descant that is English *daven'n* in everything but name. Prayerbooks in three of the four national movements have inadvertently shown the way by printing poetic passages interlineally on facing pages. A verse that is often sung communally,

> *befi yesharim tit'halal*
> the upright shall praise You,

appears that way within the Sabbath Morning introit

> *shochen ad, marom vekadosh shemo*
> Everlasting Dweller On High

in *Art Scroll Siddur* (405); *Siddur Sim Shalom* (337); and *Kol Haneshamah* (240). The same is true of numerous other poetic texts in these three prayerbooks, Psalms in particular. Only *Gates of Prayer* arranges passages like *befi yesharim tit'halal* with Hebrew and English paragraphs one above the other (299), excluding the possibility of ever enlisting bilingual *daven'n* as a means to attain the ultimate goal of Hebrew *daven'n*.

THE QUESTION OF CONTINUITY

Regarding Professor Cantor's suggestion that laypersons regularly deliver sermons, *Havurot* long ago incorporated it into their game plan. But they have otherwise failed to provide leadership beyond the founding generation. Maintaining the fiction that nobody-and-everybody is in charge has cost *Havurot* the front-runner position in spearheading any further change on the contemporary worship scene. As Bernard Reisman confided to me by way of rationalization: "Admission that one strong personality was acting as de facto leader is antithetical to *Havurah* principles."

Havurot expect that every participant be willing to serve as leader. Left to a process of natural selection, only a few regular attendees well versed in synagogue procedure might habitually volunteer. That would result in a dictatorship of the knowledgeable few, so a permanent rotation of prayer-and-study surrogates has been implemented in order to democratize the system. This conforms with the original *Havurah* view of worship as an evolving process carried forward by the active involvement of all members. But it also lowers the common denominator precipitously, for by any objective standard most of the conscripts are not qualified to lead. Yet *Havurot* refuse to admit that the policy has failed, and rather than limit leadership to those who are truly capable they persist in making everyone suffer through excrutiatingly inept—though well-meant—mangling of the liturgy and its accepted performance conventions. To discerning visitors, much of *Havurah* worship falls under the halachic heading *sakanat nefashot* ("danger of life and limb"; JT, *Terumah* 46a), to be avoided at all costs even if it entails desecrating the Sabbath.

The dearth of *Havurah* leadership is hardest on young children forced to accompany their family-minded parents on what is essentially an adult venture. With no specific assignment to complete—while Mom and Dad recreate roles once acted by their grandfathers—the youngsters are bored to distraction. Having exhausted all their books and games after the first hour, they fidget and fight, roll on the floor and eventually run wild. Predictably, their screams go unheeded by elders engaged in a spiritual battle of their own. Those who travel exclusively within the Sacred Circles of *Havurot* seem to move in a parabola that never intersects with any other, operating as it does outside of organizational parameters. Sensing that the wholeness of Jewish life described by Mark Zborowsky and Elizabeth Herzog is vanishing, *Havurah* members seek to restore what they can as family units. Adults understandably attempt to pray as (they imagine) their great-grandparents did. But their children, sharing no memories of those religiously observant forebears whom they know only from sepia-toned photo albums, must fend for themselves. That is why, aside from grade-schoolers who enjoy no say in the matter, *Havurot* have failed to attract a second generation.

DOWN BUT NOT OUT

As for the founding generation, reports feminist writer Judy Petsonk, "As they acquired jobs and young families, more *Havurah*niks began to join synagogues, where they wouldn't have to take all responsibility for choreographing their communal religious life." In turn, they infused their new congregations with some of the spiritual energy they had found in *Havurot*, whether through study or support groups that they helped organize or in pre-existent adjuncts like a *chevrah kadisha* (burial society). But the loss of members able and willing to shoulder leadership burdens has been keenly felt by many *Havurot*. Places vacated by former seasoned participants have not really been filled. Whenever newcomers step up to the plate, spirituality's batting average takes a nosedive. As for recharging one's religious batteries at weekend or week-long retreats, Petsonk finds the current leadership's grounding in traditional Judaism decidedly weak. She characterizes some of the 1990s retreats as a series of pseudo-psychological exercises having no connection to each other. The dilution of deep Jewish content is but one reason why several of the original *Havurot* have simply dissolved.

Those that remain, however, still meet a need for many who do not feel at home in denominationally affiliated synagogues. This includes many retired rabbis, cantors, and educators who find their accumulated wisdom and expertise useful to congregations only in small doses, much as one-eyed immigrants to a country of sightless individuals might sense a certain resistance among those they are attempting to help. Other square pegs who do not fit into synagogal round holes are the unmarried or divorced. Since most congregational programs revolve around family patterns that are now outdated, singles have been unsuccessful in their quest for Jewish enfranchisement through mainstream synagogues. "There is an institutional lag," notes sociologist Rela Geffen, "everyone loves the nuclear-family image and wants to pretend it still exists." The only real choice for singles has been *Havurot*, where they can aspire to leadership and decision-making roles. It is to the credit of long-time *Havurah* members that, unlike most of their fellow Baby Boomers who are accustomed to having their every whim catered to, a certain openness of spirit and willingness to accept individuals of varying ideologies still prevails among them.

WHAT *HAVUROT* HAVE TAUGHT US

That it is possible to accept the validity of other religious viewpoints within the worshiping community while maintaining one's own values is perhaps the most important lesson we have learned from *Havurot*. They have convincingly demonstrated the viability of nondogmatic worship as a workable option to the currently insular practice of our national movements. To accomplish this, each *Havurah* has had to act as an extended family, with individual factions' wishes giving way before the greater need for group survival. It remains to be seen whether this conciliatory approach—effective in smaller-scale worship—can be expanded to fill the larger confines of most synagogues. Will a "synagogue of 2000" (to paraphrase the title of a current national project created to transform the way American Jews worship) allow itself to be led as a *Minyan* is led, by one of its own, spontaneously and without hoopla?

In this regard the time has come (as Alice's Walrus said) to talk of many things, of the growing tendency for worshipers in established synagogues to act as cabbages and the willingness of officiants to accommodate them in the role of kings. This looking-glass image stands historical reality on its head; a Jewish congregation and its prayer surrogate are expected to share initiative equally. The disenfranchisement of worshipers occurred so gradually over the last three decades that we have come to regard it as normal. No matter that ours is now the only religion on earth to wrap its worship in a play-by-play simulcast; after all (we seem to be saying), the Bible itself declared our customs "diverse from those of every other people" (Esther 3:8). Yet nowhere does Scripture mandate the sacrifice of communal prayer upon an altar of unwarranted commentary, as if each service were a case of first instance.

Havurot have shown that every act and moment of worship need not be controlled to the point where spontaneity is off-limits. Perhaps the most significant by-product of *Havurah* do-it-yourself activism is the general awareness it has created of what we have a right to expect professionally from our upcoming religious leaders. If cantorially led prayers are still to be sung and rabbinically delivered sermons to be spoken in the twenty-first century, we must begin imparting to the next generation a sense of the way these worship essentials actually sounded in the past. Current practice should only be allowed to serve as a working model if and when it works. The fact that people seem willing to regularly endure several hours of what now passes for worship does not authenticate the experience; it only means that *they are not really there.*

WHERE DO WE GO FROM HERE?

Unfortunately, today's seminary graduates have never seen or heard anything other than the current tight-laced style of prayer reading in their young lives. The phasing out of a more unbuttoned synagogue chant and rhetoric predated their adolescence. That is why any search for exemplary role models today would do better to leapfrog the immediate past and focus on a retired generation of practitioners who will shortly be gone. Those avatars of a pulpit demeanor that flourished up until very recently are the ones who should be sought out as exemplars of community surrogates. Remembering what once was and having perpetuated it even fractionally during their own careers, they have a moral obligation—as well as the leisure— to pass on its essence.

Along with serving a required apprenticeship under such tutelage, student cantors-and-rabbis should turn to performances by the very best of an earlier era, filmed in situ. When the Holocaust had barely ended, Moshe Koussevitsky—the great prewar *chazan* of Warsaw—returned to the Polish capital as part of a delegation that visited its ruined ghetto. A camera recorded the scene. On the videocassette *We Who Remain* (National Center for Jewish Film, Waltham, 1993), sights of utter devastation are the only accompaniment to Koussevitsky's recital of the memorial prayer *Eil Malei Rachamim* (Merciful God on High). It is a rendition for the ages, devoid of all guile, from one who had commanded the pinnacle of Polish Jewry—the *Bimah* of Tlomacka Synagogue—and who had been spared to commemorate its destruction. His demeanor alone, one of total commitment to the enormity of his mission, speaks volumes.

Anyone wishing to appreciate just how far today's rabbis have slipped below the communicative level of their predecessors might visit the United States Holocaust Museum's *Anti-Semitism Between the Wars* archive. There a 1934 video clip shows Stephen S. Wise, founding rabbi of New York's Free Synagogue, addressing an anti-Nazi rally in New York's Madison Square Garden, just before the final calamity befell European Jewry. Decrying the barbarous and uncivilized program of *Gleichschaltung*, which decreed that neither non-Aryans nor Jews shall be citizens of the Hitler regime, he fulminated with the moral indignation of a Jeremiah:

> I thank God tonight that we who are Jews
> no longer stand alone.
> We are not the only victims of Hitlerism!

Even so forceful a speaker as Rabbi Wise would have difficulty imparting life to the moribund readings that now stand in place of Hebrew prayers, familiar words that used to leap off the page and into your consciousness. Only *poetry*, with its rhythms and symbols, "can get into a reader," wrote Pulitzer Prize–winning novelist John Steinbeck, "open him up and while he's open introduce things on an intellectual level." The poetic portions of our liturgy—*piyyutim* and *selichot*—did precisely that. They opened you up to the great moral teachings of Judaism through their beautifully wrought imagery. Your role was to garner what you could in the time allotted and wait for the cantor to impart both meaning and form to all that you had intuited, like a master painter adding needed splashes of color to your pallid canvas. Through unexpected shifts of mode and quicksilver nuancing of phrase, he spun musical midrash out of the familiar words. You were caught up in a transcendent image of the universe that penetrated to the depths of your soul.

And then, in the words of Rabbi Herbert Bronstein, a former chairman of the C.C.A.R.'s Liturgy Committee, "the cantor broke open the heart of the people in joy and yearning to the influx of the Divine." This happened when he "created an expectation which he then both skillfully and soulfully resolved by bringing the congregation into participation through a familiar, beloved melody." In the context of *tefillah* so vivid and so completely natural, parroting responsive couplets at someone else's pace would have constituted a desecration. Instead you were given the necessary elbow room to take mental note of what you were feeling, toward yourself and toward God. Prayer began and ended with you; the cantor only set a modal stage upon which you pleaded your own cause.

Yet unless *prayer's underlying modality* is properly established, the center of both our collective and individual effort will not hold. Cantors have taken the easy way out, just as their predecessors did 100 years ago, according to historian Joseph Reider. Untutored in prayer, nineteenth-century American cantors borrowed what they knew—operatic solos—for use as congregational anthems; *Eits Chayim Hee* was habitually sung to the famous tenor air from Bizet's opera *The Pearlfishers*. Today's cantors, familiar with folk-rock but still unschooled in psalmodic chant, no longer quote arias. Instead, they stack syrupy tunes one atop the other onto any text that exceeds a single line in length, no matter how unrelated the tunes are to the words or to each other.

The relatively few congregants who show up for services with any regularity are understandably content to go along with our current charade of worship as a combined lecture and sing-along. Whether rote reading or rote singing, if done nonstop it becomes largely semiconscious activity. When, for example, the traditional appeal on behalf of those who need bodily and spiritual healing is "mailed in" as synagogal Muzak, it abrogates the *dialogue* between *sheli'ach tsibbur* and congregation that has always characterized Jewish worship: one speaks, the other responds (Chapter 4 . . . "The Half-a-Loaf Rationale"; Chapter 5 . . . "The *Chazan* as Travel Guide"). More than mere convention, this is the consummation of a *ritual act*, just as when we extend our hand in greeting, someone answers in kind. Remove that social ritual and people would simply babble at each other or bump heads like animals. Dialogue is Judaism's liturgical handshake with God, the most logical and therefore desirable manner of conducting worship; continuous reading or singing leaves no room for the congregational responses so often mentioned in rabbinic literature on prayer (*Tosefta, Rosh Hashanah* 2:18; BT, *Ta'anit* 16a; *Masechet Soferim* 19:9, 11:4). As every Bar or Bat Mitzvah is taught regarding reading from the Torah after being called up to it for the first time, one cannot answer *amein* to one's own blessing.

OUR TASK

In order to preserve the religious practice our predecessors have bequeathed to us, we would do well to learn from the consensual approach of another ancient culture. Zen Buddhism asks mainly that we render

> infinite gratitude to the past,
> infinite service to the present,
> infinite responsibility to the future.

The ultimate goal for today's *Havurot* and synagogues should be to retain enough of yesterday's liturgy along with its normative modes of performance so that tomorrow's worshipers can still inherit something sufficiently viable with which to experiment on their own.

The Epilogue summarizes numerous current attempts to attain that goal and offers suggestions concerning what remains to be done.

Epilogue
Touching the Infinite

A great performance of a great work
hangs suspended in the air
like an iridescent soap bubble.
It shimmers for a moment with meaning and beauty
and then disappears, forever ephemeral,
but while it lasts it is an epiphany.
> Jonathan Miller,
> "Bidding Farewell to the Stage,"
> *New York Times*, 1983

The synagogue constitutes one of our people's signal contributions to its own history. The weekly Sabbath witnesses God's role in that history, through three seminal rituals performed in synagogues. Sanctifiying the Sabbath through *Kiddush* on Friday evening recalls Creation, when God rested from His labors on the seventh day. Scriptural *cantillation* on Sabbath morning commemorates Revelation, when God first gave the Torah to Israel. Singing *zemirot* as a community late in the afternoon during a Third Meal anticipates Redemption, an era of eternal Sabbath.

AN ISLAND OF RITUAL IN A SECULAR SEA

By now perceptive readers might be wondering where this ceremonial approach leaves Jewish worship in America, a land to whose Puritan-influenced way of thinking all religious ritual appears as *lèse majesté*, a presumptuous gilding of Divine perfection. In a difficult position, to say the least, unless it adopts the position of Maimonides (*Mishneh Torah* 2: Laws of Prayer 1:4), which asserts that neither the form of *tefillah* nor its precise wording was ever specified by the Torah. Only as a result of exile, when Jews were forced to speak the languages of their numerous diaspora host cultures and weren't able to express themselves adequately in the Holy Tongue did it become necessary to introduce fixed prayers.

In retrospect, this remedy may have created more maladies than it cured. The major drawback in repeating identical wordings every day for a lifetime is that it becomes stultifying, reversing the natural sequence of intuitive discovery followed by systematic refinement. Statutory texts are the reasoned *end-product* of biblical Revelation, the distilled essence of Israel's religious awakening, whereas Judaism's liturgy is nothing if not an attempt to recapture that *original* sense of wonder for every worshiper as if she or he were actually experiencing the event.

To unearth the initial impact of our prayerbook's statutory texts requires a creative effort equal to the one that gave them birth. Once prayers were canonized, by definition they became exiled from the circumstances that surrounded their creation. Cast from a Paradise where they had been born of artistic thoughts, they daily await the Redemption of being taught to others by sensitive individuals who approach prayer utterance with the open stare of childhood. Breathing life into them once again means removing the surface patina left by centuries of repetition, and opening a fissure down into the unconscious depths from whence they first sprang. The words that were codified so long ago are still capable of triggering a soul-searing awareness of God's Presence—even today—if we bear in mind Jacob ben Asher's dictum: One should never repeat *tefillah* without adding something new (*Tur. Orach Chayim* 107).

Yet how are we moderns to go about improving upon prayers of personal and national aspiration that have stood unaltered over the length of our people's exile? By emulating the world's Creator "Who daily renews His creative work" *hamechadesh betuvo bechol yom tamid ma'aseh bereishit* (*Shacharit* service). Daniel Matt affirms the amazing foresight shown by this liturgical statement. Once every month a new solar system forms in our galaxy out of matter that has assimilated enough gas and dust to raise pressure and temperature to thermonuclear-reactive levels high enough to light a star. Multiplying that event by 100 billion galaxies in the known universe, Matt estimates that God is actually renewing His creative work every *second* of every day.

RENEWING LITURGY THROUGH ITS PERFORMANCE

If so, surely the liturgy, which it is our solemn duty to renew morning, noon, and night—deserves no less. To go about the task, cautions philosopher Earle J. Coleman, we must "leave behind the ego so that [our] larger self, which is continuous with others, can achieve insights by moving from the provincial to the universal." As our expanding religious understanding joins forces with an ever-improving ability to express what we feel through the familiar statutory wordings, even the most unchangeable of prayer texts will take on added layers of meaning.

Should that deeply felt expression of emotion, whose freshness truly merits the adjective "creative"—bringing something forth for the first time—take the shape of speech or of song? The late composer/conductor Leonard Bernstein found an answer in the Bible's account of Creation.

> God said: "Let there be light."
> God said: "Let there be a firmament."
> He created verbally. Now can you imagine
> God *saying*, just like that,
> "Let there be light," as if ordering lunch?
> Or even in the original language: "*y'hi or*"?
> I've always had a private fantasy of God
> *singing* those two blazing words:
> "*YEHI O-O-O-R!*"
> Now that could really have done it;
> music could have caused light to break forth.

Taking our cue from the world's Creator, can we do any less in daily renewing the liturgy (Chapter 2 . . . "Words and Music")?

We surely can, whenever we content ourselves with merely speaking the watchwords of our faith—*shema yisrael, adonai eloheinu, adonai echad*—rather than singing them. And even singing can be frittered away when not accompanied by *kavanah*. One way to zero in on the words' meaning is by *singing every syllable* very, very slowly (as opposed to prolonging only the *final* one; Chapter 2 . . . "The Old Shall Be Renewed"). I have never experienced this procedure more vividly than in Conservative Congregation Agudas Achim of Alexandria, Virginia. Worshipers held the standard melody—which hardly ever registers consciously on its own merits—in seemingly endless suspension, augmented only by the increased reverberation of their own voices' overtones.

I found myself responding with all kinds of associative thoughts and feelings, and from the mien of those around me I'm certain they did as well. It was like witnessing the world's Creation instead of reading about it. The congregation's rabbi, Jack Moline, assured me that it was the same whenever his cantor (at that time), Ramon Tasat, led the *Shema* that way. Like a good part of our liturgy, the words "Hear, O Israel, . . ." are circumscribed for all time; but the way we *utter* them should never be predictable. Prayer that is continually enlivened by the varied manner in which we sing it reconciles heart and mind, liturgical gesture and rabbinic word; it is our means of touching the infinite, if only occasionally.

NEILAH AS A FORETASTE OF ETERNITY

Under the right circumstances, says Franz Rosenzweig, "eternity is stripped of every trace of the beyond . . . it is actually there!" This happens most noticeably when evening shadows lengthen across the sanctuary as Yom Kippur day nears its end, and we stand as a congregation before God wearing our shroud (in Orthodox practice) as if we were dead in the midst of life. As the Mercy Gates are "closing" (literal meaning of *ne'ilah*), we ask leave to approach God one last time with quintessential words of praise:

> *yitgadal veyitkadash shemeh raba*
> let the world magnify and sanctify the great Name of its Creator.

Only now we intone the formulaic utterances to liturgical motifs collectively known as a *reshut*, or "permission." Jewish tradition assigns the appellation *Nigunei Misinai* (Sinai tunes) to these ancient petitionary phrases, as if they had been handed down to Moses along with the other commandments. They share the same plagal/minor modal structure as Kol Nidre motifs (Chapter 4 . . . "Guilt Feelings Expressed through Religious Music"), moving between a fourth-or-fifth below the tonic and a second-or-third above. The difference lies in emphasis. Here it is *upward-thrusting protest* against the finality of whatever decree is about to be sealed, rather than *passive downward acceptance* of our fate. Leonard Bernstein opened his *Jeremiah Symphony* with the *reshut* motif, and *chazanim* cite it throughout the High Holidays when beginning a new liturgical section:

> *Ochilah la'eil, achaleh fanav*
> I look to the Lord, I entreat His Presence
>
> ```
>                            leh
> (tonic:) >o-          eil,              fa-
>                                              nav.
>          chi-      la-      acha-
>          lah
> ```

By *Neilah* time the Prophet Isaiah's "highway *for* our God" (40:3) has become a two-way thoroughfare in our lonely desert of Atonement, leading us *to*

God. In lieu of periodic tolls we offer increasingly fervent supplications (*Petach Lanu Sha'ar*).

> O Lord, let prayer's gate remain open to Thy children.

Our *Misinai* tune of entreaty expands—along with its accompanying texts—as evening draws near (*Hayom Yifneh*).

> The daylight fades,
> the sun is almost gone,
> yet we approach Thy radiant portals.

With nightfall, the musical range of our ancient chant stretches ever upward as it attempts to storm the very ramparts of God's Heavenly Palace (*Sha'arei Shamayim Petach*).

> Unlock for us the gates of repentance,
> and extend to us the bounty of Thy forgiveness;
> pardon our iniquity and rebuke us not,
> help us, save us, O God of our salvation!

At the end of the day it is not celestial entryways that open to our pleading, but the inner gateway of our own heart, which through penitent fasting and a determination to do better is at last ready to accept the yoke of God's sovereignty. We proclaim the identical Confessional (*vidui*) that a Jew recites on the death-bed—*Adonai Hu Ha'elohim*, "The Lord is God"—but in a melody that now shifts ultimately from petition to praise. Only then are we ready to resume our place among the living, having climbed one of those rare liturgical peaks where form and content are in paradigmatic symmetry.

A DISPELLER OF GLOOM

Descent from that lofty summit to the valley of the shadow of current practice can prove a sobering experience. Yet there remain crannies below where the sun still penetrates, illuminating not quite to the extent of Yom Kippur's awesome finale, but providing at least enough light for Simchat Torah rejoicing or Purim celebration. One of those bright spots is occupied by Reform Temple Beth El in Somerville, New Jersey.

Its energetic young rabbi, Arnold S. Gluck, observed the way some congregations indiscriminately invite youngsters of all ages to come dashing up onto the *Bimah* just before *Neilah*'s conclusion and then permit them to mill around aimlessly as if at a playground. He decided that his own congregation would conclude Yom Kippur in a dignified manner and yet not leave anyone out, even infants. Following the lead of Denver's Alliance Synagogue (as well as that of forward-looking churches around the country), he had his Building Committee install a glass-fronted room along one sanctuary wall. It faces toward the *Bimah* at an angle from slightly behind the congregation so as not to distract anyone from worship, and it provides comfortable seating and piped-in sound. Nothing that goes on in that "Cry Room" is heard in the sanctuary, but the message to parents is clear: "If you have small children, don't stay home; bring them to any service, including *Neilah*. You don't have to police them, only be with them." Rabbi Gluck maintains that if they hear it often enough, even two-year-olds can learn the liturgy by heart. (The corollary: so can adults who may not recall it readily from childhood; Chapter 2 . . . "What Synagogues Must Do Now").

The rabbi treats *Hakafot* circuits around the sanctuary's perimeter on the Eve of Simchat Torah in equally imaginative fashion. He has arranged it so that seating—while comfortable enough to give an impression of permanence—is fully movable. Seven Torahs are danced in processional around the cleared center of the sanctuary, after which a single Scroll is completely unrolled around the center area's perimeter so that everyone can see its closing words at one end

> *le'einei kol-yisrael*
> in the sight of all Israel

overlapping its opening words at the other end

> *bereishit bara elohim*
> in the beginning, God created.

The unfurled parchment is held aloft by fifty-four congregants who have prepared capsule summaries of every weekly portion. They review the entire Five Books of Moses orally, *sidrah* by *sidrah*, before a reader officially concludes one yearly cycle by chanting the final column of *Vezot Habrachah* (Deuteronomy 34) and immediately begins another with the initial column of *Bereishit* (Genesis 1).

The Purim Eve service is another occasion that openly invites high jinks in many synagogues. Added to ritually condoned noisemaking (Chapter 4 . . . "Enlisting the Liturgy's Built-in Motivational Devices") is the surrealism of officiants and worshipers sporting all sorts of outlandish costumes as they impersonate clowns or comic strip characters. To keep the hilarity of masquerade from turning Purim Eve's *Megillah* reading into farce, Rabbi Gluck subsumes its burlesque element into a nobler purpose: bringing together all of the generations within his congregation and providing them with a meaningful and stimulating project in whose successful outcome they share a mutual stake. As on Simchat Torah, this joint activity takes place in the synagogue's cleared center area. After *Maariv*, episodes cantillated from the *Megillah* are interpreted dramatically by different groups of players, each appropriately outfitted for its particular scenario. The casts—often entire families from grandparents to toddlers—vie with one another for weeks beforehand in devising outrageous twists of plot or hilariously incongruous endings to the familiar episodes. And the winner is: *everyone!*

ADDITIONAL POINTS OF LIGHT

The preceding eight chapters have discussed many other innovations across the United States and Canada designed to involve worshipers actively in the liturgy and its attendant rituals. Beginning in the 1970s and for twenty years thereafter, hundreds of young choristers in Dayton's Beth Abraham experienced the closest thing to a modern Levitical apprenticeship, practically living on their synagogue's premises as they studied and performed an enormous body of sacred music written specifically for them (Chapter 6 . . . "Rekindling the Flame"). In Des Moines's Tifereth Israel, hundreds more meticulously trained children and adults are still competing for the honor of leading Preliminary and Weekday services throughout the year, on a level of competence that professionals might envy (Chapter 2 . . . "Words and Music").

The Kabbalat Shabbat service at Riverdale New York's Hebrew Institute, regularly attended by a congregation 800 strong who harmonize and dance to chasidic melodies of the late Rabbi Shlomo Carlebach, has become the local Orthodox community's weekly drawing card (Chapter 6 . . . "Rekindling the Flame"). Conservative B'nai Jeshurun and Orthodox Ohab Zedek in Manhattan between them attract some 3,000 singles, young marrieds, nonaffiliates, and neighborhood couples every Friday evening by offering a Hebrew liturgy sung almost uninterruptedly. Through the efforts of lay people inspired by the Upper West Side success story, a similar worship format is being instituted with accelerated frequency in other communities, including Greater Philadelphia and Los Angeles. In the case of Reform temples, festive "singing" services may occur only once a year. Toronto's

Holy Blossom, which had always limited its Rosh Hashanah worship to one day, now boasts Standing Room Only at a Second Day service geared to full-throated communal rendering of time-honored *piyyutim* (Chapter I . . . "What Lies Immediately Ahead").

New ways of switching worshipers from passive to active mode are being devised continually. A recent article by Conservative rabbis Cathy Felix and Elliot Schoenberg proposes sparking people's interest in ethical issues by having them act out confrontational scenes from the weekly Scripture reading in English, using the printed signs as rhetorical and melodic indicators, just as in Hebrew cantillation. The authors also suggest a method for raising the energy level of worship by moving its motive force from the pulpit back to the congregation. Worshipers seated on either side of the sanctuary would alternate lines of responsive readings, at a pace, pitch, and volume more conducive to stimulating thought and eliciting rejoinders than the robotic exercises we now tolerate (Chapter 4 . . . "Enlisting the Liturgy's Built-in Motivational Devices"). Reform rabbi Herbert Bronstein goes further, advocating return to the classic synagogue norm of psalmodic dialogue between congregation and *sheli'ach tsibbur* that ripens into allusive chazanic recitative and ultimately bears fruit as uplifting communal song (Chapter 8 . . . "Where Do We Go from Here?").

In the area of ritual, many Conservative, Reconstructionist, and Reform worshipers have adopted the Orthodox custom of deferentially raising one's *tallit* fringes as the Torah is elevated during *Hagbahah*. They also find themselves in league with Traditionalists when answering an officiant's request for leave to sanctify the Sabbath over wine (*Savrai*) with the electrifying assent: *Lechayim!* Agudas Achim of Alexandria, Virginia, is among several congregations now experimenting with prolonging their singing of the *Shema* as if hearing it for the very first time. Worshipers at Philadelphia's Conservative Beth Zion-Beth Israel may now lead Weekday, Kabbalat, and Motsa'ei Shabbat prayer facing the Ark, if they so choose. The *kohanim* among them have also re-introduced Priestly *duchan'n* during Festivals, a growing trend in Conservative congregations generally (Chapter 2 . . . "The Old Shall Be Renewed").

More and more instances of crossover into a dimension of sacred time and space keep cropping up, where the aspirations of those assembled find expression through collective acts that merge religious fulfillment with aesthetic satisfaction. In a ceremony adapted to the egalitarianism that has become part and parcel of contemporary Jewish Life Cycle celebrations, baby girls—including those born to Orthodox parents—are increasingly being welcomed into the long-neglected Covenant of Mother Sarah: Brit Benot Yisrael (or more commonly, *Simchat Bat*). In the caring hands of rabbis like Linda Holtzman (Reconstructionist) it is a ritual devoid of any downside for the tiny celebrants, whose various senses awaken with as much pomp—if not pain—as do those of their baby brothers when initiated into the Covenant of Father Abraham (Chapter 2 . . . "And the New Shall Be Sanctified").

Another developing custom in Reconstructionist circles is for relatives and friends of an engaged couple to create a decorative quilt that will serve as nuptial *chupah* and later hang in the newlyweds' home. Each square tells its own story of the bride and groom's individual childhoods or of hope for their future life together. Lovingly hand-drawn or embroidered over a period of many months, the connected messages provide a lifetime of fond reminiscences (Chapter 3 . . . "Reconfiguring the Terrain").

Congregations in three of the four national movements have taken to producing liturgies customized to the exact degree of inclusivity they desire (Chapter 3 . . . "Rewriting Road Manuals to Accommodate Women Drivers"). The best of these off-print services—Temple Israel of St. Louis's *Matanat Shabbat* and Temple Beth Sholom of Santa Ana's *Siddur T'feelat Shalom*—are concise, create their own translations that are truer to the original prayers, and place helpful transliterations close to the Hebrew. Faithful and accurate translation follows the precedent of German Jewry's Liberal prayerbook of 1929, the *Einheitsgebetbuch*, which allowed individual congregations freedom of choice as to the proportion of vernacular used in a service (Chapter 3 . . . "Reconfiguring the Terrain").

Meanwhile, the various movements' official prayerbooks have been restoring *piyyutim* and *selichot* deleted earlier, while adding ones that never appeared before: Judah Halevi's *Mi Yitneini*; Hillel Zeitlin's *Av Gadol*. These moving liturgical poems create their own mythic world in which our collective folk memories, longings, and righteous indignations come alive. They are once again being set to the most exquisitely lyrical strains by composers and sung with a loving tenderness reserved for hymns that worshipers most cherish (Chapter 3 . . . "Vernacular, a Prayer Means, Not an End").

The latest official prayerbooks—including a spectacularly improved Conservative *Siddur Sim Shalom*—now offer guidelines and instructions to assist those less familiar with the service, which should significantly reduce the frequency of intrusive announcements (Chapter 4 . . . "Keeping Worship Going"). The Conservative and Reform movements are issuing self-help books and tapes to worshipers seeking to learn the choreography of prayer as well as how to cantillate from the Torah or chant an entire service (Chapter 2 . . . "Words and Music"). The resourceful rabbinical team at Temple Beth Sholom in Cherry Hill, New Jersey, engages congregants in interrelated forums spaced between portions of the Torah reading. Each segment opens with a leading question raised by current events, which elicits answers whose implications are measured against an ethical principle set forth in that week's Torah portion (Chapter 4 . . . "Utilizing the Liturgy's Built-in Motivational Devices").

In all four national movements qualified women are beginning to assume their rightful place alongside men as community surrogates in prayer or study. Within Modern Orthodoxy a phenomenally successful National Jewish Outreach Program has sprung up that educates lay people around the world in the basics of *daven'n* and brings thousands of nonaffiliates to Shabbat dinners hosted by synagogues of all denominations (Chapter 2 . . . "Prayer Therapy That Works"). In addition, many a breakaway *Minyan* is now pushing the envelope of egalitarianism within Modern Orthodoxy, encouraging female participants to prepare and deliver in-depth talks based on the weekly *sidrah* (Chapter 3 . . . "Negotiating a Roadblock"). Finally, two Modern Orthodox congregations in New York—Lincoln Square Synagogue and the Hebrew Institute of Riverdale—have each trained and then engaged a young woman as congregational intern to teach adult classes, make hospital visitations, mentor Bat Mitzvah candidates, counsel other women in spiritual matters, and deliver monthly sermons (Chapter 8 . . . "A View from the Right").

As in the past, creative energy for liturgical renewal has arisen among a few imaginative religious leaders working individually on the local level, and then radiated outward. Rabbis David Wolpe (Los Angeles) and Shelton Donnell (Santa Ana), and Cantor Faith Steinsnyder (Spring Valley) have rediscovered two short-term techniques that I see as crucial to the long-range survival of Jewish worship in our linguistically impoverished society: *offering a transliterated version of the entire liturgy, or leading at least part of the service in chanted English* (Chapter 8 . . . "*Havurot* and Bilingual/Transliterated Prayer"). Both emergency measures are life-lines being thrown to learners until they can swim on their own. Chanting in transliteration— or in English until they master Hebrew—allows worshipers of any denomination who are unfamiliar with the liturgy to approach God in the same manner that seventy generations before them did: through prayer that is wholeheartedly sung and not simply read like a newspaper. *These are surely the two common liturgical gestures most readily accessible to us at the present moment.*

NEEDED: HEART AS WELL AS MIND

No summation of current trends would be complete without acknowledging the tremendous contribution that *Havurot* have made toward fostering tolerance for opposing viewpoints within the body religious. Despite this, a wide majority of

North American Jewry continues to reject the homey ineptitude of *Havurot* in favor of vapid but socially preferable synagogal conformity. Who can fault anyone for preferring the mindless comfort of rising and sitting on cue over the meaningful discomfort of remaining mentally alert, in a kind of animated "crouch" out of which something wonderful might develop? Two prototypical images of this dynamic concept spring to mind from the world of twentieth-century painting and sculpture: Paul Cézanne's *Large Bathers* (1906, Philadelphia Museum of Art) and Henry Moore's *Reclining Figures* (1979, Philip I. Berman Collection, Allentown).

At its best, Jewish worship incorporates moments of alertness that are analogous to a baserunner intently eyeing the pitcher's motion an instant before dashing for second or retreating back to first. Those moments represent ritually ordained détentes between holding it all in and letting it all hang out. The overwhelming need for thanksgiving that accompanied ancient Israel's deliverance at the Reed Sea—and the tremendous sense of relief felt after Yom Kippur's *Avodah* ritual when a High Priest emerged unscathed from the Holy of Holies—remain the stuff of legend. In both instances, the one unplanned and the other highly structured, *masses of worshipers capped the event's dynamic with its diametric opposite.* Moses' impulsive Song of Triumph awaited the finishing touch imparted to it by Miriam-and-the-people's measured call and response. The High Priest's formulaic mention of God's unmentionable Name in the sanctum sanctorum would have been tantamount to sacrilege were it not answered by the gathered multitude's pell-mell prostration in a jam-packed Temple courtyard.

Today that balance of aesthetic polarities in communal worship has been upset. By allowing personal Greeting and Benediction from the pulpit to be the first and last things people hear, North American Judaism has flaunted the accumulated wisdom of human experience concerning two of the three pivotal moments during a service: purposeful beginning; and inspired ending. The third moment—a sermon that would transport its hearers to another world of heightened emotion—has been blunted by the proliferation of informational "sermonettes" before and after. The efficacy of a service lies in its unexpected joining of opposites: *indirect* opening versus *direct* closing; linked by a *timely* lesson rooted in *timeless* truths. Our contemporary synagogue practice has disrupted the exquisite tension of that pyramidic symmetry. Unless we are able to shore up the structural element of *surprise*, predictability will continue to swing unchecked through the ruins of our services like a wrecking ball. How are we to regain our equilibrium or, dare I add, rebuild for the future amidst the rubble?

Through reasoned expedients like those I have just recapitulated; they take minimal liberties with prayer texts while demonstrating infinite adaptability to a changing world. They also avoid dependence upon updated rewrites whose words change meanings with every passing decade. When we alter beyond recognition what was once hallowed, we run the risk of being re-edited time and again by successive prayerbook committees. Even worse, introducing new phraseology that is not in the prayerbook in order to conform with the latest dictates of overzealous political correctness only frustrates a congregation trying to follow along.

In Mishnah *Avot* (2:2) Rabbi Tarphon admonishes those who would change the world with one broad stroke: your task is not to complete the work. It is time we recognized that creativity in prayer, as in all art, swings between the *Siddur*'s broadly undifferentiated first stage of the process—statutory *tefillah*—and the congregation's narrowly focused interpretation of that "rough" draft through individual *daven'n*. Our efforts at liturgical renewal must be able to tolerate roughness and imperfection, for if nothing is left unsaid, we shall have written off any revisions that future generations must surely make. Better to keep open prayer options whose outlines appear blurred today; they will emerge in greater clarity for our children. Single out fewer words and concentrate on their pronouncement, devise more evocative musical associations, but resist the urge to remove from circulation "coins minted by our sages." Leave them alone—in what we regard as their antiquated imagery—or we rob them of a symbolism upon which their emotional effectiveness depends. Let them surprise and delight through serendipitous performance that couches the expected in an unanticipated context, for the aim of inherited formulations is to assist worshipers in fulfilling a timelessly *re-creative* role in every generation

If the creative process is ever to resume its God-ordained course within our services, one thing is certain. We must start paying attention to the thousands of lay people across the United States and Canada who have demonstrated an unmistakable desire to re-adopt normative practice. Ironically, it was a non-Jew, American poet e e cummings, who made the best case for a return to *sung* prayer, along with a loosening of the speech-driven stranglehold that has been choking synagogue worship:

> drive dumb mankind dizzy with haranguing
> —you are deafened every mother's son—
> all is merely talk which isn't singing
> and all talking's to oneself alone

"A congregation must sing or disband," wrote Israel Abrahams near the end of his life. We can greatly improve the odds for Jewish survival on this continent by empowering our congregations through *daven'n* that bursts into song of its own accord. By stimulating the creative instinct of both worshipers and their leaders in prayer, our services would recapture their characteristic interplay of feeling and thought. Worship would transform itself from obligation to privilege, from desultory compliance to energetic group involvement. Prayer would revert to the inclusive event it once was, and the voices resounding together from every synagogue in the land might even smooth over some of the ideological rifts within our divided communities.

All of this will occur automatically the moment we begin to empower our congregations through song. Although we may be too close to unfolding events to make out the headlines, it is clear that contemporary Jewish worship is ready for a return to *the age-old synagogue dynamic of sweeping exuberance alternating with studied reflection.* Only to the extent that it is allowed to do so can we again draw upon the healing power that presently lies untapped beneath the surface of our liturgy.

Glossary

(underlined words in definitions are entered separately)

Adir Hu	"Mighty God," majestic <u>Seder</u> hymn.
Adon Olam	"Eternal God," hymn to conclude a service.
aggadah	Non-halachic narrative component of the <u>Talmud</u>.
agunah	Woman whose husband has either deserted her or refused to grant her a <u>get</u>; she remains "anchored," unable to remarry.
Aleinu	"It is for us to praise," recited toward the end of a service.
Al Hanisim	Prayer of thanksgiving for God's miraculous deliverances of the Jewish people; traditionally recited on <u>Chanukah</u> and <u>Purim</u>, now also on <u>Yom Ha'atsma'ut</u>.
Aliyah	Honor of being "called up" to the <u>Torah</u> reading.
Alleluia	Melodic exclamation of rejoicing added to normal Church <u>psalmody</u> (fifth to tenth centuries).
Amidah	Standing devotion, the core of every service; <u>Amidat</u> ("the *Amidah* of"): <u>Minchah</u>, <u>Musaf</u>, <u>Shacharit</u>.
Amsterdam/ London *Minhag*	Prayer rite of Spanish/Portuguese (Western <u>Sephardic</u>) Jewry.

241

Ani Ma'amin	"I believe with perfect faith in the Messiah's coming," twelfth among Maimonides' *Thirteen Principles of Faith.*
An'im Zemirot	"Sweet Songs I Conceive," Glory Hymn whose current "standard" melody shares its march-rhythm with other well-known <u>Ashkenazic</u> hymns: <u>*Tal*</u>, <u>*Geshem*</u>, <u>*Betset Yisrael*</u>, <u>*Eder Vahod*</u>.
Apollonian	Any art form that displays calm and measured restraint.
ari'ach al gabei leveinah	Long brick over two short bricks, staggered transcription of poetic passages in Scripture Scrolls (Song at the Sea).
Ark	In <u>Ashkenazic synagogues</u>, *Aron*; in <u>Sephardic</u>, <u>*Heichal*</u>; a cabinet—often symbolically decorated—in which <u>Torah</u> Scrolls rest, positioned in front of or recessed into the Eastern wall.
Ashkenazic	Stemming from Germany (*ashkenaz* in Hebrew) and Northern Europe; from which derives *Ashkenazim.*
authentic	"Direct" music that moves between its <u>tonic</u> and an <u>octave</u> above (<u>*Hatikvah*</u>; <u>*Eits Chayim Hee*</u>; <u>*Adon Olam*</u>).
Avinu Malkeinu	"Our Father, Our King," supplicatory hymn sung on fast days, entire month of Elul, and during the <u>High Holy Days</u>.
Avodah	Liturgical reenactment of the Second Temple's <u>Yom Kippur</u> ritual when a High Priest would enter the Holy of Holies, confess that he, his tribe, and all Israel had sinned, and emerge unscathed amid great rejoicing.
avodah	"Work," literal meaning of performing a fixed liturgy.
ba'al keri'ah	Reader who has mastered Scriptural *cantillation*, often a lay person or youngster.
ba'al tefillah	Prayer leader who has mastered modal chant, often a lay person.
ba'al(ei) teshuvah	Repentee(s), newcomer(s) to traditional Jewish practice.
Bar/Bat Mitzvah	Boy/girl who enters religious maturity at age 13/12, respectively (plural: B'nei/B'not).
Barechu	Call to prayer—"Bless Ye The Lord."
baruch haba	"Blessed are you who come in the Lord's name," priestly/levitic greeting to pilgrims arriving in the Jerusalem Temple.

Bel Canto	Italian vocal technique emphasizing beauty of sound and brilliance of performance.
Bet Din	Duly constituted rabbinic court.
Betset Yisrael	"When Israel departed from Egypt's land," Psalms 114, recited during <u>*Hallel*</u>.
Bimah	Platform from which prayer is led in a <u>synagogue</u>.
Birkat Hamazon	Grace after Meals.
Birkot Hashachar	Morning Preliminary Blessings.
Brit	"Covenant," ritual circumcision of Jewish males on the eighth day after birth.
cantabile	Free-flowing vocal delivery that lies somewhere between metered song and fluid recitative.
cantillation	Half-sung/half-spoken reading of Scripture, built from tiny melodic fragments of as few as two notes each.
chacham	"Wise Man," title conferred upon a <u>Sephardic rabbi</u> who is ripe in both years and wisdom.
Chanukah	Early winter festival commemorating the Hasmonean victory over Syrian/Greek forces in second-century B.C.E. Palestine.
chasidic	Having to do with *chasidim* ("righteous ones"; singular: chasid) who follow a <u>rebbe</u>.
chazan(im)	Cantor(s), originally <u>synagogue</u> overseers, a role that modern rabbis have assumed, now the chanter(s) of prayer and Scripture, one of two clergymen within Judaism legally recognized by U.S. Government decisions of 1966, 1978.
chevra kadisha	Burial society.
chevruta	Two <u>Talmud</u> students rehearsing arguments sure to come up in their next lecture.
chorshul	"Choral-<u>synagogue</u>" rite featuring a well-ordered service led by cantor and choir.
Chumash	Pentateuch, a volume containing the Five Books of Moses (including a <u>*Haftarah*</u> for each <u>*sidrah*</u> when intended for synagogue use).
chupah	Nuptial canopy.
citron and myrtle	Two of the four species that Jews are commanded to take in hand on <u>Sukkot</u>; palm branch and willow leaves complete the bouquet.

coloratura	Roulades of many notes on one syllable that punctuate "comma" and "period" of <u>reciting tones</u> in <u>psalmody</u>.
conversos	<u>Sephardic</u> Jews who converted under duress to Christianity during the fourteenth and fifteenth centuries.
daven'n	Yiddish for praying in an undertone, often accompanied by swaying; also, "prayer" itself.
Deconstruction	Form of criticism that analyzes a literary text so as to reveal its ideological basis.
Devar Torah	Well-documented talk based on the weekly biblical portion.
didactic mode	*Magein Avot* ("Shield of Our Forebears"), typified by the sound of <u>*Haftarah*</u> <u>cantillation</u> in the United States.
Dionysian	Any art form that allows for freely expressed emotion.
dream time	Australian Aborigine term for an idyllic prehistoric period when the foundations of their culture were laid.
Dual Torah system	A synthesis of Written and Oral Law, operative at least since the second century, B.C.E.
duchan'n	Priestly benediction, pronounced by descendants of Aaron while standing on a *duchan* (platform) during worship.
d'veikut	"Clinging," meditative type of <u>*nigun*</u>.
Eder Vahod	"Homage and adoration I offer in garlanded praise," traditionally recited during <u>*Shacharit*</u> on the second day of <u>Rosh Hashanah</u>.
Ein Sof	"The Endless One," mystical designation for God.
Eits Chayim Hee	"The <u>Torah</u> is a Tree of Life," sung when the Scroll is returned to the <u>Ark</u>.
Esnoga	"<u>Synagogue</u>" in Western <u>Sephardic</u> terminology.
folk/rock sound	Achieved by combining 1960s "<u>pushed</u>" <u>beat</u> and 1930s "<u>shuffled</u>" <u>tempo</u>.
forgiveness mode	Typified by the <u>plagal motifs</u> to which <u>*Kol Nidre*</u> is sung by <u>Ashkenazic</u> Jewry; used by Christian composers in texts that ask absolution from sin: Bach (*Saint John Passion*); Handel and Haydn (*Te Deum*); Mozart and Verdi (*Requiem Mass*).
gabbai(m)	Lay synagogue official(s).

Gaon	Titular head of Jewish religious academy or community.
Gemara	Broad exposition of laws concisely set forth in the <u>Mishnah</u>; finalized in Palestine ca. 500, in Babylon ca. 600.
gematriah	Mystical discipline that derives hidden meanings from the numerical-equivalent value of Scriptural words.
geschrigen	"Shouted" rather than sung, referring to <u>chasidic</u> performance of a *tisch nigun*.
Geshem	Prayer for "rain," recited on Sh'mini Atseret, the eighth day of <u>Sukkot</u>.
get	Rabbinically issued bill of divorce, given by husband to wife.
get zikui	Special *get* granted unilaterally without the recalcitrant husband's explicit consent.
glat kosher	Higher standard of <u>*kashruth*</u> (referring to the "smooth" or unblemished organs of a slaughtered animal).
greger	Yiddish for "noisemaker," used to obliterate every mention of the villain Haman's name during <u>Purim</u> <u>*Megillah*</u> reading.
Gresham's law	Economic principle that "bad money drives out good," later attributed to Sir Thomas Gresham (1519–1579), founder of Britain's Royal Exchange.
Haftarah	Prophetic selection that follows <u>Torah</u> reading (plural: *Haftarot*).
Hagbahah	Ceremonial lifting of <u>Sefer Torah</u>—opened several columns wide—after it has been publicly read.
Haggadah	"Telling" of Passover Exodus story during the <u>Seder</u>.
Hakafot	Ceremonial circuits around the sanctuary's perimeter on <u>Simchat Torah</u>.
halachah	Jewish Law; literally "going," a continuous process.
Hallel	"Praise," Psalms of Thanksgiving (113–118) recited on <u>Rosh Chodesh</u>, <u>Pilgrimage Festivals</u>, <u>Chanukah</u>, and now <u>Yom Ha'atsma'ut</u>.
HASHEM	"The Name," substituted for "Lord" in recent Orthodox prayer books to avoid desecration in case of inadvertent damage.

Hatikvah	Israel's national anthem, a <u>minor</u> ("sad") melody in <u>authentic</u> ("direct") form.
Havdalah	Ceremonial blessings that create a "separation" between Holy Days and weekdays, over: wine; fragrant spices; braided candle.
Havurah	Intimate prayer "group" run by its members according to egalitarian and democratic principles (plural: *Havurot*).
Heichal	"<u>Ark</u>" in <u>Sephardic synagogues</u>.
hidur mitzvah	"Adorning" or exceeding the required measure in fulfilling a commandment.
High Holy Days	*Yamim Nora'im*, period from first (<u>Rosh Hashanah</u>) to tenth (<u>Yom Kippur</u>) of Hebrew month Tishrei, falling in early September to early October.
Hineni He'ani Mima'as	"Here I stand, deficient in deeds"; <u>introit</u> to <u>High Holy Day</u> *Musaf*, traditionally sung by a *chazan* from the rear of the <u>synagogue</u> as if first entering.
hitpallel	"To pray," reflexive Hebrew verb connoting intensive self-examination.
Inquisition	"Holy Office" of Spanish Catholic Church, which rooted out many thousands of suspected "Judaizers" among <u>New Christians</u> between 1478 and 1834, torturing and either burning them at the stake or reaccepting them into the Church.
introit	Opening devotional act of a religious service, usually performed rather than spoken.
Ir Hadamim	"Bloody City," referring to Vienna, which expelled its Jews in 1421 and again in 1670.
Kabbalah	"That which is received," study of the mysteries surrounding God and Creation.
Kabbalat Shabbat	"Receiving the Sabbath," service preceding *Ma'ariv* proper on Friday evening.
Kaddish	Laudation affirming God's domain over the universe that He created.
kal vachomer	*A fortiori*, exegetical principle whereby inference is drawn from a minor premise to a major one; for example, an act forbidden on weekdays is surely forbidden on Sabbath.

kashruth	Dietary laws; from *kasher*, "proper."
kavanah	Rabbinically mandated license for self-expression within the fixed forms of worship.
Kedushah	Prayer sanctifying God, built around congregational responses from Isaiah 6:3, Ezekiel, 3:12, Psalms 146:10. (<u>*Kedushat Minchah*</u> in its basic form; expands to <u>*Kedushat Shacharit.*</u>)
Kedushat Musaf	Sanctification prayer for Additional service, with added congregational responses from Deuteronomy 6:4 and Numbers 15:41.
kehillah	Organized Jewish religious community.
kenesset hagedolah	Great Assembly, first convened in Jerusalem ca. 300 B.C.E.
keva	Rabbinic principle of adherence to fixed forms in worship.
Kiddush	Ceremonial blessing over wine to "sanctify" a holy day; also, a light repast accompanying the ceremony.
Kitah	"Group" in Hebrew, more familiarly known as <u>*Havurah.*</u>
klei chomos	"Instruments of Violence"; derogatory acronym for <u>*chazan*</u>-*meshorer-singer* (cantor, bass, and boy soprano), generic trio that led German synagogue worship up until the early-nineteenth century.
klezmer	Contraction of the Hebrew *k'lei zemer* for "musical instruments," street musician hired to play at Jewish weddings in Eastern Europe.
kohanim	Priestly descendants of Aaron (singular: *kohen*).
Kol Nidre	"All Vows," atonement prayer for unfulfilled personal commitments to God.
K'ri'at Hatorah	Weekly Scripture reading.
Kumzitz	Yiddish for "come, sit" sing-along session.
Ladino	Judeo-Spanish spoken by <u>Sephardic</u> Jews.
Lamenatsei'ach	"To the Leader," heading in over a third of the Psalms, which, along with alternating subject pronoun (I/We), suggests responsive performance.
Laudatory mode	*Adonai Malach*, "The Lord Reigns," typified by <u>Ashkenazic</u> chanting of Psalm 93.
lehakriv	"Draw near" (to God), the real intent of sacrifices—*korbanot;* from the same Hebrew root *(k-r-v).*

Levites	Descendants of Aaron who sang and played musical instruments during the sacrificial rite in both Temples, and who also led prayer in the Second Temple's <u>synagogue</u>, *lishkat hagazit*.
Liberale	Moderately Liberal synagogues in German-speaking lands (as opposed to more radical Reform).
Limpieza de sangre	"Purity of Blood," racist pretext for the Spanish Catholic Church's persecution of <u>New Christians</u> in the fifteenth and sixteenth centuries.
Lineale	"Line" of aesthetic demarcation observed in Central European synagogues—no contributing element within a service crossed it by drawing attention to itself.
lishkat hagazit	"Chamber of Hewn Stone" in Second Temple, called *Solomon's Portico* in the New Testament; it doubled as a <u>synagogue</u> and as seat for the High Court of Justice (Great Sanhedrin).
liturgy	From the Greek for "public service" of God through worship.
logogenic	"Word-based" singing whose form is determined by language.
Ma'ariv	Evening service (*Arvit* in <u>Sephardic</u> terminology).
Maggid	Preacher.
Maggidischer moshel	"Preacher's parable" in Yiddish (*Osso Boiker*).
Mah Nishtanah	"Why is this night different?", four questions asked by the youngest at Passover Eve <u>Seder</u>.
major mode	"Happy"-sounding music (liturgically associated with praise of God), stemming from unconscious adult memories of pleasurable cooing that followed gratification of oral needs during infancy.
Makamat	Islamic system of musical <u>modes</u> that revolve around a fixed <u>tonic</u> (singular: *Makam*).
Maoz Tsur	<u>Chanukah</u> hymn of victory and praise.
Marranos	"Swine" in Medieval Spanish; "coerced" in Portuguese; pejorative applied by the Catholic Church to <u>New Christians</u> suspected of practicing Judaism in secret.
matbei'a shetav'u bivrakhot	Order of Statutory blessings instituted by the <u>Kenesset Hagedolah</u> and codified in the <u>Mishnah</u>.

Mazal Tov!	"Good Luck!", traditional Jewish congratulatory wish.
mechitzah	Partition separating the sexes in a <u>synagogue</u>.
Megillah	Generally, a Scriptural scroll; specifically, the Scroll of Esther read on <u>Purim</u>.
Melaveh Malkah	"Ushering-out of the Queen," post-Sabbath gathering featuring food, drink, and song, meant to prolong the Day of Rest.
merkavah	Second-century mystical school devoted to the Heavenly "Chariot" envisioned in Ezekiel I.
Meshumad(im)	Apostate(s).
midrash	Rabbinic "search" for hidden textual meaning.
mikdash me'at	"Temple-in-miniature," referring to a <u>synagogue</u>.
Minchah	Afternoon service.
Minhag	A community's worship rite.
minor mode	"Sad"-sounding music (liturgically associated with petitioning God), stems from unconscious adult memories of anguished crying that preceded gratification of oral needs during infancy.
Minyan(im)	Prayer quorum(s), traditionally ten adult males; now ten adult men or women in movements other than Orthodox.
Mi Shebeirach	"May the One Who blessed our forebears . . . ", invocation of God's blessing on behalf of a celebrant or <u>*Aliyah*</u> honoree.
Mishnah	The basic Oral Law, codified ca. 200.
mitnagdim	Staunch opponents of <u>chasidic</u> practice.
mitzvot	Biblical commandments mandatory to Orthodoxy, "sacred obligations" to Reform(singular: mitzvah).
mode	"Manner" of singing prayers according to a traditional pattern and sequence of <u>motifs</u>.
motif	Short, recurring musical phrase.
Motsa'ei Shabbat	"Sabbath's Departure," Saturday night.
muezzin	"Crier" who calls the Muslim faithful to prayer at five specific hours of the day.
Musaf	"Additional" service later in the morning, following <u>*Shacharit*</u>.
Neilah	"Closing" of the Mercy Gates, <u>*Yom Kippur*</u>'s final service.

New Christians	Spanish or Portuguese Jews who converted to Christianity in the fourteenth to sixteenth centuries.
nigun(im)	<u>Chasidic</u> tune(s) sometimes sung to words and/or danced: *dveikut* (meditative); *rikud* (lively); *tisch* (raucous).
Nigunei Misinai	"Sinai tunes," liturgical <u>motifs</u> so revered they were thought to have been handed down to Moses along with the other commandments.
octave	Span of eight musical notes.
olamim	Four (mystical) "worlds" that God established for humankind at the time of Creation: *Asiyah,* "Action"; *Yetsirah,* "Formation"; *Beriah,* "Creation"; *Atsilut,* "Emanation."
Oneg Shabbat	"Sabbath delight," collation—often with lecture—following services.
parallelistic structure	Verse form in which a consequent phrase echoes its antecedent's thought in different words.
parnas	President of a congregation.
parochet	Curtain fronting the <u>Ark</u> in a <u>synagogue</u>.
payes	Yiddish term for <u>chasidic</u> earlocks; *pei'ot* in Hebrew.
Pesach	"Passover," early spring <u>Pilgrimage Festival</u> commemorating the Israelites' Exodus from Egypt during the fourteenth century B.C.E.
Pesukei Dezimra	"Verses of Song" recited prior to the <u>*Shacharit*</u> proper of a morning service.
Pilgrimage Festivals	<u>Pesach</u>, <u>Shavuot</u>, <u>Sukkot</u>.
piyyut(im)	Liturgical poem(s) praising God, inserted into the liturgy beginning in the sixth century; from the Greek *poietes,* "poet."
plagal	"Indirect" music that moves from approximately four notes below its *tonic* to five or six above it (*La Marseillaise; Rule Brittania;* <u>*Shalom Aleichem*</u>; <u>*Yedid Nefesh*</u>).
plainsong	Basic ritual chant of all Christian Church rites (see: <u>psalmody</u>).
Posek(s)	Halachic consultant(s).
postapocryphal	Writings that relate to ideas and figures in Hebrew Scriptures and describe Jewish traditions from 200 B.C.E.

to 200 C.E., but which do not appear in the Septuagint, a pre-Christian translation of the canonized books by Jewish scholars; collectively called pseudepigrapha.

postmodern — Any art form characterized by a softening of intellectually induced rigidity and the introduction of whimsical elements previously considered embarrassingly out of date.

precentor — One who leads the singing of congregational prayer.

psalmody — <u>Parallelistic</u> form of chant—featuring <u>reciting tones</u> and <u>coloratura</u>—that pauses midway as if posing a musico-rhetorical question ("comma"), and then supplies an answer ("period").

Psalm tones — Chant formulas for liturgical recitation in the Catholic Church.

Purim — Late winter festival commemorating Persian Jewry's deliverance from annihilation in the fifth century B.C.E.

"pushed" beat — Anticipating any beat in a 4/4 bar an eighth note ahead of time and holding it through the actual beat (*the answer, my friend, is blowin' in the wind*).

rabbi — *Rav* in Hebrew; originally a teacher and arbiter of Jewish Law, now the one who oversees services, original role assigned to a *chazan* in the <u>Mishnah</u>.

Ramah songs — Sing-along melodies based on American folk and popular music, which counselors at Conservative Ramah Summer camps adapted to liturgical texts in the 1960s, many since becoming prayer staples.

rebbe — Yiddish for "rabbi" or "teacher," contemporary <u>chasidic</u> leader.

reciting tones — Pitch levels at which most voices recite the bulk of <u>psalmody</u>-style prayer; many syllables on one note.

resh galuta — Exilarch, Babylonian Jewry's civil leader during the Middle Ages.

reshut — "Permission" that the <u>*chazan*</u> requests when approaching God at the beginning of a <u>High Holy Day</u> liturgical section, by quoting <u>*Nigunei Misinai*</u>.

Ribono Shel Olam — Master of the Universe.

rikud — "Dance," lively type of <u>*nigun*</u>.

Rosh Chodesh	New Moon, signaling the first day of a Hebrew month.
Rosh Hashanah	Jewish New Year, first of the <u>High Holy Days</u>, falling in September.
sakanat nefashot	Danger to life and limb, the avoidance of which overrides most commandments.
saraf	Bronze serpent fashioned by Moses at God's command and mounted on a standard so that anyone bitten by Divinely-sent snakes (as punishment for their complaining) could look upon it and recover.
Savrai . . . Lechayim	"By your leave" . . . "to life," ceremonial request for permission to recite <u>*Kiddush*</u>, answered with whole-hearted congregational assent as wine is sipped by the <u>*sheli'ach tsibbur*</u>.
Seder	Ritual meal on <u>Pesach</u> Eve, in which every member of the family participates.
Sefer Torah	Parchment scroll on which the Five Books of Moses are handwritten in special ink, often richly mantled and crowned with silver or gold ornaments.
sefirot	Ten progressively ascendant attributes of God in the <u>Kabbalah</u>.
selichot	Penitential prayers—originally biblical—inserted into the liturgy beginning in the ninth century; from *selichah*, "forgiveness."
Sephardic	Jews originating first in Spain (*sepharad* in Hebrew), later the Levant; from which derives <u>Sephardim</u> (singular: <u>*Sephardi*</u>).
Se'udah Sh'lishit	Third Sabbath Meal, taken between <u>*Minchah*</u> and <u>Ma'ariv</u> services.
Shabbat	Sabbath (*shabbes* or *shabbos* in colloquial parlance).
Shabbat Hagadol	Sabbath preceding <u>Pesach</u>.
Shabbat Nachamu	Sabbath following <u>Tishah B'Av</u>.
Shabbat Shuvah	Sabbath preceding <u>Yom Kippur</u>.
Shacharit	Morning service.
Shalom Aleichem	"Peace Be unto You," one of several Sabbath <u>*zemirot*</u> sung prior to reciting <u>*Kiddush*</u> on Friday night.
"Shape-Note" Singing	System of sight-reading by means of four successive note symbols, each differently shaped, the notes form-

	ing a musical "template" that can be moved to cover the entire range of a hymn.
Shavuot	Late spring <u>Pilgrimage Festival</u> commemorating God's Revelation at Sinai as well as the Jewish people's acceptance of the <u>Torah</u>.
Shechinah	God's "Presence," understood by students of <u>Kabbalah</u> as the feminine component of Divinity; *sh'chineh* in Yiddish.
sheli'ach tsibbur	Surrogate of the community in prayer (feminine, *shelichat tsibbur*; plural, *shelichei tsibbur*).
Shema Uvirkoteha	Credo and its Accompanying Benedictions in <u>*Ma'ariv*</u> and <u>*Shacharit*</u> services.
Shema Yisrael	Judaism's Credo: "Hear, O Israel, the Lord our God is One!"
Shirat Hayam	"Song at the Sea," expressing thanksgiving and praise, sung by Moses—later by Miriam—and the Israelites after they had miraculously crossed through the Reed Sea on dry land.
Shirei Kavod	Glory Hymns to conclude a service.
Shir Hakavod	"Hymn of Glory" by Rabbi Judah of Regensburg (thirteenth century); its currently popular melody features a drum-beat rhythm.
shluchim	Lubavitcher <u>chasidic</u> outreach workers.
Shoshanat Yaakov	"Jacob Rejoiced," celebratory hymn that follows the *Megillah* reading on Purim.
shtetl	Small town in seventeenth- to nineteenth-century Eastern Europe.
shtibl	<u>Chasidic</u> prayer-and-study room.
"shuffled" tempo	Delaying every other eighth note in a 4/4 bar just a fraction (*every little breeze seems to whisper: Louise*).
shul	Yiddish for "<u>synagogue</u>."
Siddur(im)	Prayer book(s).
sidrah	Weekly <u>Torah</u> portion.
Simchat Bat	Naming ceremony for a newborn Jewish daughter; also *Brit Benot Yisrael*, "Rejoicing over a Girl."
Simchat Torah	The final day of <u>Sukkot</u>.
sprechgesang	Speech/song, a highly inflected style of declamation

	used by modern composers. (Bloch's *Sacred Service:* "We Therefore Hope in Thee.")
study mode	Melodic pattern that keeps repeating—with variations—for reviewing passages of Scripture or <u>Talmud</u> (*Mah Nishtanah* on <u>Seder</u> night).
Sukkot	Early autumn <u>Pilgrimage Festival</u> commemorating the Israelites' survival in temporary huts ("tabernacles") during their forty-year wandering through the wilderness.
sulam	"Ladder," a musical <u>mode</u> for singing prayers; the numerical value (*<u>gematriah</u>*) of its Hebrew letters totals 136, the same as *kol* ("voice").
supplicatory mode	*Ahavah Rabah* ("Abounding Love"), typified by the "begging" melody to which <u>*Avinu Malkeinu*</u> is sung on fast days.
"sympathetic" notes	Specific musical pitches that, when sounded, cause the interior space in narrow, high-ceilinged buildings to vibrate sympathetically.
synagogue	From the Greek *synagein*, a place for "bringing together"; open-air spaces in ancient times.
Tal	Prayer for "Dew," recited on first day of <u>Pesach</u>.
tallit	Fringed and striped prayer shawl (plural: *tallitot; taleisim* in Yiddish).
Talmud	Compilation of Jewish Oral Law including <u>Mishnah</u> and <u>Gemara</u> with multiple rabbinic commentaries; in sixty-three tractates, finalized in Palestine ca. 500, in Babylon ca. 600.
te'amim	"Neumes," Masoretic symbols indicating melody primarily, plus accent and grammar during <u>cantillation</u> of Scripture.
tefillat haderech	Prayer that travelers offer before undertaking a journey.
tefillat haregesh	Fervid improvisational style of worship (<u>Dionysian</u>).
tefillat haseder	Elegant but predictable style of worship (<u>Apollonian</u>).
tefillin	Leather phylacteries bound upon one's weaker bicep and upon one's forehead.
Teivah	Ballustraded platform upon which the *chazan* chants and <u>cantillates</u> <u>Torah</u> in <u>Sephardic</u> <u>synagogues</u>.

teshuvah	"Repentance," including acknowledgment, remorse, a resolve never to repeat the transgression, and the asking of forgiveness.
Tetragrammaton	"Four-letter" acronym for God (Y H V H), in ancient times pronounced as written only on <u>Yom Kippur</u> by the High Priest; today it is generally replaced by the reverential pseudonym *Adonai* or <u>*HASHEM*</u>, "the Name."
tikkun	Retrieving scattered sparks of Light that was there at Creation through righteous living and charitable deeds, thereby "restoring" the world's perfection (*tikkun olam*).
tisch	"Table," at which *rikud nigunim* are sung raucously during festive <u>chasidic</u> meals.
Tishah B'Av	"Ninth of Av," midsummer fast commemorating the destruction of both Temples, plus numerous other national calamities.
to'aniyot	Women "advocates" on behalf of other women in courts of Jewish Religious Law (singular: *to'anit*).
tohu vavohu	The chaotic, "empty" space of Genesis, Chapter I.
tonic	In Middle Eastern music a fixed tone toward which all chants gravitate; in Western music the principal tone of a melody, often its final one.
Torah	Originally only the Five Books of Moses, now including Prophets and Sacred Writings together with Oral Law transmitted in later commentaries.
torah umada	Motto of Modern Orthodoxy, a synthesis of religious teaching and secular knowledge.
Tosefta	Compilation of commentaries that were not included in the codified <u>Mishnah</u>.
tremula voce	Quavering-voice technique of singing or chanting; still heard in <u>synagogues</u> today, and in churches up until the mid-sixteenth century.
Tropes	Elaborate new texts and melodies added in the tenth to twelfth centuries to existent chants of the Roman Catholic Church; not to be confused with *trop*, <u>Yiddish</u> term for <u>*te'amim*</u>.
tzaddik	"One who has stood the test of righteousness," early <u>chasidic</u> leader.

Vaad Harabanim	Rabbinical council.
Vespers	Roman Catholic Evensong service.
vidui	Deathbed confessional acknowledging God.
Vota mea Domini	"I will pay my vows unto God" (Psalms 116), Scriptural Antiphon sung during Vespers.
Weekday mode	Ancient way of chanting <u>*Birkot Hashachar*</u> in the <u>synagogue</u>, Vespers in the Catholic Church.
Yahrzeit	Anniversary of a person's death.
Yang	Nature's active element in Far Eastern cosmology.
Yarmulke	Skullcap.
Yedid Nefesh	"Beloved of the Soul," one of several Sabbath <u>*zemirot*</u> often sung as an <u>introit</u> to <u>Kabbalat Shabbat</u>.
yeshivah	Religious academy; *ishiba* in <u>Ladino</u>.
Yiddish	Rich jargon of Middle High German, Hebrew, and Slavic elements spoken by <u>Ashkenazic</u> Jews, mostly from Eastern Europe.
Yigdal	"Praise the Living God," hymn to conclude a service.
Yin	Nature's passive element in Far Eastern cosmology.
Yizkor	Memorial service, held on <u>Pilgrimage Festivals</u> and <u>Yom Kippur</u> in <u>Ashkenazic</u> synagogues, only on Yom Kippur in <u>Sephardic</u> synagogues.
Yom Ha'atsma'ut	Israel Independence Day, falling between late Arpil and mid-May.
Yom Kippur	Day of Atonement, holiest event of the Jewish year, falling between mid-September and early October.
Young Israel	National chain of Modern Orthodox <u>synagogues</u> that originally stressed decorum and featured their own melodies in mass congregational singing.
zemirot	Quasi-liturgical table hymns sung during meals on Holy Days and other celebratory occasions (singular: *zemirah*).
Zohar	Book of "Splendor," Jewish mysticism's primary source, compiled by Moses b. Shemtov de Leon in the thirteenth century.

Bibliography

Prologue—Discovering a Norm

An Sky, S. *The Dybbuk* (1925). Translated by Joseph C. Landis (New York: Bantam Books, 1966).

Rosenzweig, Franz. *The Star of Redemption* (1921). Translated by William W. Hallo (New York: Holt, Rinehard, and Winston, 1971).

Chapter 1—Cycling Creatively

Abrahams, Israel. *Jewish Life in the Middle Ages* (1896). (London: Atheneum, 1969).

Adler, Israel. *La Pratique Musicale Savante dans quelques Communautés Juives en Europe aux XVIIe et XVIIIe Siècles* I, Paris: Mouton, 1966. *Synagogal Art Music*, 1978. *XIIth-XVIIIth Centuries*, two-LP album with fourteen-page annotated folio (Tel Aviv: Anthology of Musical Traditions in Israel, 1978).

Baron, Salo. *Steeled by Adversity* (Philadelphia: Jewish Publication Society, 1971).

Bresselau, Meyer Israel. *Cherev Nokemet N'kam B'rit* (1819). Michael A. Meyer. "The Early Nineteenth Century and Viennese Jewry." In *The Legacy of Cantor Salomon Sulzer.* Conference at Hebrew Union College, New York, December 8–10, 1991.

Coughlin, Charles, and Donald I. Warren. *Radio Priest* (New York: Free Press, 1996).

Donne, John. "Meditation XVII." In *Devotions upon Emergent Occasions* (1624). *The Literature of England I.* Edited by G. Woods, H. Watt, and G. Anderson (Chicago: Scott, Forseman, 1947).

Ehrenzweig, Anton. *The Hidden Order of Art* (Berkeley: University of California Press, 1967).

Gautier, Théophile. "Variations sur le Carnaval de Venise sur Les Lagunes." In *Emaux et Camées* (1852). *Nineteenth Century French Verse.* Edited by Joseph Galland and Roger Cros (New York: Appleton-Century-Crofts, 1931).

Gordon, Judah Leib. "Hakitsah, Ami." In *Kitvei Y. L. Gordon II* (ca. 1870). Edited by J. Fichman (Tel Aviv: n.p., 1960).

Green Fields (1910). Peretz Hirschbein (Vilna: B. Kletskin, 1929).

Hoffman, Lawrence. *Covenant of Blood* (Chicago: University of Chicago Press, 1996).

Lanchester, John. *The Debt to Pleasure* (New York: Henry Holt, 1996).

"Letter of Aristeas." In *The Old Testament Pseudepigrapha*, Vol. 2. Translated by R. J. H. Shutt. Edited by James H. Charlesworth (Garden City, N. Y.: Doubleday, 1985).

Leviant, Curt. *The Man Who Thought He Was Messiah* (Philadelphia: Jewish Publication Society, 1990).

Liszt, Franz. "Les Israelites." In *Des Bohémiens et de leur musique en Hongrie* (1859). (Leipzig: Breitkopf and Hertel, 1881).

Manners, Ande. *Poor Cousins* (New York: Coward, McCann, and Geoghegan, 1972).

"Mannheimer, Isaac Noah." Max Grunwald. *Vienna.* Translated by Solomon Grayzel (Philadelphia: Jewish Publication Society, 1936). Bernard Suler. *Encyclopedia Judaica,* Vol. 2. (Jerusalem: Keter, 1972), pp. 590–591.

McLuhan, Marshal. *Understanding Media—The Extensions of Man* (New York: McGraw-Hill, 1964).

Mendele Mocher Sforim. *Fishke der Krumer* (1869) (Kiev, n.p., 1929).

Nachman of Bratslav. Hillel Zeitlin. "Al Haneginah." In *Lachasidim Mizmor.* Edited by M. Geshuri (Jerusalem: Hat'chiyah, 1936).

Nietzsche, Friedrich. "The Birth of Tragedy through Music 1872–1886." In *Nietzsche.* Translated and edited by Walter Kaufmann (New York: Vintage Books, 1968).

Pepys, Samuel. *Diary* (London: H. Colburn, 1848–49).

"Protocols of the Elders of Zion." Mattvei Golovinsky (1905). Michael Lepekhine. *L'Express,* November 18–24, 1999. Douglas Davis, "Russian Aristocrat Fingered as Author of 'Protocols,'" *Jewish Exponent,* Nov. 25, 1999.

Puccini, Giacomo. *Madama Butterfly.* Libretto by Luigi Illica and Giuseppe Giacosa, Milan, G. Ricordi, 1904.

Riskin, Shlomo. "Dreaming Joseph's Dreams." *Jewish Post and Opinion,* November 29, 1991.

Rosenblatt, Samuel. *Yossele Rosenblatt* (New York: Farrar, Straus, and Young, 1954).

Roth, Henry. *From Bondage* (New York: Picador, 1994).

Ruskin, John. *Sesame and Lilies* (London: Smith, Edler, 1865).

Schick, Alfred. "The Vienna of Sigmund Freud." *The Psychoanalytic Review* (Winter 1968–1969), pp.529–551.

Sendrey, Alfred. *Music in Ancient Israel* (New York: Philosophical Library, 1969).

"Sympathetic Notes." P. H. Parkin, H. R. Humphreys and J. R. Cowell. *Acoustics, Noise and Buildings* (London: Faber, 1979).

Trible, Phyllis. "Eve and Miriam: From the Margins to the Center." In *Feminist Approaches to the Bible*. Edited by Hershel Shanks (Washington, D. C.: Biblical Archaelogy Society, 1994).

Trollope, Frances.*Vienna and the Austrians*, Vol. I (London: n.p., 1837).

Whitfield, Stephen. Thomas J. Brady. "How the 'Killer' Inspired a Jewish History." *Philadelphia Inquirer*, December 12, 1999.

Wise, Isaac Mayer. *Reminiscences.* Translated by David Philipson (Cincinnati: Leo Wise, 1901).

Chapter 2—A Few Ground Rules

"Aleinu." Text ascribed to the Academy of Rav (third century). Traditional chant notated by Aron Friedmann. *Schir Lisch'laumau* (Berlin: Deutsche-Israelischen Gemeindebunde, 1901).

Ani Ma'amin. Twelfth-century text by Maimonides. Melody by Azriel David Fastag, 1943. Arranged by Max Helfman. *Song of Faith* (New York: Transcontinental, 1948).

"Ashamnu." *Seder Rav Amram Gaon* (875). *High Holy Day Prayer Book.* Translated by Philip Birnbaum (New York: Hebrew Publishing Company, 1951), p. 547.

Bach, Johann Sebastian. "O Haupt voll Blut und Wunden." In *Saint Matthew Passion* (1729). *Chorales I.* Edited by Charles Boyd and Albert Riemenschneider (New York: G. Schirmer, 1939).

Baron, Salo. *A Social and Religious History of the Jews VI.* (New York: Columbia University Press, 1958).

Baruch ben Samuel. "Eish Ochlah Eish" (1125). *The Penguin Book of Hebrew Verse.* Edited by T. Carmi (New York: Penguin, 1981), p. 386.

Bowman Gray Study: "RX for Mental Health, Join a Synagogue?" *Philadelphia Jewish Exponent*, September 24, 1993.

Bowra, C. M. *Primitive Song* (London: Weidenfeld and Nicolson, 1962).

Campbell, Joseph and Bill Moyers. *The Power of Myth* (New York: Doubleday, 1988).

Cantors's duties. Leo Landman. *The Cantor* (New York: Yeshiva University, 1972. Hyman I. Sky. *The Development of the Office of Hazzan through the Talmudic Period.* Dissertation (Phildelphia: Dropsie University, 1977). Herbert S. Garten. "Hazzan and Constitution—Landmark Cases." In *Fiftieth Jubilee Journal* (New York: Cantors Assembly, 1998), pp. 376–392.

Cardin, Nina Beth. *A Leader's Guide to Services and Prayers of Healing* (New York: The National Center for Jewish Healing, 1996).

Chopra, Deepak. *Ageless Body, Timeless Mind* (New York: Harmony Books, 1993).

Cicero, Marcus Tullius. "De Oratore." 55 B.C.E. "Brutus." 46 B.C.E. From Moses Hadas. *A History of Latin Literature* (New York: Columbia University Press, 1952).

Cohen, Hermann. Dieter Adelmann. "Kavanah and Cantorial Background in Hermann Cohen's Philosophy." In *Voice of Ashkenaz Conference*. New York, Jewish Theological Seminary, Nov. 7–11, 1997.

Congregationalism. Conrad Arensberg. "American Communities." *Readings in Anthropology*, Vol. II. Edited by Morton E. Fried (New York: Crowell, 1959).

Demographic studies. *Chosen Voices* ("1970s-1980s"). Mark Slobin (Urbana, University of Illinois, 1989). *Emerging Worship...Trends* ("U.A.H.C. Congregations Responding"). Daniel Freelander, Robin Hirsch, and Sanford Seltzer. October 1994. *Post and Opinion* ("Conservative Survey"). October 30, 1996. *Wall Street Journal* ("The Age of Divine Unity"), Lisa Miller. Feb. 10, 1999.

Dewey, John. *Reconstruction in Philosophy* (New York: Henry Holt, 1920).

Driver, Tom. *The Magic of Ritual* (San Francisco: Harper, 1991).

"Eil Adon." *Daily Prayer Book*. Translated and edited by Philip Birnbaum (New York: Hebrew Publishing Company, 1949).

Ephraim ben Jacob. *Book of Historical Records* (twelfth century). Jacob R. Marcus, *The Jew in the Medieval World* (Cincinnati: Union of American Hebrew Congregations, 1938).

Fishman, Sylvia. *A Breath of Life* (New York: Maxwell Macmillan, 1993).

Frankel, Zacharias. Stefan C. Reif. *Judaism and Hebrew Prayer* (Cambridge: Cambridge University Press, 1993).

Geertz, Clifford. *The Interpretation of Cultures* (New York: Basic Books, 1973).

Grinstein, Hyman. *The Rise of the Jewish Community of New York* (Philadelphia: Jewish Publication Society, 1945).

Hark, the Herald Angels Sing: Words by Charles Wesley (1739). Music by Felix Mendelssohn 1840. Arranged by William Cummings (1850). *Twice 55 Plus*. Edited by P. Dykema, W. Earhart, H. Dann, and O. McConathy (Boston: C. C. Birchard, 1947).

Heilman, Samuel. *Synagogue Life* (Chicago: University of Chicago Press, 1976).

"Heiveinu Shalom Aleichem." *Manginot-201 Songs for Jewish Schools*. Edited by Stephen Richards (New York: Transcontinental, 1992).

Horodetzky, Samuel. *Yahadut Haseichel Veyahadut Haregesh* (Tel Aviv: N. Tverski, 1947).

"I Know That My Redeemer Liveth." George Frideric Handel, *Messiah* (1743). (London: Novello, 1922).

Josippon Chronicle. Solomon Zeitin. "Josippon." *Jewish Quarterly Review*. Vol. 53 (1963), pp. 277–297.

Kaplan, Mordecai. *Judaism as a Civilization* (New York: Reconstructionist Press, 1934).

Kehillah. Moshe Davis. *The Emergence of Conservative Judaism* (Philadelphia: Jewish Publication Society, 1963).

"Kinot." In *Seder Kinot le-Tish'ah be-Av* (Jerusalem: Porat Yosef, 1976).

Kovner, Abba. "Achoti Ketanah." In *A Canopy in the Desert*. Translated by Shirley Kaufman (New York: Persea, 1973).

"Manjiro, John." Lee Houchins. *Abroad in America.* Edited by Marc Pachter (Reading, Mass.: Addison-Wesley, 1976).

Mirsky, Norman. *Unorthodox Judaism* (Columbus, Ohio: Ohio State University Press, 1988).

Moynihan, Daniel. "Defining Deviancy Down." *The American Scholar.* Vol. 61, No. 1 (Winter 1993), pp. 17–30.

National Jewish Outreach Program. Ellen Pober Rittberg. "Beginners Minyans—From Prayer to Participation." *Jewish Week.* June 3, 1988. "Rave Reviews for House of Jacob's Beginners Service." *Jewish Free Press.* April 3, 1995. Gustav Niehbur. "Short Course in Judaism." *New York Times.* September 13, 1996. "Where It All Began." *Lincoln Square Synagogue Beginners Programs.* 1997 *Purim Bulletin.* N.J.O.P. March 1999.

Nicholson, Adelle. "Healing, Judaism, and Music." *Koleinu.* May 1997, pp. 1; 4–5; 7.

Pareles, Jon. "Music Moved by the Spirit Thrives Worldwide." *New York Times,* June 21, 1998.

Rabbis' duties. Jerome Carlin and Saul Mendlovitz. "The American Rabbi." *Jews.* Edited by Marshall Sklare (Glencoe: Free Press, 1957). Louis I. Rabinowitz. "Modern European Rabbinate." *Encyclopedia Judaica* Vol. 13: 1452:1453. (Jerusalem: Keter, 1972).

Reform Judaism. Wilhelm Thielmann, *Bilder aus der Synagoge,* 1899. Annotated by Abraham Sulzbach. Thiele and Schwartz, Kassel, 1900. Stuart E. Rosenberg. *"The Jewish Tidings* and the Sunday Services Question." In *The Jewish Experience in America*, Vol. IX. Edited by Abraham J. Karp (New York: Ktav, 1969). Cecil Roth. "Pittsburgh Platform." *Encyclopedia Judaica* Vol. 13:570–571 (Jerusalem: Keter, 1972). Jakob J. Petuchowski. "American" and "Ideological Developments." *Encyclopedia Judaica.* Vol. 14:24–26 (Jerusalem: Keter, 1972). Steven M. Lowenstein. *Frankfurt on the Hudson* (Detroit: Wayne State University Press, 1989).

Reik, Theodore. *The Haunting Melody* (New York: Farrar, Straus, and Young, 1953).

Rottenberg, Dan. "Editor's Notes." *Philadelphia Welcomat,* September 5, 1990.

Rousseau, Jean Jacques. "Confessions," 1781–1788. *The Norton Anthology of World Masterpieces.* Edited by Maynard Mack (New York: W. W. Norton, 1980).

Schulweis, Harold, and Marjory Zerin. "Theological Black Hole in Jewish Life." *Post and Opinion*, April 7, 1995.

Sefer Hachinuch. Attributed to Rabbi Pinchas Halevi of Barcelona (thirteenth century). Translated by Elchanan Vengrov (New York: Feldheim, 1989).

Soloveichik, Joseph. *On Repentance.* Edited by Pinchas Peli (New York: Paulist Press, 1984).

Spiro, Pincas: *A Complete Service for: Sabbath, Festivals, High Holy Days, Weekdays* (Los Angeles and Cleveland: Temple Beth Am and Congregation Beth Am, 1960–1970).

Taylor, Barbara, and Mary Otto. "Praise the Preacher." *Philadelphia Inquirer*, April 11, 1996.

Tchernichowski, Saul. "Letter to Dr. Klausner." Meyer Waxman. *History of Jewish Literature*, Vol. 4, part 1 (South Brunswick: Thomas Yoseloff, 1941), p. 264.

'Tis the Gift to Be Simple. "Simple Gifts." Arranged by Aaron Copland. *Old American Songs I* (London: Boosey and Hawkes: 1950).

Unamuno, Miguel de. "The Tragic Sense of Life." In *Men and Nations* (1921). Translated by Anthony Kerrigan (Princeton: Princeton University Press, 1977).

Weisgal, Abba Yosef. "Jewish Youth a Special Interest." *Baltimore Jewish Times*, April 16, 1926.

Wertheimer, Jack, and Shira Dicker. "Conservative Synagogues and Their Members." *JTS Magazine.* Spring 1996, pp. 12–14.

Zeitlin, Solomon. "The Origins of the Synagogue." *Proceedings of the American Academy for Jewish Research.* 1931, p. 78.

Chapter 3—The Latest Road Maps

Albright, William. *From the Stone Age to Christianity* (Baltimore: Johns Hopkins University Press, 1957).

Alter, Robert. *The Art of Biblical Poetry* (New York: Basic Books, 1985).

Av Gadol. Words by Hillel Zeitlin (1943). Unpublished music by Benjamin Z. Maissner. "Shirat Ahavah Lefanecha." Arranged by Howard Gamble (Toronto: Holy Blossom Temple, 1981).

Berlioz, Hector. *Evenings with the Orchestra* (1859), Translated by Jacques Barzun (Chicago: University of Chicago Press, 1956).

Berman, Donna. "The Feminist Critique of Language." *CCAR Journal*, 34:2 (Summer 1992), pp. 5–14.

Binder, Abraham W. "A History of American-Jewish Hymnody." *Studies in Jewish Music.* Edited by Irene Heskes (New York: Bloch, 1971).

Bloch, Ernest. *Avodath Hakodesh* (Boston: C. C. Birchard, 1934).

Descartes, René. *Discourse on Method* (1637). Translated by Donald A. Cress (Indianapolis: Hackett, 1998).

Doody, Margaret. "The New Episcopalian Liturgy." In *The State of the Language.* Edited by L. Michaels and C. Ricks (Berkeley: University of California Press, 1980).

Flender, Reinhard. *Hebrew Psalmody, A Structural Investigation.* (Jerusalem: Hebrew University, 1992).

Furman, Frida Kerner: *Beyond Yiddishkeit* (Albany: State University of New York, 1987).

Gilder, George. "The Roots of Black Poverty." *Wall Street Journal,* October 30, 1995.

Gillman, Neil. *The Death of Death* (Woodstock, Vt.: Jewish Lights, 1997).

Greenberg, Blu. "Will There Be Orthodox Women Rabbis?" *Judaism* 33:1 (Winter 1984), pp. 23–33.

Grossman, Susan, and Rivkah Haut. *Daughters of the King* (Philadelphia: Jewish Publicaiton Society, 1993).

Hartman, David. *A Heart of Many Rooms* (Woodstock, Vt.: Jewish Lights, 1999).

Horn, Wade. "Why There Is No Substitute for Parents." *Imprimis* 26:6 (June 1997), pp. 1–4.

Kallen, Horace. "Cultural Pluralism and the Jews." *The Jewish Spectator* 42 (Fall 1977), pp. 11–16.

Krauss, Simcha. "Reading Torah, Women's Group Tests Tradition." *New York Times,* February 16, 1997.

Maimonides. *Essay on Resurrection* (1191). *Crisis and Leadership: Epistles of Maimonides.* Translated and annotated by Abraham Halkin, with discussion by David Hartman (Philadelphia: Jewish Publication Society, 1985).

Mi Yitneini. Words by Judah Halevi (twelfth century). Music by Jerome Kopmar (New York: Transcontinental, 1994).

Plato. "Phaedo" (fifth century B.C.E.). In *Dialogues of Plato.* Edited by J. D. Kaplan after Benjamin Jowett's nineteenth-century translations (New York: Pocket Books, 1951).

Poller, H. Leonard. "Preparing a New Siddur." *CCAR Journal* 34:2 (Summer 1992), pp. 1–3.

Poseks. Michael Chabin. "The New 'Poseks': Orthodox Women." *Jewish Week,* October 8, 1999.

Prager, Dennis. *Think a Second Time,* citing Alexander Mitscherlisch's *Society without the Father,* 1969 (New York: Regan Books, 1995).

Rackman, Emanuel. "Justice for Agunot." *Jewish Week,* November 7, 1997. "Defending My Stand on Agunot." *Jewish Week,* February 6, 1998. "For Agunah, Leeway in the Law." *Jewish Week,* March 5, 1999.

Reimers, Paula. "Feminism, Judaism, and God the Mother." *Conservative Judaism* 47:1 (Fall 1993), pp. 24–29.

Schachter-Shalomi, Zalman. *The Encounter: A Study of Counselling in Hasidism* (dissertation) (New York: Hebrew Union College, 1968).

Sklare, Marshall. *Conservative Judaism*, 2nd edition (New York: Schocken, 1972).

Stern, Chaim. Liturgy for the Twenty-first Century. Symposium Celebrating Twenty Years of Women in the Cantorate. Hebrew Union College. February 4–5, 1996.

Stoppard, Tom. *The Real Thing* (Boston: Faber and Faber, 1984).

The Role of Laity in Worship. Janet Marder. "Praying as One." *Reform Judaism.* Summer 1999, pp. 24–29.

Wagner, Renee Rabinowitz. "You Just Don't Understand Women." *Jewish Post and Opinion*, November 13, 1991.

Wieseltier, Leon. "Jews and Books—The Ties That Bind." Speech accepting the National Jewish Book Award for Non-Fiction, 1998. *The Jewish Week*, March 26, 1999.

Whitmont, Edward. *Return of the Goddesses* (London: Routledge and Kegan Paul, 1983).

Wolf, Arnold Jacob. "The New Liturgies." *Judaism* 46:2 (Spring 1997), pp. 235–242.

Yoffie, Eric. Keynote Address. Symposium Celebrating Twenty Years of Women in the Cantorate. Hebrew Union College, February 4–5, 1996.

Chapter 4—Changing Lanes

"Adon Olam." Text attributed to Solomon ibn Gabirol (eleventh century). "Standard" Ashkenazic melody by Eliezer Gerovitch, *Schirei Zimroh.* (Rostow on Don: Self-published, 1904).

"Al Hanisim." *Weekday Prayer Book.* Edited by Gershon Hadas (New York: Rabbinical Assembly, 1962).

Armenian Chorale. "Khorhoort Khoreen." Magar Yegmalian. *Divine Liturgy of the Armenian Apostolic Church* (New York: Armenian Prelacy, 1983).

"Ashreinu." William Sharlin and Max Helfman. *Let There Be Song.* (New York: Transcontinental, 1981).

"Avinu Shebashamayim." *Art Scroll Siddur*, Rabbinical Council of America edition (Brooklyn, N. Y.: Mesorah, 1987).

Beatles. "Eleanor Rigby." Written by John Lennon and Paul McCartney (1966). In *The Ultimate Pop Rock Fake Book.* Joel Whitburn (New York: Hal Leonard Publishing, 1986).

Berlin, Irving: "God Bless America," *Yip, Yip, Yaphank* (1918). (Delaware Water Gap, Pa.: Shawnee Press, 1969).

Birkat Hamazon. Moshe Nathanson (1954). Arranged by Sholom Secunda (New York: Cantors Assembly, 1962).

Burgess, Anthony. *This Man and Music* (London: Hutchinson, 1982).

Cahan, Abraham. *The Rise of David Levinsky* (New York: Harper, 1917).

Cooke, Deryck. *The Language of Music* (London: Oxford University Press, 1959).

Copland, Aaron. *Music and Imagination* (Cambridge, Mass.: Harvard University Press, 1952).

"Deus Genitor Alme." *Liber Usualis*. Edited by Benedictines of Solèsmes Abbey (Tournai, Belgium, and New York: Desclée, 1956).

Dylan, Bob. "Blowin' in the Wind." *The Answer, My Friend.* (1962). In *Great Songs of the Sixties*. Edited by Milton Okun (New York: Quadrangle Books, 1970).

Einstein, Albert. *Special Theory of Relativity* (1916). "Person of the Century," *Time*, December 16, 1999. Walter Isaacson, *The Century of Science and Technology*, pp. 54–60. Frederic Golden, *Relativity's Rebel*, pp. 64–65. Stephen Hawking, *A Brief History of Relativity*, pp. 67–81. J. Madeleine Nash, *Unfinished Symphony*, pp. 83–87.

"Eits Chayim Hee." Text from Proverbs 3:18, 17 and Lamentations 5:21. Today's "standard" melody in *Gesaenge fuer Synagogen*. Edited by H.. Goldberg (Braunschweig: Friedrich Biewig, 1845).

Ellison, Ralph. *Invisible Man* (1947). (New York: Random House, 1952).

Emerson, Ralph Waldo. "Nature" (1836). *The Heritage of American Literature*. Edited by L. Richardson, G. Orians, and H. Brown (Boston: Ginn, 1951).

"Every Little Breeze." Richard Whiting. *Louise* (New York: Famous Music, 1929).

Felix, Cathy, and Elliot Schoenberg. "Worship for the 21st Century" (based on Daniel Benedict and Craig Miller, *Contemporary Worship for the 21st Century*, 1994). *Conservative Judaism* 52:4 (Summer 1998), pp. 97–79.

Freud, Sigmund *Civilization and its Discontents* (1930). Translated by James Strachey (New York: W. W. Norton, 1961).

Funk, Virgil. "Building a Relationship with God, While Enabling the Congregation to Pray through Music." Academic Conference Commemorating the School of Sacred Music's Fiftieth Anniversary, Hebrew Union College, November 24, 1998.

Generations. Coupland, Douglas. *Generation X* (New York: St. Martin's Press, 1990). Petersen, Andrea, "All the Hot Gen X Pundits, Like, Vanished." *Wall Street Journal*, August 31, 1999. Wolfe, Tom. "The 'Me' Decade and the Third Great Awakening." *New York Magazine* 9:34 (August 23, 1976).

Halleluyah (Psalms 150). Folk tune. Arranged by Benjamin Z. Maissner (Toronto: Holy Blossom, 1985).

Hatikvah. Words by Naphtali Herz Imber. Words in Joseph Megilnetzky, *Songs of Zion* (Philadelphia, 1903). (1878). Music arrangement in Carl Schrag. "High Hopes." *Jerusalem Post*, May 8, 1992. Courtesy of Israel Music Publications.

Heisenberg, Werner. "Theory of Quantum Mechanics" (1925). In *Physics and Beyond*. Translated by Arnold J. Pomerans (London: G. Allen and Unwin, 1971).

Hoffman, Lawrence. *The Art of Public Prayer* (Washington, D. C.: The Pastoral Press, 1988).

Homer. *The Iliad* (eighth century B.C.E.) Translated by Richmond Lattimore, 1951.

Idelsohn, Abraham. *Jewish Music in Its Historical Development* (New York: Henry Holt, 1929).

"In Germany at the End of World War II." Members of Kibbutz Buchenwald, *Kol Haneshamah*. Edited by David A. Teutsch (Wyncote, Pa.: The Reconstructionist Press, 1994), p. 812.

In a one-horse open sleigh. "Jingle Bells." *Golden Song Book*. Edited by Katharine Tyler Wells (New York: Simon and Schuster, 1945).

Isidore of Seville. "De Ecclesiasticis Officiis." Salo Baron. *A Social and Religious History of the Jews VII* (New York: Columbia University Press, 1958).

"Kadesh Ur'chats." (Constantinople). *Antologia de Liturgia Judeo-Española III*. Edited by Isaac Levy (Jerusalem: Ministry of Education and Culture, 1968).

Lamm, Norman. "Memorial Address for Prime Minister Yitzhak Rabin." *Yeshiva University Review* 2:2 (Winter 1996), insert.

Leibowitz, Nechama. *New Studies in the Bereshit*. Translated by Aryeh Newman (Jerusalem: Ministry of Education and Culture, 1993).

Levy, Richard. "The Holy Makes Us Whole." *Reform Judaism*, Fall 1997, pp. 19–22.

Logogenic Singing. Curt Sachs. *The Rise of Music in the Ancient World* (New York: W. W. Norton, 1943).

Maggid of Koznetz. Martin Buber. *Tales of the Hasidim I* (New York: Shocken, 1947).

"Mah Nishtanah." Judith Kaplan Eisenstein. *Heritage of Jewish Music*, 2nd edition (New York: Union of American Hebrew Congregations, 1973).

"Maoz Tsur." Translations. *Hymns and Anthems*. Edited by Gustave Gottheil (New York: Temple Emanuel, 1887). *Gates of Prayer*. Edited by Chaim Stern (New York: Central Conference of American Rabbis, 1975).

Marines' Hymn ("To the Shores of Tripoli"). *All-American Song Book*. Edited by Joseph E. Maddy and W. Otto Miessner (New York: Robbins, 1942).

"La Marseillaise." Claude Joseph Rouget de Lisle (1792). *Music of Many Lands and Peoples*. Edited by O. McConathy, J. Beattie, and R. Morgan (New York: Silver Burdette, 1932).

Masses of Requiem. Mozart, Wolfgang Amadeus. *D minor* (1791). (Kassel: Verlag Baerenreiter, 1965). Verdi, Giuseppe. *Manzoni* (1873). (Frankfurt: C. F. Peters, 1937).

Melville, Herman. *Moby-Dick* (1851). Edited by Harold Beaver (London: Penguin Books, 1986).

Michener, James. "Barcelona." *Iberia* (New York: Fawcett Crest, 1969).

Milton, John. *Paradise Lost* (1667). *The Literature of England*, Vol. I. Edited by G. Woods, H. Watt, and G. Anderson (Chicago: Scott, Forseman, and Co., 1947).

Neusner, Jacob. *Introduction to American Judaism* (Minneapolis: Fortress Press, 1994).

"Pazer" and "Zarka." Salomon Sulzer. *Schir Zion* (1865). Edited by Joseph Sulzer (1905) (Frankfurt am Main: J. Kauffman, 1922).

"Polly Wolly Doodle." *New American Song Book*. Edited by Anne and Max Oberndorfer (Chicago: Hall and McCreary, 1941).

Psalms 93. "Adonai Malach." Abraham Idelsohn. *Thesaurus of Hebrew Oriental Melodies VII* (Leipzig: Friedrich Hofmeister, 1932).

Reform Biennial: Eric Yoffie. Keynote Address to UAHC. Dallas, Anatole Hotel. October 29–November 2, 1997.

Romberg, Sigmund and Oscar Hammerstein II. "Stout-Hearted Men." *New Moon* (London: Chappell, 1940).

Rosenbaum, Samuel. "The American Synagogue—A Work in Progress." *Journal of Synagogue Music* 24:2 (1995), pp. 22–33.

Rosenberg, Bernhard, and Fred Heuman. *Theological and Halakhic Reflections on the Holocaust* (Hoboken: Ktav, 1993).

Rubin, William. *Primitivism in the Twentieth Century* (New York: Museum of Modern Art, 1984).

"Rule Brittania" (1750). Thomas Arne and James Thompson (London: Preston and Son, 1803).

Saint John Passion. "Ruht Wohl." Johann Sebastian Bach (1722) (Kassel: Baerenreiter, 1973).

Seeger, Pete. "Where Have All the Flowers Gone?" (1961). In *Great Songs of the Sixties*. Milton Okun (New York: Quadrangle, 1970).

"Shabbat Hamalkah." Words by Hayyim Nahman Bialik. Melody by Pinchas Minkowsky (1920). *Zamru Lo I.* Edited by Moshe Nathanson (New York: Cantors Assembly, 1955).

"Shalom Aleichem." Author unknown (seventeenth century, based on BT, *Shabbat* 119b). Melody by Israel Goldfarb and Samuel E. Goldfarb. *Friday Evening Melodies* (New York: Bureau of Jewish Education, 1918).

"Shalom Rav." Jeff Klepper and Daniel Freelander. *Shiron L'Shalom.* Edited by Ann Carol Abrams and Lucy Joan Sollogub (Brookline: Jewish Educators for Social Responsibility, 1986).

Shehashalom Shelo. Author unknown. *Sabbath and Festival Prayer Book.* Traditional melody unattributed (New York: Rabbinical Assembly, 1946).

Shehu Noteh Shamayim. Ramah version. Unattributed oral tradition (1960). *Psalmodic version.* Pinchas Spiro. *A Complete Weekday Service* (*Minchah* section) (Cleveland: Congregation Beth Am, 1970).

"Shuffled" tempo and "pushed" beat. Jeffrey Gutcheon. *Improvising Rock Piano* (New York: Amsco, 1983).

Simon, Paul. *All your dreams are on their way.* "Bridge over Troubled Water." (1969). In *Great Songs of the Sixties*. Milton Okun (New York: Quadrangle, 1970).

Singer, David. "What Do American Jews Believe?" Symposium. *Commentary*. August 1966, pp. 83–84.

Springsteen, Bruce. "I Was Born in the U.S.A. Now." *Born in the U.S.A.* n.p. 1984.

"Tal Bo Tevarech Mazon." Salomon Sulzer. *Schir Zion* (1865). Edited by Joseph Sulzer (1905) (Frankfurt am Main: J. Kauffman, 1922).

Te Deum Celebrations. "Keep Us This Day without Sin." George Frideric Handel (*For the Peace of Utrecht*, 1713) (Berlin: Verlag Merseburger, 1958). "Dignare, Domine die ista." Franz Josef Haydn (*For Empress Maria Theresa*, 1800) (London: Oxford University Press, 1932).

"The Teensy Weensy Spider." *Fireside Song Book of Birds and Beasts*. Edited by Jane Yolen (New York: Simon and Schuster, 1972).

Telisha gedolah. Abraham Baer. "Neginoth (*peshutah*)." *Baal T'fillah* (1877) (New York: Sacred Music Press, 1954).

"That Old Time Religion." George Pullen Jackson. *Spiritual Folksongs of Early America* (New York: J. J. Augustin, 1937).

Toch, Ernst. *The Shaping Forces in Music* (1948) (New York: Dover, 1977).

"Twinkle, Twinkle, Little Star." Katharine Tyler Wessells. *The Golden Song Book* (New York: Simon and Schuster, 1945).

"Veshamru." Steve Reuben. *Let There Be Song* (New York: Transcontinental, 1981).

Veyeira'eh Kippureinu. "Ya'aleh." *Schir Lischlaumau*. Aron Friedmann (Berlin: Deutsch-Isrealitischen Gemeindebunde, 1901).

Vogt, Von Ogden. *Art and Religion* (1921) (Boston: Beacon Press, 1948).

Voss, Richard, and William F. Allman. "The Musical Brain." *U. S. News and World Report*. June 11, 1990, pp. 56–60.

"Vota mea Domini." *Liber Usualis*. Edited by Benedictines of Solesmes Abbey (Tournai, Belgium and New York: Desclee, 1956).

Werner, Eric. "Practical Applications of Musical Research." *From Generation to Generation* (New York: American Conference of Cantors, 1967).

"Yedid Nefesh." Eliezer Askari (sixteenth century). Melody traditional. *The Harvard Hillel Sabbath Song Book* (Boston: David R. Godine, 1992).

Yehon Sharan. "Kol Nidre." Louis Lewandowsky. *Kol Rinnah Ut'fillah* (Berlin: n.p., 1871).

"Yigdal." Text by Daniel ben Judah of Rome (fourteenth century). "Standard" Ashkenazic melody by Meyer Leoni; 1760). Abraham Zvi Idelsohn. *The Jewish Song Book* (Cincinnati: Publications for Judaism, 1951).

Zim, Sol. "Ledor Vador." *The Joy of Sabbath* (New York: Tara, 1978).

CHAPTER 5—CASTLES IN TIME

Acropolis of Athens. *Architecture of Ancient Greece*. William J. Anderson (London: B. T. Batsford, 1927).

"Adir Hu" and "Shoshanat Ya'akov." *The Songs We Sing*. Edited and arranged by Harry Coopersmith (New York: United Synagogue Commission on Jewish Education, 1950).

Amichai, Yehuda. *Travels.* Translated by Ruth Nevo (New York: The Sheep Meadow Press, 1986).

"An'im Zemirot." Melody unattributed. *Zamru Lo II* 135:b. Edited by Moshe Nathanson (New York: Cantors Assembly, 1960).

Avenary, Hanoch. "Formal Structure of Psalms and Canticles in Early Jewish and Christian Chant." *Musica Disciplina* Vol. 7. (1953), pp. 1–13. *Studies in Hebrew, Syrian, and Greek Liturgical Recitative* (Tel-Aviv: Israel Music Institute, 1963).

Benson, Herbert. *The Relaxation Response* (Boston: G. K. Hall, 1976).

Browning, Robert. "Pippa Passes" (1841). *The Poems and Plays of Robert Browning* (New York: The Modern Library, 1934).

Camhy, Ovadiah. *Liturgie Sephardie* (London: World Sephardi Federation, 1959).

Chaucer's Prioress. "Prologue." In *The Canterbury Tales.* Geoffrey Chaucer (1396). Edited by Daniel Cook (Garden City, N.Y.: Doubleday, 1961).

"Eder Vahod." Text by Simon ben Isaac ben Abun (eleventh century). Melody transcribed by Abraham Baer. *Baal T'fillah.* No. 1274b (1877) (New York: Sacred Music Press, 1954).

Exoo, George. "The Church Main Speaks." *Milwaukee Magazine* 19:2 (February 1994), pp. 16–27.

Forsyth, Michael. *Buildings for Music* (Cambridge, Mass.: The Massachusetts Institute of Technology Press, 1985).

Frymer-Kensky, Tikva. *In the Wake of the Goddesses* (New York: The Free Press, 1992).

Gordon, Mary. "Waste, and Want Not." *Forbes ASAP.* November 30, 1998, pp. 113–114.

Hamakdishim. After "Voyez Sur Cette Roche." Daniel Francois Auber. *Fra Diavolo* (1830) (Leipzig: C. F. Peters, 1925).

Hansel and Gretel. Libretto by Adelheid Wette. Music by Engelbert Humperdinck (1893). Edited by L. Artok (London: Schott and Co., 1924).

Heschel, Abraham. *The Sabbath* (New York: Harper Torchbooks, 1951).

Idelsohn, Abraham. *Jewish Music* (New York: Henry Holt, 1929).

Jacob, Benno. Commentary on Exodus (MS 1935). Nehama Leibowitz. *New Studies in Shemot.* Translated by Aryeh Newman (Jerusalem: Haomanim Press, 1993).

Josselit, Jenna. *The Wonders of America* (New York: Hill and Wang, 1995).

Judgment Day. Judy Petsonk. *Taking Judaism Personally* (New York: The Free Press, 1996). Petsonk cites Rabbi Nancy Fuchs-Kremer, who learned from Rabbi Lionel Blue, after a kabbalistic teaching of Rabbi Joseph Weiss, around 1960.

Kevodo Malei Olam. After *Reb Dovidl.* Folksong arranged by Zavel Zilberts (Newark: M. Mansky, 1924).

Marcello, Benedetto. "Betset Yisrael." *Estro Poetico-Armonico* (1727) (Weisbaden: Breitkopf and Haertel, 1983).

Mimekomo. After "Erev Shel Shoshanim." M. Dor and Y. Hadar. *Great Songs of Israel.* Edited by Velvel Pasternak (New York: Tara, 1976).

Rimsky-Korsakoff, Nicolai. "Flight of the Bumble Bee." *Tsar Saltan* (after Alexander Pushkin 1900) (New York: C. Fischer, 1940).

Salmen, Walter. "Viennese Jewry." *The Legacy of Cantor Salomon Sulzer.* Conference at Hebrew Union College, New York. December 8–10, 1991.

Scott, Michael. *The Record of Singing to 1914* (London: Gerald Duckworth, 1977).

Sherman, Richard and Robert. *It's a Small World, after All* (Glendale: Wonderland Music, 1964).

Smith, Huston. "Judaism." *Religions of Man* (New York: HarperCollins, 1958).

Solis-Cohen, Solomon. Translation of "Maoz Tsur." *Authorized Daily Prayer Book.* Edited by Joseph Herz (New York: Bloch, 1941).

Tal and Geshem. "Chatsi Kaddish" (*ba'agala uvizman kariv*). Abraham Baer. *Baal T'fillah* (1877) (New York: Sacred Music Press, 1954).

Zalman, Shneur. Abraham W. Binder. "Jewish Music." *Jewish Encyclopedia Handbooks* (New York: Central Yiddish Cultural Organization, 1952.

Vigoda, Samuel. *Legendary Voices* (New York: M. P. Press, 1981).

CHAPTER 6—MELODIES IN SPACE

Aaron, David. *Endless Light* (New York: Simon and Schuster, 1997).

"Adonai, Sefatai Tiftach." *Amidah* text. Melody unattributed. *Gates of Song.* Edited by Charles Davidson (New York: Transcontinental, 1987).

Almagor, Dan. *Ish Chasid Hayah* (1968). Text reproduced by Hebrew Cultural Council of Greater Philadelphia, 1970.

"Al Shloshah Devarim." Chaim Zur. *The Best of the Chassidic Song Festivals.* Edited by Velvel Pasternak (New York: Tara, 1989).

Al-tira Avdi Ya'akov. Author and date unknown. *Art Scroll Zemiroth* ("Amar Hashem L'Yaakov"). Edited by Nosson Scherman and Meir Zlotowitz (Brooklyn, N.Y.: Mesorah, 1979).

Asch, Sholom. *Salvation.* Translation of *Der Tehillin Yid* by Willa and Edwin Muir (New York: G. P. Putnam's Sons, 1936).

"Avinu Malkeinu." *Shirei Erets Yisrael.* Edited by Yaakov Shenberg (Berlin: Juedischer Verlag, 1936).

"Bemotsa'ei Yom Menuchah." Ya'akov Manui (thirteenth century). *Antologia de Liturgia Judeo-Española* I. Edited by Isaac Levy (Jerusualem: Ministry of Education and Culture, 1964).

Benedict, Ruth. *Patterns of Culture* (New York: Penguin Books, 1934).

Carlebach, Shlomo. "Elimelech." *In the Palace of the King.* Liner note for CD recording (Santa Monica, Ca.: Vanguard, 1965). "Song of Shabbos." *Shlomo Carlebach Anthology* (New York: Tara, 1995).

Dov Baer of Mezhirech. "Likutei Amarim." Edited by Solomon of Luzk (1781). *Magid Devarav le Ya'akov* (Brooklyn, N.Y.: Kehot, 1986).

Dubnow, Simon. *History of the Jews in Russia and Poland I.* Translated by I. Friedlaender (Philadelphia: Jewish Publications Society, 1916).

Eisenberg, Robert. *Boychiks in the Hood* (San Francisco: HarperCollins, 1995).

Elohei Hamerkavah. "Aneinu Elohei Avraham, Aneinu." *Liturgie Sephardie.* Edited by Ovadiah Camhy (London: World Sephardi Foundation, 1959).

Elohim Yis'adeinu. Avraham. Date unknown. *Art Scroll Zemiroth* (Brooklyn, N.Y.: Mesorah, 1979).

Goldberg, J. J. "Missionary Passions." *The Jewish Week,* July 2, 1999.

Green, Morton. "The Aesthetic Dimension of Prayer." Great Lakes Regional Conference of Assembly Cantors at Adath Israel Synagogue in Toronto, Canada. April 2–3, 1990.

"Havah Nagilah." Words by Moshe Nathanson. Melody after the chasidim of Sadigora, Hungary. *Manginot Shireinu.* Edited by Moshe Nathanson (New York: Hebrew Publishing Co., 1939).

Huxley, Aldous. *Brave New World* (London: Chatto and Windus, 1932).

"I Been Wukkin' on de Railroad." *Fireside Book of Folk Songs.* Edited by Margaret Bradford Boni. Arranged by Norman Lloyd (New York: Simon and Schuster, 1947).

I'd Like to Coo. "Too Darn Hot." Cole Porter. *Kiss Me, Kate* (New York: T. B. Harms, 1948).

Israel of Ruzhin. *Keneset Yisrael* (Warsaw: n.p., 1906).

Kahana, Abraham. *Sefer Hachasidut* (Warsaw: n.p., 1922).

Kamenetz, Rodger. *The Jew in the Lotus* (San Francisco: HarperCollins, 1994).

Leon, Moses de. *Zohar* (thirteenth century). Translated Harry Sperling and Maurice Simon (London: Soncino Press, 1934).

Liebman, Charles. "Orthodoxy in American Jewish Life." *Dimensions of Orthodox Judaism.* Edited by Reuven Bulka (New York: Ktav, 1983).

Lorch, Steven. *The Convergence of Jewish and Western Culture through Music.* Dissertation given at Columbia University, New York, 1977.

Lurianic Kabbalah. Marcos Ricardo Barnatan. *La Kabala* (Barcelona: Barral Editores, 1974).

Magnes, Judah. Norman Bentwich. *For Zion's Sake* (Philadelphia: Jewish Publication Society, 1954).

Mason, Jackie. "Man of Many Barbs." Interview with Jennifer Weiner. *Philadelphia Inquirer,* April 7, 1996.

Matt, Daniel. *God and the Big Bang* (Woodstock, Vt.: Jewish Lights, 1996).

Nachman of Bratslav. Hillel Zeitlin. "Al Haneginah." *Lachasidim Mizmor.* Edited by M. Geshuri (Jerusalem: Hat'chiyah, 1936).

National Population Surveys. Barry Kosmin (New York: Council of Jewish Federations, 1990). Sidney Goldstein (New York: City University of New York, 1993). Gary Tobin (Waltham: Brandeis Institute for Community and Religion, 1997).

Nochlin, Linda. "The Couturier and the Hasid." *Too Jewish.* Edited by Norman Kleeblatt (New Brunswick, N.J.: Rutgers University Press, 1996).

Pasternak, Velvel. *Songs of the Chassidim II* (New York: Bloch, 1971).

"The People in My Neighborhood." Adapted by Nancy Rubin and Julie Jaslow Auerbach from Jeffrey Moss. *The People in Your Neighborhood* (1969). *Manginot.* Edited by Stephen Richards (New York: Transcontinental, 1992).

Peretz, Isaac Leib. *A Gilgul fun a Nigun* (Vilna: n.p., 1922).

Podhoretz, John. "The Decline of Broadway." *Inside*, February 2, 1987, pp. 12–15.

Rejoice and Sing: Compiled and arranged by Sholom Kalib (New York: Tara, 1976).

Rubens, Alfred. *A History of Jewish Costume* (New York: Funk and Wagnalls, 1967).

Schatz, Rivka. "Contemplative Prayer in Chasidism." *Studies in Mysticism and Religion.* Edited by E. Urbach, R. Werbloski, and C. Wirzubski (Jerusalem: Magness Press, 1967).

Scholem, Gershon. *Major Trends in Jewish Mysticism* (New York: Schocken, 1941).

"Shape-Note" Singing. William Little. *The Easy Instructor* (Albany: Webster's and Skinner and Daniel Steel, 1802). After John Tufts, *An Introduction to the Singing of Psalm Tunes* (1721).

"Shema Yisrael." Tsvikah Pik (1972). *The Best of the Chasidic Song Festivals.* Edited by Velvel Pasternak (New York: Tara, 1989).

Shneur Zalman. Abraham Wolf Binder. "Jewish Music." *Jewish Encyclopedia Handbooks* (New York: Central Yiddish Cultural Organization, 1952).

Sharvit, Uri. *Chasidic Tunes from Galitzia* (Jerusalem: Bar-Ilan University, 1995).

Sklare, Marshall. *Conservative Judaism*, 2nd ed. (New York: Schocken, 1972).

Soloveitchik, Haym. "Rupture and Reconstruction—the Transformation of Modern Orthodoxy." *Tradition* 28:4 (Summer 1994), pp. 65–130.

The Sorcerer's Apprentice: Paul Dukas. Based on Johann Wolfgang von Goethe. *Der Zauberlehrling* (1897) (New York: Kalmus, 1933).

Uri of Strelisk. Abraham Ber Birnbaum. "Song in the Chasidic Courts of Poland." *Haolam* (1908). Abraham Idelsohn. *Jewish Music* (New York: Holt, 1929).

"Vetaheir Libeinu." Solomon Rosowsky. *Chansons d'Erets Israel* (Paris: Editions Salabert, 1935).

Weiss, Avraham. Citing Rabbi Abraham Isaac Kook. "Open Orthodoxy." *Judaism* 46:4 (Fall 1997), pp. 409–419.

Yitzchok Isaac of Kalev. Abraham Zvi Idelsohn. *Thesaurus of Hebrew Oriental Melodies X.* No. 192 (Leipzig: Friedrich Hofmeister, 1932).

CHAPTER 7—A STATE OF MIND

"Abram Batka Nash." Platon Brounoff. *Jewish Folk Songs* (New York: Charles K. Harris, 1911).

A Maisele. Peretz Hirschbein and Lazar Weiner (1936) (New York: Transcontinental, 1953).

Avenary, Hanoch. "Music: Consolidation of the Oriental Style of Jewish Music." *Encyclopedia Judaica* Vol. 12 (Jerusalem: Keter, 1972), pp. 623–626.

Baer, Jean. *The Self-Chosen* (New York: Arbor House, 1982).

Baruch, Bernard. *Baruch* (New York: Holt, 1957).

Berlin Reforgemeinde. The Musical Tradition of the Jewish Reform Congregation in Berlin. Edited by Hermann Schildberger, 1928–1930. CD liner notes by Avner Bahat (Tel-Aviv: Beth Hatefutsoth Museum, 1997).

Birmingham, Stephen. *The Grandees* (New York: Harper and Row, 1971).

Borges, Jorge Luis. "I, the Jew." (*Megafono*, 1934). Translated into Hebrew from the Spanish by Yoram Bronowsky. "A Longing for the Epic." *Ha'aretz*, August 20, 1999.

Brain, Robert. *The Last Primitive Peoples* (New York: Harper and Row, 1976).

Catholic Practice. *Ceremonies and Religious Customs of the various Nations of the Known World.* Translated anonymously at St. John's College, Oxford (London: William Jackson, 1733).

Cohen, Martin. *The Martyr—The Story of a Secret Jew and the Mexican Inquisition* (Philadelphia: Jewish Publication Socieity, 1973).

Dobrinsky, Herbert. *A Treasury of Sephardic Laws and Customs* (New York: Ktav, 1988).

Don Quixote. Miguel de Cervantes, Part I (1615). Translated by Magda Bogin (New York: Stewart, Tabori, and Cheng, 1991).

Eliot, George. *Daniel Deronda* (1876). Edited by Barbara Hardy (London: Penguin Books, 1967).

"Esta Noche es Alevada." Alberto Hemsi. *Coplas Sephardies* X (Paris: n.p., 1973).

"Et Sha'arel Ratson Lehipatei'ach." Emanuel Aguilar and David de Sola. *Talelei Zimrah* (1857). *Sephardi Melodies* (London: Oxford University Press, 1931).

Faur, Jose. "Spain on the Eve of the Expulsion." Lecture at Washington Hebrew Congregation, November 3, 1991.

Gampel, Benjamin. *The Last Jews on Iberian Soil* (Berkeley: University of California Press, 1989).

Gill, Sam. *Sacred Words* (Westport, Conn.: Greenwood Press, 1981).

Green, Arthur. *Seek My Face, Speak My Name* (Northvale, N.J.: Jason Aronson, 1992).

"Hodu Ladonai." Chasidic. Velvel Pasternak. *Songs of the Chassidim II* (New York: Bloch, 1971). Sephardic. E.M. Jessurun. *Sephardic Melodies* (London: Oxford University Press, 1931).

Horowitz, Sara. "Simchat Torah Intimations." *Kerem* (Winter 1994), pp. 54–57.

Joyce, James. *Ulysses* (Paris: Shakespeare and Co., 1922).

Judah Halevi. "Ye'iruni Ra'ayonai." *Shirei Yehudah Halevi.* Edited by Simon Bernstein (New York: Shulsinger Brothers, 1944).

La Mujer de Terach. "Childbirth Songs among Sephardic Jews of Balkan Origin." Susana Weisch-Shahak. *Orbis Musicae* Vol. 8 (1982/1983), pp. 87–103.

Maslin, Simeon. "Hewers of Wood, Drawers of Water." *CCAR Journal*, Vol. 22 (Fall 1975), pp. 1–6.

Mendelssohn, Felix. *Lieder ohne Worte* (1830–1845) (New York: G. Schirmer, 1893).

"Mizmor Ledavid." Ovadiah Camhy. *Liturgie Sephardie* (London: World Sephardi Foundation, 1959).

Moroccan and Tunisian Synagogues. See Dobrinsky entry. Avivah Luri. "The Tunisian Djigan. *Haaretz*, December 3, 1999.

Musleah, Rahel. "The Sephardic Renaissance." *Hadassah* (November 1999), pp. 14–18.

Netanyahu, Benzion. *The Origins of the Inquisition* (New York: Random House, 1995).

Osso Boiker. Joel Engel. Op. 24, No. 1 (Moscow: O. E. M., 1921).

Paz, Octavio. *The Labyrinth of Solitude.* Translated by L. Kemp, Y. Milos, R. P. Belash (New York: Grove Weidenfeld, 1985).

Perera, Victor. *The Cross and the Pear* (New York: Alfred A. Knopf, 1995).

Reform Torah Processional. Jakob J. Petuchowski. *Prayerbook Reform in Europe* (New York: World Union for Progressive Judaism, 1968).

Serotta, Edward. *Survival in Sarajevo* (Vienna: Verlag Christian Brandstaetter, 1996).

Seroussi, Edwin. *Spanish-Portuguese Synagogue Music in Nineteenth-Century Reform Sources from Hamburg* (Jerusalem: Magnes Press, 1996).

Snyder, Patricia Giniger. "The Long Road Back." *Hadassah*, January 1992, pp. 18–20.

Stern, Malcolm H. *Americans of Jewish Descent* (New York: Ktav, 1960).

de Torquemada, Tomas. Simon R. Schwarzfuchs. "Spain; Steps toward the Expulsion." *Encyclopedia Judaica* Vol. 15 (Jerusalem: Keter, 1972), pp. 240–41.

Weinberg, Joseph. "New Mexico's Secret Jews Emerging." *Post and Opinion*, July 21, 1999.

Wiernik, Peter. *History of the Jews in America* (New York: Jewish History Publishing Co., 1931).

Wischnitzer, Rachel. *The Architecture of the European Synagogue* (Philadelphia: Jewish Publication Society, 1964).

"Yedidi Ro'i Mekimi." Isaac Levy. *Antologia Judeo-Español I* (Jerusalem: Ministry of Education and Culture, 1964).

"Yitzchok . . . Farhert Zaine Bonim." Lyrics by Itzik Manger (*Chumesh-Lieder* 1935). Music by Israel Alter. *Maine Lieder* (Johannesburg: n.p., 1957).

CHAPTER 8—SACRED CIRCLES

Alice's Walrus. Lewis Carroll. *Through the Looking Glass* (1872) (Chicago: Children's Press, 1969).

Aleichem, Sholem. *Gantz Tevya Der Milchiger* (1895–1915) (Buenos Aires: Alter Rozental Fund, 1961).

Bellah, Robert. *Habits of the Heart* (New York: Harper and Row, 1985).

Bronstein, Herbert. "The Elu V'Elu (both/and) of Synagogue Music." *CCAR Journal*, Vol. 46 (Summer 1998), pp. 76–83.

Buber, Martin. *I and Thou* (1937). Translated by Walter Kaufmann (New York: Scribner, 1970).

Buber, Martin. *Paths in Utopia.* Translated by R. F. C. Hull (New York: Macmillan,1950).

Cantor, Norman. *The Sacred Chain* (New York: HarperCollins, 1994).

Congregational Interns. Laurie Goodstein. "Unusual, but Not Unorthodox." *New York Times,* February 6, 1998.

Cyberia. Richard Appignanesi and Chris Garratt. *Introduction to Postmodernism* (New York: Totem Books, 1995).

"Daniel's Band." Edited by Philip Paul Bliss. *Gospel Songs* (Cincinnati: J. Church, 1874).

Finney, Jack. *Time and Again* (New York: Simon and Schuster, 1995).

"Follow the Drinkin' Gourd." *Folksing.* Edited by Herbert Haufrecht (New York: Berkley Medallion, 1959).

Geffen, Rela, and Andee Hochman. "The Changing Face of the Jewish Family." *Inside,* (Summer 1994), pp. 62–71; 80–85.

Greenberg, Blu. *On Women and Judaism* (Philadelphia: Jewish Publication Society, 1981).

Herberg, Will. *Protestant, Catholic, Jew* (Garden City, N.Y.: Doubleday Anchor, 1955).

Hertzberg, Arthur. *The Jews in America* (New York: Simon and Schuster, 1989).

Heschel, Abraham. *The Earth Is the Lord's* (New York: Harper Torchbook, 1966).

Hoffman, Lawrence. "From Ethnic to Spiritual—A Tale of Four Generations." (New York: Synagogue 2000 Project, 1995).

Jick, Leon. *The Americanization of the Synagogue* (Hanover, N.H.: University Press of New England, 1976).

Lerner, Laurence. "Introduction." *Reconstructing Literature* (Oxford: Basil Blackwell, 1983).

Lévi-Strauss, Claude. *Structural Anthropology.* Translated by Monique Layton (Chicago: University of Chicago Press, 1983).

Lewandowsky, Louis. "Kedushoh li-N'iloh, *Deutsche Kedushoh, Todah Wesimrah II* (1883). Neil F. Blumofe. Program notes based on eyewitness testimony for the concert, *Soul of Ashkenaz: The Lost Heritage of the German Synagogue.* Alice Tully Hall, New York. November 10, 1997.

The Lord Is My Shepherd (Psalms 23). Hebrew chant in F# minor by Max Wohlberg (ca. 1970). Piano accompaniment and English translation by Lawrence Avery (New York: School of Sacred Music, 1979).

"Michael, Row the Boat Ashore." *Folksing.* Edited by Herbert Haufrecht (New York: Berkley Medallion Books, 1959).

Nadell, Pamella. "Women in the American Synagogue." Lecture at Washington Hebrew Congregation. March 8, 1992.

Neusner, Jacob. *Contemporary Judaic Fellowship in Theory and Practice* (New York: Ktav, 1972).

Pearlfishers, The: "Je Crois Entendre Encore." George Bizet (1863) (Paris: Choudens, 1975).

Petsonk, Judy. *Taking Judaism Personally* (New York: The Free Press, 1996).

Petuchowski, Jakob. *Understanding Jewish Prayer* (New York: Ktav, 1972).

Pittsburgh Principles. Arnold Jacob Wolf. "Reforming Reform Judaism." *Judaism* 48:3 (Summer 1999), pp. 367–372.

Pogrebin, Letty C. *Deborah, Golda and Me* (New York: Crown, 1991).

Prell, Riv-Ellen. *Prayer and Community* (Detroit: Wayne State University Press, 1989).

Reider, Joseph. "Secular Currents in the Synagogal Chants in America." *Jewish Forum* 1:13 (December 1918), pp. 583–594 .

Reisman, Bernard. *The Havurah* (New York: Union of American Hebrew Congregations, 1977).

Rosenberg, Shelley Kapnek. "Counterculture Goes Mainstream." *Jewish Exponent*, February 12, 1993.

de Saussure, Ferdinand. *Cours de Linguistique Générale.* Notes of lectures (1916). Translated by Wade Baskin (London: Fontana, 1974).

Schiffman, Lisa." 'Generation J' Finding a Cyber Home." *The Jewish Week*, July 23, 1999.

Schwartz-Bart, André. *The Last of the Just.* Translated by Stephen Becker (New York: Atheneum, 1960).

Shneur Zalman. Lucy Davidowicz. "Politics, the Jews, and the '84 Election." *Commentary*, Vol. 79 (February 1985), pp. 25–30.

Stark, Edward. "Let Us Adore." *Anim Zemiroth* (New York: Bloch, 1911).

Steele, Shelby. "Baby Boom Virtue." *Wall Street Journal*, September 25, 1998.

Steinbeck, John. Letter to Herbert Sturz (1953). "The Author on 'Grapes of Wrath.'" *New York Times*, August 6, 1990.

Strassfeld, Sharon, and Michael Strassfeld. *The Jewish Catalogue II* (Philadelphia: Jewish Publication Society, 1976).

de Tocqueville, Alexis. *Democracy in America* (1835). Edited by Richard D. Heffner (New York: Mentor Books, 1956).

"Va'anachnu Kor'im." After Salomon Sulzer (1842). *Gates of Song.* Edited by Charles Davidson (New York: Transcontinental, 1987).

"Wayfaring Stranger." *A Treasury of Folk Songs.* Edited by Sylvia and John Kolb (New York: Bantam Books, 1948).

Wesley, John. Robert Southey. *Life of Wesley* (New York: Harper and Brothers, 1847).

Women's Tefillah Network. "What Made Women's Prayer Groups Expand." *Post and Opinion*, February 12, 1997. "Reading Torah, Women's Group Tests Tradition." *New York Times*, February 16, 1997. "A Turning Point for Orthodox Jewish Women." Naomi Grossman. *Post and Opinion*, March 10, 1999.

Yolkoff, Arthur. "Tov Lehodot." *Shirat Atideinu* (New York: Transcontinental, 1966).

Zborowski, Mark, and Elizabeth Herzog. *Life Is with People* (1952) (New York: Schocken, 1962).

"Zen Buddhism." Huston Smith. *The Religious of Man* (New York: HarperCollins, 1958).

EPILOGUE—TOUCHING THE INFINITE

Abrahams, Israel. *Poetry and Religion* (London: G. Allen and Unwin, 1920).

"Adonai Hu Ha'elohim." Israel Alter. *The High Holy Day Service* (New York: Cantors Assembly, 1971).

Bernstein, Leonard. *Jeremiah Symphony* (1943) (New York: Harms, 1949). *The Unanswered Question* (Cambridge, Mass.: Harvard University Press, 1976).

Coleman, Earle. *Creativity and Spirituality* (Albany: State University of New York Press, 1998).

cummings, e e. *73 Poems* (New York: Harcourt, Brace, and World, 1963).

Hayom Yifneh." Abraham Zvi Idelsohn. *Thesaurus of Hebrew Oriental Melodies VIII* (Leipzig: Friedrich Hofmeister, 1932).

"Ochilah La'eil." Abraham Baer. *Baal T'fillah.* No.1230a (1877) (New York: Sacred Music Press, 1954).

"Petach Lanu Sha'ar." David Nowakowsky. *Schlussgebet für Jom-Kippur* (1895) (New York: Sacred Music Press, 1954).

"Sha'arei Shamayim Petach." Joseph A. Levine. *Emunat Abba* (1981). Edited transcriptions of Abba Yosef Weisgal's habitual chazanic practice, ca.1950.

"Yitgadal." Israel Schorr. *N'ginoth Baruch Schorr.* Edited edition of Baruch Schorr's compositions, ca. 1880 (New York: Bloch, 1928).

Index

About the Author

Dr. Joseph A. Levine lectures extensively on the aesthetic dimension of synagogue life. His standard text, *Synagogue Song in America*, soon to be republished by Jason Aronson Inc., was termed "the most important study of Jewish music to appear in English in the past fifty years." His articles have appeared in the *Encyclopedia of Jewish/American History and Culture*, *Gratz College Centennial*, *Journal of Synagogue Music*, *Maryland Jewish Historical Society Journal*, *Midstream*, *Musica Judaica*, and *National Jewish Post and Opinion*. He has also written monographs on the life and times of Cantors David Kusevitzky, Josef Rosenblatt, and Abba Yosef Weisgal. An active cantor himself for thirty-five years, he taught sacred music at the Jewish Theological Seminary and is currently a faculty member at the Academy for Jewish Religion. Dr. Levine serves on the Cantors Assembly editorial board as well as on the Rabinical Assembly committee preparing a new High Holiday *Machzor* for the Conservative movement.

RECOMMENDED
RESOURCES

Blessed Are You: A Comprehensive Guide to Jewish Prayer
by Jeffrey M. Cohen   0-7657-5974-8

The Encyclopedia of Jewish Prayer: Ashkenazic and Sephardic Rites
by Macy Nulman   1-56821-885-0

Every Person's Guide to Jewish Prayer
by Ronald H. Isaacs   0-7657-5964-0

Jewish Liturgy as a Spiritual System:
A Prayer-by-Prayer Explanation of the Nature
and Meaning of Jewish Worship
by Arnold S. Rosenberg   0-7657-6134-3

Kavvana: Directing the Heart in Jewish Prayer
by Seth Kadish   0-7657-5952-7

Prayer in Judaism: Continuity and Change
edited by Gabriel H. Cohn and Howard Fisch
                                                 1-56821-501-0

Service of the Heart: A Guide to the Jewish Prayer Book
by Evelyn Garfiel   1-56821-041-8

The Structure of the Siddur
by Stephen R. Schach   1-56821-974-1

A Treasury of Thoughts on Jewish Prayer
edited by Sidney Greenberg   1-56821-937-7

Available at
your local bookstore, online at www.aronson.com
or by calling toll-free 1-800-782-0015